THE **WAITE GROUP**®

C000007281

3D
Modeling
Lab

Create Beautiful
3D Photorealistic Models
on Your PC

Philip Shaddock

WAITE GROUP PRESS™
Corte Madera, California

Publisher • *Mitchell Waite*
Editor-in-Chief • *Scott Calamar*
Editorial Director • *Joel Fugazzotto*
Content Editor • *Heidi Brumbaugh*
Technical Reviewer • *Mike Halvorson, Igor Plotnikov*
Production Director • *Julianne Ososke*
Design • *Cecile Kaufman*
Production Coordinator • *Michele Cuneo*
Production • *Marlyn Amann*
Illustration • *Pat Rogondino*

© 1994 by The Waite Group, Inc.®
Published by Waite Group Press™, 200 Tamal Plaza, Corte Madera, CA 94925

Waite Group Press™ is distributed to bookstores and book wholesalers by Publishers Group West, Box 8843, Emeryville, CA 94662, 1-800-788-3123 (in California 1-510-658-3453).

Printed in the United States of America
94 95 96 • 10 9 8 7 6 5 4 3 2 1

Library of Congress Cataloging-in-Publication Data
Shaddock, Philip.
   3D modeling lab : learn to build 3-D models on your PC / Philip Shaddock.
     p. cm.
   Includes index.
   ISBN 1-878739-52-2 : $39.95 ($55.95 Can,)
    1. Computer graphics. 2. Three-dimensional display systems.
  I. Title.
  T385.S384 1993
  006.6--dc20   93-46272
                 CIP

DEDICATION

For Lyla Shaddock, artist before me

ABOUT THE AUTHOR

Philip Shaddock is an award-winning artist, writer, and director of video, multi-image and multimedia. He has worked for such clients as Coca-Cola, Mattel, Procter & Gamble, Olgivy & Mather, Apple, and IBM. He created the multimedia disk for Waite Group Press's *Nanotechnology Playhouse,* which uses 3D animations to simulate nanotechnology machines. He is also designer and producer of the Spring 1994 Waite Group book catalog, an interactive 3D space station the user can explore. He has created 3D art for video, print, multimedia, and kiosks.

His previous book for Waite Group Press, *Multimedia Creations,* is a practical, hands-on tutorial in integrating and producing sound and animation productions on PCs, including the integration of 3D animations in multimedia productions.

He lives and works in Vancouver, B.C. He may be contacted on CompuServe (70274,2146) or on the Internet (Philip_Shaddock@mindlink.bc.ca.).

Dear Reader:

What is a book? Is it perpetually fated to be inky words on a paper page? Or can a book simply be something that inspires—feeding your head with ideas and creativity regardless of the medium? The latter, I believe. That's why I'm always pushing our books to a higher plane; using new technology to reinvent the medium.

I wrote my first book in 1973, *Projects in Sights, Sounds, and Sensations*. I like to think of it as our first multimedia book. In the years since then, I've learned that people want to experience information, not just passively absorb it—they want interactive MTV in a book. With this in mind, I started my own publishing company and published *Master C,* a book/disk package that turned the PC into a C language instructor. Then we branched out to computer graphics with *Fractal Creations,* which included a color poster, 3-D glasses, and a totally rad fractal generator. Ever since, we've included disks and other goodies with most of our books. *Virtual Reality Creations* is bundled with 3-D Fresnel viewing goggles and *Walkthroughs and Flybys CD* comes with a multimedia CD-ROM. We've made complex multimedia accessible for any PC user with *Ray Tracing Creations, Multimedia Creations, Making Movies on Your PC, Image Lab,* and three books on Fractals.

The Waite Group continues to publish innovative multimedia books on cutting-edge topics, and of course the programming books that make up our heritage. Being a programmer myself, I appreciate clear guidance through a tricky OS, so our books come bundled with disks and CDs loaded with code, utilities and custom controls.

By 1994, The Waite Group will have published 135 books. Our next step is to develop a new type of book, an interactive, multimedia experience involving the reader on many levels. With this new book, you'll be trained by a computer-based instructor with infinite patience, run a simulation to visualize the topic, play a game that shows you different aspects of the subject, interact with others on-line, and have instant access to a large database on the subject. For traditionalists, there will be a full-color, paper-based book.

In the meantime, they've wired the White House for hi-tech; the information super highway has been proposed; and computers, communication, entertainment, and information are becoming inseparable. To travel in this Digital Age you'll need guidebooks. The Waite Group offers such guidance for the most important software—your mind.

We hope you enjoy this book. For a color catalog, just fill out and send in the Reader Report Card at the back of the book. You can reach me on CIS as 75146,3515, MCI mail as mwaite, and usenet as mitch@well.sf.ca.us.

Sincerely,

Mitchell Waite

Mitchell Waite
Publisher

Waite
Group
Press™

ACKNOWLEDGMENTS

Mike Miller contributed to this book in many ways not obvious in the text. He was a partner in its creation. You're generous to a fault. My heartfelt thanks.

Alan Henry must have been thinking about this book in his cockpit, because it shows in the details of his contributions. Your enthusiasm was infectious.

Mike Halvorson provided the motivation for much of what is good about this book. Thank you for making this project possible. I also want to thank him for providing some of the cover images.

Thanks to the Waite Group team for being patient with a book that had a long birth: Scott Calamar, Joel Fugazzotto, Cecile Kaufman, Julianne Ososke, Mitch Waite, Heidi Brumbaugh. Scott often threatened execution. I'm still here. He must have been kidding. I taught Joel a new word. Ask him sometime.

Other people who helped include Bill Allen (*3D Artist* magazine), Chuck Jameson, Mabyn Martin, Fred Thompson, Bill Knoedel, James Kaplan and Jason Gibbs.

Colby Shaddock drew the house.

Valérie was amused by the title of the opening chapter.

INTRODUCTION

At the time *3D Modeling Lab* is being written there are no books that teach you how to actually build 3D models. There are many books that teach you 3D math, books that act as tutorials for particular features of specific programs, and books that survey the field. But no books provide a general introduction to modeling with practical hands-on tips for building objects like honeybees or modeling surfaces with maps and procedural textures.

This book gives you the background knowledge necessary to understand 3D modeling. In the tradition of Waite Group Press books, you learn 3D modeling by doing. The book includes a complete version of Impulse Inc.'s Imagine 3D modeling and animation program which you use as a laboratory to explore 3D concepts and object construction techniques.

I give you a dash of theory, then illustrate its application in step-by-step tutorials. The tips and techniques you learn here can be applied to the program of your choice: the shareware program POV-Ray, Autodesk 3D Studio, NewTek Lightwave, and a host of others.

What makes Imagine a particularly good choice as a laboratory is its robust tools. Imagine is one of the most sophisticated 3D modeling and rendering programs for desktop animators. It is an aptly named product, because the program allows you to model just about anything you can imagine. The program contains such advanced modeling and rendering tools as procedural texturing, magnetism, particle animation, ray tracing, fog, and skinning. Imagine has entered its ninth year as a tool for 3D artists, and it shows.

Because the focus is on general theory and practical model building tips and techniques, I do not cover all of Imagine's features. In particular, a single chapter is devoted to animation; I could have devoted an entire book to this subject. I do not cover Imagine's Cycle Editor, a self-contained module that is used to animate parts of objects. Also, the complete Imagine version 2 comes with this book.

This book is broken into major themes, beginning with a general introduction to 3D that places it in the context of representational art. From there, it moves on to such topics as giving objects surfaces; the intricacies of lighting; building detailed, photorealistic objects; and image processing the final image.

Also bundled with the book is Picture Man for Windows, a shareware image processing program that acts as an excellent companion for Imagine. Chapter 8, on image processing, shows you what to do with the image after it has been created.

The first part of the book introduces concepts and their applications. The second part contains two projects that take you step-by-step through object construction and animation. Appendixes include a glossary and descriptions of how the train and bee models commissioned for the book were created by Mike Miller and Alan Henry, two distinguished 3D artists.

Each chapter stands alone and is broken into sections that are tightly focused on a single modeling concept. If you are new to 3D, I encourage you to read the chapters in order and complete all of the exercises. If you already know your way around 3D, you might want to skip to the section that interests you most.

If you have long had the desire to express yourself artistically, you've come to the right place. By the end of the book, you will have learned to create scenes of extraordinary realism and beauty.

The lab is open. Welcome to the *3D Modeling Lab*.

INSTALLATION

This book is bundled with two high-density disks containing Imagine, Picture Man for Windows, and sample files. The files have been compressed to save space. This means that you cannot run Imagine from the floppy. You must use the installation batch files (INSTALL1.BAT and INSTALL2.BAT) to copy the files onto your hard drive.

EQUIPMENT REQUIREMENTS

This book is written for Imagine on the PC. Version 2 of the program is included with the disks. Here are the basic requirements for an IBM-compatible computer:

- 386 computer with a math coprocessor
- 4 megabytes of system (RAM) memory
- 10 megabytes of hard disk space
- 256K VGA card
- Mouse

Creating 3D images on a 386 computer is up to ten times slower than creating images on a 486 computer. On average, your work flow will be slowed down by a factor of two to three times. The recommended requirements for a system are

- 486 computer
- 16 megabytes of system memory
- 30 megabytes of hard disk space
- Hi-Color or True Color VGA system
- MS-DOS's HIMEM.SYS memory manager

INSTALLING THE PROGRAMS

Installation of the programs to your hard drive is automated. Each of the disks must be installed separately.

1 Verify that you have 5 megabytes free on the designated hard drive by typing the following at your hard drive prompt:

`dir`

2 Assuming you've placed the installation disk in drive A, make the first installation floppy the current directory.

`a:` (ENTER)

3 Run the installation program, designating the drive where the files are to be installed.

`install1 c:` (ENTER)

Installation proceeds automatically. The installation program sets up the necessary directories on your hard drive, copies the files to these directories, and decompresses them. Please be patient while this happens.

4 Place the second installation disk in the floppy drive.

5 Run the second installation program, designating the destination drive.

`e.g. install2 c:` (ENTER)

Once again, the files on the second floppy disk will be copied and decompressed to the hard drive.

Directory Structures

Impulse's Imagine program, all its subdirectories, and the subdirectories for vendors and guest artists are in the root directory, \IMAG.

Picture Man for Windows and its subdirectories are in the root directory, \PICMAN.

SETTING UP YOUR PC'S MEMORY FOR IMAGINE

If your computer came supplied with extended memory, you probably already have an *extended memory manager* installed. Extended memory managers make the computer's extended memory available to the programs you use. They use special routines that trick DOS into using the additional memory.

Altering the CONFIG.SYS file

Memory managers are usually installed by a special file in the system *boot* directory (usually c:\) called CONFIG.SYS. When you first turn on the computer, the disk operating system looks for this file and configures your system according to instructions found there. You must alter this file to run Imagine efficiently. First, back up the existing CONFIG.SYS file. If you are a novice user of computers, you should seek the help of your computer dealer or a knowledgeable friend before altering this file. Buy a book that teaches you the basics of managing memory on your computer system, for example, *Up and Running with DOS*, by Alan Simpson. Appendix B lists ordering information for Simpson's book.

Recommended Memory Management Setup

Here are the recommendations for memory setup:

1. Use the MS-DOS memory manager HIMEM.SYS for memory management.

2. Add or modify a stacks device driver to CONFIG.SYS.

   ```
   STACKS=9,256
   ```

The following is the CONFIG.SYS file used to develop this book. If you use this file, you will have to tell DOS where to find the HIMEM.SYS, SETVER.EXE, and MOUSE.SYS files. Your mouse driver may be different from the one I used.

```
DEVICE=HIMEM.SYS
BUFFERS=10,0
FILES=20
DOS=UMB
LASTDRIVE=K
FCBS=16,0
DEVICEHIGH =SETVER.EXE
DEVICEHIGH =MOUSE.SYS /Y
STACKS=9,256
```

This configuration allows you to run Windows and Imagine without having to reconfigure the system. (Imagine cannot run under Windows enhanced mode. Do not try to run Imagine from within Windows.)

Freeing Memory

The most important advice I can give you is to free up as much system RAM as possible for Imagine. That means removing TSR (terminate and stay resident) programs and other programs that use up RAM, such as the SMARTDRV.SYS device driver that is usually installed by Windows. If you have a RAM drive installed, remove it.

Virtual Memory

Imagine does *not* use virtual memory. This makes it especially important that you free up the RAM resources on your computer. If necessary, write special CONFIG.SYS and AUTOEXEC.BAT files for Imagine. Make sure you save your existing files before doing this.

RUNNING IMAGINE

Once you have installed Imagine and configured your computer to run Imagine, change to the \IMAG directory and type

```
imagine
```

If you have an expanded memory manager installed in your system (not recommended), and Imagine refuses to run, try typing

```
imagine /noxms
```

RUNNING PICTURE MAN FOR WINDOWS

Picture Man for Windows runs under Microsoft's Windows 3.0 or 3.1 operating environment. The files for Picture Man take up about 1.2 megabytes of hard disk space. You will need at least 2 megabytes of RAM to run Picture Man. More is better. Images take up a lot of memory and must have a contiguous area of memory, not bits scattered around like other programs.

Installing Picture Man on the Windows Desktop

This section describes how to install a Picture Man icon on the Windows desktop. If you know how to install Windows programs in the Program Manager, skip this section.

1 Run Windows.

`C:\win`

2 Click on the File menu.

3 Click on New.

A New Program Object box pops on the screen. Program Item is highlighted.

4 Click on OK.

A Program Item Properties box pops on the screen.

5 Type the words `Picture Man` in the Description box. Don't press (ENTER).

6 Press (TAB).

This moves the text cursor from the Description box to the Command Line box.

7 Type the following, substituting the drive letter where you installed Picture Man:

`c:\picman\pman.exe`

A warning message titled "Invalid Path" appears on the screen if you specify the wrong drive or directory. Make sure the spelling is exact. There are no spaces in this line. If you do get an error message, start over. Check to see if you have installed Picture Man on another drive. If you do not get an error message, proceed to the next instruction.

8 Click on the Change Icon button.

The Change Icon box pops on the screen. There is a series of small, colorful icons at the center of this box. Choose an icon. (I like the little picture of the monitor with the blue, yellow, and red colored circle.) Once this is installed in your Windows environment, all you have to do to run the program is double-click on this symbol.

9 Click on the icon you want to use for Picture Man.

You are returned to the Program Item Properties box. You are finished and ready to return to the Program Manager.

10 Click on OK.

This completes installation of Picture Man for Windows.

Windows Setup

Picture Man will use the existing Windows drivers and settings. For best results, allow Picture Man to use all the available Windows resources. Don't run other programs while running Picture Man and do not attempt to run Imagine and Picture Man simultaneously. Exit from Windows to run Imagine; exit from Imagine to run Windows.

Video Setup

Although you will be able to display images in fewer colors using the bundled Picture Man for Windows, scenes with metal surfaces, refractions, and reflections will display better if your video system supports 32,000 colors (Hi-Color) or 16.7 million colors (True Color). Some users have VGA color systems installed in their computers but fail to use all of the available colors because they do not have the correct drivers installed. Ask your dealer or an expert computer user for help in determining if your system is using its resources optimally.

Caution: Windows 3.0 Users

Picture Man uses the Windows 3.1 file COMMDLG.DLL to handle boxes for opening files and choosing colors. This file did not come with Windows 3.0 or with Picture Man. Most Windows software packages that have come out since Windows 3.1 will install this file. If you are using Windows 3.0 and Picture Man doesn't respond when you first try to open a file, you probably do not have COMMDLG.DLL on your hard disk. Use the DOS directory command (DIR) to see if it is in your Windows SYSTEM subdirectory.

TABLE OF CONTENTS

CONTENTS

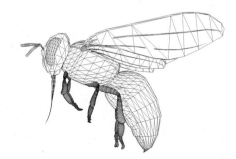

Part 2   Projects

Appendixes

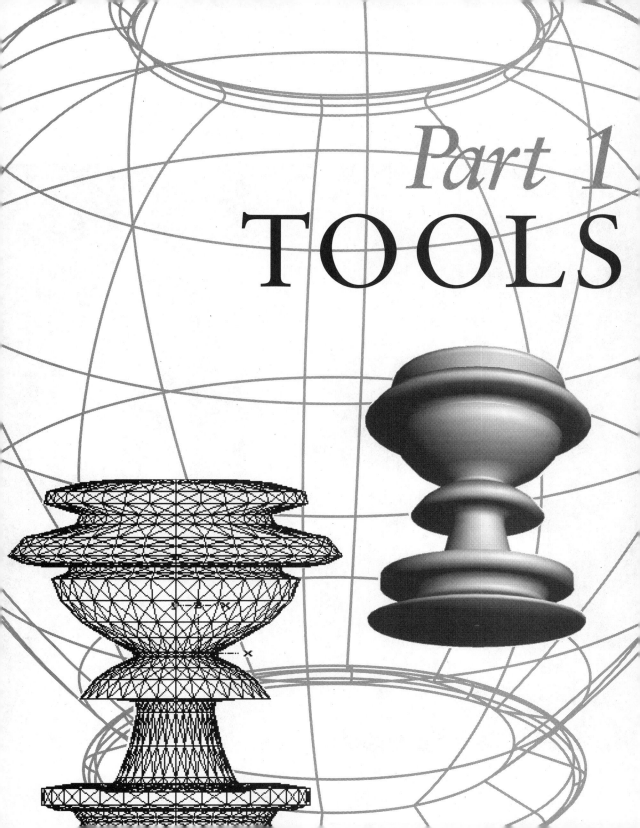

Part 1
TOOLS

Learning to See in 3D

This chapter journeys back to the studios of those old visual magicians, the Renaissance masters. They are the ones who first learned how to fool the eye into seeing depth on a flat two-dimensional surface. The illusion rested on a body of knowledge that reached back to the Greeks: geometry. Geometry is a branch of mathematics devoted to discovering the relations, properties, and measurement of solids, surfaces, lines, and angles. It is also a theory of space and of figures in space. The Renaissance artist learned to transform that knowledge into works of striking realism. Up until the Renaissance, artists used art to express ideas. The Renaissance artist used art to mimic reality. That was a breakthrough.

Over a century of films and photography have taught us to be more blasé about the representation of 3D space on a flat surface, except in one area: 3D art and animation. Movies that blend 3D art and animation with traditional photography and cinematography have revived the appetite for art that accurately models the physical and optical properties of the world. History has repeated itself. Once more the mathematician and artist have colluded to enchant and transport the observer. Today, it is called *photorealism.*

Photorealism describes computer-generated images that model the optical and physical properties of the world so well that some people are fooled into seeing the computer image as a photograph. An example is the image shown on Color Plate 1 created by the ray-trace artist, Mike Miller.

Mike has created a compelling resurrection of an old steam engine. He created this scene using the program bundled with this book, Imagine.

The computer's ability to mimic photographic images is mystifying to people who think of computers as the playthings of mathematicians and spreadsheet wizards. A computer-generated image is magic, in the sense meant by the science fiction writer Arthur C. Clarke when he wrote, "Any sufficiently advanced technology is indistinguishable from magic."

This chapter will tear the veil of illusion away from the world of 3D art and reveal it for what it is: technology in the service of art. You'll see how 3D programs, like Imagine, are used to create photorealistic images. Geometry lessons will be reduced to a few dozen clicks of the mouse. 3D programs encode in algorithm the laws of perspective and the complex interplay between surfaces and lights. By burying modeling algorithms behind a point-and-click interface, the 3D program puts technology in its place, as another tool in the artist's studio. You don't need a degree in math to create 3D images, but you do need basic computing skills to tap into the buried intelligence of 3D programs. You'll learn those skills along the way.

You should also have some basic knowledge of the techniques long used by representational artists. An image like Mike Miller's train was coaxed from the silicon reaches of the computer, but his eye is a trained artist's eye. The latter part of this chapter provides tips on using color, detail, light, and elevation to make your own 3D graphics rich and convincing.

By the end of this chapter, you'll have a good understanding of the roots of 3D in representational art, what the 3D creation process is, and how modern artists use 3D to create photorealistic scenes.

ORIGINS OF 3D DISPLAY IN THE RENAISSANCE

Let's put the Renaissance artist's accomplishment in perspective. If you have ever tried to draw a three-dimensional shape, you know how difficult it is to create the illusion of depth on a flat surface. In fact, the concept of three-dimensional space is so abstract that a child has no innate understanding of such concepts as depth and volume. An example: Pour the same amount of water into two containers (see Figure 1-1), and adults have no trouble understanding that both glasses contain the same volume of water.

A child thinks the taller glass contains more water. Try as you might, you cannot convince the child that when an object changes shape, it still occupies the same volume in space.

Even after you've learned how to think in 3D, you still have to learn to apply that knowledge. Figure 1-2 shows a ten-year-old's drawing depicting his home.

Figure 1-1 The fact that both glasses contain the same volume of water is incomprehensible to a child

Figure 1-2 Colby's portrait of his home is seen without an observer's viewpoint in space

In this picture there is little awareness that the appearance of objects in the scene are affected by the observer's position in space. Colby's drawing expresses his ideas about his home and the people in it, but that picture does not give us many clues about how the house actually appears to the eye.

Learning to model objects in three-dimensional space is so basic to classical art training, that we have forgotten that the principles underlying it had to be discovered. Figure 1-3 provides an interesting contrast between Renaissance art and the medieval art that preceded it.

The panel on the left was created by the Florentine artist Cimabue (c. 1240-1302) sometime around 1280. The panel on the right was created about 30 years later by the artist Giotto (1266-1336). The two panels hang in the same room at the Uffizi Gallery in Florence, but they are about half a dimension apart. You can see that Cimabue was interested in three-dimensional representation. Look at the shape of the throne and the arch below it. But Cimabue didn't quite get it right. If you were looking at a photograph, you wouldn't see the inside walls of all three arches at once.

Compare that to the panel on the right. In the 30 years that elapsed between Cimabue's treatment of the theme and Giotto's, artists had discovered a powerful new way of orienting the observer to the picture. When you look at Cimabue's Madonna, you are not quite sure where you are. Giotto makes it clear. Giotto gives the viewer a vantage point.

The laws of perspective were not laid down until long after Giotto's death, and his *Madonna Enthroned* is not quite right, but it is a major step forward.

Two centuries later the Renaissance artist Giorgione (1478-1510) shows how much artists and mathematicians had learned in the intervening years (see Figure 1-4).

The Madonna appears to be smaller than the figures standing before the throne. This is a reversal of the medieval canon that made the most important figure in the painting the largest. Is this sacrilege? Apparently not. The contemporary viewer understands that the Madonna only appears to be smaller because she is farther away from the observer.

The throne's three-dimensional solidity stands out in relief against the natural, panoramic view in the background. The artist has discovered some of the subtleties of representing objects in three-dimensional space. For example, there is a mist in the distant scene that enhances the feeling of depth in the painting. There is more detail in the foreground than the background. Far objects are lighter in color. There is attention to the relative sizes of things. For example, you can barely make out two people in a field to the right of the throne, in the distance. We know they are far away by their relatively small size compared to the figures in the foreground.

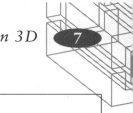

Figure 1-3 The medieval world was two-dimensional, the Renaissance three-dimensional

LEARNING TO IMITATE NATURAL PERSPECTIVE

The Renaissance artist had discovered how to imitate what is now called *natural perspective*. Figure 1-5 shows how this works. The world is always seen from a viewpoint, the viewpoint of the eye. Notice that the lines converge as they move away from the picture frame to a vanishing point.

Seen from the point of view of the eye, a scene with natural perspective looks like Figure 1-6. This scene was created in Imagine. All the lines in the picture recede to a vanishing point in the distance. This tricks the eye into seeing

Figure 1-4 Giorgione's Madonna shows mastery of perspective

depth where there is no depth. Let's see how the Renaissance artist used this knowledge. Figure 1-7 shows Giorgione's image of the Madonna.

Giorgione knows exactly how to orchestrate the image for the eye. Imagine that Giorgione's work is hanging above you and your eye has picked up the vertical lines on the floor. You follow the path of the lines up to the Madonna. The line of the horizon is high, so that the lines in Figure 1-7 should recede to a vanishing point *behind* the throne, in the distant hills. In placing the

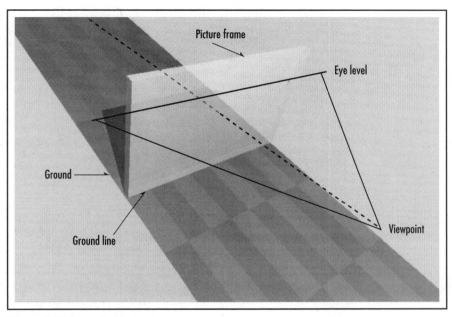

Figure 1-5 Natural perspective

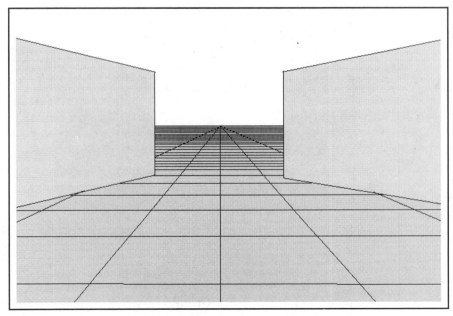

Figure 1-6 A 3D program easily creates the illusion of depth

Figure 1-7 Lines of perspective in Giorgione's painting

Madonna along the path of the distant vanishing point, Giorgione is using perspective to bring the natural world into line with the spiritual world represented by the Madonna. There is mathematical coordination between the divine and the mundane. Giorgione's audience would have delighted in the philosophical meaning of the image.

Technology and Art

You may think that when technology elbows its way between the artist and the canvas, art becomes mechanical and uninspired. But the Renaissance artist's happy marriage of science, technology, and art contradicts this view. Figure 1-8 shows that art and technology do make good partners.

Paolo Uccello, the Renaissance Florentine artist, is reported to have worked through the night to finish this study of perspective. The chalice is entirely composed of line segments and looks exactly like a computer model! Now compare Figure 1-8 with Figure 1-9, the chalice modeled in Imagine.

Uccello divided the surface of the chalice into square geometric shapes that look like the polygons that underlie computer images. Polygons are three- or four-sided line segments intersecting at vertices. A common way of describing a 3D object modeled with polygons is a *wireframe*. Uccello's "wireframe" is almost *six centuries* old.

Uccello's sketch was meant as a drawing aid. Entrepreneurial artists at the dawn of the industrial age found an easier way to model objects. Figure 1-10

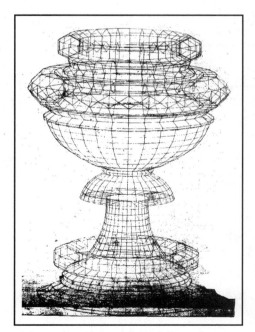

Figure 1-8 Paolo Uccello's chalice

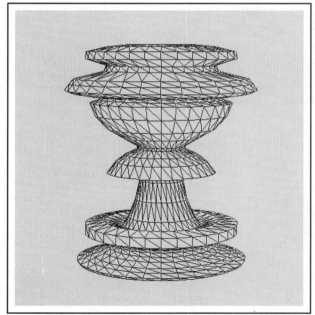

Figure 1-9 The computer wireframe version of Uccello's chalice

Figure 1-10 Albrecht Dürer's mechanical drawing aid

shows a device created by the German Renaissance artist and genius, Albrecht Dürer.

The image comes from Dürer's manual for artists. The image shows how to bring technology to perspective drawing. He has chosen a lute because its curves make it difficult to model. Look at the drawing held in the out-stretched hand of the man standing. This object anticipates the computer wireframe view.

What's Ahead

In the next section you'll learn how artists use 3D computer programs to model scenes and create animations.

THE COMPUTER 3D CREATION PROCESS

In the beginning, 3D computer art was generated on mainframe computers with mathematical formulas. Uccello would have been fascinated by this development.

There is a group of dedicated (some might say fanatical) 3D artists who still use code to generate 3D images: devotees of the shareware POV-Ray 3D program. But most 3D artists prefer a less arduous approach. Modern drag-and-drop menu systems provide that. They allow users to ignore the underlying mathematical complexity. Instead of writing code, the artist points and clicks or enters simple coordinates in dialog boxes. Imagine uses a modern graphical user interface that makes access to program functions easy and makes working with objects visually intuitive (see Figure 1-11).

Figure 1-11 shows a computer-generated version of Uccello's chalice, seen from above (a), from the front (b), from the side(c), and from a perspective view (d). 3D artists look at their creations through windows and use mice or digitizing tablets to create 3D objects. Albrecht Dürer's mechanical drawing aid has its modern equivalent.

Four Steps of the Creation Process

Modern graphical interfaces free the artist to concentrate on the art of 3D rather than the science. Figure 1-12 shows the four steps the artist takes to create a scene.

- **Step 1: Planning**–In planning and visualizing the scene, the artist sketches it on paper.

- **Step 2: Modeling**–The artist creates a computer-generated version of the sketch using modeling tools. The artist then sets parameters that give the model color, shading, and other surface attributes.

- **Step 3: Staging**–The artist arranges the objects in the scene. A point of view is created by placing a camera in the scene. Lighting is added for photorealistic effect.

- **Step 4: Rendering**–Finally the scene is rendered. Rendering converts the 3D data generated during the previous steps into an image the artist can save to disk as a paint image or output to videotape as a series of frames in a movie or video.

Color Plate 2 shows the evolution of Uccello's chalice according to this four-step process.

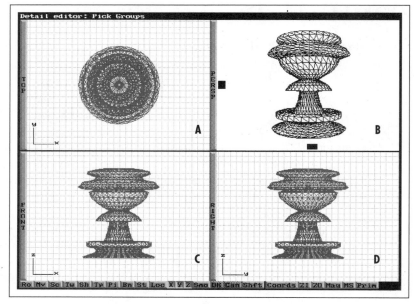

Figure 1-11 The graphical interface for Imagine buries math in mouse clicks

The way that the modeling process is implemented in 3D programs varies widely. Some programs attempt to simplify the interface for artists by incorporating all the program functions into one or two program modules. Imagine divides the task of modeling scenes into five main modules (see Figure 1-13), two devoted to object creation and two to staging the scene. A fifth contains rendering commands. There are two more modules, the Cycle Editor and Preferences Editor, not covered in this book.

The next sections review the steps in the 3D creation process in detail.

PLANNING

Storyboards are commonly used in film, television, and audio-visual productions as a planning aid. They are a kind of comic strip that documents the action in a scene so that directors, actors, lighting technicians, and prop people can determine what scene elements are required, how they are arranged, and how they change over time. The storyboard helps anticipate problems. What you see in your head might not look good on paper, or ultimately, the screen. A storyboard helps identify problems that might result in halting the

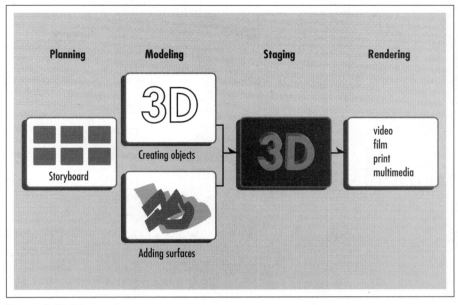

Figure 1-12 3D creation process

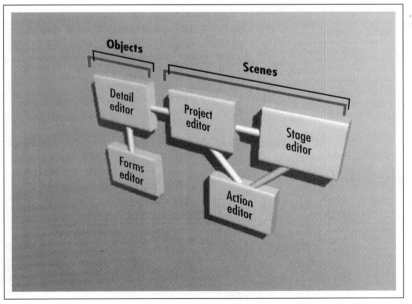

Figure 1-13 Imagine divides the modeling task into program modules

action, as the camera is moved, the scene rebuilt, and new scene elements are purchased or made. For the 3D artist, a storyboard is most useful for planning the complexities of 3D animations and getting client approval before costly production begins.

Even when the goal is to create a single image, a sketch of the scene is helpful in planning the work. Working from a technical drawing, the artist can develop an accurate scale model of the object in the computer. The technical drawing provides the correct proportions and relations between parts.

MODELING

Modeling is the process of creating the geometry of objects in the computer's memory and giving them surfaces. Over the years the computer has taken on more and more of the labor of generating 3D scenes. In the beginning, computer artists had to actually draw all of the line segments defining an object on the screen. Today, a number of modeling techniques are used to automatically generate 3D objects.

Using Extrusion to Generate 3D Shapes

One of the most common methods of creating 3D objects is to draw an object profile on the screen and then *extrude* it. Extrusion taps into the computer's power to transform objects. A 2D square is extruded to become a 3D box. The profile of a wine glass is spun on its axis to become a 3D wine glass. A hollow circle becomes a cylinder, capped at both ends. A hollow square becomes a box. A circle spun along an axis becomes a garden hose. Figure 1-14 shows the word "3D" extruded into a 3D object.

Cross-sectional Modeling

Another modeling technique divides the object into 2D cross sections over which a surface is drawn, like cloth over the hoops of a lamp. The shape of the object can be changed by changing the shape and size of individual slices defining the object's cross section. The program then interpolates the surface that is "drawn over" the individual slices. This is how Imagine's Forms Editor works. It is also implemented in Imagine's Detail Editor as a program function called *skinning*.

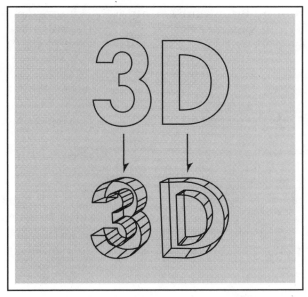

Figure 1-14 Extruding "3D" into three dimensions

Sculpting

Extrusion and cross-sectional modeling generate 3D objects from 2D shapes. Programs also offer tools that allow you to start with a 3D shape and sculpt it, much as a sculptor chips way at stone. Other tools allow you to mold objects in a manner similar to modeling in clay.

Procedural Modeling

Procedural modeling lies at the leading edge of 3D modeling. In this case, complex objects like trees are generated by computer procedures (mathematical models). Particle systems simulate such natural phenomenon as wind, fireworks, explosions, and lens-flare effects.

Animation Tools

There are many techniques particular to animation and its needs. For example, *bones* is a relatively recent innovation in which a model is developed, and then a separate object is developed that acts as the object's skeleton. By animating the skeleton, the object's movements and surface structure change in tandem. Collision detection determines when objects are in contact.

Adding Surfaces to Objects

3D objects have surfaces composed of triangles or polygons. This quiltlike cover of line segments (sometimes called a *polygonal mesh*) looks like a wire cage. It is the default view of objects in most modelers.

There are three basic ways of adding surfaces to 3D wireframes: by applying a layer of pixels to the surface of the object using a reference map, by applying a mathematically generated pattern to the surface, and by modeling the effect of light on the surface. Each of these will be covered in turn.

Image-mapping

The surface of an object can be assigned a texture derived from a 2D image. The image is created in a paint program, a scan, or even a video frame grabbed from a camera or VCR. Image-mapping is a process similar to wrapping a plain white box with gift wrap. The 3D program puts a layer of pixels on the object, automatically projecting the reference image (such as a scan of wood) onto a 3D object. Figure 1-15 shows a cube, a cylinder, and a sphere wrapped with the same wood-grain texture.

Notice that the same 2D image is mapped very differently on the three different types of objects. The streaking lines you see along the sides of the cube, for example, are the result of projecting the map along one axis of the cube. With careful planning, and a few tricks, you can overcome the limitations of projecting two-dimensional surfaces on three-dimensional objects. You'll learn these tricks in Chapter 6.

Procedural Textures

Procedural textures use mathematical formulas to simulate natural surfaces, such as wood. Whereas in the previous example, an actual scan of wood was used, in the case of procedural texturing, a mathematical formula is used to simulate the patterns in wood. Fractal algorithms are popular for producing such patterns as clouds, rocks, or water.

Figure 1-15 Three types of image-mapping

Shading

Shading is another method of defining the way surfaces in the final image appear. The object is assigned a color, and the program determines how the object will be shaded, based on the way light strikes the surface of the object. There are four principal types of shading algorithms: wireframe, flat, Gouraud, and Phong. In Figure 1-16 a sphere has been mapped with each of the types of surfaces. There is a single light illuminating each of the spheres. You can see its reflection in three of the four spheres.

Wireframe Shading

In wireframe shading only the edges of polygons are rendered. When computers were first used for 3D display, they created objects as wireframes.

Flat Shading

In flat shading, the entire surface of a polygon is given a single level of illumination. In Figure 1-16 you can see the shape of the polygons in the flat-shaded sphere that make up the surface of the sphere. The sphere does not look smooth because the polygons are each given a different color. Flat shading is not very natural, but objects with this kind of shading can be quickly rendered.

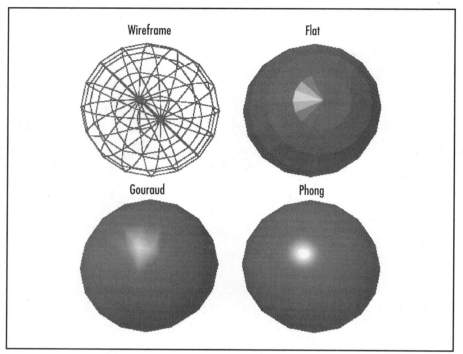

Figure 1-16 The four types of surface shading

Gouraud Shading

Gouraud shading is the simplest form of *smooth* shading, where the light's intensity is averaged across an entire polygon, usually from values measured at vertices. On the Gouraud-shaded sphere in Figure 1-16 you can see the blurred outline of the polygons where the highlight occurs, but the sphere looks much smoother than the sphere rendered with flat surface shading.

Phong Shading

The Phong-shaded sphere reflects the light most realistically. In Phong shading, each pixel on the object's surface is calculated in relation to the light source. The number of calculations that need to be performed on a Phong-shaded object is vast compared to Gouraud, flat, or wireframe shaded objects. The number of calculations multiplies exponentially as the spatial resolution of the image increases. As a general rule in 3D computing, the more realistic the final scene, the longer the render time it takes to create that scene. Choose the shading appropriate to an object.

Using Image Maps in 3D Scenes

Just as the gunfight in a movie may occur on a street that is lined with painted backdrops, a 3D scene might also be composed of scanned photographs or 2D patterns prepared in programs like Corel Photopaint, Adobe Photoshop, or the Picture Man program bundled with this book. Hollywood's visual magicians know that distant objects will be seen imperfectly by the camera, so they do not have to be created in exact detail. By placing live action in the foreground, the audience will be fooled into seeing the painted backdrop as a three-dimensional reality. The same logic applies to 3D production. As long as the 3D camera never zooms into or travels close to the 2D surface, the audience will quite happily accept the illusion.

STAGING

Staging a scene is a lot like staging a theatrical production. First of all, objects are arranged and a camera view of the scene is established. Then lighting is added to the scene. Animation is defined. After the puzzle of creating 3D objects, staging the scene with lights and action gives the 3D artist an opportunity to become the director in his or her own virtual movie. These are subjects that will be thoroughly treated in the chapters ahead.

Establishing the Camera View

The observer's point of view is established with a digital tool whose name is borrowed from photography: the *camera* view. In 3D programs users can create a virtual camera with a lens that *sees* the scene in a manner similar to a real camera. The focal length (angle of view) of the scene is adjusted. The camera is moved through the scene, just as a real movie camera moves through a movie set.

Using Lighting for Photorealism

In the natural world, light reveals the shape and texture of objects around us. Adding lights to a scene and adjusting ambient light values are integral to the scene's photorealism. Most programs include a variety of lighting options.

For example, Imagine allows you to create cylindrical lights that behave like theatrical spotlights, or conical lights that behave like headlights. There is also a variety of lighting models used by 3D software, including scanline rendering, ray tracing, and radiocity. These methods are discussed in Chapter 5 and Chapter 7.

Animating the Scene

Animation techniques take advantage of the way our eyes respond to light. Rods and cones in the eye are not fast enough in responding to changing light values, so the eye compensates by mentally merging successive images. If a series of images are rapidly shown to the eye, it is easily fooled into seeing continuous motion rather than a series of discrete images. The traditional animator working with paints, plastics, film emulsions, and camera stands must laboriously create a series of pictures to achieve this effect. Often the master animator draws only key images. The *key frames,* as these are called, are passed to assistants who fill in the *in-between* frames straddling consecutive key frames.

In computer 3D animation, *key frame animation* describes the 3D program's ability to interpolate scene changes from one frame to another. A frame is a single image in an animated series. If you tell a computer where an object is at the beginning of a series of frames, what path it follows, and where it moves to, the computer calculates the shape and size of the object as it moves from one key frame to the other. The computer automatically keeps track of the way light interacts with the object as it moves.

Most advanced 3D programs like Imagine allow you to animate more than the movement of objects. A bouncing tennis ball squashes as it hits a surface and rebounds to its spherical shape after it leaves the surface. You can also animate cameras and lights.

RENDERING

Rendering is the conversion of the object, including its attributes and its transformations, into an image or animation saved to the hard drive. A wireframe image of a chalice is transformed into a gold chalice brimming with wine and glistening in the evening light. All the complex elements that make up the final image or visual sequence are brought together and married to form a flat two-dimensional image that can be output to video, film, print, or multimedia.

An image may exceed the display capabilities of your system (some images destined for the printed page can exceed 4K-by-4K resolution), so most 3D programs provide the option of rendering the image to disk.

The computer must make millions of calculations in order to transform a scene from the 3D wireframe view on the monitor to a fully rendered 2D image. In the development stage, when you preview the final image, most programs allow you to specify different levels of detail in the rendered image. You may want to see a very quick outline of the scene or animation to study motion or the effects of lighting decisions. One strategy is to render a low-resolution version of the image, such as VGA's 320 by 200, 256-color mode.

Rendering is the least labor-intensive activity for 3D artists and the most calculation-intensive for the computer. The chapters that follow provide tips on how to reduce rendering time.

Output Options for 3D Scenes

A 3D image or animation usually forms part of a larger project. It may form part of a print collage. It may be imported into a 2D program like Adobe Photoshop for embellishment and exported from there to become part of a multimedia sequence. A 3D animation sequence might become part of a film or a television advertisement.

At first you will be tempted to make the 3D program produce the final image. However, it is often faster and easier to use other programs to add elements to the final composition. This book includes an image processing program, Picture Man for Windows, as a convenience for readers who may not have an image processing program. If you need to add animation to a complex product demo, you would use the 3D program to generate the parts of the scene that must simulate movement in three-dimensional space. But a 2D animation package like Animator Pro or Paul Mace's GRASP would do 2D animations (for example, a bird flying across the screen) more efficiently.

SIMULATING DEPTH IN 3D SOFTWARE

You may be able to quickly create an image with correct perspective, but the most important source of exceptional art is creativity. Figure 1-17 shows the Renaissance artist Andrea Mantega's *Dead Christ,* a classic example of the use of *foreshortening* to give an image depth. Mantega mastered the rules of perspective enough to fudge the picture. Can you see where the rules have been broken?

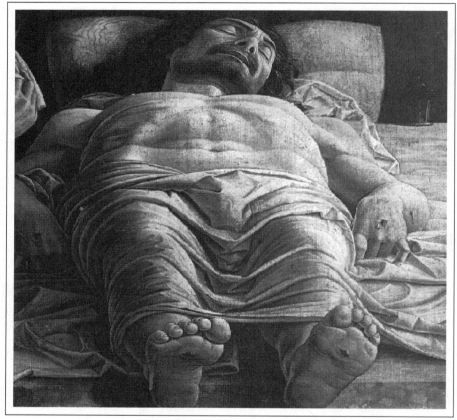

Figure 1-17 Andrea Mantega's Dead Christ shows foreshortening

Mantega made Christ's feet smaller than they would be if this were a photograph. If he had made the feet larger, the picture would have produced a lighthearted titter in its audience rather than a hushed reverence. Learning to creatively break the laws of perspective still requires knowing the laws in the first place.

The strategy is to use the computer to perform the calculations on the image that give it the illusion of solidity and depth. Then use the rules of perspective to enhance the effect. Besides vanishing points, some of the techniques used by 3D artists include shading, elevation, brightness and color, detail differences between foreground and background objects, the relative sizes of known objects, motion parallax (or blur), and binocular vision.

Shading

Shading is discussed briefly here because it is the subject of an entire chapter (Chapter 3). Shading is defined as the way colors on an object's surface interact with light. The side of an object turned in the direction of the light is the brightest. As the surface of the object rotates and recedes from the light, it becomes darker. Figure 1-18 shows the chalice rendered with a default white surface.

Phong-shading objects creates models with smooth surfaces, subtle shading, and detailed highlights. The observer uses this information to interpret the position of the object in 3D space. It gives an almost tactile sense of the shape's contours and its volume.

Elevation

Objects seen from a high angle seem smaller than objects seen from a low angle. Figure 1-19 shows the chalice seen from below. Notice how large the chalice looks. Figure 1-20 shows the object seen from above. Notice how small it now looks. The angle of the point of view is an important clue about size.

Figure 1-18 The chalice shaded and lit with one light

Figure 1-19 The chalice seen from below

Figure 1-20 The chalice seen from above

Altering the Horizon Line

To give a scene a feeling of tremendous depth, make the horizon high in relation to the foreground. Then objects that are closer to the horizon will appear to be the farthest away. Figure 1-21 is titled *Uccello's Study* (see also Color Plate 2). The horizon line is quite high in the picture, giving the scene a feeling of depth.

Overlapping

Superimposing objects is a very basic 3D clue. This can be demonstrated very simply (see Figure 1-22). The eye will tend to see the circle and square as two-dimensional objects lying on a plain. However, as soon as the circle overlaps the square (Figure 1-23), the eye sees one as being in front of the other. When the circle interrupts the outline of the box, the sensation that the circle is on top of the box is much stronger (see Figure 1-24).

You can enhance the sense of depth in 3D computer art by artfully overlapping objects. Adding some kind of ground or vertical backdrop in 3D scenes helps the audience to interpret the size and orientation of objects in space. In *Uccello's Study* (Figure 1-21), objects rest on a table, giving the viewer a sense of the object's weight and solidity.

Figure 1-21 Uccello's Study has many depth cues

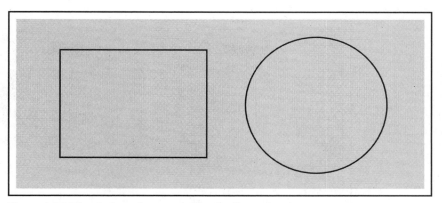

Figure 1-22 The circle and square look two-dimensional

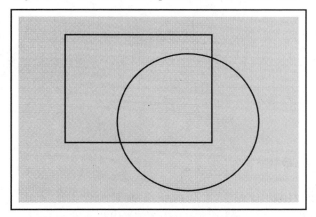

Figure 1-23 Offsetting the circle creates depth

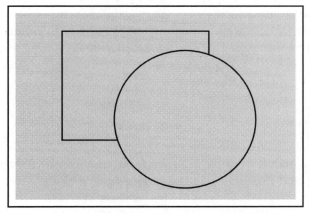

Figure 1-24 The 3D effect is enhanced when one shape completely overlaps another

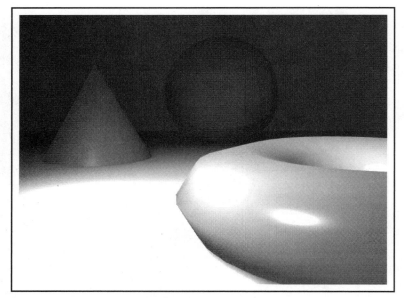

Figure 1-25 Image created using distance cueing

Brightness and Color

As a rule, brighter objects appear to be closer, darker objects farther away. The colors of objects also change as they recede. Trees and mountains become bluish, for example. *Uccello's Study* uses the play of darkness and light. The candle's light casts shadows and models the surface of the chalice with light. 3D programs often include the ability to simulate the fall-off of light over a distance. This is often called *distance cueing*. Figure 1-25 shows an example of this. Notice how depth is enhanced by the falling off of the brightness of the spotlight.

Shadows

Shadows are one of the most popular methods in 3D for giving scenes depth. A more dramatic example is Figure 1-26, *Title Against Background.*

Most modeling software incorporates shadow-casting, and some allows you to adjust the granularity and edge softness of shadows. Figure 1-27 shows another example of the use of shadows. Notice the shadows cast by the router and the shadows on the legs of the table.

Figure 1-26 Title Against Background

Figure 1-27 Shadows on 3D router table add realism

Detail

Sharp edges and high levels of detail distinguish objects close at hand. Fog or haze effects in 3D programs, combined with some sort of distance cueing that increases the effect as the view recedes, are powerful methods of simulating depth. If you plan your scenes carefully, you should be able to give distant objects less detail right from the start. This has the advantage of reducing the time it takes to build and render scenes.

Many image processing programs, including Picture Man, which is included on your disk, allow you to simulate photographic blur with image processing procedures called *filters*. You could, for example, composite a sharply detailed image on top of another image that has been blurred. This will make the sharp image appear to be on top or in front of the blurred image.

Color Plate 5, Alan Henry's bee, has blurry back feet to give the scene depth. The blur was added in an image processing program.

Relative Size of Known Objects

One of the favorite tricks of the photographer is to put an object of known size beside an object less familiar to a viewer, a penny beside a microchip, for example. You know how big the chalice is in *Uccello's Study* because there is a candle and a piece of paper lying near it. You unconsciously judge distances by your knowledge of the size of known objects.

Motion Blur

Motion blur simulates the photographic effect produced when the film emulsion cannot react quickly to the image of a fast moving object. The object is smeared.

Binocular Vision

Each eye sees a slightly different scene. You can test this by putting your index finger in front of your face, closing your eyes, and then rapidly opening and closing each eye in succession. This exercise works well for objects up to 100 feet from your eyes. The principle has been extensively exploited in the different approaches to 3D viewing on the screen and the page. The most common method is to create two images that are slightly offset in relation to each other and assign them different colors, usually red and green. When viewed through glasses that have one red and one green lens, each eye sees a slightly different view of a scene. The brain interprets the view as three-dimensional.

What's Ahead

These are the most common methods used by 3D artists to simulate depth and photorealism in computer-generated scenes. The next section reviews some of the compositional issues associated with 3D creation.

COMPOSING 3D IMAGES

The discussion so far has talked about 3D without reference to the frame: the implicit frame around the computer monitor. And yet, the frame's influence on composition in art is total. The frame itself is a geometric shape. It has a size and a proportion. It's the stage where all the action inherent in the picture is acted out, and the artist's decision about the frame shape will determine the placement and proportions of all the other elements of composition in the picture.

The rectangle with a base longer than its sides has had such a longstanding influence in picture making that images oriented to this shape are called *landscape*. When the same rectangle is turned on in its side, it is called *portrait*. (see Figure 1-28).

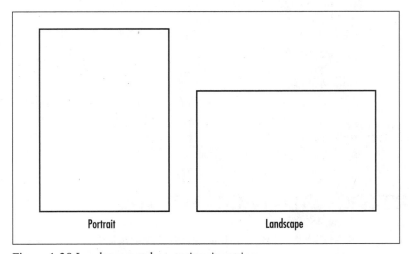

Portrait   Landscape

Figure 1-28 Landscape and portrait orientation

Portrait orientation dominated the Renaissance world, and artists led the eye upward, a suitable direction for pious admiration. Landscape orientation has dominated electronic and film media. Hollywood discovered that the panoramic view, in filling the audience's field of vision, created an experience called *telepresence*. When the image is wrapped completely around the field of view, as in the case of IMAX film technology, the audience becomes immersed in the film to the point where people's emotions are aroused by the action. An increasingly common sight is that of the virtual reality headset, where the viewer's entire field of vision is filled with an image at close range, and the scene changes as the viewer turns his or her head. The virtual reality world appears to exist independently of the viewer's point of view. In effect, the frame has disappeared entirely.

A major difference between 3D art and virtual reality is that 3D art is largely still reproduced on 2D surfaces: glossy pictures, monitors, television sets, and movie screens. Virtual reality worlds must be seen through headgear. But the 3D artist works in the same virtual space as the virtual reality artist. The composition begins somewhere in an open virtual space infinite in potential. The artist can imagine a nanomachine composed of a few atoms many thousands of times smaller than the tip of an eyelash. Or imagine the Milky Way from a trillion kilometers away. Figure 1-29 doesn't show the full dimension of the workspace, but it does show the 3D artist's relationship to the digital canvas.

The monitor is a floating window in a mathematical universe. It can be turned in any direction. Objects can appear and travel from any point to any other point in the virtual space, even past and behind the viewer. The traditional artist establishes a frame, then works within its boundaries. As soon as a dot is applied to the canvas, the view is fixed. The 3D artist creates a universe that he or she can navigate around at will. Even where the goal is the creation of a single scene with a single point of view, the 3D artist can always modify the view through the monitor and regenerate hard copy. The artwork itself retains its three-dimensional identity.

This has some important consequences that will be explored in the chapters ahead. Because so much of the world is seen through wide-angle and telephoto lenses, the 3D artist has as much to learn from the great cinematographers as the masters of traditional art.

REBIRTH OF 3D IN OUR TIMES

When Renaissance artists first mastered perspective, their audiences were enthralled by the magic wrought by the skilled illusionists. But audiences are

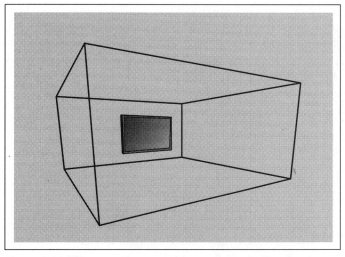

Figure 1-29 The screen is a portal into an empty virtual universe

notoriously fickle. Photography dealt a major blow to the craft. Cubism and other forms of abstract art are in some ways a reaction to photographic realism.

The interest in 3D representational art is undergoing a minor rebirth, a renaissance, now that 3D computer programs like 3D Studio, Real 3D, and Imagine have led the parade in the migration of 3D down from mainframes to the PC. Suddenly, one of the most difficult and time-consuming aspects of representational art has become very easy. Complicated math and careful measurement of space have been replaced by the dialog box, the drop-down menu, and electronic drawing tools. This has created a new generation of artists obsessed by realistic depiction of natural and fantasy worlds. You have to reach back to the Renaissance to find an equivalent period of time when so many people delighted in the artifice.

For the 3D artist, the flat screen of the computer monitor has opened a vista on a new Xanadu, a world entirely constructed in the imagination. Freed from the need to accurately portray everyday objects, 3D artists have created fantastic worlds that only give the illusion that they are real. (See the work at the center of this book for examples.)

The medieval mind thought the spiritual world was more real and everlasting than the world of mere appearances. Now we use computers to create illusory worlds just beyond the looking glass of the monitor. When the interface itself disappears and we become totally immersed in the 3D world—lost to our own—the circle with the past will be complete.

3D art embodies ideas and worlds that it would be difficult to envision, let alone re-create with a saw, hammer, or camera. Whether you are creating something as mundane as a product, a fly-through of a proposed architectural project, or just giving reign to an imaginary flight in a virtual world, you have much to learn from the grand old masters of the art of illusion. But the future is digital and the tools you'll use are rapidly evolving. It's time to go into the workshop now and learn the tools of the trade.

CHAPTER TWO

Cross-sectional Modeling

You can learn a lot about modeling by thinking about the way things are manufactured in the world around you. If you mentally take apart objects around you, you'll get a good idea of how to approach the problem of modeling them in 3D. Let's take the example of your living room. Think about the steps you would take, using common tools and materials, to create a miniature model of it. The model will include walls, floor, rug, and furniture.

Here are the tools and materials in your model kit:

- A package of modeling clay
- Balsam wood
- Thin sheets of colorful fabric
- A tiny drill
- Scissors
- A tiny lathe
- Glue
- Paint

- Decals

- Needle and thread

- A cookie cutter tool

- A chisel

Your modeling kit includes some basic wooden building blocks:

- A round wooden ball

- A wooden platform

- A wooden cone

- A long tube

- A donut-shaped object

- A thin wooden disk

How would you build the coffee table? Out of balsam wood and glue? How about the lamp? Perhaps you would begin with the wooden cone shape and chip away the excess shape with the chisel. The couch? Build the frame and then stretch material over it? *This is exactly how the problem is approached in 3D software.*

In thinking about how objects are built in the real world, you learn a lot about how to build them in the more abstract world of 3D software. For example, in mentally breaking down the coffee table to legs, top, and finish, you come up with a parts list for a 3D modeling project. If you ever do build your living room in 3D space, you will have become an accomplished model maker. That's because a living room presents the entire gamut of challenges you face as a 3D modeler.

You know instinctively that building a coffee table shape is easier than building a sofa. That's because most coffee tables are made up of flat surfaces that can be defined with straight lines. The sofa's curves are difficult to create. You would build the miniature coffee table using balsam wood. You would use modeling clay to build the sofa.

Instead of hand tools, the contact made between you and 3D computer objects is indirect: a mouse and a graphical interface. Your mouse and program commands become *virtual* tools. Instead of a hand drill, you work with a tool that allows you to use one shape to subtract a hole in another: a cylinder to drill a hole in a square. Instead of scissors, you use a tool called *split;* instead of needle and thread, you use a tool called *merge.*

What's Ahead

The next section is a technical discussion about how objects are stored and displayed in 3D programs. Read it as a general background for the chapters ahead. You do not have to know the details of what goes on behind the scenes while working in a 3D program, but knowing the general principles does help.

THE GEOMETRY OF 3D WORLDS

3D tools help you create a 3D world that has many of the optical and physical properties of the real world. The 3D living room built in the memory space of the computer is a scale model of a real living room. You look at this 3D living room through a special viewing window: your monitor. This monitor is like the view screen inside a camcorder. You can walk around the 3D room, zoom in on a vase, and look at it from above, and below.

A simple object in 3D space will illustrate how objects are viewed in the 3D world. Figure 2-1 shows a donut-shaped object lying on a plane. This is how the donut shape appears on the monitor, but the actual 3D object is stored internally as a three-dimensional object as shown in Figure 2-2.

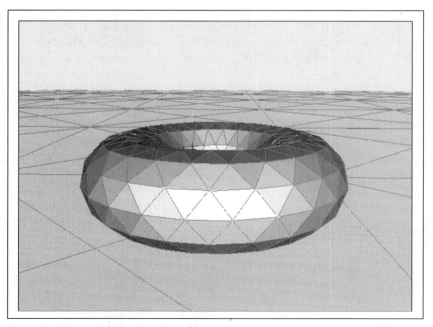

Figure 2-1 Donut object in 3D world

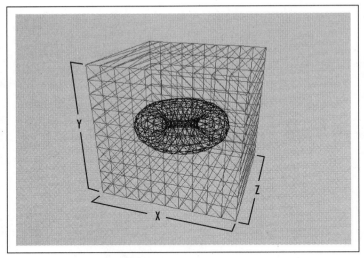

Figure 2-2 Visualization of 3D donut data

Figure 2-2 is a visualization of the database stored by a 3D program. The donut is a true 3D entity; it has a known position in 3D space. It can be measured along three axes, called X, Y, and Z by convention. It is made up of lines and points with precise coordinates. The 3D program uses the record of this object's position in space to draw a two-dimensional version of it on the monitor.

Figure 2-3 provides another way of looking at the relationship between 3D databases and the viewing window. The viewing window shows the scene as the eye would see it in the real world. But the computer actually stores the object independently of this point of view. You can move the point of view around in this world, and you can move, rotate, and size objects in this world. Let's see how this is done.

Manipulating 3D Objects

You do not have direct control over the objects in the 3D world. A 3D interface mediates between you and the 3D object you create. You may have seen pictures of special rooms in research laboratories that are too dangerous for humans to enter. Scientists look into this room through a window. They manipulate objects in the room using robot arms operated by remote control.

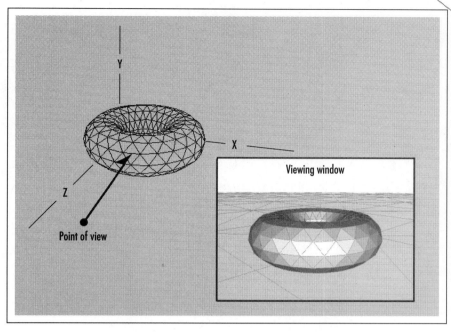

Figure 2-3 The relationship between a 3D object and a viewing window

The mouse and the 3D interface give you the same kind of control over objects. Your robot arms have a certain amount of intelligence built in: more of an assistant than just arms. Instead of attempting to draw a donut object with a mouse and a line tool, you ask the 3D robot to do it for you. The robot *knows* how to do this. You can move either the donut around in the 3D world, or your virtual window in this world.

How 3D Objects Are Displayed

Even though objects are stored as 3D data, they are represented on the screen as 2D images. Figure 2-4 shows how a line is displayed on a computer screen.

The square dots that make up the surface of your monitor are a lot smaller than the dots shown in Figure 2-4. The line itself is not stored in the internal 3D database. Rather, the instructions for creating the line are stored. For example, a line on the screen might be drawn by the computer by adding horizontal and vertical values to a start point (marked *A* in Figure 2-4) until an end point is reached (*B*). In the language of simple arithmetic, each new dot on the screen,

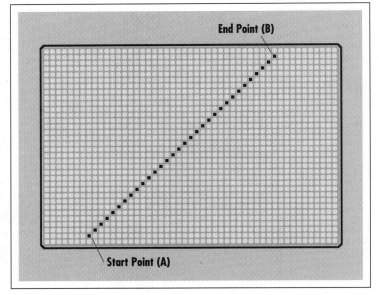

Figure 2-4 A line drawn on the screen

P(x,y), is created by adding d_x units to the X axis and d_y units to the Y axis. The new point is created with the following formula:

$$x_1 = x + d_x \qquad y_1 = y + d_y$$

This is the language spoken by the robot that is buried in the software.

Today's graphical interfaces save the 3D artist from having to laboriously work out the math. But it is helpful to know that when you move or reorient an object, at a certain level, you are asking the program to instruct the hardware to perform addition and multiplication to modify the coordinates of the object stored in the database. In effect, you are supplying data used by the program to transform the scene's database.

Mapping

The beauty of 3D software is this: Once you have built the 3D object, the program automatically figures out how it is displayed on the screen. This is called *mapping* and is analogous to shining a round light on a surface (see Figure 2-5).

The cone of light that comes out of the flashlight is circular. But because we see the wall at an angle, it appears that the bright spot on the wall is oval. In

Figure 2-5 The round light from the flashlight is mapped as an oval on the crooked wall

the language of 3D, the round cone of light is *mapped* onto the wall. The term mapping comes from the practice of projecting the surface of the earth onto flat paper. All the points on the surface of the earth are spread out, and remapped on the flat surface of the paper.

The Problem of Curves

Drawing a straight line on the screen is relatively straightforward. You give the program the starting point of the line and the ending point, and the program fills in the line between the two points. Things get a lot more complicated when the object you want to build is composed of curves (see Figure 2-6).

The mathematical formula required to reproduce a curve requires substantially more computing cycles and consequently, more time to create. That's what makes objects with a lot of curves, like cars, difficult to create and more demanding on computer resources (see Figure 2-7). Compare the car to a simple object like a cube sitting on a grid shown in Figure 2-8.

Now imagine a moving car in a 3D animation. Add a moving viewpoint, such as a camera following the car from a helicopter. The millions of calculations required to represent objects on the screen multiply exponentially.

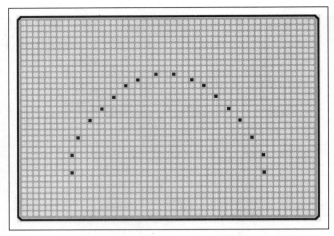

Figure 2-6 A curve presents a challenge to 3D programs

Color Plate 3 (*Utah Teapot*) is a famous example of a complex 3D object. This ray-traced 3D model would be extremely difficult to create using traditional computer drawing tools. It is also very challenging for 3D modelers.

The Geometry of 3D Objects

Objects composed of curves are challenging for 3D programs that must reside on desktop PCs. Storing, translating, and transforming objects with curves is computationally expensive. 3D software designers have come up with a very clever way of getting around this problem. The solution is to cover the object with 2D shapes called polygons. Figure 2-9 shows the Utah Teapot stripped of its chrome finish. Notice that the teapot is made entirely of two-dimensional triangles. They are *patched* onto the surface of the teapot in a similar way that facets are pasted on a mirror ball. Figure 2-10 shows a sphere made up of triangular polygons

Here, the triangles have been filled in to give the mirror ball solidity. The advantage of using polygons to define object surfaces is that they can be defined using relatively simple math. A triangle is composed of three points connected by straight lines. The points are located at three different coordinates in 3D space, but they lie on a single plane. Confining basic object geometry to points and lines on a 2D plane keeps the object simple to create and store. Programs that use triangular polygons, like Imagine, are also very fast.

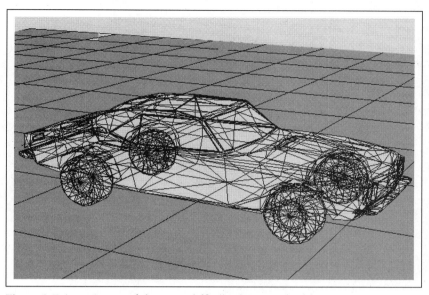

Figure 2-7 A car is one of the most difficult objects to build

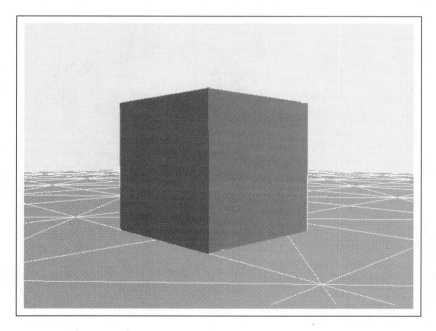

Figure 2-8 Cube on a grid

Figure 2-9 The wireframe Utah Teapot

Figure 2-10 Sphere composed of triangular polygons

Shading Polygons

As mentioned, the object's surface is composed of points and line segments. The area that they enclose is called a *face*. It is the face that is filled with color and shaded to create the illusion that the object is solid. In Figure 2-11 compare the wireframe version of the teapot (*a*), with the solid mesh version (*b*), and the shaded version (*c*).

Faces are transparent in the wireframe teapot, opaque in the solid mesh version, and shaded in the final version. The shaded teapot looks most natural to the eye because it's closest to the appearance of objects in the real world. Let's explore each of these modes within Imagine. The teapot object is in the Imagine \IMAG\OBJECTS directory on your hard drive. Load it into the Detail Editor with the following steps:

1. Run Imagine and enter the Detail Editor by choosing it from the Editor menu.

2. From the \IMAG\OBJECTS directory, load TEAPOT.OBJ into the Detail Editor.

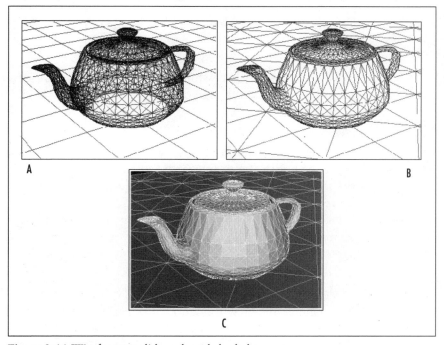

A

B

C

Figure 2-11 Wireframe, solid mesh and shaded teapots

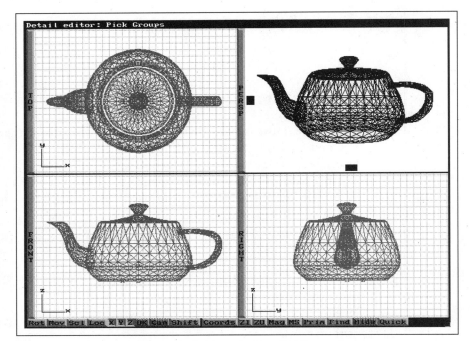

Figure 2-12 The teapot object loaded into the Detail Editor

When you have successfully loaded the object, your screen will look similar to Figure 2-12, although the perspective view will be different.

Wireframe Mode

In a wireframe representation of a 3D object like the teapot, you see the polygons but the faces are transparent. You see through to the other side of the object. This gives you access to the points and lines that make up the object.

In Imagine, the Top, Front, and Right views are editing views. The PERSP (perspective) view allows you to preview the object in 3D. Right now the perspective window is in its default wireframe viewing mode.

Solid Mesh Mode

Let's change the view mode to solid. Press the hot key combination (right) (ALT)-(H) or choose Solid from the Display menu. The perspective window changes to solid view. Your screen should now look like Figure 2-13.

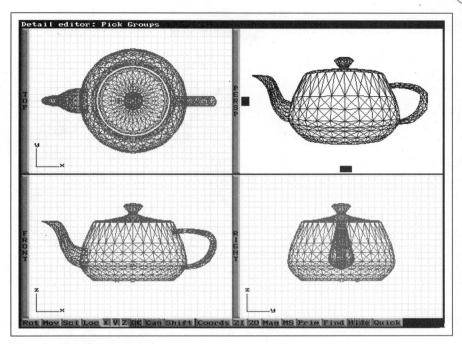

Figure 2-13 Solid view mode

You can go back and forth between wireframe and solid view by alternately pressing (right) (ALT)-(W) and (right) (ALT)-(H).

A solid display of an object is arrived at through hidden line removal. The software uses a formula to decide which lines would be hidden if the object were solid. The parts of the picture that are hidden are simply removed from view.

Shaded Mode

Imagine also allows you to view an object as shaded. You must change to full-screen mode in the perspective window to see a shaded version of the object. To do this, follow these steps:

1   Click on the vertical yellow bar marked "PERSP" along the left side of the perspective window.

2   Choose Shaded from the Display menu.

Your screen should now look like Figure 2-14. Sometimes it's easier to make sense of a 3D scene when the objects in it are shaded. Imagine does this by fill-

Figure 2-14 Shaded teapot

ing in the faces of the object with color. Faces perpendicular to the user's point of view are given a lighter shade. As the faces rotate away from the user's point of view, they are shaded darker and darker. In effect, the teapot is lit by a light placed at the user's point of view.

The viewing system allows us to edit the points, lines, and faces of objects in the editing windows (Top, Front, and Right) and to see a simple rendition of the result in the perspective view. The next section shows how objects are constructed in the editing windows.

USING 3D SOFTWARE TO DRAW 3D OBJECTS

Artists trained in perspective drawing can create convincing simulations of 3D objects on paint canvases and in such computer graphics programs as Corel's CorelDRAW and Zsoft's paint programs. This is laborious, however, and if you change the orientation of the object, you have to start all over again. 3D programs allow you to create three-dimensional objects that are displayed on the screen. Once these objects are created, they can be viewed from any angle by moving, rotating, or scaling them. The 3D program automatically determines how to represent the object on the two-dimensional surface of the monitor. This frees the artist to concentrate on the design of the object rather than its representation on the screen.

You can use point and line tools to construct 3D objects. A bee's wings, for example, can be constructed out of lines, points, and faces. However, it would be impractical to construct entire objects this way. Over the years, 3D program designers have come up with a variety of methods for generating complex 3D objects using modeling tools. One of the most basic methods is to use point and line tools to create a shape and then have the program automatically generate a 3D object from this shape. You can create a cylinder, for example, by drawing a circle on the screen and then extruding it along an axis (see Figure 2-15).

What's Ahead

The next section introduces you to a special Imagine modeling tool that has its own module: the Forms Editor.

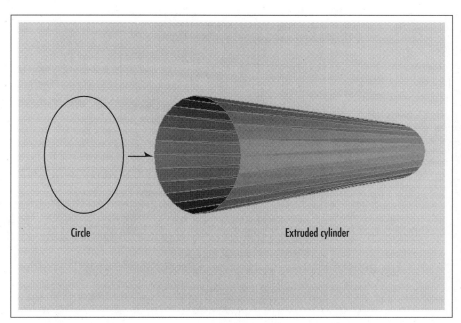

Circle   Extruded cylinder

Figure 2-15 3D programs generate 3D objects out of 2D shapes

WORKING WITH THE VIEWING SYSTEM

In the first part of this section, we'll practice viewing objects in the Forms Editor. Figure 2-16 shows an object created in the Forms Editor.

If we were creating a helmet for a space creature, we might create this shape as a starting point and add detail to it later. (Our alien warrior has rather large ears and a pointed forehead.) A copy of the helmet object is included on disk. Let's load it into the Forms Editor:

1   Run Imagine and start the Forms Editor by choosing it from the Editor menu.

2   From the \IMAG\OBJECTS directory, load HELMET.FRM into the Forms Editor.

Your screen will now look similar to Figure 2-17, although the perspective view will be different.

Let's practice manipulating the helmet in the perspective view. First, we'll make the object easier to visualize by choosing shaded mode in the Display menu.

3   Choose Shaded from the Display menu.

The helmet appears as a solid object in the perspective view. Now adjust the perspective view so that the point of view is just below and to the right of the helmet. Use the small black squares, labeled "Sliders" in Figure 2-17.

4   Move the sliders in the PERSP window until the perspective view of the helmet is the same as in Figure 2-17.

As you move the sliders in the perspective window, the object will spin up and down or from side to side. Objects in the Forms Editor are centered in 3D space. They cannot be moved to new coordinates. In the perspective window, you move the point of view closer or farther away from the object.

5   Press (right) ⒜ⓛⓣ-ⓘ or click on the ZI (Zoom In) button at the bottom of the screen to move the point of view closer to the object. Press (right) ⒜ⓛⓣ-ⓞ or click on the ZO (Zoom Out) button at the bottom of the screen to move the point of view farther away.

The zoom and slider controls allow you to view the object as a camera might view it. This is helpful in visualizing what the object might look like in the final rendered scene.

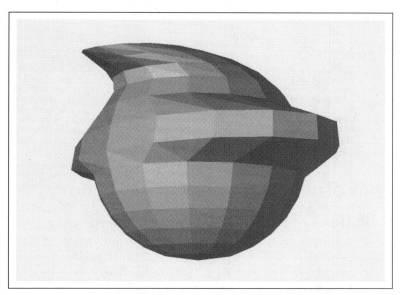

Figure 2-16 Warrior helmet created in the Forms Editor

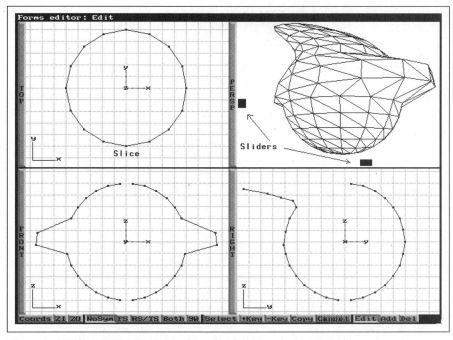

Figure 2-17 The HELMET.FRM object loaded into the Forms Editor

Hint: Zooming

You can change the zoom ratio by choosing Set Zoom on the Display menu or by pressing the forward slash key on your keyboard (/). A data entry box will pop on the screen. You can make fine adjustments by subtracting or adding a small decimal fraction from the current zoom ratio.

Using the Forms Editor for Cross-sectional Modeling

The way that objects are created and manipulated in the Forms Editor is rather unique. Instead of using point and line tools to construct objects, you load a predefined 3D object, a sphere or cylinder. The object is defined using a parameters box. You use the editing views (Top, Front, and Right) to shape the object. The process is analogous to working with clay on a pottery wheel. Instead of building the pottery in parts or from the ground up, you begin with a lump of clay and shape it into the final object.

You can see the circle that was used to form the helmet shape in the Top view of Figure 2-17. Imagine calls the object's cross section a *slice*. Forms Editor objects are slices stacked one on top of the other, in the same way a loaf of bread is composed of slices. Figure 2-18 shows the way the slices that make up the helmet are organized.

You can see that the helmet is a stack of slices of various sizes. At the middle of the helmet, the slices are very wide. Imagine covers the surface of the helmet with polygons, using the slices to define the helmet's contours. Figure 2-19 shows the polygons making up the helmet's surface.

Changing the Shape of Objects

A way of describing the Forms Editor is to say that it is a cross-sectional modeler. Instead of building the object using line and point tools, you load a slice and then change its shape or its profile by adding, deleting, or moving the points that define its surface. This makes the Forms Editor useful for creating organic shapes that have distinct profiles. Figure 2-20 shows the relationship between the helmet and the editing windows.

Notice that the editing windows do not provide a view of the helmet's surface, but rather the object's slice or profile. In order to perform detailed work

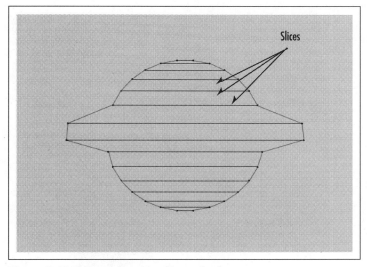

Figure 2-18 Helmet slices seen from the front

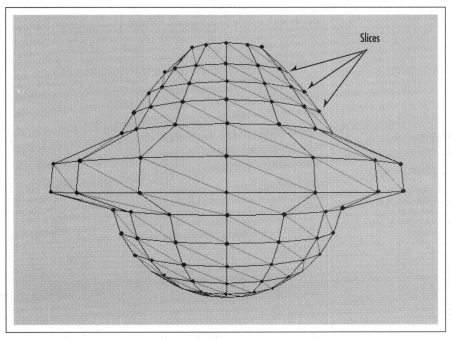

Figure 2-19 Imagine covers the perimeters of slices with a surface of polygons

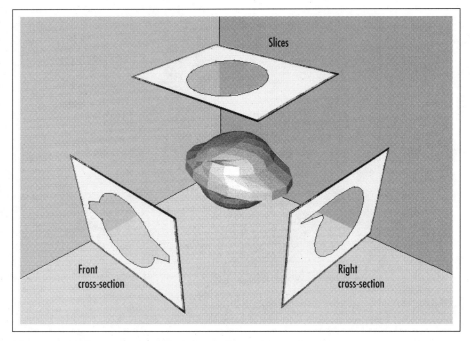

Figure 2-20 Editing windows and their relationship to the object

on individual polygons, you must export the object from the Forms Editor and import it into Imagine's Detail Editor, where surface modeling is performed.

Exercise: Modifying the Helmet Object

You'll get a better feel for the way Imagine's cross-sectional modeling tool works in this exercise. Watch the perspective window as you move points around in the Front and Right views of the Forms Editor. (This exercise assumes you are in the Forms Editor with the helmet loaded.)

1   Click on and move points in the Front and Right views.

Notice that when you move points on slices, the polygons attached to these points move with them. Points in a Forms Editor object are connected to neighboring points. Pulling on one point affects the geometry between that point and the surrounding points.

Each slice has the same number of points because of the way the slices are connected. You cannot have eight points in one slice and six points in the next.

The basic building block of a Forms Editor is a slice made up of a fixed number of points.

Experiment by changing the shape of the slice and observing the new shapes in the perspective window.

2 In the Top view, move the points defining the slice. Try changing the shape to a square. Elongate it in one or more directions.

CREATING FORMS EDITOR OBJECTS

When you create a new object in the Forms Editor, Imagine uses a circle to define the slices. A circle is a primitive out of which spheres are made. The other object created in the Forms Editor is a cylinder. A cylinder is merely a stack of circles with identical sizes. Uccello's chalice is a stack of circles of varying widths. A loaf of bread is an irregularly shaped cylinder. It is a circle extruded along the length of the loaf, like toothpaste extruded from a tube. A soda can is a stack of circle slices. Whether the Forms Editor creates a circle or a cylinder, the basic geometry derives from a circle.

You might think that a circle is a rather limited shape. Not so. A circle can be bullied into being a cube if you flatten its top and bottom and pinch in its sides. It can be shaped into a teardrop or a pencil. This is exactly the kind of object you can easily create in the Forms Editor. It's a kind of digital clay studio where you can model organic shapes.

The Object Specifications Box

All objects in the Forms Editor are created by entering parameters in a pop-up box. Let's create an object from scratch using the Object Specifications box.

Choose New from the Object menu or press (right) (ALT)-(N). If you have an object already loaded, Imagine will ask if you want to save it. Answer *no*. An Object Specifications box like the one shown in Figure 2-21 pops on the screen.

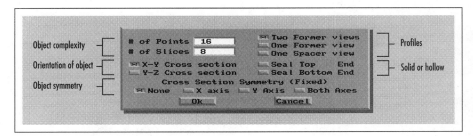

Figure 2-21 Object Specifications box

Hint: Keep It Simple

You can add or remove slices and points from your object as you create a shape. It's best to begin with a simple object and add points and slices to it. A complex object with a lot of points is difficult to edit.

The Object Specifications box has a number of parameters that you can modify. You can make decisions about object complexity, object shape, which profiles will be edited, horizontal or vertical orientation, and what kind of symmetry the object will have. Each of these parameters will be explained in turn.

Specifying Slices and Points

The first decision is about complexity of the object. Notice that the object can be defined in terms of how many slices it has and how many points. The data entry boxes have a default value of 8 slices and 16 points. The more slices and points added to an object, the smoother and more complex the object becomes. Compare the spheres in Figure 2-22. The sphere on the right has three times as many points and slices.

The Former and Spacer Controls

By default, you can modify an object's shape by altering the front and right profiles. This facilitates the creation of objects like the helmet, which has distinctive side and front profiles. But some objects have a single profile: The chalice is a good example. The Former and Spacer views give you three kinds of shaping controls:

- Two Former
- One Former
- One Spacer

Two Former View

Two Former view is the default view. It creates objects whose front and side profiles can be altered (or in the case of an object created in horizontal orientation, the top and front). Figure 2-20 shows Two Former view. Notice that the front profile and the side profile are different shapes. Figure 2-23 shows the Two Former view screen.

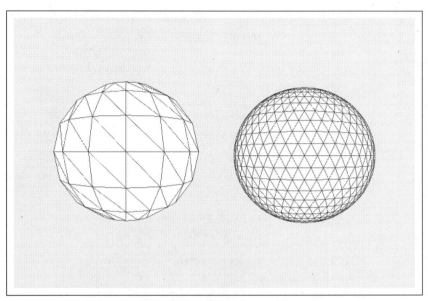

Figure 2-22 Specifying more points and slices creates smoother circles

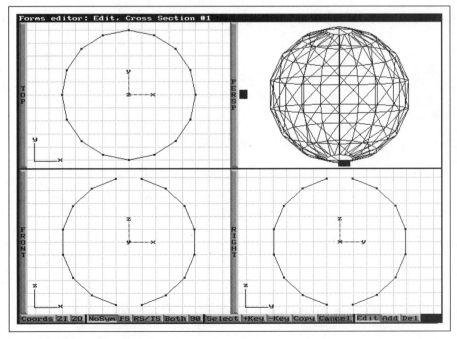

Figure 2-23 Two Former view program interface

The Top view shows the sphere's cross section. The Front and Right views show the front and side profiles of the sphere. Notice that the circles that outline the profiles are broken at the top and bottom. By default the objects that are created have a hole running down the middle of the object.

One Former View

Uccello's chalice was created in One Former view. Let's load the chalice into the Forms Editor:

1 Press (right) (ALT)-(L). The program will ask if you want to save the current object. Answer *no*.

2 Load CHALICE.FRM into the Forms Editor.
It's in the \IMAG\OBJECTS directory.

Figure 2-24 shows the relationship between One Former view and the chalice. One Former view creates objects that you can alter in only one profile. Whereas Two Former view allows you to make changes to the front and side of an object independently. One Former view allows you to form an object as you might shape clay on a spinning platter. As you modify a point, you are modifying all the points around the object's circumference. A teardrop is easily created in this view.

One Spacer View

One Spacer view allows you to only alter the slice, not the profile of the object (see Figure 2-25).

1 Load an object called ONESPACE.FRM into the Forms Editor,
(It's in the \IMAG\OBJECTS directory.)

Notice that the Front view shows a line of vertical points connected by a line. One Spacer gets its name from the fact that you can alter slices and the spaces between them but not their profile.

2 Experiment with this view by altering the shape of the slice.

Summary of View Controls

The Forms Editor has been designed to give you three levels of control over an object: slice only (One Spacer), slice plus a single profile (One Former), and slice plus independent front and side profiles (Two Former).

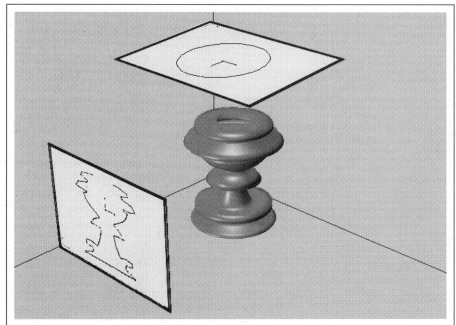

Figure 2-24
One Former view
diagram

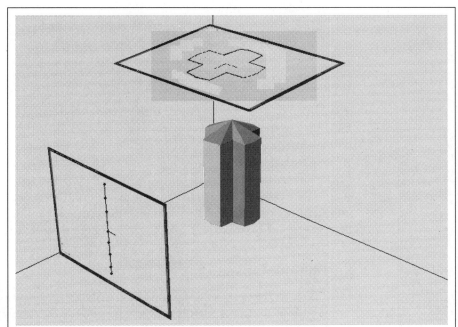

Figure 2-25
The One Spacer
view

Working with More than One View

View controls can be used interactively. You can create an object in one view and then load it into another view.

1   Load ONESPACE.FRM into the Forms Editor.

2   Select shaded mode from the Display menu.

3   Adjust the sliders in the perspective window until you see a three-quarter view of the object.

4   Call up the Object Specifications box with (right) (ALT)-(N).

5   Select Two Former view.

6   Click on OK.

7   When you are prompted: "Keep the old cross section points?" answer *yes*.

Your screen should now look like Figure 2-26. Notice how the shape has been made to conform to the default circular profiles in the Front and Right views. You could have created the same object in the Two Former view. However, once you learn some of the subtleties of each of the views, you'll find yourself popping from one view to another to create unique shapes.

Let's continue with our exploration of the object specifications controls in the Forms Editor. Pop the Object Specifications box back onto the screen by pressing (right) (ALT)-(N).

Cross-section Orientation

The X-Y and X-Z Cross-section buttons in the Object Specifications box determine the orientation of the object in the views (see Figure 2-21). The two alternatives are vertical (X-Y) and horizontal (Y-Z). A loaf of bread would be created with the Y-Z Cross-section button selected, so that the slices in the loaf run vertically from left to right. If the object is tall and narrow, such as a skyscraper, you choose the default X-Y orientation. Experiment by calling up the Object Specifications box and changing the cross-section orientation from the default vertical orientation (X-Y) to the horizontal orientation (Y-Z).

Sealing the Object

Let's move to the next set of options in the Object Specifications box. The Seal Top and Seal Bottom controls are right beside the cross-section controls. An empty paper roll has unsealed ends, a soda can has two sealed ends. If you choose

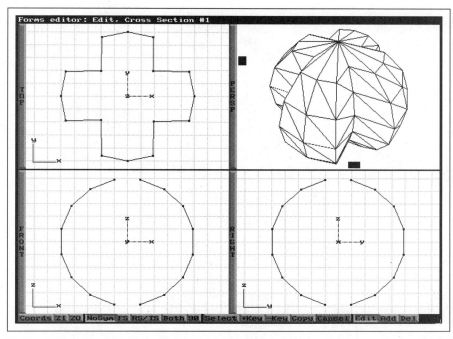

Figure 2-26 One space object loaded into Two Former view

to seal the object, the ends will shrink down to a single point. You can later delete this point in the Detail Editor if you choose to change the object to hollow. Experiment with this option by creating objects with open and closed ends.

Cross-section Symmetry

The last option in the Object Specifications box, Cross Section Symmetry, determines how the object's shape will be edited. Remember that the basic shape of the object is determined by the slice. Cross Section Symmetry allows you to make symmetrical changes to the slice's shape. Figure 2-27 shows each of the slice symmetry editing options.

- **None:** This is the default. It allows you to move each point on the slice independently.

- **X Axis Symmetry:** The point opposite the one you move on the X axis will move in tandem. You must define an even number of points to make this possible, since each point in the slice must lie opposite another.

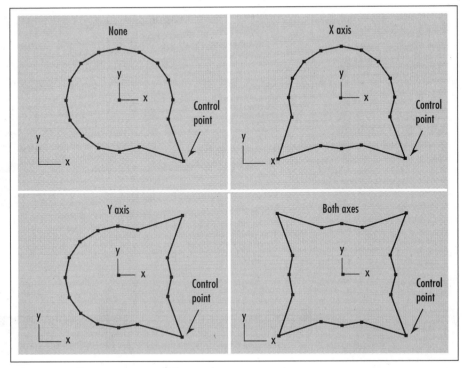

Figure 2-27 Slice symmetry editing options

- **Y Axis Symmetry:** This option offers controls along the Y axis similar to those for the X axis.

- **Both Axes Symmetry:** Four points move in tandem. The value you enter for points must be divisible by four.

Altering Symmetry Options

The symmetry controls are listed as "fixed" because the control you have over the points in the slice view is predetermined by the option you selected in the Object Specifications box. However, you can change the slice's symmetry at any time by calling up the Object Specifications box and changing the Cross Section Symmetry option. Let's begin with a new object:

1   Call up the Object Specifications box.

2   Use the defaults for points, slices, view, orientation, and sealing. Select Both Axes under Cross Section Symmetry.

3   Create a star shape by selecting a point in the Top (slice) view and moving it out and away from the circle.

4   Call up the Object Specifications box. A box will pop on the screen warning you that the current object is not saved. Indicate that you want to create a new object by answering *yes*.

5   Select None under Cross Section Symmetry.

6   Click on OK. You are asked if you want to keep the old forms (profiles). Answer *yes*. You are asked if you want to create the old cross-section points. Answer *yes*.

7   Now select a point on the slice and move it out and away from the circle. Watch the perspective window. Notice that you now have a five-armed star shape.

Changing Profile Symmetry

The Object Specifications box allows you to determine the slice's symmetry. Control over the object's profile symmetry is found outside of the Object Specifications box, in the Symmetry menu at the top of the Forms Editor screen. Let's see how this works:

1   Call up the Object Specifications box.

2   Create a new object using the default settings.

3   Click on the Symmetry menu.

The Symmetry menu provides the following options:

⊛   **Off:** Points move independently (shown in Figure 2-28).

⊛   **Front view:** Points opposite each other move in Front view. Right view points move independently (shown in Figure 2-29).

⊛   **Right view:** Points opposite each other move in the Right view. Front view points move independently (shown in Figure 2-30).

⊛   **Both:** Front and Right views are symmetrical, but not with each other (shown in Figure 2-31).

⊛   **90 degree:** Front and Right views are symmetrical with each other. This option allows you to create circular shapes in profile (shown in Figure 2-32).

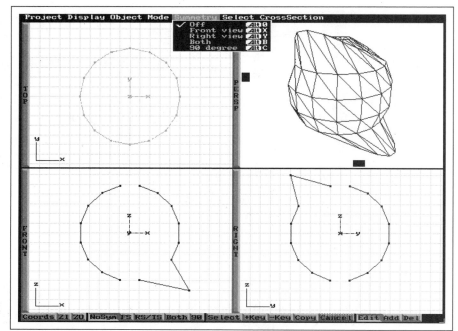

Figure 2-28
Symmetry off

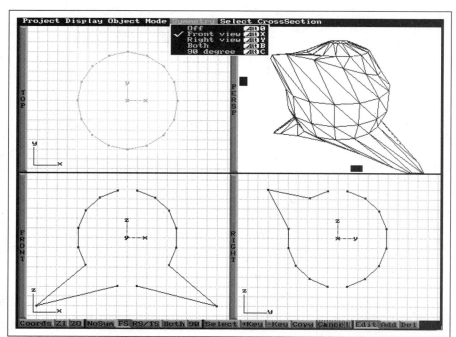

Figure 2-29
Front profile
symmetry

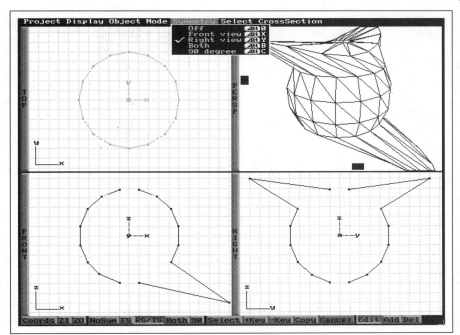

Figure 2-30
Right profile
symmetry

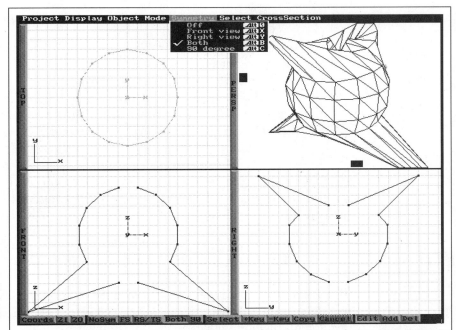

Figure 2-31
Both profiles are
independently
symmetrical

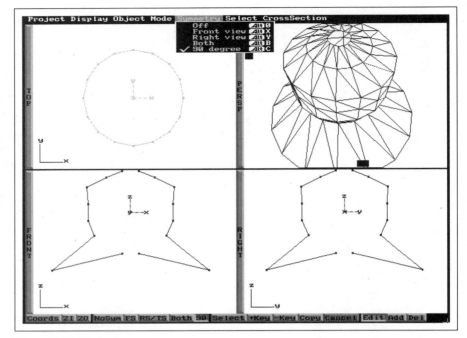

Figure 2-32 90 degree symmetry

This covers symmetry for profiles in Two Former view in detail. The Symmetry menu is different for each of the other views (One Former and One Spacer). One Former view allows you to modify the object's Front profile only. As a result, the Front, Right, Both, and 90 Degree options are grayed out (disabled) in the Symmetry menu. All options are grayed out in the One Spacer view because you cannot edit an object's profile in this view.

What's Ahead

So far we've been changing the shape of existing objects by moving points. Imagine allows you to add and delete points from objects. In the next section, we'll create a new object, an igloo, and learn to use object editing tools.

EDITING FORMS EDITOR OBJECTS

An Eskimo igloo is a dome with a hole in the top of it. It's very easy to create this shape with Imagine. All that's required is that you specify a sphere and then lop off the bottom half by deleting points from the bottom.

Editing Tools: Edit, Add, Delete

Imagine is a modal program. In the Forms, Detail, Stage, and Action editors, you can switch the program from one editing mode to another. If you click on the Edit menu at the top of the screen, you will see that there are three Forms modes: Edit, Add, and Delete. Clicking on one of these three modes determines what will happen when you click on a point on the object. You will either move it (Edit mode), add a new point beside it (Add mode), or delete the point (Delete mode). A check mark beside Edit indicates that Edit mode is currently selected. There is also a keyboard shortcut listed for each mode.

There is another way of moving between the three operating modes of this editor. If you look at the row of yellow buttons at the bottom of the screen, you'll notice that at the far right there are three buttons called Edit, Add, and Del. The Edit button is depressed, signifying that you are in Edit mode.

Let's modify an object using these modes.

Creating the Basic Object

We'll use the Object Specifications box to create the initial shape and Two Former view to create a sphere with a hole in it. First specify the object:

1   Call up the Object Specifications box and enter the following specifications:

   ⊕   16 points

   ⊕   8 slices

   ⊕   Two Former view

   ⊕   X-Y Cross section

   ⊕   Unsealed Top and Bottom

   ⊕   Cross Section Symmetry: None

2   Click on OK.

Make sure symmetry is off in the Symmetry menu. (There should be a check mark beside Off.)

3   Click on the ZI button at the bottom of the screen to zoom in on the sphere.

Your screen should look like Figure 2-33. Notice that the Front and Right views show the sphere with a hole in the top and the bottom. Hollow objects is the default for the Forms Editor.

Altering Shapes by Deleting Points

Now remove the bottom of the sphere by clicking on the yellow Del button at the far right of the button bar at the bottom of the screen. Notice that the information line at the top of the screen changes to read, "Forms Editor: Delete."

Two points that lie at the bottom of the sphere in the view labeled "Front" define the bottom slice of the sphere. Use your mouse cursor to click on either one of these two points. Notice that the point on the opposite side of the sphere is deleted simultaneously with the point you selected. In deleting the point, you remove the slice at the bottom of the sphere.

Delete the next pair of points. Then delete the pair of points after that. The shape should now look like a dome as shown in Figure 2-34. Notice that the Top view is still a circle, while the Right view is the same shape as the Front view.

Experimenting with the Editing Modes

Experiment by adding or deleting points in the igloo shape using the three different modes of the Forms Editor. For example, in Front view, you can create a lamp shade by deleting the points along the sides of the igloo. View the object you have modified in the shaded full-screen perspective mode. You can create fairly elaborate—and strange—shapes using the Forms Editor cross-sectional modeling.

OTHER OBJECT MANIPULATION TOOLS

In the previous sections you were introduced to some of the basic object creation and editing tools found in all of Imagine's editors. This section presents editing tools that help you edit shapes with a great deal of precision. Learning how to use these tools in the Forms Editor makes it easier to use them in the other object editors.

Create a new object and then change its shape using the following commands.

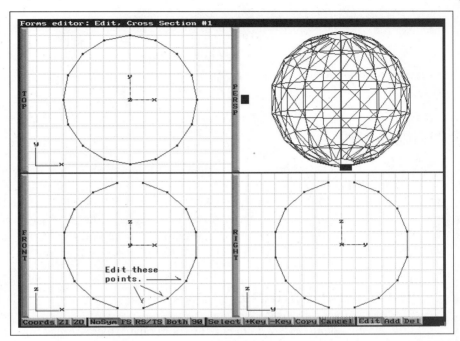

Figure 2-33
The zoomed
sphere

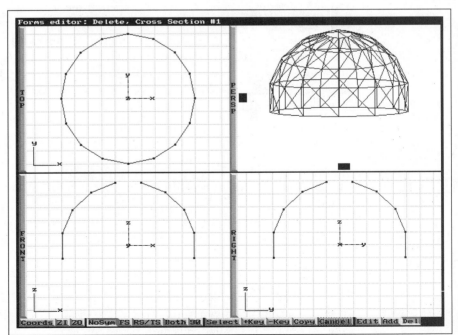

Figure 2-34
The igloo shape

Undoing Mistakes

If you make a mistake while working with Imagine, use the (ALT)-(U) key combination to undo the mistake or use the menu command, Undo, in the Project menu.

Saving Objects

To save an object, press (right) (ALT)-(S) or select Save from the Object menu. It's a good idea to give Forms Editor objects special extensions, such as the extension .FRM (as in CAR.FRM) when you save them. The .FRM extension will remind you that the object was created in the Forms Editor. In most cases, Imagine does not care what extension you add to objects, scenes, attributes, and so on. This can lead to confusion unless you follow a naming convention.

Zooming and Panning Views

Zooming is like adjusting the zoom on a camera or telescope. The ZI (Zoom In) and ZO (Zoom Out) buttons at the bottom of the screen allow you to see less or more of the object you are working on. Under the Display menu in all editors where objects or scenes are created is a menu choice called Set Zoom. This allows you to set the zoom factor. By default the zoom factor is 1. Entering .5 in the Zoom factor dialog box cuts the zoom factor in half. Entering 2 in the Zoom factor dialog box doubles the zoom factor. You can also call up the Zoom factor box by pressing the forward slash key (/).

Centering

Change the center of a selected view by clicking on Re-Center in the Display menu, or press the period key (.). Then click on the screen. Where you click will become the new center for the viewing window.

Panning

The arrow keys on the keyboard are used to pan the view. *Panning* moves the viewing window up, down, right, or left. The view moves one-half screen at a time. Zoom in for smaller pans and out for larger pans.

Selecting and Moving Points

Imagine allows you to select and move more than one point at a time. The following selection tools are found on the Select menu:

- **Click:** Select one point. Notice that when you move a point, the point becomes red in color. Because points are dynamically related to other points, connecting lines and points are brown in color as you move a point.

- **Drag Box:** Select several points by dragging a box around them.

- **Lasso:** Surround a group of points using a lasso. A lasso is made by using your mouse to drag a rough circle around the area.

- **Lock:** Confine movement of points to grid intersections.

Multi-mode

Multi-mode allows you to select a group of objects simultaneously. It's activated by pressing the (SHIFT) key. Keep the (SHIFT) key depressed as you select the points.

Drag Box and Multi-mode

Drag Box is usually used in Multi-mode. To test this, switch to Delete mode by pressing the Del button at the bottom of the screen (or select Delete from the Mode menu, or press the right (ALT)-(D)). Then click the mouse cursor on a spot near a group of points. While keeping the mouse button depressed, drag a box over the selected group of points. Release the mouse cursor. The group of points disappear. You cannot use Drag Box in Add mode, since points must be added to an object one point at a time.

Using the Grid for Precision Drawing

Imagine uses some of the drawing conventions found in traditional paint or draw programs such as CorelDRAW or Adobe Illustrator. One of those conventions is the use of a grid for precise placement of points, lines, or objects.

You can see the grid in the Top, Front, and Right views. It's visible as light-gray lines. You can turn the grid on or off by pressing the equal sign (=) on your keyboard. Normally when you move points from one spot to

Hint: Snap to Grid

You can convert a circle to a square faster by moving all the points in the circle to the nearest grid intersection.

- Create a sphere.
- Click on the Edit button at the bottom of the screen.
- Choose Drag Box in the Select menu.
- Drag a box around the sphere in one of the views.

When you do this, the points on the screen turn red and the lines turn blue. This indicates that these points have been selected.

- Then click on Snap to Grid.

All the points you have selected snap to the nearest grid intersections. Snap to Grid works like Lock in the Select menu. While in Click or Lasso modes, you can perform the same operation on one or more points.

another, they can be placed anywhere. You can lock points to the intersections on the grid by toggling the Lock switch under the Select menu. Click on Lock now to turn it on.

Make sure that you are in Click mode. (The word *Click* should have a check mark beside it in the Select menu.) Now when you move points around on the screen, the points will snap to the nearest grid intersections. Start with a new object, then try to create a square by moving the points in each of the views out to four corners. Keep an eye on the perspective view as you do so.

Altering the Grid Size

You can alter the grid size by selecting Grid Size from the Display menu or pressing the minus sign (-). Enter a new value in the box that pops on the screen and press (ENTER). The grid size changes. You can then make finer or coarser adjustments.

What's Ahead

The previous sections have covered Imagine's editing tools. The next section gives you practice in using them.

Creating Uccello's Chalice Using the Editing Tools

In this section, we re-create Uccello's chalice. We start with the default sphere and then edit its points until we have re-created the chalice. Before creating the chalice from scratch, look at the one stored on your disk.

1 Use the (right) (ALT)-(L) keyboard combination to pop the file requester on screen. (Or choose Load from the Object menu.)

2 Navigate to the \IMAG\OBJECTS directory. Load CHALICE.FRM.

Your screen should now look like Figure 2-35. Notice that there is no view of the chalice in the Right view. That's because the chalice was created in One Former view. Let's look at the object creation specifications used to create the chalice.

3 Press (right) (ALT)-(N). This brings up the Object Specifications box. The chalice has been created with:

- 32 points

- 42 slices

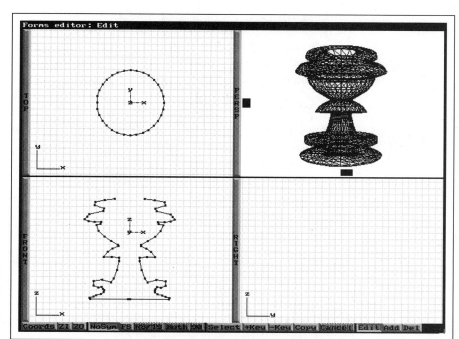

Figure 2-35
The chalice
loaded into the
Forms Editor

⊕   One Former view

⊕   X-Y Cross section

⊕   No sealed ends

⊕   Cross Section Symmetry: None

4   Click on OK. When the information box pops on the screen asking if you want to keep the old forms, click on No. Answer *no* to the question asking if you want to keep the cross sections.

You now have the original object used to create the chalice on the screen: a sphere. Using the shape of the chalice as shown in Figure 2-36 as a guide, you are going to move the points in the front view.

5   Select Front View from the Symmetry menu. This allows you to make the two sides of the chalice symmetrical.

6   Change to full-screen Front view by clicking on the yellow bar along the right side of the view.

7   In Front view, click on the two points that lie at the very bottom of the circle and move them out until they are the same width as the base of the chalice seen in Front view.

8   Switch back and forth between Front view and perspective view by clicking on the view's name along the right side of the view window. You will be able to watch the chalice develop.

9   Add and delete points as necessary.

There are enough points to model the chalice, but you may place some of them too close together or too far apart. Note that when you add points, sometimes they are created so close together that you cannot see the new point. Zoom in to move the new point into place.

You may want to test render the object as it develops:

10   Choose Quick Render from the Project menu. Answer *no* to the query about lights. The chalice is previewed on the screen.

11   Click on the screen with the left mouse button to return to the Forms Editor screen.

In this section you have practiced using some of the editing tools you will use again and again as you work in Imagine's object editors. The next section introduces you to the use of multiple slices.

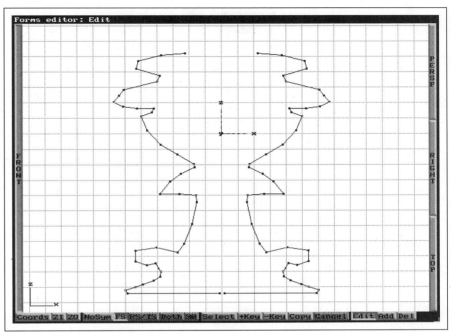

Figure 2-36 Shape of the chalice

Working with More than One Slice

Up until now, when you changed an object's slice, all the slices connected to it changed simultaneously. Not all objects have this kind of symmetry. A car's cross section, for example, changes from the front to the back. In this section you will learn how to use the Forms Editor to create complex shapes by modifying individual slices. You'll learn about the concept of key slices.

Think of a car passing through an automatic car wash. As its nose pushes up against the rollers, the rollers accommodate themselves to the boxy shape of the front end. The rollers move along until they encounter the slope of the windshield. Then they travel up the windshield until they reach the roof. They travel along the roof for a while and then find the slope at the back of the roof (this is a hatchback). Figure 2-37 shows this shape.

A car is a difficult shape to model because of its complex curves. Herein lies the strength of the Forms Editor. You can model the car by assigning slices to points where the shape changes and then let Imagine compute the changes from one slice to the next. In the car in Figure 2-38 the slices run from the front to the back of the car. You can see the shape of the slices in the Right view.

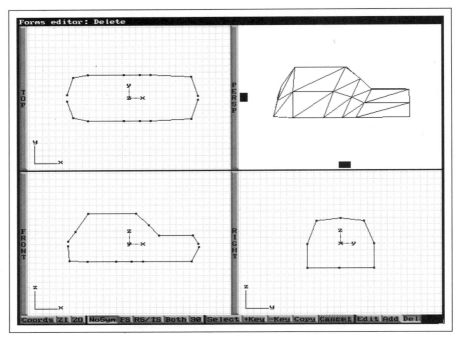

Figure 2-37 The car shape

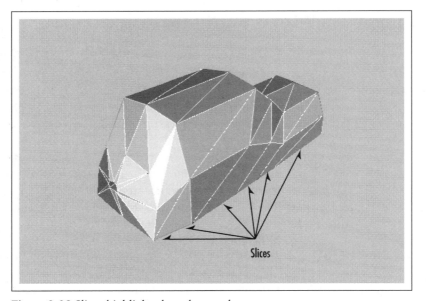

Figure 2-38 Slices highlighted on the car shape

Tip: View the Car Shape

A car shape is included in the \IMAG\OBJECTS directory. You may want to load it into the Forms Editor and experiment with it throughout this section. You will find it listed as CAR.FRM.

The Concept of Key Slices

The slices where the car changes shape are called *key slices*. The term *key* is borrowed from *key frame animation*. In key frame animation the animator specifies a key frame in an animation, and the computer interpolates changes to the object between that key and the next key. In the example of the car, the program draws a skin of polygons over the slices that make up the car. The next section presents an exercise in using key slicing.

Modifying a Cylinder Using Key Slices

Let's modify a cylinder using key slices.

1 Use the hot key combination ((ALT)-(N)), or choose New from the Object menu, to bring up the Object Specifications box.

2 Enter the following specifications in the Object Specifications box. (Don't forget to press (ENTER) after typing in values.)

⊕ Points: 16

⊕ Slices: 8

⊕ One Spacer view

⊕ X-Y Cross section

⊕ Cross Section Symmetry: None

⊕ Click on OK

Your screen should now look like Figure 2-39. The result is a simple cylinder, open at both ends. You can see how the slices that make up the cylinder are arranged in the perspective view. The horizontal lines show the location of slices.

The vertical line shown in Front view is not an orthogonal view of the cylinder. Rather, it shows figuratively how slices are stacked on top of each other

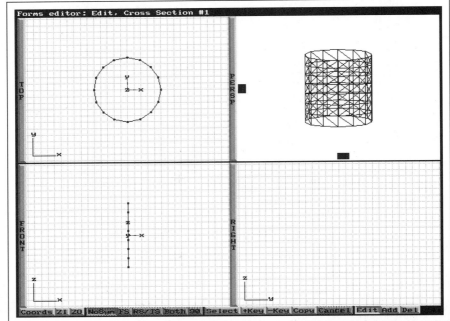

Figure 2-39
The cylinder
shape

from the top of the cylinder to the bottom. The points along the vertical line show where slices are located along the length of the cylinder and how far apart they are spaced (hence the name One *Spacer*).

In order to modify the individual slices that make up the cylinder, you must first designate slices as key slices, using the button on the yellow button bar labeled "+key."

3   Click on the +key button and watch the Front view.

Notice how the top point turned red. This is the slice whose shape is shown in the Top view.

4   Now click on the bottom point in the Front view.

When you do so all the views redraw. The top point is no longer red. You have just made the bottom slice a key slice.

5   Press the Select button.

The Select button causes two red dots to appear in the Front view, one at the top of the cylinder and one at the bottom. The Select button allows you to choose which slice to modify in the Top view.

6   Click on the bottom red dot.

Now the Top view shows the shape of the bottom slice. It happens to be the same shape as the top slice, but you can change that.

7   Move the points that make up the circle in the Top view out to form a square. (Go to the Select menu and toggle Click and Lock on. They are on when check marks appear beside them.)

Watch the perspective view as you do this. You should see the bottom of the cylinder become square in shape. When you are finished, your screen should look like Figure 2-40.

8   Click on the PERSP button bar beside the perspective view, make sure Shaded is turned on (there should be a check mark beside Shaded in the Display menu), and look at the cylinder from various angles.

Notice how the square bottom of the cylinder gradually transforms into the round circle that forms the cylinder's top.

9   Return to the Quad view by clicking on the PERSP button at the left of the screen.

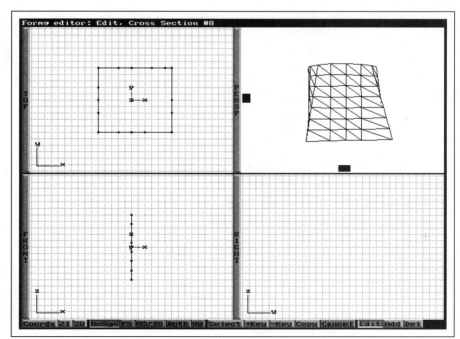

Figure 2-40
The round cylinder with a square bottom

10 Click on the Select button.

You are now going to select the top slice again. Watch the Top view. It now shows a square shape.

11 Click on the red dot at the top of the vertical line in the Front view.

The square changes to a circle. That's because what you see in the Top view is the "floor plan" of each slice as you select it for viewing with the Select button.

Exercises

Try altering the shape of the cylinder by defining new key slices between the top and bottom slices and giving them new shapes. Try moving some slices farther apart.

SUMMARY

Cross-sectional modeling provides an intuitive way for creating and modifying basic shapes that are organic or geometric. Instead of building objects from the ground up, a base object is loaded and edited. Complex shapes, like cars, that have smooth surfaces bending and twisting along three axes are ideally suited for cross-sectional modeling.

Each 3D artist adopts a unique approach to planning and building models. If you take the time to master the Forms Editor, you will find that it can be an extremely productive tool. But there are other methods of model building ahead. These will be covered in Chapter 6, which is devoted to the other model-building techniques.

The next chapter will cover surface modeling techniques.

CHAPTER THREE

Shading Surfaces

The scientific quest to develop mathematical models for natural processes has spawned an interesting side effect: computer programs that model the physical and optical properties of the world. The Newtonian laws of physics have been patiently coded by programmers and offered to users as features available at the click of a mouse. The mathematical models that describe the way light bounces off a surface, accounting for such optical effects as shininess, transparency, reflections, refraction, and shading, are at the heart of every 3D program.

Using 3D software to model the surfaces of the world around us is a matter of knowing the limits imposed by computer hardware and software. The temptation is to think that 3D software can definitively imitate nature's generative powers. But nature has woven a tapestry of detail out of these laws that overwhelms the computer's limited memory space and narrow bandwidth. Let's take the example of silk. Silk has a shiny, smooth surface soft to the touch. But take a look at it under a microscope (see Figure 3-1). Seen magnified by a ratio of 50 times, it is rough and porous. This is detail not obvious to the naked eye.

The weave of fibers gives silk its flexibility and allows it to flow over the contours of the body.

Figure 3-1 Silk looks very different under a microscope

Modeling the motion of silk as it bends, twists, and flows overwhelms the computing horsepower of desktop PCs. Programs like Imagine allow you to make a polygon mesh conform to simple surfaces like spheres, but the calculations involved in conforming a mesh with thousands of polygons to irregular surfaces slows even super computers to a crawl.

The telltale sign of a computer model is the lack of detail on surfaces. The surfaces of 3D models are too smooth, too regular to fool the eye consistently. They lack the nicks, scratches, and imperfections that give natural objects their gritty reality. That's because the underlying structure, the geometry of models, is relatively simple compared to such surfaces as silk.

Faced with this situation, 3D artists have responded with the tricks long used by artists, beginning in the Renaissance. They model the *appearance* of objects rather than the underlying structure. Fortunately, the eye is crude compared to the resolving power of microscopes and telescopes. The complex weave of silk is well beyond the resolving power of our eyes, even seen close up. This makes silk relatively easy to imitate, especially since it is smooth and regular in texture.

It's relatively easy to create the colors and patterns of surfaces using conventional 2D paint programs like Adobe Photoshop. But even pure white silk has a sheen and subtle shade that only experienced artists using such techniques as airbrushing can model. Fortunately, this an area where 3D modeling programs come to the aid of the artist seeking the elusive goal of photorealism. The mathematical models built into programs that simulate the interaction between surfaces and light have become extremely sophisticated, giving modelers a great deal of control over how surfaces appear to the eye. The subtle shading produced by light glancing off of a round surface is automatically generated by a computer algorithm.

THE ART OF MODELING SURFACES

This is the first of two chapters that initiates you into the art of modeling surfaces. In this chapter, you'll learn how to color objects and shade surfaces. You'll learn how to:

- Make objects flat or round shaded

- Color objects

- Make them reflective

- Make them transparent

- Give them specular highlights

- Give their surfaces detail

- Make them shiny

Chapter 4 will show you alternate methods for giving objects surfaces.

For the exercises, we'll create a simple pottery vessel and then give it color and shading. Pottery is a particularly appropriate subject for surface modeling. The 3D potter uses digital clay and digital paint to give virtual pottery its shapes and surfaces. The bowls, vases, jars, plates, and vessels that are the potter's expression of artistry can be easily modeled in 3D software.

In this chapter we will use Imagine's Attributes Requester as a laboratory for exploring the art of modeling surfaces (see Figure 3-2).

The way 3D programs implement object coloring and shading varies widely. However, the fundamental principles are the same.

Learning about basic surface controls will help you understand the properties of 3D surfaces. The other controls, including textures, brushes, and fog objects, are covered in Chapter 5.

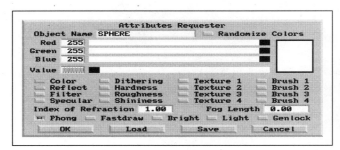

Figure 3-2 Imagine's Attributes Requester allows you to control the way surfaces interact with light

What's Ahead

Surface modeling has two aspects: the underlying geometry of the surface and the way the surface interacts with light. The discussion begins by describing the geometry of surfaces.

THE GEOMETRY OF SURFACES

Computer models are hollow objects whose surfaces imitate the behavior of natural objects like wood, plastic, and glass. The fundamental unit out of which all surfaces are created is the polygon (see Figure 3-3).

A polygon is three or more line segments connected by vertices or points. As you learned in Chapter 2, the interior of a polygon is called a face. It is this face that is given a surface of color during final rendering. Figure 3-4 shows the chalice we created in the last chapter as a polygonal mesh and the final rendered image.

The previous chapter showed one way of generating surfaces, by cross-sectional modeling. Chapter 6 will show you how to create objects with complex surfaces. Whatever method is used to generate the volume of the object, all surfaces can be reduced to the fundamental unit, the polygon.

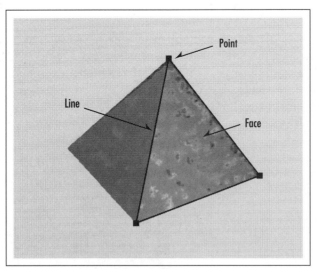

Figure 3-3 Polygons are the fundamental unit of surface geometry

Figure 3-4 The chalice is constructed out of polygons and then shaded

It's extremely efficient for computers to model objects with lines and points. Instead of having to store the color of each point on the surface of a model, the program stores the location in 3D space of lines and points. The area between the points and lines is then defined mathematically using a variety of procedures, including shading. Instead of accounting for every point that lies inside the polygon, an algorithm is used to color the face. The formula may calculate how the surface is colored when a blue light is added to a scene. Or it may use an algorithm to simulate the bands of color in bark. (These other ways of filling in the face are discussed in the next chapter.) This makes the storage of 3D objects more efficient than the paint images they generate as output. It also makes it easy to revise the color, transparency, or shininess of a surface. A simple sphere can become a glass ball, a pool ball, or an eyeball.

Types of Shading Surfaces

The process of giving a face color is called shading. In Imagine, there are four basic methods of shading: wireframe, solid, flat, and Phong. Figure 3-5 shows a pyramid shaded in each of these modes.

- **Wireframe:** Wireframe objects have transparent faces that allow you to see through to hidden lines and points. This is the shading method used when constructing objects in the orthogonal views of 3D modelers.

- **Solid:** Solid shading removes hidden lines and points. This makes the object easier to visualize. Solid shading is usually used in the editor's perspective or camera view.

- **Flat:** The faces of the model are given solid colors. Faces at right angles to a light source in a scene are made brighter than faces at angles to the light source.

- **Phong:** In Phong shading, the individual points on the face of the polygon are colored according to the placement of the light source. This creates objects that have smooth, rounded faces.

Figure 3-6 shows a teapot shaded using each of the four shading methods. The Phong-shaded teapot is the most realistic because each of the points on the polygon is given a specific color. The Phong-shaded teapot also shows how the other surface attributes of polygons can be manipulated to make the teapot

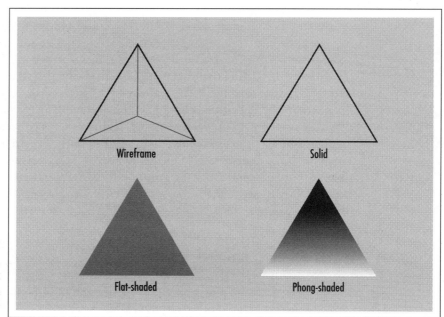

Figure 3-5
Wireframe, solid, flat, and Phong shading of a pyramid

Wireframe

Solid

Flat-shaded

Phong-shaded

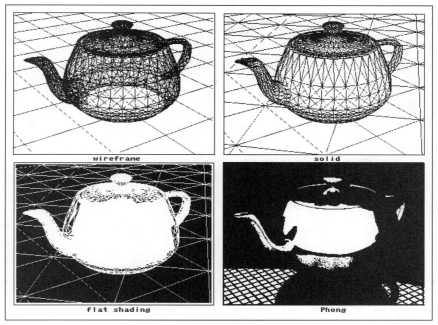

Figure 3-6
The different shading methods create dramatically different views of the teapot

look like a photograph. Notice how smooth the surface of the teapot is. The flat two-dimensional polygons making up the surface of the teapot are *smoothed* by Phong shading. Phong shading is the method used to create the final image.

What's Ahead

The next section shows you how to use Imagine's Phong shading button to alter the interaction of the object's surface with light sources in the scene.

Flat and Smooth Shading

Not all surfaces of an object need to be Phong-shaded. Because each point on the surface of an object must be calculated in Phong shading, objects using this shading method take a comparatively long time to render. A floor, for example, is usually assigned flat shading.

When a surface is first modeled, the first decision you make is the shading method. Imagine's shading controls are found at the bottom left of the Attributes Requester (see Figure 3-7), the Phong button. The Phong button toggles between flat and Phong shading.

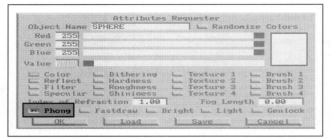

Figure 3-7 Imagine's Phong shading button is used to make a surface flat- or Phong-shaded

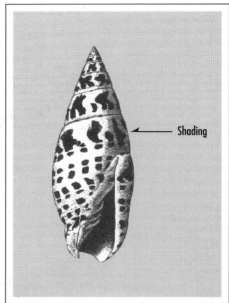

Figure 3-8
The eighteenth century
artist uses shading to
give the miter shell
roundness

Illustrators have long used shading as a technique for simulating roundness. Figure 3-8 shows a miter shell created by an unknown artist in the eighteenth century. Phong shading works like the shading on the miter shell, creating the impression of roundness without actually changing the geometry of the flat polygon. When the Phong button is on (it has an X beside it), the object is shaded as a round object; when it is off, it is shaded as a flat object.

How Shading Simulates Roundness

Using shading to make an object appear round mimics the effect of light. Figure 3-9 shows how flat surfaces and round surfaces reflect light. The top part of the figure shows the *incidence* of light, and the bottom part shows the corresponding shading achieved.

This incidence, or angle of light on a surface, determines the brightness or darkness of the surface at that point. The larger the angle, the weaker the intensity of light, because fewer rays of light are bounced back in the observer's eye. In the case of a flat surface, the rays of light have a common angle. When you click the Phong button off, Imagine gives the object surface an even level of illumination. Similarly, in the case of a rounded surface, Imagine makes the surface appear round by making the illumination uneven.

Flat Shading and Lighting

If you render the helmet object we created in the last chapter with the Phong button off, as in Figure 3-10, you tell Imagine to treat each face on the object as a flat surface. You can see the shape of the individual polygons that make up the helmet's surface. Objects with facets, such as chandeliers, may be assigned this type of surface. You can give this type of surface to any object that does not have bright highlights, such as a flat latex-painted wall in a room. Choosing flat shading can save hours of rendering time for complex scenes.

Phong Objects

In the case of Phong objects, the polygons are treated as round surfaces. Figure 3-11 shows the helmet Phong-shaded. You no longer see the shape of the polygons. One polygon smoothly blends into another.

What's Ahead

The exercise that follows takes you through the steps of modeling the surface of an object.

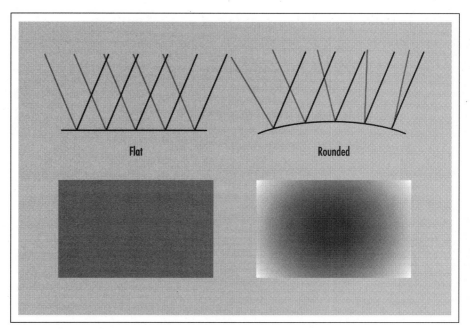

Figure 3-9 Flat and round surfaces reflect light differently

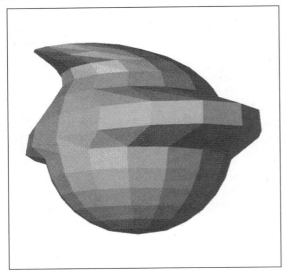

Figure 3-10 The helmet flat-shaded

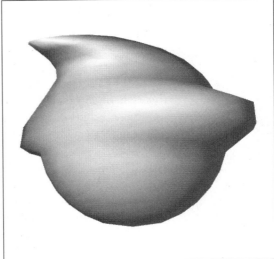

Figure 3-11 Phong-shaded helmet

Modeling the Surface of the Pottery Object

Surfaces are very rarely constructed polygon-by-polygon. In Imagine's cross-sectional modeler, the Forms Editor, you model surfaces by altering a default shape's profile and cross section. This automatically generates the polygons of the surface of the pottery vessel. The pottery vessel we'll shade is first created in the Forms Editor and then imported into the Detail Editor for surface definition.

   1   Enter the Forms Editor.

   2   Call up the New Object box, (right) ⒜ⓁⓉ-Ⓝ.

In this exercise, we create a small, squat pottery vessel with about twice the number of polygons as the default. This gives the object a smoother surface. We'll seal the bottom and create the object in One Former view. Because the vessel is perfectly symmetrical around its axes, One Former view allows us to change the shape of the default sphere in one view.

   3   Enter the following in the New Object box:

     🌐   32 points

     🌐   16 slices

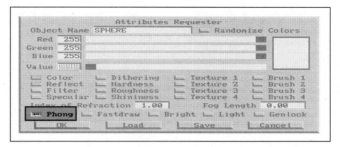

Figure 3-12 Settings for pottery vessel

⊕   X-Y Cross section

⊕   One Former view

⊕   Seal Bottom End

⊕   Cross Section Symmetry: None

Don't forget to press (ENTER) after entering numbers in the boxes. The New Object box should look like Figure 3-12.

4   Click on OK.

Clicking on OK returns you to the Forms Editor. Zoom in on the sphere.

5   Click on the ZI button at the bottom of the screen.

Now go to full-screen mode in the Front view.

6   Click on the Front bar along the left of the Front view.

The sphere now occupies the full screen. Your screen should look like Figure 3-13. Figure 3-14 shows the pottery shape in profile.

7   Select Front symmetry from the Symmetry menu so that when you move points on opposing sides of slices, they move in tandem.

Now flatten the bottom of the vessel. First make the points snap to the grid intersections.

8   Click on Lock in the Select menu. A check mark appears beside Lock, indicating it is selected.

9   Move points at the bottom of the screen until they are in the same position as those seen in Figure 3-14.

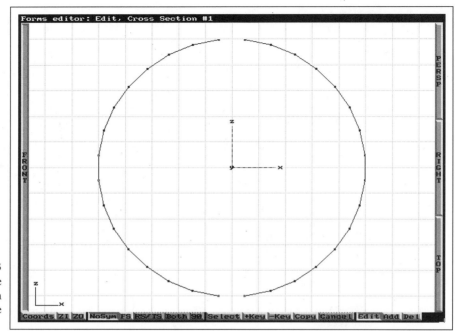

Figure 3-13
The default sphere in full-screen mode

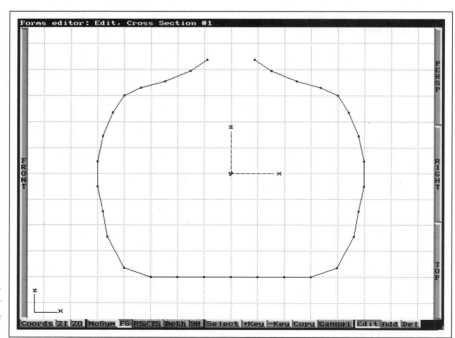

Figure 3-14
The pottery vessel's profile

Tip: Naming Conventions

> The .FRM extension identifies the object as a Forms Editor object. You can load a Forms Editor object into the Detail Editor, but once it is saved in the Detail Editor, the object's geometry changes, so it cannot be loaded back into the Forms Editor. It's best to save a Forms Editor object with a .FRM extension and a Detail Editor object with a .OBJ extension.

Do the same for the points at the top of the sphere. This time, the points shouldn't lock to the grid, so turn Lock off.

10 Click on Lock.

11 Move points along the top of the sphere to the positions shown in Figure 3-14.

Switch to the perspective window to see how the pottery shape looks so far.

12 Click on the PERSP button on the right of the screen.

13 Select Shaded from the Display menu.

14 Adjust the perspective window sliders.

Your screen should look like Figure 3-15. The flat-shaded vessel shown in the perspective window is a very rough preview of the object. Save the object.

15 Press (right) (ALT)-(S). Navigate to the objects directory and save the object as POTTERY1.FRM.

Shading the Surface of the Pottery Object

Load the POTTERY1.FRM object created in the previous exercise into the Detail Editor. The surface attributes of objects are created in the Attributes Requester of the Detail Editor.

1 Enter the Detail Editor.

2 Load the POTTERY1.FRM object from the OBJECTS directory.

When the vessel is loaded, its wireframe is brown, indicating that it is selected automatically.

3 To Pick the vessel press (F1).

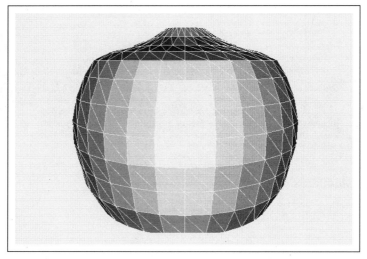

Figure 3-15 The pottery vessel in shaded view mode

Now that the object is picked, you can activate the Attributes Requester.

4   Select Attributes from the Object menu or press (F7).

The Attributes Requester box pops on the screen (see Figure 3-16). Notice that the color swatch at the top right of the box is white. By default, objects in Imagine are created with a white surface. Notice also that the Phong button at the bottom left of the Attributes Requester box is selected. Imagine gives new objects a Phong surface by default. You can see this default surface in quick render mode.

5   Click on OK to return to the Detail Editor.

6   Select Quick Render from the Editor menu or click on the Quick button at the bottom right of the screen.

The vessel renders as a white, Phong-shaded vessel (see Figure 3-17). Now render the object as a flat-shaded object.

7   Click on the screen to return to the Detail Editor.

8   Press (F7) to activate the Attributes Requester.

9   Click on the Phong button to deselect it. Click on OK.

10   Click on the Quick button at the bottom right of the screen.

This time the sphere renders as a flat-shaded object (see Figure 3-18).

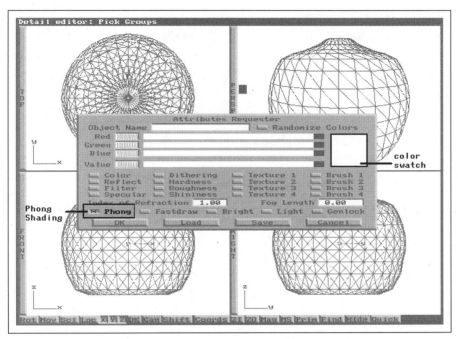

Figure 3-16 The Attributes Requester is Imagine's surface "paint box"

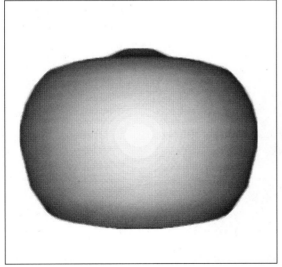

Figure 3-17 Phong-shaded vessel

Figure 3-18 Flat-shaded pottery vessel

What's Ahead

The Phong button allows you to define the polygons on an object as flat or rounded. Right now, the pottery vessel has a flat, matte surface. In the next section, you'll see how to give surfaces other surface attributes, such as shininess or reflections.

ALTERING THE SURFACE ATTRIBUTES

Look around the room and notice how flat objects and round objects reflect light differently. Materials reflect light in quite different ways. The rug absorbs light and has a rough surface. The walls are mildly reflective and smooth. Pick out an object in the room. What color is its surface? Is the surface hard or soft? Is it shiny or dull? Does it absorb or reflect light?

3D modelers provide extensive control over these surface attributes. Attributes highlighted in Figure 3-19 (Color, Reflect, Filter, Specular, Dithering, Hardness, Roughness, Shininess) provide control over the way an object interacts with light.

Editing Attributes

Working with the Attributes Requester is like revising a text document on a computer. In a word processing program a document is loaded. Changes are made to text or formatting. The document is proofread on the screen and printed. When you are satisfied with editing changes, the document is saved over the old document on disk.

Changing object surfaces is an analogous process. The Attributes Requester provides the same types of editing functions. Let's walk through the process of changing an object's Color attribute as an example of an attribute editing session.

1   Load the POTTERY1.FRM object if it is not already loaded.

2   Pick it by pressing (F1) or clicking on the axis at its center.

3   Press (F7).

How the Attributes Are Organized

An object usually has a combination of attributes. A glass dish is blue, shiny, has soft highlights, and passes light rays right through it. A stoneware dish has

Hint: Practice

Practice with the controls as you read how to use them.

a strong, dominant color, low reflectivity, and a certain roughness to it. Imagine organizes attributes into eight different categories, which are represented by buttons. Each button either changes the object's color characteristics or its surface features.

Buttons that affect an object's color are

- *Color* changes its color.

- *Reflect* makes it reflective.

- *Filter* makes it transparent.

- *Specular* changes the size of its highlights.

Changes that affect the object's surface features are

- *Dithering* reduces the amount of colors it uses.

- *Hardness* changes the hardness of its highlights.

- *Roughness* changes the roughness of its surface.

- *Shininess* changes the shininess of its surface.

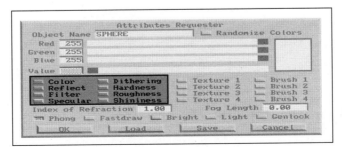

Figure 3-19 The surface attributes buttons

Changing Attributes: Three Steps

An attribute is altered in a three-step process.

1. Choose the attribute by clicking on its button.

2. Use the sliders or data entry boxes to change the attribute's values.

3. Click on OK.

This saves the changes to object attributes in a temporary area of memory. You can now use Quick Render to see the changes you have made. If you are satisfied with the changes, save the object.

Exercise: Changing an Object's Color

In this exercise, we'll change an object's color. Let's begin by reloading the vessel. (Don't save the current version of the vessel.)

1. Load POTTERY1.FRM. The pottery vessel loads back into the Detail Editor.

The vessel is automatically selected. Pick it to let Imagine know the object will be edited.

2. Press F1. The object turns purple.

Now call up the Attributes Requester.

3. Press F7. The Attributes Requester pops on the screen.

Notice that the color swatch is white. To change the pottery vessel to dark blue, select the Color button.

4. Click on the Color button.

Figure 3-20 shows the attributes. When Color is selected, the Color controls are activated. Notice that the Value control is grayed out. This means the settings are disabled. Now change the vessel's color, either by entering new values in the data boxes or by using the color sliders. In changing these values, you are *color mixing*.

Using RGB Color Mixing

Computer artists add together combinations of red, green, and blue color values to make new colors. Varying the intensity of each of the three colors lets

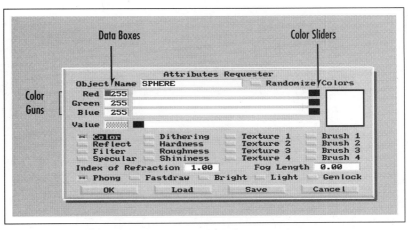

Figure 3-20 Adjusting the color of an object

you produce all the colors of the spectrum. Color Plate 4 shows the classic RGB color wheel, a visual guide to mixing colors.

Notice that when you first click on the Color button after creating a new object, a value of 255 is placed in the data box beside each color name. That's because the default color of objects is white. Try experimenting with the sliders.

1 Move the color sliders all the way to the left.

The color swatch turns to black. Notice that the color swatch changes color interactively as you move the color sliders. Notice also that the values in the data boxes change. A value of 0 in each of the data boxes makes the object black.

Each of the colors, red, green, and blue, has a maximum color value of 255 assigned to it. The range of intensities associated with each color is from 0 to 255.

Now make the pottery vessel blue. In order to make it blue, remove red and green from the object's color and set the blue value at a positive value.

2 Move the red and green sliders to the left. Move the blue slider all the way to the right.

Notice that as you do this, the color swatch becomes bluer and bluer.

Let's give the vessel a red hue by adding 100 units of red using the red color slider.

3 Adjust the sliders until the Green value reads 0 and the Red value reads 100.

Hint: 24-Bit Color Processing

Imagine internally processes colors using 24 bits of computer data—8 bits for red, 8 bits for green, and 8 bits for blue. Eight bits of computer data can store a total of 256 values, so red, green, and blue can have 256 distinct levels of intensity associated with them. Since in computer programming 0 is treated as an integer, the range is from 0 to 255, not 1 to 256.

Hint: Dithering

If your system does not support 24-bit color (sometimes called True Color), you will see a *dithered* version of the color in the color swatch. Instead of seeing a light shade of blue, for example, Imagine will attempt to simulate the shade by mixing blue and white pixels. If the pixels are small enough, or you are far enough away, the eye will not see the individual colors, but will combine them.

You can also enter values directly into the data boxes by clicking in them, removing the current value, and typing in the new value. Press (ENTER) after typing in the new value.

Now let's see what the new color looks like on the surface of the object.

4   Click on OK to return to the Detail Editor.

5   Click on the Quick button. The vessel renders with a deep-blue color.

Let's now save the pottery vessel with its new Color attribute.

6   Click on the screen to return to the Detail Editor.

7   Press (right) (ALT)-(S). The save box pops on the screen. The POTTERY1.FRM object name is currently selected for saving.

When you change an object in the Detail Editor, it can no longer be loaded into the Forms Editor. Change the name extension from .FRM to .OBJ. This helps keep objects organized.

8   Name the object POTTERY1.OBJ. Click on OK.

The vessel is now saved as a Detail Editor object, and you have made the pottery object blue.

IMPULSE, INC.

8416 Xerxes Avenue North

Minneapolis, MN 55444

- FOLD HERE -

Imagine 3.0 Order Form

I want to be a 3D Modeling wizard. Since I've bought *3D Modeling Lab,* please send me Imagine 3.0 for only $300.00 plus shipping and handling. That's a savings of $395.00, over 55% off the retail price of $695.00! I am enclosing my check or Visa/Master Card number.

To order by phone call 800-328-0184 or 612-425-0557

or return this form to Impulse, Inc.

Name

Company

Address
Street Address Only, No P.O. Box

City   State   ZIP

Daytime Phone

Quantity and Type

Name	Quantity	Price
IMAGINE 3.0		x $300.00=
		Sales Tax
Shipping—Add $5 USA, and Canada, $10 Europe, Asia and Middle East, $15 Australia for shipping and handling. Standard shipping is UPS Ground. Allow 2 to 3 weeks for delivery. Purchase orders are subject to credit approval.		Shipping
		Total Due

Format: (Please check one) ☐ **Amiga**   ☐ **PC**

Method of Payment

Checks or money orders, payable to Impulse, Inc. To pay by credit card, complete the following:

☐ Visa   ☐ MasterCard   Card Number

Cardholder's Name _____   Exp. Date

Cardholder's Signature _____

Phone Number _____

What's Ahead
In the next section we make the pottery vessel reflective.

Making Objects Reflective

In order to make objects appear reflective, 3D software mimics the physics of light. There are three main ways of modeling light in 3D software:

- **Scanline:** An algorithm determines the path of a light ray from the light source to an object and then to a point on the screen. Reflections, refracted light, and shadows are not modeled, with the exception of ground, which will show up in scanline reflections.

- **Ray tracing:** An algorithm traces the path of a light ray from a point on a screen to all the objects in a scene and then back to the light source. Reflections, refracted light, and shadows are modeled.

- **Radiocity:** All the interactions between objects, lights, and the screen are determined. Even light rays that never reach the screen are rendered. For example, a red wall may cast a reddish hue on the matte surface of an object (like a bench) sitting beside it. This reddish hue would be missing in a scanline or ray-traced scene.

Radiocity is the most accurate model, scanline the least accurate. However, radiocity is not used in desktop 3D programs because it can take hours, even days, for a program to determine the complex paths of light in a scene. Some programs allow you to simulate reflections, shadows, and other effects in scanline mode. This is often called *reflection mapping*. This provides a compromise between rendering time and accurate light modeling.

Imagine supports both scanline and ray-tracing modes. It also supports reflection mapping. In reflection mapping, a 2D image, like the scan of a real sky, is assigned to an object like a silver sphere. The scene does not include the sky as an object in it. Rather the sky is used as a reference map by the sphere. It appears as a reflection.

How Reflections Are Modeled

Reflections are modeled after the optical properties of light. Colors absorb or reflect rays of light (see Figure 3-21).

Black absorbs all the colors in the color spectrum, and white repels all the colors in the spectrum. All other colors selectively absorb and repel colors.

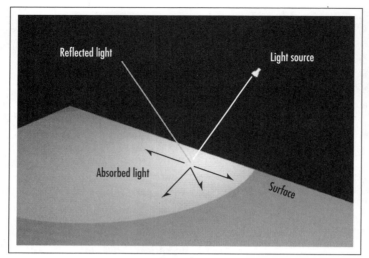

Figure 3-21 Reflected and absorbed light rays

Look around the room you are in and observe reflective objects. A mirror is fully reflective. A black wool carpet has no reflectivity. A varnished wooden floor falls somewhere in between: It is somewhat reflective, but the color and grain of wood show through.

"Pure" Versus "Impure" Reflections

Imagine actually uses two different attributes to create objects that have reflective properties: Reflect and Shininess. The Reflect attribute creates objects that have the properties of mirror surfaces. That is, the surface reflects a sharp image, the colors of which you can adjust. The Shininess attribute creates objects that have the reflective property of metals. That is, the reflection is blurry and is heavily tinted by the reflecting object's color. Steel, for example, distorts and tints reflections blue. Color Plate 5 shows the pottery vessel reflected in the two types of surfaces (Reflect on the left and Shininess on the right).

Color Sliders

You can adjust an object's reflectivity by using the Attributes Requester color sliders. If you make an object in a scene 100 percent reflective (255 units of red, green, and blue), it will disappear because it will have no color. It will merely reflect other objects in the scene. If you make it partially reflective, it will partially reflect light rays hitting it, and the object's own color and surface features will show through. If you make the red, green, and blue sliders unequal in the Attributes Requester, the object's reflection will be *biased* toward these colors. Biasing towards blue, for example, creates blue-tinted reflections. This might be useful in a night scene. Let's experiment with this attribute.

Exercise: Making the Pottery Vessel Reflective

Call up the Attributes Requester. If the pottery vessel is not currently picked (it is not blue or purple), pick it.

1. Pick the pottery vessel by clicking on its axis. It turns blue.

2. Now call up the Attributes Requester by pressing (F7).

Notice that the color swatch is violet, indicating the object's current color. Click on the Reflect button. The swatch turns black, and the values in the data boxes are 0. This indicates that the sliders now are associated with the Reflect button. The black color indicates that the object has zero reflectivity. Let's change that.

3. Drag the color sliders all the way to the right. The color swatch turns white.

Now the pottery vessel completely reflects all the light that strikes it. In other words, it has the reflectivity of a mirror. Let's do a test render.

4. Click on OK to return to the Detail Editor.

5. Click on the Quick Render button. The pottery vessel disappears. The screen is blue.

The vessel has disappeared. What happened? A completely reflective object, like a mirror, reflects its environment. The scene has only the pottery vessel in it. It sits in a black, empty void. In quick render mode, Imagine gives the void a default blue color. (In the Stage Editor the sky is black by default.)

Simulating Reflections

If you look at the chrome legs of a chair or the handle of a refrigerator, you see that they distort and reflect the environment around them. You could fill the

3D world with objects, but this would be tedious and computationally expensive. Imagine, like most 3D software, gives you a way of creating reflections without having to build a complete scene around the object. The technique, called reflection mapping, was outlined briefly in a previous section. It is the use of 2D images to simulate reflections in an object. There are two ways you can do this in Imagine:

- *Global brush map* stretches an image (such as clouds) over the whole scene.

- *Object reflection map* projects an image onto a selected object or part of an object.

Global Brush Map

Imagine calls the image that is stretched over the world a global brush map. *Brush* is an Amiga term for 2D paint images, such as those you create in paint programs. The global brush map does not actually exist as an object in your scene. It only appears as reflections in objects when the scene is rendered. Think of it as an invisible dome on a 3D scene (see Figure 3-22).

Exercise: Creating a Global Brush Map

In order to apply a global brush map, you enter Imagine's Action Editor and apply the reflection map to the entire scene. It's usually applied after you open a project in Imagine and set up a scene in the Stage Editor. These are subjects covered in the chapters ahead. Rather than take you through all the staging and rendering steps now, we'll use the special project called VESSEL that has the staging and rendering parameters already set. This will allow you to experiment with reflections without having to learn staging and rendering first.

Projects are created and rendered in the Project Editor.

1   From the Project menu select Project Editor. The Project Editor screen appears.

2   From the Project menu in the Project Editor select Open. The Project Name box pops on the screen.

Project files are stored in the \IMAG root directory. Navigate to that directory. Scroll through the list of project files until you find VESSEL.

3   Select VESSEL from the \IMAG root directory. The Rendering Subproject screen appears.

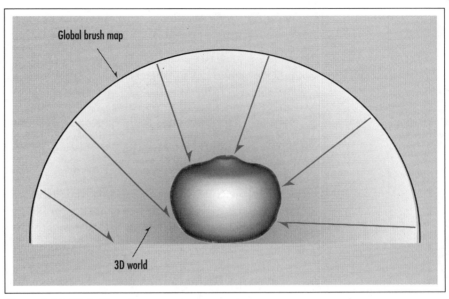

Figure 3-22 Global brush map

Subprojects are like file drawers in a filing cabinet. They store the images that you render.

4 Click on the Open button on the Rendering Subproject screen. The Rendering Project Name box appears.

5 Select REFLECT from the Rendering Project Name box. This opens the rendering subproject with its preset rendering parameters.

Now let's return to the Detail Editor to prepare the pottery vessel for reflection. We've stored a Forms Editor object in the \IMAG\OBJECTS directory. Load the object into the Detail Editor.

6 From the Object menu select Load. Navigate to the \IMAG\OBJECTS directory and load VESSEL.FRM. A brown pottery vessel appears in the viewports.

7 Click on the ZI button to zoom in on the pottery vessel.

8 Press (F1) or choose Pick Select from the Pick/Select menu. The object becomes purple.

This lets Imagine know that you want to make editing changes to the object. Use Quick Render to see what the default object looks like.

9   Select Quick Render from the Editor menu. The Quickrender Lighting box appears. Click on OK.

The vessel renders as a white, matte pottery vessel. The object is shown with the default surface given to objects when they are first created. In order to change the surface, enter Imagine's Attributes Requester.

10   Press (F7). The Attributes Requester box pops on the screen.

Notice that the color swatch shows the vessel as white. Change the vessel to black, so that it has no color.

11   Click on the Color button. Move the red, green, and blue sliders all the way to the left. Alternately, enter a value of 0 in each of the data boxes beside the color names. The color swatch turns to black.

Now make the pottery vessel 100 percent reflective.

12   Click on the Reflect button and move all the sliders to the right. The color swatch turns white.

The vessel will now reflect all light rays striking it. To see the result of the change, use Quick Render to view the scene.

13   Click on OK to make the changes and select Quick Render from the Project menu. The vessel disappears. The screen is totally blue.

The pottery vessel sits in an empty 3D world. It has no color. In quick render mode, the world is given a default blue color. The default light model is scanline rendering, so even if there were objects in the 3D world, they would not appear as reflections on the vessel surface. In order to see reflections, we'll need to add a global reflection map to the scene. We'll do that in the Action Editor. First save the object.

14   Select Save from the Object menu or press (right) (ALT-S). Save the object as VESSEL.OBJ.

Figure 3-23 shows the Action Editor screen. The Action Editor allows you to make global changes to entire scenes or animations. Placing a global brush map on a scene is this kind of change. Located in the Action Editor is a pop-up box where you activate the global brush map. The line added to Figure 3-23 (connecting the word *Actor* in the right column with the frame number in the top row) shows where you click to bring up the Globals Info box, shown in Figure 3-24.

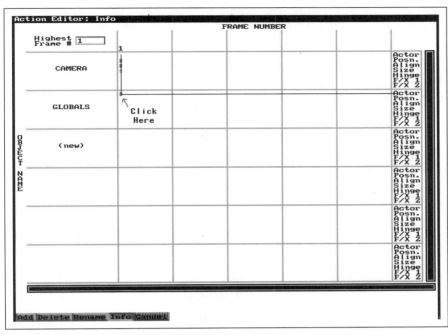

Figure 3-23 The Action Editor

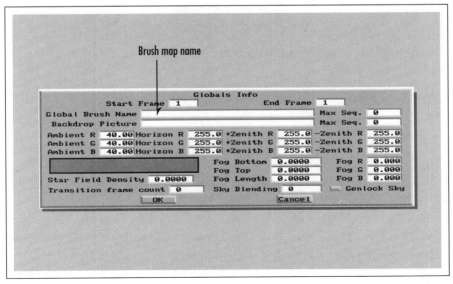

Figure 3-24 Globals Info box

To add a global brush map to a scene, enter the brush map name (including the DOS path to it) to the Global Brush Name data entry box in the Action Editor's Globals Info box.

Figure 3-25 shows the clouds global brush map that we'll use for the pottery vessel. The image was copied from the clip art collection of images available from Aris Entertainment on the CD-ROM "Wild Places."

15 Click on the Global Brush Map box and enter the path name to the reflection map: \IMAG\MAPS\CLOUDS.TIF. (Don't forget to press ENTER.)

16 Click on OK to exit from the Globals Info box. Select Save Changes from the Project menu.

This saves the changes you made to the scene. Now enter the Project Editor to render the scene.

17 Select Project Editor from the Project menu.

The Project Editor allows you to render an entire animation or a single frame (image) in an animation. The project has only one frame in it. It shows up as the number 1 in the series of rectangular boxes at the center of the screen. It's in the box above the Generate button.

18 Click on the number 1 to select the frame for rendering. The number 1 is highlighted.

19 Click on the Generate button to start the rendering process.

A progress indicator on the information line at the top of the screen shows the progress of the render. When rendering is complete, display the finished image on the screen.

20 Click on the Show button.

Your screen will look similar to Figure 3-26. You can see the clouds in the pottery vessel and the land mass at the bottom.

Reflection Map

The second method of adding reflections to scenes is to place a reflection map on the object itself. This method works well for simple scenes or logos where precise control over the reflection is important. The brush map might look like Figure 3-27.

The blurry, undefined shapes in this image are ideal for metallic surfaces that have an uneven, dull finish. Images like these are commonly called *maps,*

Figure 3-25 Clouds global brush map from Aris Entertainment's "Wild Places" CD-ROM clip collection

Figure 3-26 The pottery vessel reflecting the clouds

Figure 3-27 A paint image used as a reflection map for an object

Tip: Making Maps

Picture Man for Windows (included with this book) has a blur tool that makes these images easy to create. Imagine also allows you to layer image maps, creating interesting effects. Chapter 8 shows you how to do this.

because they are projected onto 3D surfaces. The maps themselves are flat and two-dimensional. Think of maps as slides projected onto a 3D surface (see Figures 3-28 and 3-29).

The 2D image of the blur is projected on the rounded shape of the clay vessel. It helps give the reflection interest and detail.

Reflection maps are applied to objects in the Attributes Requester, using the Brush 1, 2, 3, or 4 buttons. We return to this subject in the next chapter, in the section titled "Reflect Map Type."

What's Ahead

Reflective surfaces bounce light rays off the surface of objects. The next type of surface passes light rays through surfaces.

Making Objects Transparent

The Filter button in the Attributes Requester is used to make objects transparent or semitransparent. The Filter attribute gets its name from the fact that it filters light in a very special way. What it does is this:

- First it temporarily converts the surface to grayscale.

- It then filters the light through this grayscale.

- The darkest areas of the grayscale filter the light out.

- In the whitest areas of the grayscale, all the light is let through.

Setting the Filter color sliders to pure white will make an object totally transparent. The blues and reds at one end of the color spectrum tend to convert to very dark colors when Imagine converts them to grayscale. All colors have at least some white component, with the exception of pure black. For example, light blue is more transparent than dark blue.

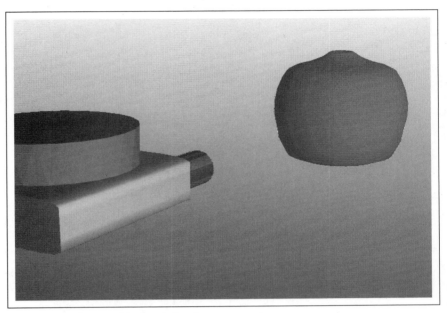

Figure 3-28 The vessel before it has been mapped

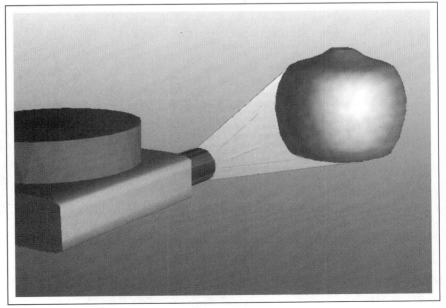

Figure 3-29 Blur map projected onto a 3D surface

Caution: Do Not Make a Transparent Object Shiny

The Shininess attribute disables the Filter attribute as a transparency control. When Shininess values are set, the object is rendered as opaque. To make a transparent object shiny, use the Specular and Hardness attributes.

Figure 3-30 shows the violet pottery vessel with the red, green, and blue sliders set at the halfway point. The pottery vessel has been placed in front of pinstripes. You can see the stripes through the vessel.

Refraction

When light passes through air or glass, its path is bent as shown in Figure 3-31. Imagine has a button called Refraction Index that allows you to adjust the way an object bends the light that passes through it (see Figure 3-32).

To make objects refract light, first make them transparent using the Filter button and then enter a value for refraction. By convention the range of refraction is between 1.0 and 3.5. Air has an index of 1.0, glass has an index of about 1.52, and diamond has an index of 2.4. You enter a value between 1.0 (the default) and 3.5 (the maximum). Compare Figure 3-30 with Figure 3-33. Notice how refraction bends the stripes.

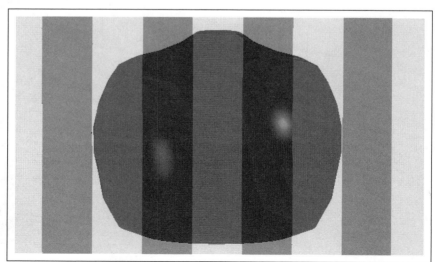

Figure 3-30
Half-transparent
blue pottery vessel

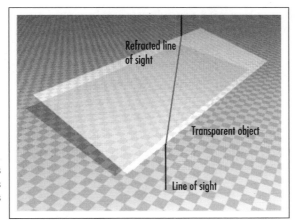

Figure 3-31
Light bends
when it passes
through glass

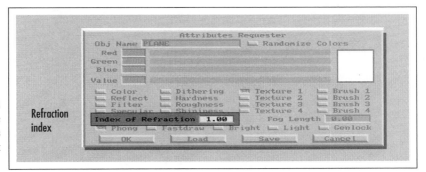

Figure 3-32
The Attribute
Requester's
Refraction Index

Refraction
index

Figure 3-33
Ray-tracing
programs allow
you to make light
refract through
an object

Giving an Object a Specular Highlight

Specular highlights are the small, intense circles of light formed when light rays fall on a shiny surface. A cue ball has a very intense, small highlight close to the color of the light shining on it. A flat latex-painted door has no highlight. A pure white light source lighting a shiny surface will overpower the object's surface color, producing a white highlight. The same object with a dull finish has a large, diffuse highlight with much of the surface color showing through.

Specular highlights are associated with light sources. They provide a visual clue as to the location of light sources in a scene. For example, the pottery vessel will render with a highlight on the curve at right angles to the light source.

There is another kind of shininess that is the result of diffuse light rays striking the object. A varnished hardwood floor, for example, reflects all light rays striking it, producing a bright, glossy look. (This type of shininess is discussed shortly.)

An object when it is first created has a matte finish. Most programs allow you to make an object look shiny by controlling the size and intensity of the specular highlight. Figure 3-34 shows three spheres with different specular highlight settings.

The sphere in the middle has no specular setting. The sphere on the left has the specular highlight set at maximum width. The sphere on the right has the specular highlight set at minimum width. Notice how shiny the right sphere looks.

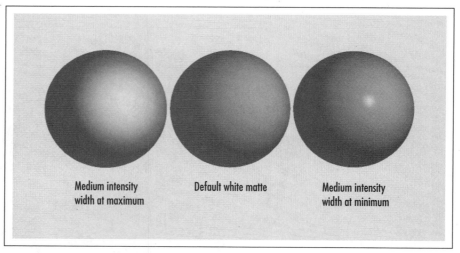

Medium intensity   Default white matte   Medium intensity
width at maximum   width at minimum

Figure 3-34 Adjusting the specular highlight changes the viewer's perception of shininess

Tip: Ignore the Dithering Button

> Imagine does its internal color processing using 24 bits of color (True Color). In this book, all images are rendered as 24-bit Targa images. When you render an object as a 24-bit image, the settings in the Dithering button are ignored.

Imagine's Specular attribute controls the intensity and color of the highlight. Objects that have a clear plastic or clear varnish finish have white highlights. On other surfaces, such as an orange, the highlight will be a lighter shade than the object's base color. Change the color of the highlight with the color sliders. The Hardness attribute is used to change the width of the specular highlight.

Exercise: Adding a Specular Highlight to the Vessel

Experiment with the Specular and Hardness settings using the VESSEL.OBJ created in the previous exercise (load the VESSEL project). Click on the Reflect and Filter buttons and change their values to 0. Click on the Color button and adjust the color of the vessel to a blue or red color. Then click on the Specular button and adjust the intensity of the specular highlight using the color sliders. Adjust the size of the highlight by clicking on the Hardness button and moving the Value slider. The greater the value of the slider, the larger the specular highlight.

You can also adjust the color of the highlight using the color sliders in conjunction with the Specular button. Many modelers prefer to work with neutral colored highlights, but it is possible to light an object with a gray or white highlight and then create the impression of a colored light source by changing the color of the specular highlight.

Changing the object's roughness also contributes to the character of a specular highlight. A rough surface has a more textured look than a smooth finish. The next section has more about this attribute control.

Changing an Object's Surface Roughness

The surface of an orange is not as smooth as that of a light bulb. Imagine's Roughness attribute allows you to manipulate this surface characteristic. Figure 3-35 shows the pottery vessel with Roughness set to its maximum.

Figure 3-35 Pottery vessel with Roughness set at maximum

Roughness does not penetrate into the geometry of the object. It's a layer of pixels placed over the object that looks like the bumpy or dirty surface of an object. If you try to animate an object that has been made rough with the Roughness attribute, the surface will not be the same from one frame to another. This makes animated rough surfaces random and noisy. Don't use the Roughness attribute in animated scenes.

Change the roughness of the object using the Roughness button in the Attributes Requester. Use Quick Render to see the effect of the changes.

Making an Object Shiny

The "Making Objects Reflective" section discussed the physics behind reflections. Shininess models the diffuse reflections created by all the light sources in a scene. Pure, mirrorlike reflections are created with the Reflect attribute. The kinds of impure, tinted, and diffuse reflections of metals are created using the Shininess attribute. Refer to the comparison between Reflect and Shininess reflections in Color Plate 7.

Like objects created with the Reflect attribute, objects created with the Shininess attribute must reflect *something*. You can add a global reflection map

Plate 3 Utah Teapot

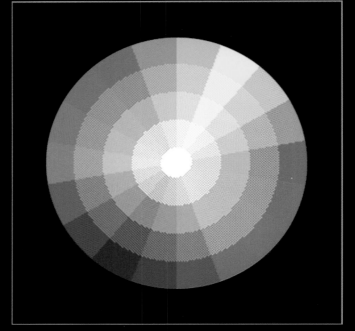

Plate 4   RGB Color Wheel

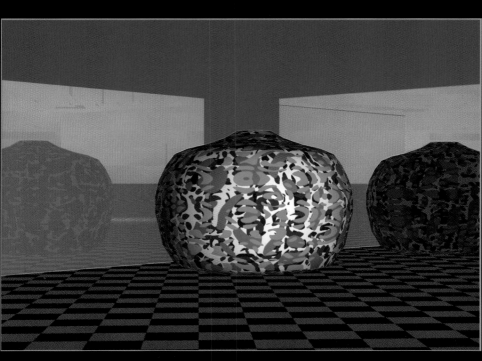

Plate 5   Reflection and Shininess

Plate 6 Alan Henry's Honey Bee

Plate 7   Mike Miller's 35mm Camera

Plate 8   Chalice with 50% Fog

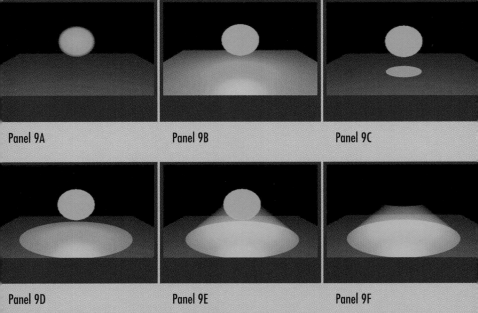

Panel 9A

Panel 9B

Panel 9C

Panel 9D

Panel 9E

Panel 9F

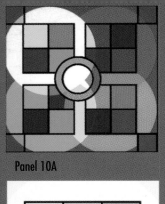

Panel 10A

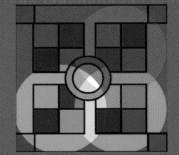

Panel 10B

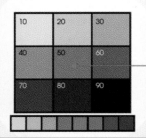

10	20	30
40	50	60
70	80	90

Panel 10C

10	20	30
40	50	60
70	80	90

Panel 10D

Plate 10   Color Test Panels

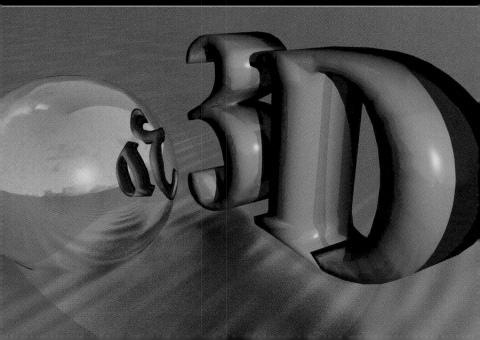

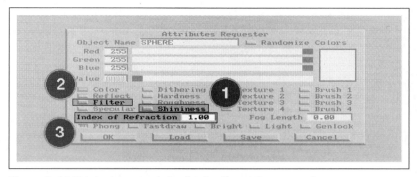

Figure 3-36 Shininess controls in the Attributes Requester box

to a scene or give reflections interest by adding a reflection map to the surface of an object.

The Shininess attribute creates more complex reflections than the Reflect attribute. You can alter

- ⊕ The intensity of the reflection
- ⊕ What colors are reflected by the object
- ⊕ How soft or sharp the reflection will be

Figure 3-36 shows where you make these alterations.

Imagine uses the Reflect and Index of Refraction buttons for a different purpose here. Here's what the buttons do:

- ⊕ *Shininess button* (1) controls intensity of reflection
- ⊕ *Filter button* (2) controls color of reflection
- ⊕ *Index of Refraction* (3) controls the amount of light aberration

The Shininess attribute is especially useful for creating metallic surfaces.

Once again, experiment with Shininess using the VESSEL project. Remember that the shininess of the pottery vessel will not become apparent until you render the object in the Project Editor.

Saving Attribute Settings

Imagine allows you to save the changes made during an Attributes Requester editing session by clicking on the Save button at the bottom of the box. When you have created a surface characteristic that looks realistic, save it in the

Imagine subdirectory called \IMAG\ATTRIBS. You will find a number of exist-ing surface attributes stored on your disk, including such surfaces as chrome, gold, red plastic, and oak wood texture.

SUMMARY

The attributes discussed in this chapter control the way light interacts with sur-faces. So far those surfaces have been very simple. The next chapter will add another layer to the discussion by showing you how to model complex surfaces using image-mapping, procedural textures, and other special effects.

Applying Textures to Surfaces

The main obstacle in creating photorealistic surfaces is detail. The detail of the natural world is practically inexhaustible, and it extends well beyond the limits of our senses. As far back as the turn of the century, photographers, such as Arthur E. Smith, combined microscopes and cameras to peer down at the rich tapestry of textures just outside the range of human vision (see Figure 4-1).

Smith's microphotographs fed a public appetite for new ways of looking into the details of life. The honeybee's tongue magnified 20 times reveals structures underlying the world just beyond our gaze (see Figure 4-2).

If you were modeling a honeybee, one of the most important decisions you would make is how much detail to include. This is especially important in models that will be animated later. The more complex your model, the longer each frame of the animation will take to render. Animation rates of 30 frames a second are common for sequences transferred to video. If your image takes an hour to

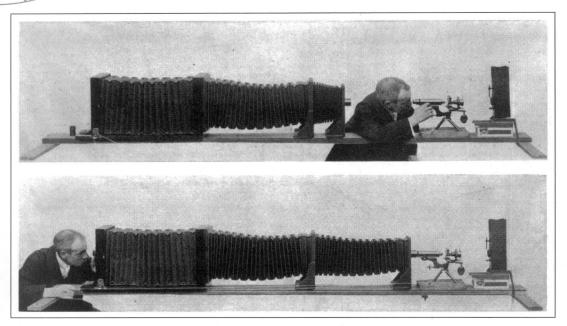

Figure 4-1 Arthur E. Smith in his studio at the turn of the century

render, it will take close to 30 hours to make the bee fly for 1 second. A 6-second animation would take more than a week!

Nature has given the honeybee's leg a lot of detail (see Figure 4-3). An engineering masterpiece, the honeybee's leg is more intelligent, better tooled, and more versatile than the most elaborate robot arm or leg built to date. There is a limit to any computer's ability to model the deep complexity of reality. In 3D graphics the art is knowing what detail to leave out of an object or a scene. A 3D bee doesn't have the fine detail of the original, although most people will accept the computer-generated version as a simulacrum. See Color Plate 6.

This may be all the detail required to animate the bee. The period at the end of this sentence may be all the detail required to animate a swarm of bees from a distance. Or a bee zooming by at close range may require no more detail than Alan Henry's bee to look absolutely real. Moving graphics are very forgiving of detail. Again, the art of modeling is to know what detail to leave out.

Much 3D art lacks the dents, dirt, grime, and grittiness of real objects. People are also finely tuned to the movements of objects they know well. This

Figure 4-2 Honeybee's tongue magnified 20 times

Figure 4-3 Honeybee's leg magnified 25 times

is the reason why the face is a most challenging object to model and animate (see Figure 4-4).

The face is a moving target for 3D artists. Its surfaces and myriad complex rhythms we humans know all too well. Computer imitations, even those laboriously re-created by super computers, lack the details and fine nuances of reality.

The same organic machines that conspire against 3D artists, the eye and the brain, can come to their aid. Artists use their gray matter to overcome the limitations of their digital tools. Mike Miller creates scenes of incredible beauty and fine detail using an ordinary desktop PC and a freeware ray-tracing program. Color Plate 7 shows a photorealistic camera entirely constructed in the program POV-Ray.

How to Build a Bee

Alan Henry, the 3D artist who created this bee, tells you how he did it in Appendix D.

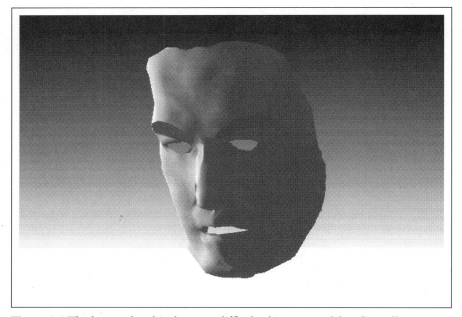

Figure 4-4 The human head is the most difficult object to model realistically

This is the ultimate surreal image: a simulation of a 35mm camera that captures simulations of moments in time. In the virtual reality of 3D art, the canvas for artistic expression is quite unlimited.

SURFACE MODELING TECHNIQUES

The previous chapter showed you how to model surfaces using shading. You learned how 3D programs fool the eye by simulating the effect of virtual light on the surface of virtual objects. The magic act continues in this chapter. You will see how 3D artists make simple surfaces look complex by covering them with a carpet of detail. There are two basic methods:

- *Procedural textures* that use an algorithm to selectively apply color and pattern to the object.

- *Image maps* (2D paint images) mapped onto the surfaces of objects.

Procedural textures are special mathematical formulas used to add color to polygons. Image maps are similar to the reflection maps discussed in Chapter 3. A reference image is mapped onto a surface.

There is a variety of other ways surfaces can be treated by 3D programs. Objects can be self-illuminated, they can be rendered as dummy objects (no surfaces), or given other special properties during animation. For example, Imagine's explode special effect uses particle system technology to cause object surfaces to shatter and disintegrate.

In this chapter we will use Imagine's surface modeling tools to illustrate the primary techniques.

Imagine's Surface Modeling Tools

Figure 4-5 shows the location of procedural texture (1), image-mapping (2), and special-effects tools (3) in Imagine's Attributes Requester. (Imagine calls image maps brush maps as you learned in Chapter 3.) The special-effects tools include the following:

- *Fastdraw* is used during object editing to cause selected objects to be viewed as bounding box displays. *Bounding boxes* substitute line segments around the perimeters of objects. The hundreds or thousands of lines that make up the wireframe model are hidden until the object is rendered. This speeds up redraw time in the viewing windows.

- *Bright* creates objects that do not cast shadows or have shading.

- *Light* turns an object into a light-emitting object.

- *Fog* causes the object to become a fog or partially obscured in fog.

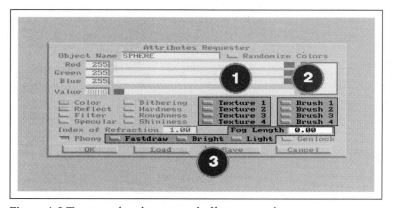

Figure 4-5 Textures, brush map, and effects controls

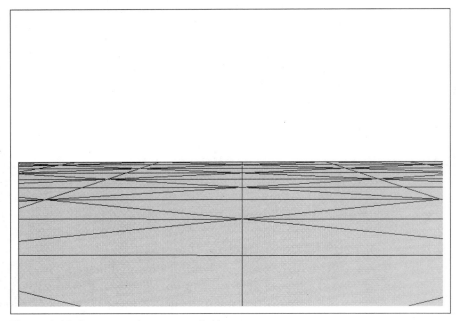

Figure 4-6 Polygons on the wave surface

COVERING SURFACES WITH PROCEDURAL TEXTURES

Procedural textures use mathematical formulas to color the individual pixels that make up the surface of an object. The procedure can be as simple as placing a grid of lines on an object or as complex as animating ocean waves. The key is that the geometry of the object is not modified. Rather, the way the surface is *colored* is modified.

Figure 4-6 shows a flat plane. To simulate ocean waves on this flat surface, Imagine places a layer of pixels on the polygonal mesh consisting of adjustable bands of dark and light blue (see Figure 4-7).

In the next section you'll learn how to use these procedural modeling tools.

Applying Procedural Textures

In most cases, the first thing you do before selecting a procedural texture is specify the surface highlights on the object. These attributes are applied "on

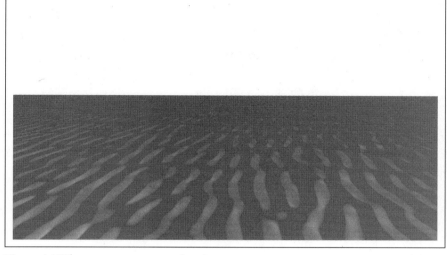

Figure 4-7 The waves pattern on the plane

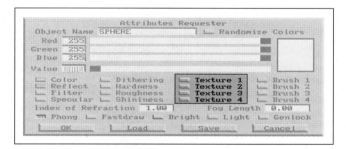

Figure 4-8 You can layer up to four textures

top" of textures to give them realism. For example, a texture that simulates wood grain is given a shiny surface using specular lighting parameters.

After working out the object shading, the texture is then applied. In many programs, including Imagine, you can layer up to four textures on top of each other. They are applied sequentially. The Attributes Requester has four buttons corresponding to each of these layers (see Figure 4-8).

Think of the textures as successive overlays, like the sheets of acetate a presenter uses to build up a chart on an overhead projector. The parts of the acetate that are clear will show the layer underneath. White is the transparent color in computer graphics and black is opaque. In the case of procedures that use transparency, the white component of a color makes the object semi-transparent.

Here are the steps for creating textured surfaces in Imagine:

- Call up the Attributes Requester box.

- Set the object's surface attributes.

- Click on one of the Texture buttons (beginning with Texture 1).

- Select a texture from the TEXTURES subdirectory.

- Change the texture parameters in the texture parameters box.

- Click on OK and save the object.

Some of the textures, like Camo (camouflage), layer spots on top of the object's current color. Other textures completely cover the object's surface.

Texture Surface Attributes

Some textures allow you to use the same types of surface attributes as the object attributes (color, reflection, transparency) discussed in the previous chapter. For example, the grid texture allows you to apply the texture as a color, reflection map, or filter map.

Texture Axes

All Imagine objects have axes, and when you move, rotate, or scale an object, you automatically change the axes as well. Textures can also have axes.

Think of textures as being mapped onto the surface of an object, like a slide projected onto an object. Imagine will automatically guess at how to wrap the texture around your object, but sometimes, the default size, rotation, or position of the texture will appear to be wrong. Usually the problem lies with the orientation of the object's axes relative to the world axes. The world axes remain fixed. If the object is not in line with the world axes, the texture may appear to be askew. It's always a good idea to keep an object's axes in line with the world axes.

Realigning an Object's Axes to the World Axes

To realign an object with the world axes:

- Pick the object.

- Call up the Transformation Requester ((ALT)-(T)).

- Click on the Transform Axes Only button.

- Click on the Alignment button.

- Set all the values in the X, Y, Z data entry boxes to 0.

- Click on Perform.

This returns the alignment of the object's axes to coincide with the world axes. When you apply a texture, it will be oriented to the axes of the world.

Changing the Orientation of the Texture Axes

There are some cases where you want to change the orientation of the object's texture relative to the object rather than the world. You may decide to put a brick patio on an angle, rather than at the default right angle. Imagine supplies the tools for reorienting texture maps. Figure 4-9 shows where these controls are located on the Pastella parameters box.

Transform Axes provides an accurate way of changing an object's axes. Figure 4-10 shows the Transformation Requester box that pops up when you

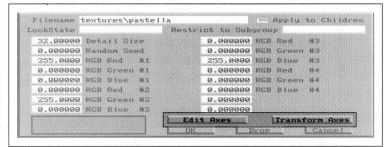

Figure 4-9
Edit Axes and
Transform Axes
controls

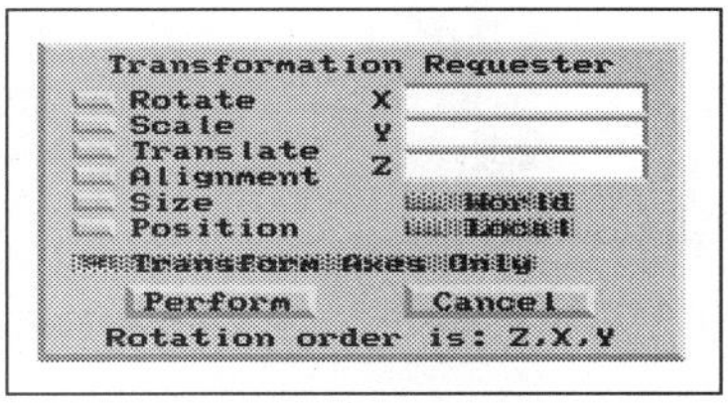

Figure 4-10 The
Transformation
Requester box

click on the Transform Axes button. You see this box often while working in Imagine. It allows you to precisely change the size, position, or scale of the object or axes.

Edit Axes allows you to change the axes interactively. When you click on the Edit Axes button, the screen changes to a view of the object with the axes superimposed on it as a bounding box as shown in Figure 4-11.

It's a little difficult to see the box surrounding the pottery object in a diagram. Figure 4-12 visualizes the size and orientation of the texture axes for the texture called Pastella found in the \IMAG\TEXTURES subdirectory.

To change the scale, rotation, and position of the texture map, use the same keys or buttons used for scaling, rotating, or moving objects in the Detail Editor:

- Rot button or (R) key rotates the texture.

- Mov button or (M) key moves the texture relative to the object.

- Scl button or (S) key scales the texture.

Once the object's texture map axes have been adjusted, press the (SPACEBAR) to confirm the changes and return to the parameters box. Pressing (ESC) cancels the editing session and returns you to the parameters box.

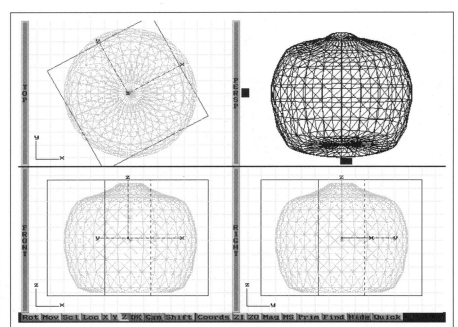

Figure 4-11 Axes superimposed as a bounding box on the pottery object

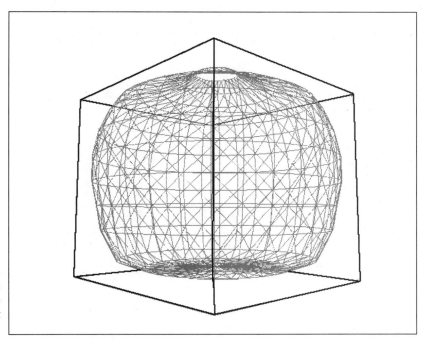

Figure 4-12
The texture axes
enclose the
pottery object

Tip: Axes Manipulation

Editing axes is treated in depth in the image map section "Changing Map Size, Position, and Orientation" later in the chapter.

Exercise: Applying a Texture

Let's practice by applying the Pastella texture to the pottery object created earlier.

   1   Enter the Detail Editor.

   2   Load POTTERY1.FRM or create a new pottery object.

The texture in this example is called Pastella. The texture's name derives from the colors it places on the object: random swirls of soft pastel colors. Figure 4-13 shows the pattern created by Pastella.

To apply this texture, pick the object and call up the Attributes Requester.

   3   Pick POTTERY1.FRM by pressing F1.

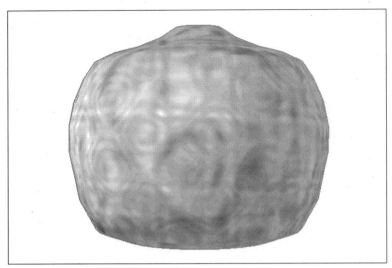

Figure 4-13
Pattern formed
by Pastella

Tip: Digging Out a Texture

Sometimes a texture map will become partially buried in an object after you have moved it. The grid texture, for example, will become spotty in some places. Move the texture slightly off of the surface to correct this.

4   Press (F7) to bring up the Attributes Requester.

Select the first texture layer by clicking on its texture button.

5   Click on Texture 1. A file load box pops on the screen.

The file load box allows you to select the subdirectory where textures are located.

6   Select the \IMAG\TEXTURES subdirectory.

7   Select Pastella from the \IMAG\TEXTURES directory. The Pastella parameters box pops on the screen (see Figure 4-14).

Each of the textures has an associated parameters box. In the case of Pastella, you can change the following parameters:

- *Detail Size* controls size of the swirls

- *Random Seed* makes the pattern random

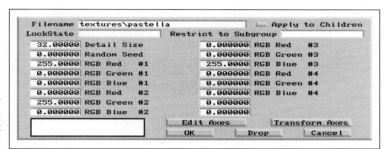

Figure 4-14
The Pastella
parameters box

⊕ *RGB Colors* allows you to specify each of the four colors

Now let's enter values into the parameters boxes. Remember to press ENTER after typing in each of the values.

8 Enter the following in the parameters boxes:

⊕ Detail Size: 32

⊕ Random Seed: 22

⊕ Pink:

RGB Red #1: 255
RGB Green #1: 95
RGB Blue #1: 95

⊕ Medium Gray

RGB Red #2: 120
RGB Green #2: 120
RGB Blue #2: 120

⊕ Medium Blue

RGB Red #3: 120
RGB Green #3: 120
RGB Blue #3: 255

⊕ Turquoise

RGB Red #4: 155
RGB Green #4: 155
RGB Blue #4: 155

Notice that as you change the color settings, the color swatch changes accordingly.

Hint: Experiment

The best way to master textures is to experiment with texture parameters.

Pastel colors have a high level of white in them. The white component of a color is increased by adding equal amounts of red, green, and blue to it. This will tone down the contrast between colors, for a more subtle effect than the default colors. Use the Random Seed setting to make the default pattern (as seen in Figure 4-9) more random, less structured. Increase the pattern size to further soften the pattern.

After entering the parameter values, quick render the pottery object.

9   Click OK to exit the parameters box.

10   Click OK to exit the Attributes Requester.

11   Click on the Quick button to quick render.

The image in Figure 4-15 has a much softer pattern and more diffuse color than the default pattern and colors.

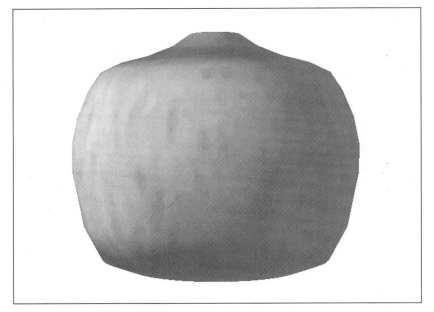

Figure 4-15 The altered Pastella texture

Hint: Removing Textures

An X beside a Texture button indicates that you previously added a texture to an object. Texture parameters boxes have a Drop button at the bottom center. To remove a texture from an object, simply click on the Drop button. The X beside the texture disappears.

Experiment with the other textures in the \IMAG\TEXTURES library on your disk.

What's Ahead

The next section introduces you to the second method of adding two-dimensional detail to surfaces: image-mapping. Imagine calls image-mapping, *brush-mapping*.

COVERING SURFACES WITH IMAGE MAPS

Procedural textures mathematically define the object's surface coloring. The alternative method for giving objects surface color is image-mapping. An image map wraps an object with a 2D paint image prepared in a paint program. Instead of giving the surface geometry of an orange the bumps and pits of an orange peel, you wrap a sphere with the image of an orange peel. The orange peel image is prepared in a paint program or scanned from a picture.

The way objects are wrapped with images varies widely between 3D modeling programs. The basic methods, however, are similar. You assign an image to an object, and the program figures out how to wrap it around the object. This is rather straightforward for flat surfaces, but wrapping flat images around curved objects is more complicated. This is where 3D programs diverge in the techniques they use for wrapping such basic shapes as cubes, spheres, and cylinders. You'll learn how to use Imagine's mapping parameters to cover these three types of objects. Once you get the hang of it, you'll master one of the 3D modeler's most valuable modeling tools.

Sources for Image Maps

Image maps are paint or bitmapped images. You can capture the images from a video input device or color scanner. You can also create (or manipulate) images with a paint program such as Adobe Photoshop, CorelPHOTO-PAINT, Zsoft paint programs like PC Paintbrush, or Aldus Photostyler. Finally, there are many vendors who sell image maps specifically designed for 3D modeling. For example, CorelDRAW supplies maps (marble and stucco and others) as clip art on the CD-ROM disc accompanying the package. All images must be TIFF (.TIF), not compressed and 24-bit.

Wrapping Objects with 2D Paint Images

Imagine imports these images you supply and *maps* them onto objects. The process is analogous to the way a map is projected onto a globe. Figure 4-16 shows how the points on a 2D image are mapped onto a curved surface.

Programs use mathematical formulas that translate coordinates on the 2D plane of the image to the coordinates on the curved surface of objects. Figure 4-17 shows a 2D grid pattern projected onto a sphere.

Notice the way the grid lines are bent to fit the contours of the sphere. Some distortion is going to occur to maps wrapping round surfaces. This is similar to the challenge of covering a round object with Christmas wrapping

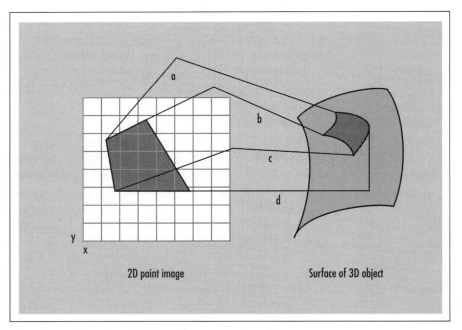

Figure 4-16 Mapping a 2D image on a curved surface

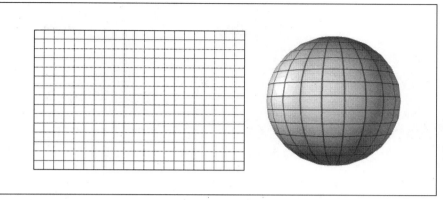

Figure 4-17 3D programs are quite clever in figuring out how to put a 2D surface on a curved object

paper. Fortunately, many 3D programs provide a lot of user control over how maps are applied to objects.

Mapping Techniques

Programs like Imagine give you explicit control over the way maps are projected onto 3D surfaces. Mapping parameters address such issues as: Will the map be applied to the entire object or placed like a decal on part of the object? Will it be applied at an angle? How will it reflect light? Will it be semitransparent? Programs provide interactive tools for specifying these options.

Imagine is particularly helpful in this area. Once you tell Imagine what the basic shape of the object is, it will try to figure out how to wrap it with the map. For example, by default the map will be applied as a flat image on a flat surface. Imagine will try to cover the entire object unless you specify otherwise. If you specify a sphere, Imagine will project the map as a curved surface rather than a flat surface. The next section introduces you to the Imagine mapping system.

IMAGINE'S MAPPING SYSTEM

Imagine's mapping system is found in the Attributes Requester. Figure 4-18 shows the location of the mapping buttons on the Attributes Requester. Like procedural textures, you can apply up to four image maps to an object. The image maps are applied sequentially.

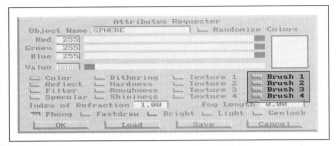

Figure 4-18 Buttons used in brush mapping

Tip: *Layering Brush Maps on Top of Texture Maps*

Brush maps go on *after* texture maps. This means you can apply an image on top of a texture map. Where the image is white, the underlying texture map will show through. This allows you to build up complex textures. However, for users with limited system memory, this practice is not recommended. Each map is loaded into memory at render time. The more maps you use, the more memory required.

Tip: *Processing Maps*

Use Picture Man for Windows, included with this book, to prepare images for Imagine. Images can be sized, converted to the correct file format, and sharpened, blurred, or converted to grayscale.

Preparing Image Maps for Imagine

To be used in Imagine, pictures created in paint programs and used for image maps must have the following characteristics:

- They must be in TIFF (.TIF) format.

- They must be uncompressed.

- They must be 24-bit (True Color).

- They can be any size, but 320 by 200 is recommended for most objects.

Procedure for Applying Brush Maps

The procedure for applying brush maps is similar to that for applying textures. Adjust the object's surface attributes, then apply the brush map using a mapping parameters box. These are the steps:

- Adjust the surface attributes.
- Click on one of the four Brush map buttons. (Maps are applied sequentially.)
- Using the file selector box, select an image to use as a map.
- Adjust the mapping parameters.
- Test render the image.

What's Ahead

In the next section we'll apply an image to a sphere using Imagine's default mapping parameters.

Exercise: Image-mapping a Sphere

We are going to map a picture of a lion's head onto a sphere. First we'll prepare the image.

Preparing the Image Map

You'll find an image called LION.JPG in the MAPS directory. This is a picture of a lion's head (from a statue in Rome). The extension .JPG indicates that the image is stored as a JPEG image. JPEG (Joint Photographics Expert Group) is a file compression standard that allows large images to be stored as very small files. Imagine does not support this file format. You have to convert the lion image into TIFF (.TIF) 24-bit or True Color format. If you have a file conversion utility that supports JPEG, convert this image and save it as LION.TIF.

Picture Man for Windows, bundled with this book, converts images from JPEG to TIFF format. To convert the image using Picture Man follow these steps:

1. Run Picture Man for Windows.
2. From the File menu select Open. The File Open dialogue box pops on the screen.
3. From the Open File menu navigate to the \IMAG\MAPS directory.

4　From the Type dialog box select JPEG. (The Type dialog box specifies the image format.)

5　Select LION.JPG from the file list.

6　Click on OK.

7　From the File menu click on Save As.

8　From the Type dialog box select TIFF Revision 5.0.

9　Enter the name LION.TIF in the File Name box.

10　Click on OK. The file compression options box pops on the screen.

11　Click on OK to accept the default (No compression).

A dialog box appears with a progress gauge (Converting...). When it is finished, the file has been resaved as LION.TIF. You can now import it into Imagine.

Creating the Object

Enter Imagine's Detail Editor. We'll use a sphere primitive as the surface for the lion's head.

1　Select Add from the Functions menu.

2　Select Primitive from the submenu.

3　Select Sphere from the Primitives Type pop-up box.

4　Accept the default size by clicking on OK. A sphere is created.

5　Click on the ZI button until the sphere is full frame.

The sphere is loaded as a brown object, indicating it is selected but not picked.

6　Pick it by clicking on its axis or pressing (F1).

7　Call up the Attributes Requester by pressing (F7).

Let's add a light-yellow highlight to the lion's head.

8　Click on the Specular attribute and adjust the color sliders until the swatch turns yellow:

● Red: 220
● Green: 220
● Blue: 80

9   Click on the Hardness attribute button. Adjust the Value slider about halfway along its travel.

This will make the specular highlight smaller. Now let's add the lion's head to the sphere.

10   Click on the Brush 1 button. The brush parameters box pops up.

Notice that Color is the default map type. Let's use all the default settings in this box.

11   Click on OK. You are returned to the Attributes Requester.

12   Click on OK. You are returned to the Detail Editor.

13   Select Quick Render from the Project menu.

When the image renders, it should look like Figure 4-19. The lion's face has been wrapped around the surface of the sphere. We will be using this map and object a little later in the chapter. Save it as LION.OBJ.

14   Save the object as LION.OBJ in the OBJECTS directory.

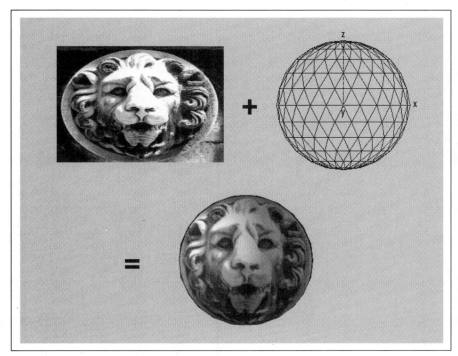

Figure 4-19 The lion's head mapped onto the sphere

USING IMAGINE'S MAPPING PARAMETERS

Accepting the default settings for the map parameters simplifies image-mapping. Once you tell Imagine what kind of object you want to cover (flat surface, cylinder, or sphere), the map is automatically fitted to the object as an opaque layer.

There are situations, however, where specifying the mapping parameters is necessary. Here are some of the situations:

- Make the white areas in the map transparent.

- Tile the map onto the surface.

- Make the map smaller and move it relative to the object.

- Selectively apply the map to faces on the object.

- Remove the map.

Imagine's mapping parameters box gives you control over mapping parameters. It is called up automatically right after you select an image map. Figure 4-20 groups the controls into types. Here is what you can do with the controls:

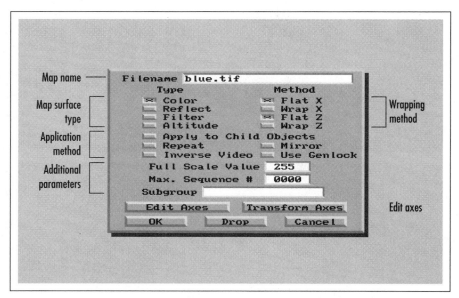

Figure 4-20 Map parameter controls by type

⊛ *Map surface type* specifies how the map image responds to light.

⊛ *Wrapping method* specifies how the image is mapped on the surface of the object.

⊛ *Edit or Transform Axes* specifies the size, orientation, and position of the map on the surface.

⊛ *Application method* specifies whether the map is applied to groups or individual objects and specifies whether the map is applied to the whole surface or tiled as smaller maps.

What's Ahead

The next sections discuss each of the mapping parameter groups.

Map Surface Type

Imagine allows you to specify how the map responds to light. You can make the map reflective, transparent, or use it to simulate bumpiness (altitude).

Color Map Type

By default, Color is selected. The image map replaces the current surface of the object, as shown in Figure 4-21.

This is the simplest brush map. It is completely opaque, hiding the surface underneath. Like all brush maps, it takes on the shading assigned to it in the Attributes Requester.

Reflect Map Type

The Reflect selection makes the pixels on the object's surface reflective. Reflect uses the grayscale information in the image to determine how much of the surrounding environment is reflected on the surface of the object. (Imagine obtains the grayscale information by temporarily converting the image to a grayscale image.) A black map would make the object reflect no light, a white map would turn the surface into a mirror, and a blue map would make the object reflect the blue component colors (see Figure 4-22).

Figure 4-22 shows a brush map (batik pattern) wrapped around an object reflecting a sky. Notice that where the batik design is white, you can see the clouds clearly. Where the batik pattern is black, the reflection is absent.

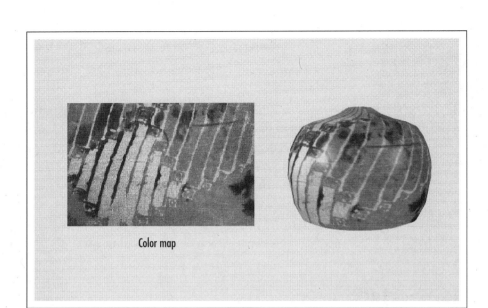

Color map

Figure 4-21 A color map wraps an opaque layer around an object

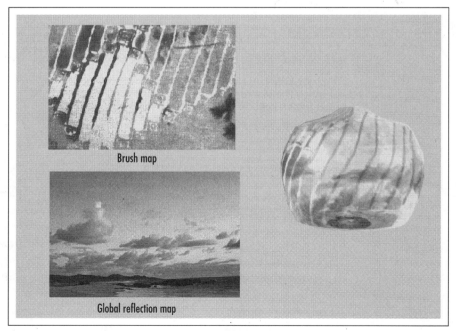

Brush map

Global reflection map

Figure 4-22 A reflection map selectively mirrors the environment

Filter Map Type

The Filter selection uses the grayscale information in an image to filter light. Darker areas of the image let very little light through; lighter areas are almost transparent. In Figure 4-23 an image from the Aris Entertainment Batik Designs Media Clips™ CD-ROM, called "mask" is used as the filter map.

When the filter map is the first map on the object's surface, it makes the object transparent in the white areas of the image map. That's why you can see to the batik design on the other side of the vessel. This makes filter maps ideal for stained glass windows.

You can layer filter maps for interesting effects. Look at Figure 4-24. Shown on the left are the image maps, consisting of white-on-black and black-on-white versions of the word *Beans*. Notice that in reversing the order in which the maps are applied, you produce dramatically different effects. The effects are a result of the way filter maps work. Black areas of the map filter out light (opaque), while white areas allow light to pass through (transparent).

A word of caution: filter maps, like all image maps, eat system memory. Use them sparingly.

Filter map

Figure 4-23 The filter map makes the surface of an object selectively transparent

Figure 4-24 Layering filter maps allows you to create interesting effects

Tip: How the Filter Maps Were Prepared

The word *Beans* was prepared in Picture Man for Windows. The word was created as black letters on white, then the inverted white letters on black were created by reversing the colors in the first image. The maps are exactly the same size. This is important.

Note: Full Scale Value

The Full Scale Value control in the mapping parameters box is associated with the filter map surface type, but it is not functional on the PC version of Imagine. On the Amiga, it helps scale the color palette for systems that do not process or display 24-bit color.

Altitude (Bump) Map Type

Altitude is one of Imagine's most valuable tools. You may hear altitude maps referred to as *bump* maps. That's because they are used to simulate uneven, or bumpy, surfaces. The object's geometry is not actually changed, rather, Imagine uses the red tones in the image to simulate bumpiness. Depressions in the surface are at the black end of the scale, and bumps are at the white end of the scale. Figure 4-25 shows a vessel wrapped with an altitude map.

The top left side of the picture shows an image that was created with a spray-paint tool in a paint program. Then the image was blurred. Imagine takes into account the direction of the light when it creates the bumpy look. If you look closely at the small pits on the pottery vessel in Figure 4-25, you'll see that the white highlights on the edges of the pits are oriented properly to the light. Imagine not only figures out how to create virtual bumps and depressions, it figures out how light will play across the bumpy surface. Smart program!

If you enter the Transformation Requester and change the value for the Y axis of the altitude map, you can scale up the height of the bumps on the object surface.

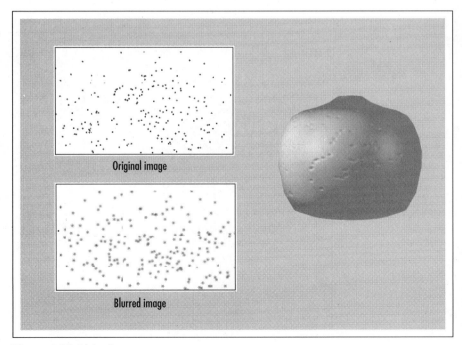

Figure 4-25 Altitude map type

Tip: Keep the Size Under 10 Percent

As a rule, make the Y size 10 percent or less of the size of the object. Anything over 10 percent creates unpredictable results.

Normally 3D surfaces are too smooth because they lack the underlying geometry to give them detail. An altitude map helps give the object the gritty look of reality.

Many of the planets you see in 3D animations use this type of mapping. Terrain on a distant planet is simulated with a bump map instead of being built out of polygons, saving the 3D artist hours and hours of model building. Building a complex planet would consume too much system memory and would take weeks to render.

Bump maps are also valuable when creating metallic surfaces. Metallic surfaces come alive when a subtle bumpiness is given to them. For example, subtle effects can be achieved by using altitude maps with little red component in them. Figure 4-26 is an image with blue as its dominant color.

Altitude map

Figure 4-26 Altitude map with little red component in it

Tip: Creating a Planet

Mike Halvorson, Imagine's designer, provides this tip. Altitude works especially well as a brush map layer on top of another brush map. To create a planet with a bumpy terrain, first create or scan an image of the planet's surface. Then apply the image to the surface of a sphere as a color map. Finally, apply the same map to the sphere as an altitude map. Give the altitude map a Y axis value of 9. This will make the planet look like it has a 3D surface. Try this technique with titles and patterned textures.

Image processing programs like Picture Man for Windows are excellent surface workshops. They can quickly blur and randomize images or computer-generated patterns.

Suggested Exercises

Experiment with the mapping types. Import images into Picture Man, save them as 24-bit TIFF images, and use them as surfaces. Experiment with the map surface types.

What's Ahead

The next set of mapping parameters allows you to specify what type of surface the map will cover.

Wrapping Method and Direction

Very few objects have simple shapes. A rug is a flat surface, so applying a map to it is relatively simple. You just have to size the map to the rug's perimeter. But organic objects like rocks offer a challenge. One of the ways 3D modeling programs overcome this difficulty is to develop projection methods suited for different types of objects.

Flat and Wrap Projections

Imagine uses two different methods for projecting maps on surfaces. *Flat projection* works like a slide projector. Think of projecting a slide onto a curved surface. The 2D slide image will conform to the sphere, but it will be distorted. *Wrap projection* works like shrink wrap. Because the mathematical formulas used are different, wrap projection works best for curved surfaces, and flat projection works best for flat objects.

Mapping Directions

A box is composed of six flat surfaces. But a soda can has two flat surfaces (the top and bottom of the can) and a round surface (the perimeter of the can). In order to fit the map to the can, it would have to be applied as a flat map in the Z (vertical) direction and as a wrap map in the X (horizontal) direction. Imagine allows you to do this.

Imagine allows you to toggle two of four buttons at the right side of the mapping parameters box. Clicking on one button in a group turns the other button off:

- Flat X or Wrap X

- Flat Z or Wrap Z

Figure 4-27 shows the basic types of objects you can specify using the toggle switches.

A flat surface uses flat wrapping in both directions. A cylindrical surface uses flat projection in one direction and wrap projection in the other direction. A sphere uses wrap projection in both directions.

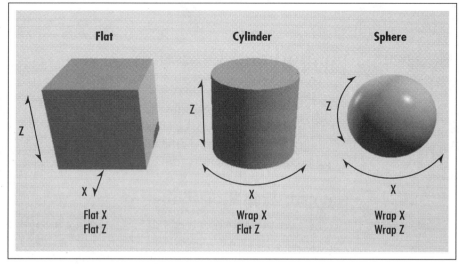

Figure 4-27 Projection map types: flat, cylinder, and sphere

Caution: Drop Maps When Map Types Are Changed

Objects that have been previously mapped with an image have an X beside one of the Brush map buttons. When you change the mapping type, click on the Brush map button to bring up the mapping parameters box. Then drop the previous version of the map by clicking on the Drop button at the bottom of the map parameters box. This resets mapping axes. If you don't do this, the new map type might appear highly distorted because the previous map settings were retained.

All the objects in a room can be sorted into these three geometric shapes. A table is composed of flat planes. A lamp shade is flat along its Z axis and curved along its X axis. A light bulb is curved in both directions.

To prevent distortions, it's a good idea to match the mapping method and direction to one of the three basic shapes, cube, cylinder, or sphere. However, in some cases, you may want to break the rules.

Experiment with these controls using the lion map from the previous exercise. As you do so, you'll notice that by default Imagine tries to fit the map over the entire object. In the next section you'll learn how to control the size and orientation of maps.

Changing Map Size, Position, and Orientation

When you select an image map for a surface, Imagine automatically positions, sizes, and orients the map on the surface of the object. In many cases, you don't have to modify the default map placement. There are cases, though, when you will want to change the default map size or placement. Figure 4-28 shows the cloudy scene mapped as a decal on the front of a cone. If the map had been applied using the default parameters, it would have entirely covered the cone.

Remember that the Top, Front, and Right views are *orthogonal* views, meaning they show the object from viewpoints at right angles to the object. Because the map is not visible until you render the image, keeping track of the location of the map is difficult at first. The Front view is the most natural orientation. Impulse, Imagine's creators, recommends that you make major changes in the Front view and make adjustments in the Top and Right views.

Maps can also be projected onto objects at an angle. For example, you may want a cloud scene to appear as a continuous image on two sides of a cube as shown in Figure 4-29. In this case, the image has been mapped on the cube *at an angle*. The map orientation was changed by changing the map's axes.

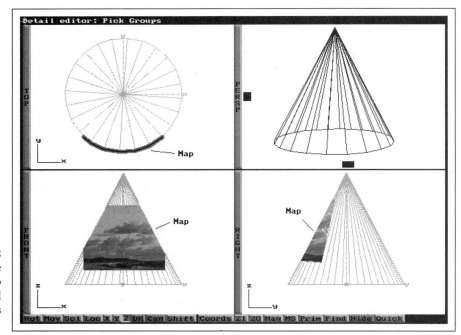

Figure 4-28
Location of the
map relative to
the orthogonal
views

Figure 4-29
Cloud scene
mapped at an
angle onto two
sides of cube

Using Map Axes to Manipulate Maps

Image maps, like 3D objects, have their own axes. As with object axes, when you move or rotate a map axis, you move and rotate the accompanying map. The map axes controls are found at the bottom of the mapping parameters box (see Figure 4-30).

Imagine provides two different methods for changing a map's size and orientation. You can interactively change the axes using a viewing system (Edit Axes), or you can use a numerical entry box for precision manipulation (Transform Axes).

Let's begin with the interactive method of manipulating map axes.

Map Axes Display

When you click on the Edit Axes button, Imagine presents you with a new screen, the Edit Axes display. Figure 4-31 shows how the map axes applied to a cube are displayed.

Notice that the cube, shown in the Top, Front, and Right views, is located inside the top right quadrant of a bounding box. This is a bit confusing, because the bounding box does not show the size of the map, it shows the size of the map's axes (see Figure 4-32).

Also notice that the object's axes are much smaller than the map's axes, and there is a line drawn between the intersection of the map's axes and the intersection of the object's axes. This indicates that the center of the map is coincident with the center of the object. If the map's axes were made the same size

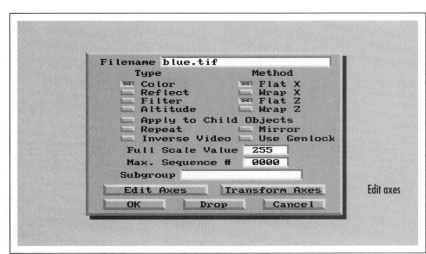

Figure 4-30
Axes editing
buttons

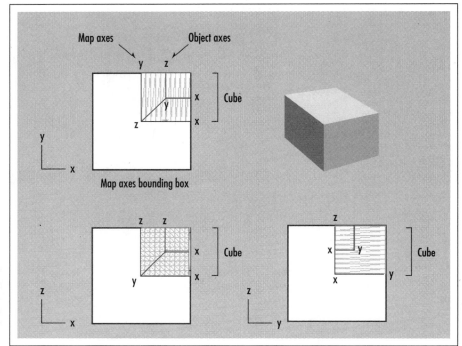

Figure 4-31
The Edit Axes display allows you to alter a map's axes interactively

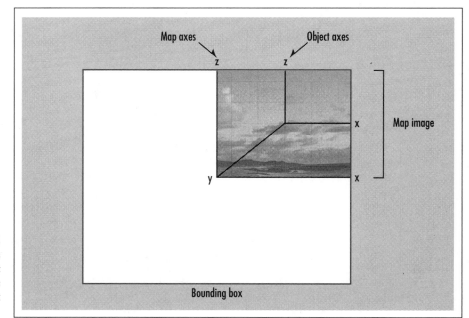

Figure 4-32
The map sits in the top right quadrant of the bounding box

as those of the box, the map's axes would overlay the object's axes, obscuring them.

When you size a map to an object, it is this top right quadrant that represents the size, orientation, and placement of the map, not the bounding box. When you move the bounding box around interactively, you move the map relative to the surface of the cube. For example, moving the quadrant to the right moves the map to the right. Making the quadrant four times smaller makes the map four times smaller.

Flat, Cylindrical, and Spherical Map Axes

Because maps are wrapped around cubes, cylinders, and spheres in different ways, Imagine displays their axes in unique ways. You have just seen how the axes for flat maps are displayed. The other two types are cylinder and spherical maps.

Cylindrical Map Axes

Figure 4-33 shows the cylinder map type. The cylinder object appears in the top right quadrant of the display. The Front and Right views are shown.

Spherical Map Axes

Figure 4-34 shows the spherical map type. The axes for spherical maps are located at the center of objects.

What's Ahead

The next section will show you what controls to use when manipulating maps.

Using the Transformation Commands to Alter Maps

Applying a map as a decal to a surface requires that the map be scaled to a smaller size. While in the edit axes mode, you can interactively change the size, orientation, and position of the map relative to the object, using the normal object manipulation tools:

- Rot button or ®️ key rotates the map axes.

- Mov button or Ⓜ️ key moves the map axes relative to the object.

- Scl button or Ⓢ key scales the map axes.

- (SPACEBAR) confirms changes made to the map's axes and returns you to the mapping parameters box.

- (ESC) cancels changes and returns you to the mapping parameters box.

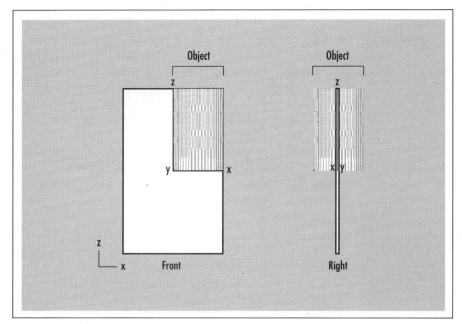

Figure 4-33 Cylinder map type axes

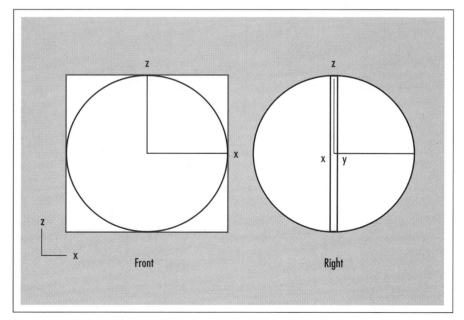

Figure 4-34 Spherical map type axes

Caution: Sizing Maps

> Always make the map a few pixels larger than the area it covers. This is insurance against a map that doesn't quite cover the object. Be careful when scaling the Y axis. The Y axis governs the thickness of the map. If you *scale down* the Y axis, it may disappear.

What's Ahead

In the next section we'll practice moving, scaling, and rotating a map.

Exercise: Creating a Decal

In this exercise, we are going to load an Imagine primitive called a cone, map a picture of a lion's face on it, and scale it to become a decal on the cone's side.

1 Enter the Detail Editor.

If you presently have objects in the Detail Editor, delete them by selecting Pick All from the Pick/Select menu and selecting Delete from the Function menu.

The Detail Editor's Primitive Type submenu is found under Add in the Functions menu. We'll use a shortcut to it:

2 Press (F5). The Primitive Types box pops on the screen.

3 Click on the Cone button. When the cone parameters box comes up, click on OK to accept the defaults.

4 Click on the ZI button to zoom in and fill the windows with the cone.

5 Pick the cone by pressing (F1).

6 Call up the Attributes Requester with (F7).

Now we are going to map the lion's head to the cone.

7 Click on the Brush 1 button. The file load box comes onscreen.

8 Navigate to the \IMAG\OBJECTS directory and load the LION.TIF image map.

This assigns the lion's head to the cone. By default the lion's head is applied flat on the cone. If you quick render the image right now it will look like Figure 4-35.

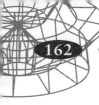
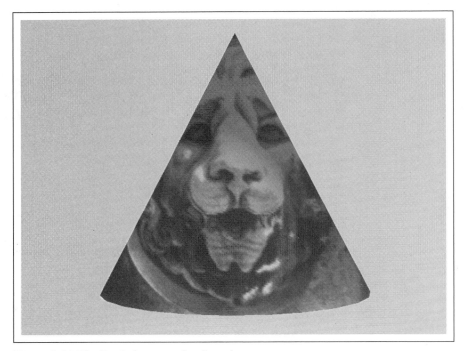

Figure 4-35 The lion's face as a decal on the cone

Not bad! The lion's face is somewhat distorted because of the shape of the cone. Let's make the map smaller so that it looks like a label on the cone. To resize the map smaller, we need to edit its axes.

9   Click on the Edit Axes button.

Your screen should look like Figure 4-36. The mapping quadrant encloses the cone in all three orthogonal views. This indicates that Imagine automatically positioned and sized to the image to cover the entire cone. This is the reason why part of the lion's face is exaggerated. Let's make the map smaller.

10   Click on the Scl (scale) button or press ⓢ. Using your mouse, scale the map to about half size.

Now we'll reposition the map.

11   Click on the Mov (move) button. Click and drag to position the map so that it is centered on the front side of the cone. Remember to adjust the map in the Front view first, and then move to the other views (see Figure 4-37).

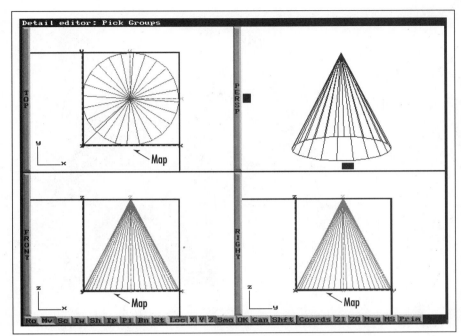

Figure 4-36
Cone with
the map size
indicated

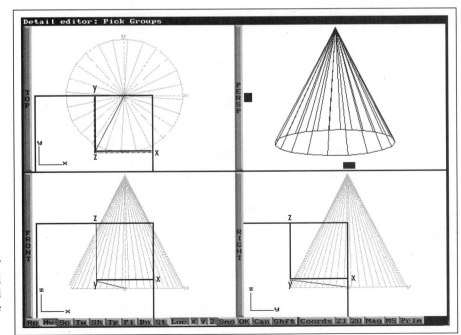

Figure 4-37
The map resized
and repositioned
on the cone

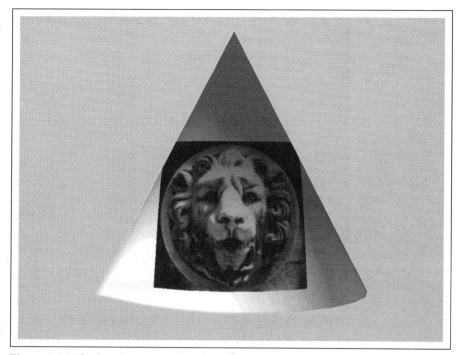

Figure 4-38 The lion image as a decal on the cone

12 Press the (SPACEBAR) to confirm the changes.

13 Click on OK to exit the Attributes Requester.

14 Perform a quick render. The lion image now appears as a decal on the cone (see Figure 4-38).

Suggested Exercises

Experiment with the map type and axes manipulation controls. Figure 4-39 shows the lion's head mapped using the Wrap X, Wrap Z spherical map type.

Tiling Maps

Creating maps that cover entire areas, such as walls, can create huge image files that gobble memory. 3D software programs usually allow you to *tile* a map on a surface. The Repeat and Mirror buttons in the mapping parameters box perform this function.

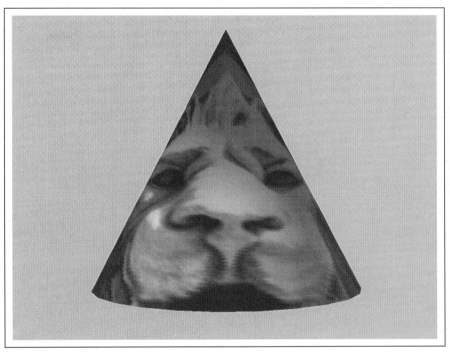

Figure 4-39 This lion is tired of being pushed around!

Map tiling works like tiling a floor: The map is repeated over and over again on a surface (see Figure 4-40). The wall on the right is the same size as the wall on the left. The wall on the left shows the map full size. The wall on the right shows the brick image map sized at 25 percent and repeated.

The map size is the same in both cases. The tool used to map the tile smaller is the Transform Axes button. It is found beside the Edit Axes button in the mapping parameters box. When you click on Transform Axes, the Transformation Requester box pops up (see Figure 4-41).

To scale the map, click on Scale and enter new values for the X (width) and Z (height) dimensions of the map. (Don't forget to press (ENTER) after changing each value.) Notice that you do not change the value of Y. This is the depth of the map. You don't want to modify the map's thickness. If you do, the map might disappear.

If you look carefully at the brick texture in Figure 4-40, you will see that this map has been created so that the top, bottom, right, and left edges join to form a seamless surface. As an alternative to the Repeat tool, Imagine provides a Mirror button that causes the map to mirror along its four sides. This

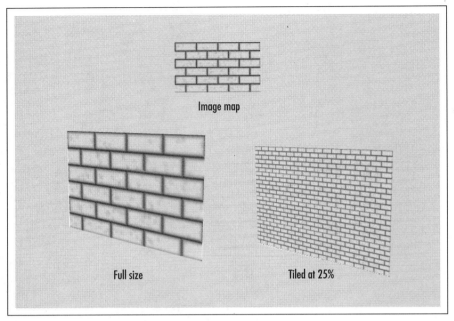

Figure 4-40 Tile maps

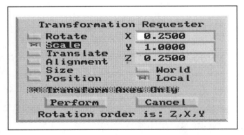

Figure 4-41 Transformation Requester box

guarantees that a seam is not created between tiles. Tilable maps are not easy to make because regularities in the map will show up as a distinctive pattern in the surface. Tilable maps can be purchased from third-party sources. Because tile maps consume very little memory, they are an extremely valuable tool for modelers.

What's Ahead

Mapping all the objects in a scene can be time-consuming. The next section outlines modeling strategies for reducing this labor.

Tip

You cannot tile a map on a sphere.

Modeling Strategies for Maps

Break down the object to its constitute parts and image-map these first. The temptation in building objects is to create the entire object and then map its individual surfaces. You will save a lot of time if you map the individual parts of an object as you build them. For example, to build a blade for an airplane propeller:

- Build the propeller.

- Apply a wood image map to it.

- Copy and paste a copy of the propeller.

- Use the Transformation Requester to rotate the copy around the axis.

- Group the parts to form the propeller using the Detail Editor's Group command.

Placing Maps on Objects with Multiple Surfaces

A cube is an object with multiple surfaces. It is not possible to put a different map on each surface of the cube because of the way Imagine's mapping system works. (Some programs do allow you to wrap a cube.) To create a cube with the same map on every face:

- Start by creating a plane with the Primitive Types box (F5).

- Copy (ALT)-(C) and paste (ALT)-(P) to the plane.

- Use the Transformation Requester (ALT)-(T) to rotate the copy into place around the cube.

- Group the copies to form the cube object using the Detail Editor's Make Subgroup command.

Mapping Objects with Mirror Parts

Some parts of objects, like wings, are mirror images of each other. Build one wing, map it, copy it, paste it, and then use the Transformation Requester to mirror it. When you enter a negative value for Scale in the Transformation

Requester, a copy of the part is mirrored in the opposite direction. The next chapter covers this technique in more detail.

Apply to Child Objects

You can group a number of objects and then apply the same map to them. This works best with objects that are identical, like the slats in a picket fence. The next chapter introduces you to grouping objects, but it is simple enough to preview here:

- Pick the object you want to make the parent. (Click on its axes.) Pick the other objects in the group by clicking on their axes while holding down the (SHIFT) key. These become the children.

- Select Group from the Object menu in the Detail Editor. A yellow line appears connecting the child objects to the parent objects (see Figure 4-42).

Now all you have to do to apply an image map to all the objects at once is apply the image map to the parent. The children will automatically be mapped. The objects have to have the same geometry for this method to work.

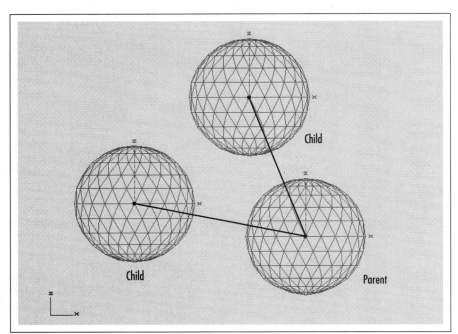

Figure 4-42
Parent and
child objects

Tip: Reduce Map Size

One way to overcome memory limitations is to keep maps small. If the image is applied to a distance object, size the map accordingly. You can also tile a surface with image maps. Some vendors sell maps that seamlessly join along all four sides of the map.

ADVANTAGES AND DISADVANTAGES OF BRUSH MAPPING

You might ask first, "When do I use a paint image in place of shading or procedural texturing?" Here are the advantages of image maps:

- *Images are easy to capture or create.* To get exactly the right kind of surface, like oak wood, you could scan a section of board into a computer. In the case of procedural textures, you're limited to what textures are available from Impulse, Inc. or third parties.

- *Object geometry remains simple.* A picture of grass is much less demanding on computer resources than the millions of polygons necessary for real grass. Image-mapping reduces memory usage significantly, since you do not generate complex models.

Here are the disadvantages of brush maps:

- *A brush map's texture detail is fixed.* In animations, as you move closer to a surface, the individual pixels that make up the map become apparent. Procedural textures are generated mathematically, so they retain their detail as you move close to a surface.

- *Increased memory is required.* Imagine uses 24-bit True Color images that are over 1 megabyte in size at 640 by 480 screen resolution. Procedural textures use small chunks of code. Compared to procedural textures, image maps consume enormous quantities of system memory.

What's Ahead

Applying procedural textures and image maps to surfaces are the most common methods for modeling surfaces. The next section covers some other common methods and special effects.

SPECIAL-EFFECT SURFACES

Some of the other ways of treating surfaces include:

- *Bright* creates objects that do not cast shadows or have shading.

- *Fog* causes the object to become a fog or partially obscured in fog.

Bright

Bright removes shading and shadow-casting attributes from an object. The object renders with the color you assign it in the Attributes Requester, but it renders as a flat color. This treatment is very useful for creating such objects as brightly lit windows in a building at night. A cat's eyes might be rendered with Bright. This surface type is discussed in the next chapter. The Bright button at the bottom of Imagine's Attributes Requester performs this function.

Creating a Fog Object

Fogged surfaces look like they are seen through mist. Fog is a special effect applied after the surface of the object is modeled. It has a number of parameters that determine how the object is colorized.

Imagine provides two ways of adding fog to a scene: globally or on an object-by-object basis. Global fog lays a bank of fog over an entire scene. Global fog is discussed in the next chapter, along with global lighting effects. A fog object created in the Detail Editor is quite different from global fog. A single object is colorized, and you can build up a scene full of fog objects, but global fog is best used for this effect.

You can make a shapeless blob foggy and then attach it to an old steam engine's smokestack. You would get very realistic steam. Color Plate 8 shows the chalice with 50 percent fog assigned to it.

The chalice appears as a ghostly image in a fog of white light. That's exactly how it would appear if it were a real chalice in a real fog. Notice that the chalice is a pure color with no reflections and no specular light areas. In fact the only surface attribute you can alter when you have fog activated is the Color attribute. This makes sense. In a bank of real fog, the water and dust floating in the air scatter light and obscure the object. The object's color also changes due to the physics of light absorption and reflection.

The Fog Length box in the Attributes Requester has a default value of 0.00. This means there is no fog assigned to the object. As soon as you enter a positive value in this box, you activate fog and turn off all surface attributes except the Color attribute. You can still assign a texture and a brush image to the fog object.

Fog Length provides a means of determining the *thickness* of the fog surrounding an object. An object half-obscured by fog is given a Fog Length value half its depth (measured front-to-back). Higher numbers make the fog less dense; lower numbers make the fog more dense, almost making it disappear into thin air. Fog is easier to understand when you work with it.

Exercise: Creating a Fog Chalice

Let's load the chalice (included on disk) into the Detail Editor and then fog it.

1 Load CHALICE.FRM from the OBJECTS directory.

In order to use fog, you will need to measure the chalice front-to-back. Imagine has a built-in measuring system that uses your mouse and a coordinate display area.

2 Turn on the coordinates display by choosing Coordinates from the Display menu.

Figure 4-43 shows the chalice loaded, with the coordinate readout activated. The current mouse coordinates are at the very top and right side of the screen on the information line. As you move the mouse, you will see these values change. The first number is the X (side-to-side) location of the mouse. The second coordinate is the Y (front-to-back). The third coordinate is the Z (top-to-bottom) location. We're only concerned with the depth of the fog as seen from the front, so take note of the middle (Y) number.

3 In the Top view, move the mouse to the front edge of the chalice (see Figure 4-43). Note the value for the Y position of the mouse (-135).

4 In the Top view, move the mouse to the back of the chalice. Note the Y value for the back of the chalice.

The Y value should change to positive 135. The distance between the front and the back of the object is 270.

5 Record the front-to-back or Y size of the chalice (270).

We're going to make this object appear half-obscured by fog. If we divide 270 in half, the midpoint between the front and back of the chalice is 135.

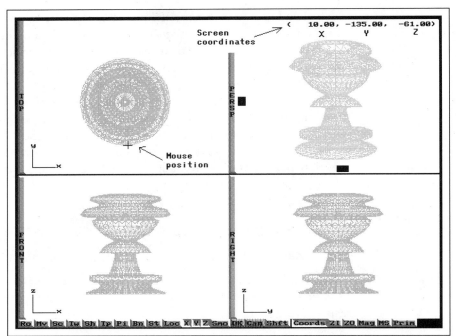

Figure 4-43
Measuring the
chalice's depth

It's this number we'll enter into the Attributes Requester Fog Length data box.

6   Pick the chalice.

7   Call up the Attributes Requester ((F7)).

8   Enter 135 in the Fog Length data box. Press (ENTER).

If you render the chalice right now, it would not appear, because it would be a white object in a white fog. You need to give it color. Let's give it a gold color.

9   Click on the Color attribute button and enter the following values for the color sliders:

   Red: 241

   Blue: 208

   Green: 0

10   Press (ENTER) after each value is entered in the data boxes. The swatch turns gold.

That's all there is to it. You have now created a gold chalice sitting in a mist. Exit the Attributes Requester and use Quick Render to view the chalice.

SUMMARY

We now pass through the very heart of 3D modeling: from surface modeling to lighting. This is a good point to recap the story so far. In Chapter 2 you learned how to use 3D sculpting tools to form organic and geometric objects (the Forms Editor). In Chapter 3 you took a "close" look at 3D object surface structure. You learned how 3D software simulates the action of light on surfaces. You learned how to use Imagine's digital paint box, the Attributes Requester, to add color, shading, reflection, and other surface attributes to objects. In this chapter you were introduced to two methods for making simple surfaces look complex: procedural textures and image-mapping.

The next chapter focuses on lighting. If you're in the dark about modeling objects with 3D software, the next chapter shines a light on the subject.

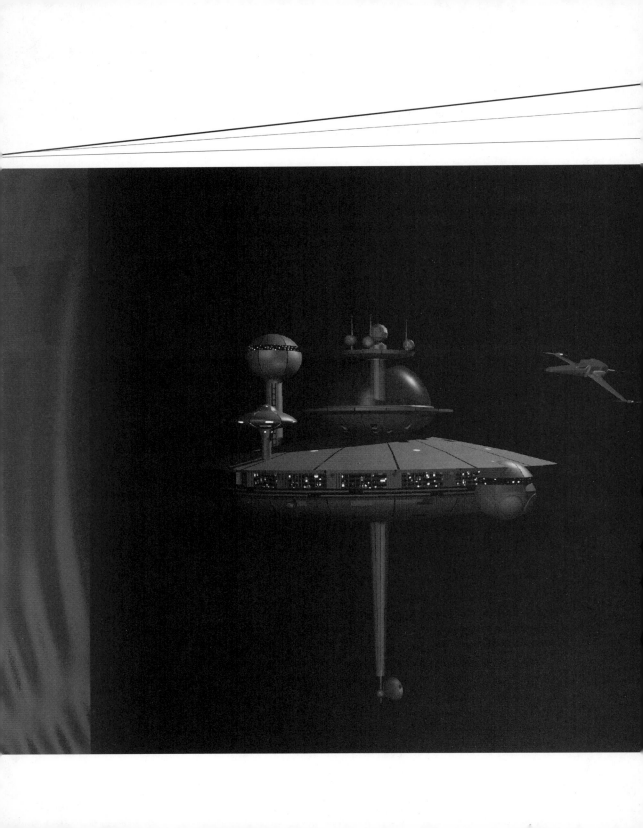

Lighting Surfaces

Without lights, we would live in a world of total darkness. Beyond the end of the power lines, the natural world is illuminated by the sun, the stars, and the moon. In the concrete tunnels of cities, artificial electric light brightens gloomy, sunless places. After sunset, artificial light bathes dwellings in a greenish or yellowish light that allows us to extend our lives into the deep of the night.

Although 3D software can produce excellent lighting simulations, the effect is not perfect. Getting the lighting right is an art as well as a science. Limitations imposed by computer light models become spurs to creativity. In the hands of a skilled artist, 3D lighting can be stunning. This chapter provides tips and techniques for creating a broad range of lighting effects on objects. Lighting scenes and animating lights are treated in Chapter 7. In this chapter you'll learn how to light surfaces, create light sources, and use lights to color objects.

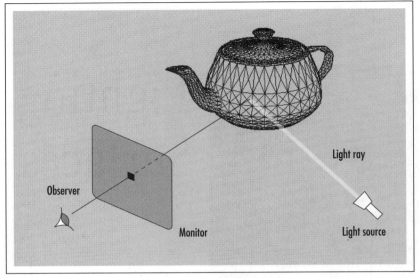

Figure 5-1 3D software reproduces the physics of light

LIGHTING TOOLS AND TECHNIQUES

Of all the tasks in 3D modeling, lighting has the most profound effect of the look of the final image. Moving a light slightly and changing its intensity can dramatically transform a scene from a dull lifeless image to a scene vibrant and scintillating.

3D software models the action of natural light. An object is illuminated by a light source. The ray of light traveling from the light source bounces off an object and intersects the screen at an angle (see Figure 5-1).

Another way of picturing this is to look at the way a light ray bounces off a polygon (see Figure 5-2). A ray of light strikes the surface of a polygon at an angle, and bounces off it at an angle to the observer. The greater the *angle of incidence,* the dimmer the pixel on the screen illuminated by the light source. If a light strikes the surface at right angles and the observer is at right angles to the surface, the ray of light is at its brightest.

The four different shading methods (wireframe, solid, Gouraud, and Phong) were discussed at the beginning of Chapter 3. When a scene is rendered, the program first determines which surfaces are visible. Then the color, intensity, and position of the light is calculated in relation to the object's surface attributes. There are two common algorithms used to determine how the object is shaded:

- **Scanline:** The color of a point on the object is determined by its relationship to the observer and the light sources in the scene.

- **Ray trace:** Each pixel on the object is calculated based on all the light (including reflected light) striking it.

Figure 5-3 shows how the two different models work. In the case of scanline rendering, the program calculates the brightness and color of a point on the object by measuring the intensity and angle of incidence of light sources striking the object. Notice that the path of the light is calculated from the light source to the object and finally to the observer.

In the case of ray-trace rendering, the light ray is traced in the reverse direction, from the observer to objects, and thence to the light source. Light rays bouncing off of objects can create complex interactions between objects in a scene. Ray tracing allows you to create such lighting effects as refraction (the bending of light in a semitransparent medium), shadows, and reflections. This makes ray tracing calculation-intensive, and therefore time-consuming. But the images created by ray-tracing programs look very natural. Figure 5-4 shows a comparison between a scanline-rendered scene and a ray-traced scene.

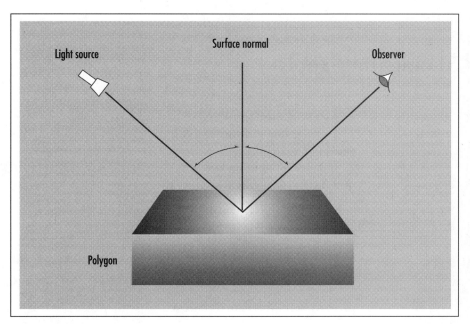

Figure 5-2 Light rays and surface normals

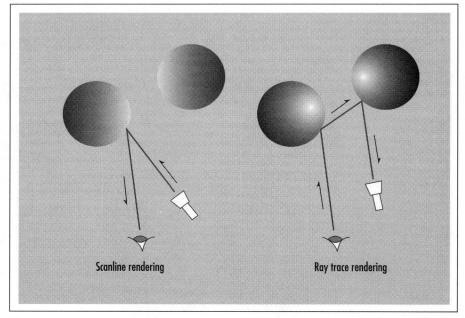

Figure 5-3 Ray tracing produces a more accurate model of the path of a light ray in a scene

3D Lighting Tools

When you light objects, you see them through a photographer's eyes. In fact many of the metaphors and tools used in 3D lighting are based on the language of photography. In this section, we'll open up the 3D lighting kit to see what tools are available.

Imagine's "lighting kit" is full of special-purpose lights and filters. You can add the following light sources to a scene:

- An adjustable ambient light level

- Spherical lights that shine in all directions

- Conical lights that shine a cone of light like a flashlight

- Cylindrical lights that shine a long focused tube of light like a laser

- Self-illuminated objects

- Lighting effects

Scanline   Ray trace

Figure 5-4 Ray tracing creates true reflections and refractions

Adding Ambient Light to a Scene

Ambient light level is the total of all diffuse light bouncing around a scene. This is usually adjustable. In the case of Imagine, the ambient light level is set in the Globals Info box in the Action Editor. It's discussed in Chapter 7. Adjusting ambient light levels helps lighten shadows.

Using Spherical Lights

Spherical lights cast light in all directions. In most programs they can be made to cast shadows. When used as shadow-casting lights, they simulate point light sources, like light bulbs or the sun. They can be colored and in many programs animated. They are often used as fill lights in scenes, as light sources that illuminate selected areas of the scene, or offset a brighter main light. Shadow-casting is turned off; intensity is turned down. The color of the light can be adjusted.

Using Conical and Cylindrical Lights

Conical and cylindrical lights have light paths shaped like light cones and cylinders, respectively. This makes them useful for creating spotlights in scenes or as headlights or street lamps.

These lights can be colored. Light brightness can be made to fall off over a distance. Conical and cylindrical lights can be adjusted. For example, you can adjust the size of the spotlight formed by the conical light.

Self-Illuminated Objects

Most programs allow you to make an object self-illuminated. This does not usually mean the object casts a light. Rather, the surface of the object is rendered as a flat area of color. A window in a night scene, for example, may be made bright yellow.

Special-Effects Lighting

There are a number of other special-effects lighting tools. Fog was introduced at the end of the last chapter. One of the differences between 3D lighting and natural lighting is that 3D lighting does not fall off over a distance. Programs allow you to simulate fall-off. Global fog might be used for this purpose. Other objects, like a flame on a candle, can be made to behave like a light source. Imagine allows you to turn objects into light sources in the Attributes Requester.

What's Ahead

The next section reviews an object's surface attributes from the perspective of lighting controls.

LIGHTING AND SURFACE ATTRIBUTES

You can use shading to make an object brighter or darker without changing the brightness of light sources in the scene. You can also adjust the size, intensity, and color of the highlights on objects. This will influence the viewer's perception of the scene. For example, making the specular highlight larger and less intense gives the viewer an impression of softer, more diffuse lighting.

Surface shading was discussed in Chapter 3; here, more attention is given to the way the light is modeled on the surface of the object, and what that tells us about the object's composition. You'll also learn how to combine settings to produce specific effects.

The six surface attributes that directly affect surface lighting are

- Color
- Specular
- Hardness
- Bright

- Light

- Fog

These settings are shown in Figure 5-5. Color, Specular, and Hardness are related. Let's look at these first.

Giving Objects Specular Highlights

Soft and hard surfaces reflect light in a very different way. You also need to pay attention to the color of the highlight itself. Adding red highlights to an evening scene, for example, simulates the color of the setting sun.

The Specular and width (Imagine's Hardness button) settings are governed by two general rules:

- A very soft or rough surface should have a very large specular highlight. Lower the specular color sliders to simulate light absorption by the object surface.

- To make hard or smooth surfaces, create tighter and more reflective specular highlights. This means that very hard, glossy plastic should have a very small specular highlight that is close to the color of the light source. Adjust the color of the specular highlight with the color controls to accomplish this.

Imagine can produce many of the surface textures you see in the real world using Color, Specular, and Hardness surface attribute controls. Experiment with them by trying to match the settings of the Attributes Requester to the color and specular reflection of real-world objects.

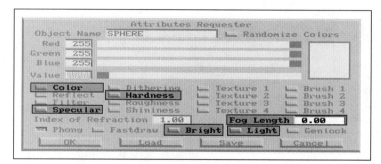

Figure 5-5 The surface lighting attributes

Making an Object Self-Illuminated

Selecting Bright in the Attributes Requester shuts off shading or shadows on the object. Bright renders your object as a self-illuminating object. Although the Bright object does not transmit light, it glows as pure color in the absence of light.

Exercise: Making a Neon Light

Let's make a glowing neon sphere.

1   Create a sphere in the Detail Editor. (Press (F5) and select Sphere.)

2   Pick the sphere by clicking on its axes or pressing (F1).

3   Press (F7) to pop up the Attributes Requester.

4   Set the Color attribute to Red 0, Green 255, Blue 0. This produces a neon green color.

5   Select Bright and click on OK.

6   Select Quick Render to render the object.

Figure 5-6 shows what the sphere looks like.

The Bright control creates objects with no surface shading, giving this green sphere the appearance of a flat disk that glows in the dark. Hardness and Specular settings are ignored when the Bright setting is used. The Filter setting controls how transparent your Bright object appears. Bright objects produce glowing objects like light bulbs, stars in the sky, lit windows in office buildings, and so on.

CREATING A LIGHT SOURCE

In most 3D programs, light sources such as spotlights are added to the scene one at a time. Imagine allows you to add lights to a scene either in the Detail Editor or the Stage Editor. The Light button in the Detail Editor's Attributes Requester turns the current object into a light source. When you click on the Light button, a Light Source Data box pops on the screen (see Figure 5-7).

The three different light types, spherical, cylindrical, and conical, govern the shape of the light that is cast. You can make the object cast shadows or have

Figure 5-6 Bright neon green sphere

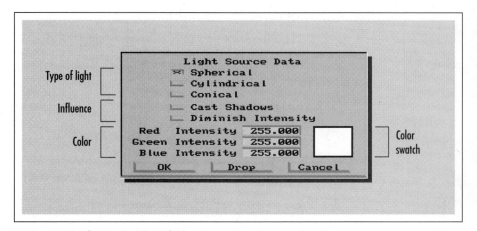

Figure 5-7 Light Source Data box

its intensity diminish over distance. You can also change the light's color from its default white by entering new values in the color data boxes.

Light-source objects work in the same way as lights created in the Stage Editor using the Add Light Source command.

Exercise: Creating a Bright Object

Turning on the Light button in the Attributes Requester along with the Bright button makes your object both self-illuminating and light-emitting. This creates objects like headlights and street lamps. In this tutorial you'll learn how to create light objects and combine Bright, Color, and Fog to produce colored spotlights. Color Plate 9 shows the type of lighting scenes we will create.

Enter the Detail Editor or clear it of objects. (Select Pick All from the Pick/Select menu and use the (ALT)-(D) key combination to delete all the objects from the scene.) In the first part of this exercise, we are going to create the Bright scene pictured in Panel 9A in Plate 9.

1 Press (F5) to pop up the Primitives Type box.

2 Select Sphere.

3 Enter 100 for the radius and click on OK.

This creates the round globe to use for the light. Now turn the sphere into a light.

4 Press (F1) to pick the sphere.

5 Press (F7) to call up the Attributes Requester.

6 Click on the Color button and set Red 0, Green 255, and Blue 0. Select OK.

This creates a neon green globe. Now create a surface to shine the light on.

7 Press (F5) to bring up the Primitives Type box.

8 Select Plane. Enter 300 for both Width and Height and 5 for both Horizontal and Vertical Sections and click on OK.

9 Press (F1) to select the new plane object.

10 Press (F7) to enter the Attributes Requester.

11 Click on the Color button and drag the color sliders to Red 100, Green 100, Blue 100.

12 Click on Specular and drag its color sliders to Red 200, Green 200, Blue 200.

13 Set Hardness to 50 and click on OK to return to the model.

Now adjust the rotation and position of the plane relative to the neon globe. Use the Transformation Requester.

14 With the plane object still picked, press (right) (ALT)-(T) to call up the Transformation Requester.

15 Set Rotate to X -90, Y 0, Z 0 and click on World for the axis system. This makes the plane rotate to a flat position.

16 Set Position to X 0, Y 0, Z -200. This moves the plane down.

17 Click on Perform.

The plane object is now rotated and translated under the sphere. In Quad view set your windows up so they come close to matching Figure 5-8. Note that the Top view is shifted up, not centered. This pushes the sphere and plane object farther back in perspective view. Adjust the view so that it looks like Figure 5-8.

18 Press the ○ key, then click in the Top view to shift your view to match that of Figure 5-8.

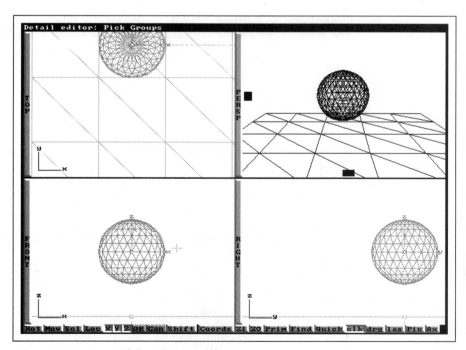

Figure 5-8 Location of the sphere and floor

19   Slide up the left slider in the perspective view so the point of view is slightly down toward the floor.

We will reuse the elements in this group of objects, so save them to the hard drive. Use the Group command to save all the objects in the scene.

20   Hold the (SHIFT) key down and pick the plane and sphere.

21   Press (right) (ALT)-(G) (or select Group from the Object menu) to group the objects.

22   Press (right) (ALT)-(1) or select Pick Groups from the Mode menu.

23   Press (right) (ALT)-(S) to save the grouped objects to your drive.

24   Use Quick Render to view the scene.

The resulting render is a soft-green sphere floating over a gray panel. See Panel 9A in Plate 9. The scene is lit by the default light Imagine uses when it quick renders the scene. This is a light directly in front of the scene at full brightness.

What's Ahead

The next section provides some guidelines for lighting objects. Some of these rules are specific to Imagine, but the rest of them are general enough to be applicable to any program.

Lighting Objects: Some Guidelines

The following are some general issues you should keep in mind when lighting objects.

- Unlike real light, computer 3D lights do have constant radiation over their length of travel.

- You can toggle shadows on or off. You must be in ray-trace mode to render shadows.

- Lights at full intensity wash out a scene. Lights at three-quarter intensity are a good starting point. As you add more lights to a scene, reduce the intensity of each light.

- Make lights close to objects less intense than lights farther away. This will prevent "burns" from appearing on objects.

⊕   As a rule, do not place lights close to objects. (In Imagine, keep lights at least 1000 units away from objects.) This will produce more natural-looking lighting.

⊕   Most programs allow you to create visible or invisible light sources. In Imagine, you can create an object and then turn it into a light. Or you can add an axis to the Detail Editor (using the Add Axis command in the Functions menu) and then turn this axis into a light. The axis will not be visible in the rendered scene. Lights are automatically created invisible in the Stage Editor.

Let's create each of the three light sources.

Exercise: Creating a Spherical Light Object

A spherical light object is like a light bulb. It casts its light in all directions. See Panel 9B (spherical light) in Color Plate 9 for a picture of the effect of this light on a surface.

Begin by creating the sphere used for the light object.

1   Select Pick Objects mode.

2   Pick the sphere object.

3   Press (F7) to pop up the Attributes Requester.

4   Click on the Bright button and then on the Light button. The Light button pops up the Light Source Data box.

5   Select Spherical for light type and change the color intensities to Red Intensity 50, Green Intensity 200, Blue Intensity 50.

6   Click on OK twice to back out of both menus.

7   Use Quick Render to view the scene.

Your image should look like Panel 9B (spherical light) in Color Plate 9. The Bright switch renders the sphere as self-illuminating. The Spherical light setting turns the object into a light object that emits light equally in all directions.

Notice the overall greenish shade on the formerly gray plane. Any object added to the scene would also have a green specular cast, providing it is in the path of the light.

Conical and Cylindrical Lights

Conical and cylindrical lights are similar. Figure 5-9 compares a conical light and a cylindrical light. The light is represented by a sphere, but it could be any light object.

Cylindrical light objects project a long tube of light over a distance. The diameter of the tube of light is controlled by the X axis. It remains constant throughout the length of the tube. The light is directed by the orientation of the Y axis. The only thing that makes conical lights different is that the cone of light starts as a single point at the light source and expands out to the X size. In the diagram you can see that changing the length of the Y axis changes the shape of the cone.

Exercise: Making a Cylindrical Light

This section gives you practice working with a cylindrical light first.

1   Pick the sphere created in the previous exercise by clicking on its axes.

2   Press (right) (ALT)-(T) to call up the Transformation Requester.

Right now the sphere's Y axis is pointing to the back at 3D space. Rotate the Y axis down so that it is pointing to the floor.

3   In the Transformation Requester set Rotate to X -90, Y 0, Z 0.

4   Click on Transform Axes Only and then Perform.

The local Y axis of the sphere is now pointing down. Now turn the sphere into a cylindrical light.

5   Press (F7) to bring up the Attributes Requester.

6   Click on Light and change the light type to a cylindrical light.

7   Click on OK twice to back out to the Detail Editor.

Use Quick Render to view the scene. Your screen should now look like Panel 9C in Plate 9 (cylindrical light). The sphere emits a cylinder-shaped beam of light that strikes the gray floor. Notice that the gray floor has a green specular reflection within the boundaries of the cylindrical light. The remaining dif-

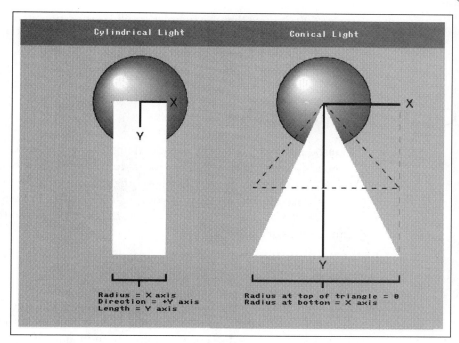

Figure 5-9 A conical and cylindrical light compared

fused light that illuminates the gray panel comes from the Quick Render default light.

Changing the Cylinder Light Radius

Let's now change the size of the spotlight. The cylindrical light radius size is based on the X (width) and Z (height) size of the axes. The effect we will create can be seen in Panel 9D of Color Plate 9.

1. With the sphere object picked, press (right) (ALT)-(T) to call the Transformation Requester.

2. Select Size. Change the axes sizes to X 300, Y 100, Z 300. Click on Transform Axes Only and then Perform.

3. Use Quick Render to view the scene.

Your screen should now look like Panel 9D in Color Plate 9. The radius of the cylindrical light that strikes the gray panel is now 300 units, or a diameter of 600. Notice that the light looks like it is casting a cone of light. This is deceiving. We changed the object's axes independently of the object size (by using Transform Axes), so the large spotlight reflects the size of the axes rather than the size of the object.

Creating Conical Lights

Conical lights create a cone of light along the Y axis. The cone of light grows from a single point to a diameter equal to the light object's X axis. Increasing the X axis increases the size of the spotlight formed by the conical light.

In the exercise we are about to do, we'll not only create a cone of light, we'll see a bit of modeling magic. We're going to fool viewers into thinking that they can see the cone of light.

Adding a Light Haze to the Spotlight

When a flashlight is shone through fog, you can see a milky-white cone of light. In the clinically sterile environment of a 3D rendering program, dust and water particles are not used to create fog effects. In Imagine, fog is simulated by colorizing an object. You can colorize a single object (the Fog object button in the Attributes Requester) or the entire scene (Global Fog in the Action Editor's Globals Info box). In order to make the cone of light visible, we'll create a stand-in for it: a tapered cylindrical object. Then we'll turn it into a fog object and attach it to the sphere. This will simulate a cone of light in fog. See Panel 9E in Color Plate 9 for the final effect.

Exercise: Creating a Conical Light in a Fog

Remember from the last chapter that you can change the density of fog in the Attributes Requester by entering a value in the Fog Length data box. The fog density is a factor of the object's depth.

1   Press (F5) for Primitive Types.

2   Select Tube.

3   Set Radius to 100 and Height to 200 and click OK.

4   Press (F1) to pick the tube.

5   Press (right) (ALT)-(T) to call the Transformation Requester.

Now let's orient the tube to the path of light between the sphere and the plane.

6 Set Position to X 0, Y 0, Z -200 and then click on Perform.

We are now ready to change the shape of the tube to match the light pattern that would form if the sphere were casting light down in fog. We'll widen the tube at the spotlight end and narrow it at the sphere end. Do this by switching the Detail Editor into points mode and editing the points that make up the ends of the tube.

7 With the tube object still picked, Press (right) (ALT)-(3) for Pick Points.

Imagine allows you to pick points in an object and move them. Notice the screen changes to a view of the points that make up the object's geometry. Next, select a group of points for manipulation using Drag Pick.

8 Press (F8) to select Drag Pick.

9 While holding the (SHIFT) key down, select the bottom part of the tube in Front view. There 24 points that touch the plane object at -200 Z.

10 Press (right) (ALT)-(T) to call the Transformation Requester.

11 Set Scale to X 3, Y 3, Z 1 and then press Perform.

The tube is now tapered to match the radius of the light beam. Now let's create and colorize the fog.

12 With the tube object picked, press (F7) to change the object attributes.

13 Set Color to Red 180, Green 255, and Blue 180.

14 Set Fog Length to 600 and then click on OK.

15 Use Quick Render to view the scene.

We now have a light-emitting globe that seems to be casting its light through illuminated dust particles.

Exercise: Making Invisible Objects

The method just used to create a shining light in a fog can be used in conjunction with an invisible light source. This allows you to create lighting effects like headlights. Panel 9F in Color Plate 9 shows what happens when you make the sphere invisible, while retaining its color and axes characteristics.

To make the object completely transparent, we'll remove all the faces from the object. Remember that it is the faces on an object that are rendered, not its points and lines. This is an elegant way of making objects disappear while retaining their characteristics.

First let's save the sphere as it now exists.

1　With only the sphere selected, press (right) (ALT)-(S) to save it. Save the sphere with a unique name such as NEONBALL.OBJ.

2　Press (ALT)-(5) to change to Pick Faces.

3　Press (F1) for Drag Pick.

4　Hold the (SHIFT) key down and drag a box around the entire sphere to select all faces.

5　Press (right) (ALT)-(D) to delete the selected faces. Press (right) (ALT)-(2) to return to Pick Object.

6　Use Quick Render to view the scene.

Your screen should match Panel 9F in Color Plate 9. The cone of light looks like it is projected from a darkened lamp. Use this technique to model the exhaust for a space ship.

What's Ahead

This chapter began by reviewing the effect of lights on surfaces. Then you learned how to create and shape light sources. The third section turns to coloring lights.

COLORING OBJECTS WITH LIGHT

So far, white lights have been used to illuminate objects. A red sphere turns pink under the influence of a white light source. The pink is a result of the fact that the object has absorbed some of the white light. A red sphere reflects red light and absorbs green and blue light. When using white lights, the lighting model is close to the optical properties of real light. Things get a lot more complicated when the color of the 3D light source changes to gray or some other tone. That's because 3D lights do not have true light intensity. A gray 3D light source is not a dim light; it's a light with less color in it.

Adding gray to a light source is a common method for lowering the intensity of a light source in a scene. However, natural lights lighten objects; while gray 3D lights actually darken objects because the gray colors of the object surface will tend to absorb the gray of the light source.

The key is this: *Any light source color other than white will darken the object's surface.*

Color Plate 10 makes this clearer. The plate shows two sets of color-test panels created in a paint program. The plates were imported into Imagine. Panels 10A and 10C are lit by a white light. Panels 10B and 10D are lit by a 50 percent gray light (Red 128, Green 128, Blue 128).

The panels provide us a visual reference for the interaction of lights and surfaces. The panels on top show how gray surfaces respond to white and gray lights. The panels on the bottom show how colored surfaces react to colored lights.

Gray Surfaces/White and Gray Lights

The white light illuminating Panel 10C renders the colors accurately. The border color is white, and it reflects the white light. There is a smooth gradation of grays in the color panel. Look what has happened to Panel 10D. The fall-off between the light-gray and dark-gray squares is much more rapid and less even than the squares in Panel 10C. The border around Panel 10D is accurate. That's because it has a white surface. The white surface in Panel 10D reflects the 50 percent gray light completely.

Colored Surfaces/Colored Lights

Now let's look at the way colors react to colored lights. There are four lights shining on Panel 10A and Panel 10B. You can see the color of the lights in the white areas of the panel illuminated by white light (Panel 10A).

- Top left: Red 255, Green 255, Blue 255 (White)
- Top right: Red 0, Green 0, Blue 255 (Blue)
- Bottom left: Red 0, Green 255, Blue 0 (Green)
- Bottom left: Red 255, Green 0, Blue 0 (Red)

The way colored lights interact with colored surfaces is complex. Multiple lights compound the problem, something you can see in the areas where colored lights overlap. The combination of a red, green, and blue light in a scene produces a white light when their rays illuminate the same area on a surface. Panels 10A and 10B both have a small area in the center circle of the panel that is illuminated by all three (RGB) lights.

The mixing of colored lights in Imagine is identical to RGB mixing in video and computer graphics. See the RGB color wheel (Color Plate 4) for a visual color mixing guide.

Colored lights in a 3D scene should be added as special effects, and should not be used to illuminate an entire scene.

SUMMARY

In this chapter the focus has been on lighting objects. The next chapter will also include the subject of lighting by showing you how to add lights in the Stage Editor, attach lights to objects, animate lights, and create such global light effects as fog and ambient light.

Building Photorealistic Objects

Photorealistic images fool the eye—or almost fool the eye. You know that you are not looking at a real dinosaur, but it looks like a real dinosaur. That's photorealism.

Photorealistic images mimic the structural and optical characteristics of the real world. The subject may be an alien landscape made to look "real" or a realistic-looking insect, like a bee. Alan Henry's bee (Color Plate 6) looks so real, you can almost hear it buzz.

Let's lift the cover of illusion and look at the geometry underneath. When you strip the 3D bee of its surface, you see a polygonal mesh of lines as shown in Figure 6-1.

The wireframe bee is a good model. While surface modeling using shading, image-mapping, and texturing adds realism to the bee, the detail in the underlying geometry shown in Figure 6-1 is important as well. The bee is composed of 25,520 polygons—typical for a photorealistic model with this

Figure 6-1 The wireframe view of the bee looks complex

level of detail. It would be impractical to construct this bee line-by-line, point-by-point. Fortunately, 3D programs provide tools for generating complex models.

This chapter introduces modeling techniques to create and edit detailed objects. You'll see the step-by-step process followed by professional modelers. You'll learn how to plan a project and how to break down the subject into simple modeling tasks. You'll see how to harness the computer's mathematical muscle to generate 3D objects. Exercises illustrating the modeling techniques of extrusion and surface editing are provided. Let's begin by reviewing the steps taken in a modeling project for a photorealistic rendering.

THE MODELING PROCESS FOR PHOTOREALISTIC OBJECTS

The most important part of modeling photorealistic objects occurs before you turn on the computer. You need to give a lot of thought to how the model will be built and to what level of detail you want to achieve. You need to ask the following questions:

1   What will I use as a visual reference for the model?

2   How detailed can I make the model given the limitations of the project and my own computer resources?

3   How can I break the modeling project down to smaller, easier modeling tasks?

4   What modeling tools will I use?

Use a Visual Reference to Design the Model

Most artists use some kind of visual reference for the subject they will reproduce on canvas, paper, or the monitor of a computer. When the subject is an object like a camera, you may have the visual reference right at hand (Color Plate 7). Sometimes objects can be modeled from illustrations (see Figure 6-2).

Your visual reference can be a sketch, a plastic model, or a picture from a book. A technical drawing is an accurate scale model of the subject's parts and their relationships. These measurements are used in the construction of the 3D

Figure 6-2 An illustration provides a good visual reference

model. For this reason, it's best to work from illustrations that show the object in two or three profiles: front, top, and side.

Model Sources

The hobby store is often an excellent source for visual references. Plastic models have the advantage of coming in parts that you can pick up, rotate, and measure with a ruler. Book stores are also excellent haunts for modelers. The art section contains photography and art books themed around subjects like Italian product design or English pewter. Many used book stores near colleges or universities contain inexpensive used science texts. Children's stores, antique shops, secondhand stores, and bargain stores often yield miniature versions of the objects you want to reproduce.

Sketching the Model

Make a sketch of the object on paper. In the process of sketching the object, you'll soon identify the modeling challenges the object proposes.

When working from another artist's work, be careful of copyright infringement. Some product designs and logos, for example, cannot be reproduced. Figure 6-3 shows a copyright-free fish.

The fish comes from a book called *Treasury of Animal Illustrations From Eighteenth-Century Sources*. It is published by Dover Publications, Inc., a specialist in the publication of copyright-free illustrations.

Specify the Level of Modeling Detail

After choosing a visual reference for the object, you are immediately faced with the most important issue in the modeling project: How detailed will the finished model be? Visual detail in the real world is inexhaustible. In the computer world, there is a limit imposed by the maximum speed and memory capacity of your computer hardware. An 80486 equipped with 16 megabytes of RAM is now considered entry level for photorealistic models. A workstation-class computer, such as a Pentium or Silicon Graphics Indigo, is standard issue for the type of photorealistic animation common in TV logos and commercials.

Before attempting to model a scene, you should have a mental picture of how many polygons you expect will be in the final scene. Each polygon is stored as data. The more data the 3D program has to process, the slower the model is displayed and redisplayed on your system. Rendering can take hours, days, or weeks.

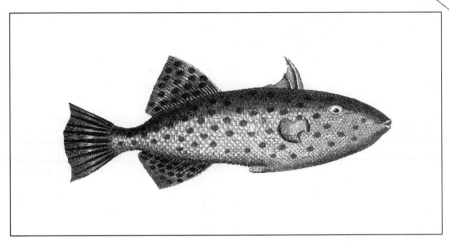

Figure 6-3 Copyright-free fish can be modeled as a fantasy life form

Determining Your System's Limits

Here's a method for determining the limits of your system when running the version of Imagine bundled with this book:

- Load the BEE.OBJ into the Detail Editor. It is in the \IMAG\OBJECTS directory.

- Repeatedly load BEE.OBJ until you see an out-of-memory error message.

- Delete one of the bees and quick render the swarm of bees. If you succeed, go to the next step. If you fail, delete another bee and re-render. Repeat this step until the object renders.

- Count the bees and multiply by 25,000.

This will provide you a rough count of the polygons your system can render before running out of memory. This is the practical limit to the polygonal detail

Caution: You May Not Be Warned

3D software does not always warn you about memory problems. When rendering, the program may randomly drop polygons. Holes will appear in objects, or entire objects may disappear.

of the scene. Add more RAM to your system if you find yourself bumping up against the limit.

Memory Conservation Tips

You can conserve memory in the following ways:

- Free up the maximum amount of extended memory. Remove disk caches, TSRs, and other device drivers that consume memory. Delete them from your CONFIG.SYS file and AUTOEXEC.BAT file. (Back up the old CONFIG.SYS and AUTOEXEC.BAT files first!)

- If possible, model surfaces using shading and procedural textures rather than image maps. Check the file size for the map. A map 1.2 megabytes in size will consume 1.2 megabytes of system memory. Reduce the map to a much smaller size.

- Use tilable image maps. These are small, seamless, repetitive patterns. Some vendors specialize in tilable maps.

- Use the smallest number of polygons to create an object.

The last point is important. The resolving power of the human eye places a limit on the amount of detail we see in distant objects. Our brain fills in the missing detail. In a field outdoors, a distant swarm of dots around a honeycomb is seen as a hive of bees. If the swarm of bees is never seen up close, they should be rendered as simple spheres. As the bees are seen from a shorter distance, the level of detail goes up (see Figure 6-4). Seen from a distance, colored and animated, this simple assembly of shapes could easily fool the eye.

Remember that an image map can often add visual detail to an object while keeping the polygon count down. For example, the bee's hair in Color Plate 6 was modeled using a filter map (called an *opacity* map in other programs). Creating the individual hairs on the bee using polygons would have made the bee too complex. (See Appendix D for a description of how Alan Henry created the bee.)

Tip: Using Backdrops to Create Complex Scenes

Most 3D programs allow you to use a previously rendered scene as a backdrop in the current scene. You could for example, create a landscape and render it. Then use the rendered landscape as a backdrop for a bee or other object. A favorite program for generating the backdrop is Vista Pro, a 3D landscape-generating program.

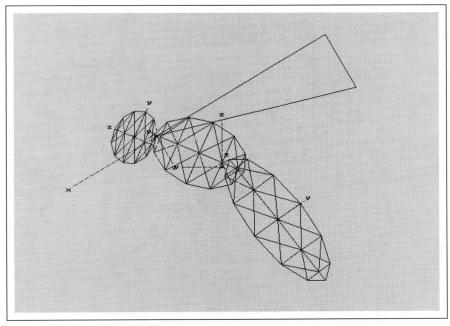

Figure 6-4 Seen from a distance, this simple bee could easily fool the eye

The art of producing models is like Einstein's rule about theories: "Make things as simple as possible, but no simpler."

Rendering Time

When planning a modeling project, you should also take into account time. This is especially true of projects that have multiple frames, like animations.

Divide the Modeling Task into Smaller Steps

After finding a visual reference for the subject and determining how much detail you are going to include in the computer model, it's time to come up with a plan of attack. After all, buildings are not built all at once. The general contractor breaks the construction project into distinct parts and then calls in specialized trades to handle specific tasks. A modeling project proceeds in a similar manner. The model is divided into its parts and then each part is modeled separately using the most efficient modeling tools for the job.

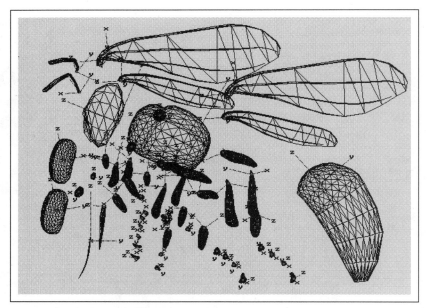

Figure 6-5 The bee is simply a collection of geometric shapes

Building Objects from Parts

Most objects are made of parts, or they can be dissected into parts. The bee is a collection of fairly simple geometric shapes. Figure 6-5 shows the bee's parts.

The parts look like the plastic parts to a modeling kit purchased at a hobby shop. Indeed the bee's parts are assembled in a similar fashion. Some parts are created and "glued" to other parts, some are assembled more loosely. The bee's wings, for example, are created so that they can be flapped in an animation.

Keeping moving parts independent makes the model suitable for animation. Even if you don't intend to animate parts of the body, keeping the model in parts makes later editing of isolated pieces easier.

There are advantages to selectively linking parts of models or parts of entire scenes. You can snap objects or parts together or pull them apart, like a tinker toy.

Editing Advantages of Building Objects with Parts

One advantage of building an object in parts is that you can change parts without having to change the entire object. You can give different parts of composite objects unique textures or brush maps. The floor will use a wood tile map. The rug on the floor is tiled with its own map. The rug can then be grouped with the floor and saved as one object. If you don't like the color of the rug, you can always break the rug and floor apart, fix the rug, and group them again.

Creating a model with many small parts has another advantage. It makes the model easier to build. The bee looks hopelessly complex until you begin to see the simple shapes that it encompasses. It is composed of three main body

Tip: Using Imagine's Group Command When Saving

Imagine's Detail Editor creates and saves single objects. An object with many parts like the bee must be grouped as a single object to be saved. Use Imagine's Group command in the Mode menu to link objects. When the bee is later reloaded back into the Detail Editor, it can be ungrouped using the Ungroup command. To group all the objects in a scene:

- Change to group mode by selecting Pick Groups from the Mode menu.
- Select Pick All from the Pick/Select menu.
- Select Group from the Object menu or press (ALT)-(G). The objects in the group are linked.

Imagine draws yellow lines between grouped objects. The first object selected becomes the **parent** object. It's this object you control when manipulating the group. The child objects follow suit (see Figure 6-6).

Notice in Figure 6-6 that the lines emanate from one object. The Ungroup command breaks the bonds between objects in a group. In group mode, click on the parent object and then select the Ungroup command from the Object menu.

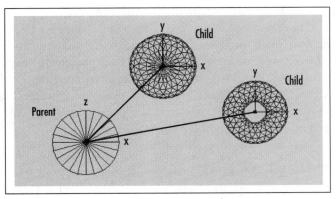

Figure 6-6 Grouping objects creates a parent linked to child objects

parts (head, thorax, and abdomen), with two wings and two legs. Taken individually, the parts of the bee are relatively easy to model. Seen at stages in its evolution, a 3D modeling project looks very much like a construction project in the real world.

Options for Generating Parts of the Model

There are many sources for ready-made 3D parts. These can be assembled and modified. Options include

- Use built-in 3D primitives.

- Import objects from specialized modeler.

- Import objects from other CAD or render programs and customize them (DXF import).

- Import objects from public domain and third-party sources (mesh libraries).

Using 3D Primitives

Most 3D programs come with a standard set of ready-made 3D objects (see Figure 6-7). These *primitives* can then be linked and modified to become more complex shapes. A tube becomes a pillar. The bee's eyes, for example, were created by loading and modifying a simple sphere primitive.

Importing Objects from Specialized Modeling Tools

Specialized modeling tools like Imagine's cross-sectional modeler, the Forms Editor, or Vista Pro's landscape generation program allow you to work efficiently. In the case of Imagine, the modeling strategy is to use the Forms Editor to generate the basic shape and then finish that shape in the Detail Editor. Let's use the example of a car. You could create the entire shape of the car in the Detail Editor. But it's much easier and faster to create the complex curves of the car in the Forms Editor using key slicing. (See Chapter 2 for the details) The car is then imported into the Detail Editor for finishing. Figure 6-8 shows the evolution of a car using this approach.

Importing DXF Files

Many 3D programs allow you to load 3D objects in Data Exchange Format (DXF). It is a standard sponsored by Autodesk to facilitate the exchange of 3D

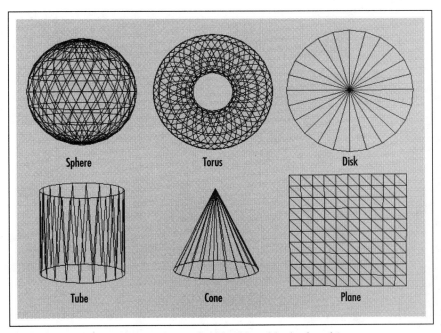

Figure 6-7 Imagine comes with standard building blocks for objects

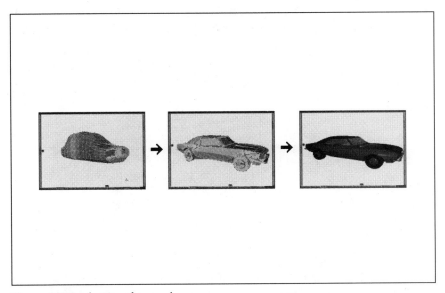

Figure 6-8 Evolution of a car shape

shapes between CAD programs. (The Load and Save DXF options are found in Imagine's Object menu.) You could model an object in Imagine and then import it into Autodesk's 3D Studio for finishing and rendering.

Mesh Libraries

A *mesh* refers to the geometry of an object. Many public domain 3D meshes are available from BBSs, CompuServe, sites on the Internet, or on CD-ROM from mesh library vendors. Appendix B lists sources for libraries of objects. There are several objects on the included disk.

Select and Apply the Modeling Tool

The final stage in the modeling project is the construction of the model using 3D modeling tools. Building the object will easily consume 80 percent of project time from inception to final render. The rest of this chapter will be devoted to modeling tools and techniques.

Objects imported from another program may be edited using surface editing tools. Objects created from scratch are modeled using 3D drafting tools and a variety of modeling techniques. This section provides an overview.

Basic 3D Drafting

Users entering the 3D modeling world from CAD (computer-aided design) will find that 3D programs have a familiar interface. At its most basic level, a 3D program is a drafting tool. Here are the common tools used for drawing shapes on the screen:

- A world coordinate system (X,Y,Z).

- A world viewing system arranged in four or more windows.

- A grid system for precisely laying out objects.

- Editing tools such as cut, copy, and paste.

- Tools for selecting parts of objects.

- Basic object transformation tools: moving, rotating, and scaling.

Figure 6-9 shows Imagine's Detail Editor viewing system. The viewing system has general characteristics common to most 3D programs.

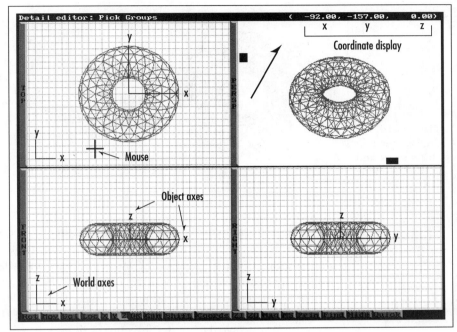

Figure 6-9
Imagine's Detail Editor has the key elements of a 3D program interface

3D Viewing

The screen is divided into three orthogonal views (Top, Front, and Right) that allow you to build and modify objects in each of its three dimensions. There is also a camera view (called the perspective window in the Detail Editor), which shows the object as the eye might see it.

The orthogonal views show a grid system that can be turned on or off. This system is useful as digital grid paper for laying out and moving, scaling, and rotating objects. You can also turn on a "lock to grid" function. This is sometimes called "snap to grid." The element (point, line, or polygonal mesh) can be forced to attach to intersections in the grid of lines. You can also set the size of the grid.

Usually the viewing system can be customized in some fashion. For example, in Imagine, you can switch the display to full-screen mode. By clicking on the long buttons along the left side of the views, you can make the view overtake the entire screen. This facilitates detailed work in one of the views.

The viewing system shows objects in one of two basic ways: object mode or surface mode (see Figure 6-10). In object mode, the object is shown as a polygonal mesh without vertices. In surface mode, the vertices and lines that make

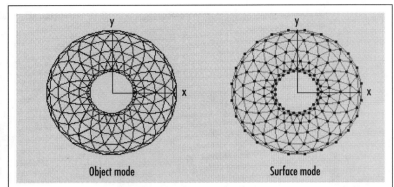

Figure 6-10 The torus is shown in object mode and surface mode

up the object are shown. This reflects the two different ways of working with objects. In the case of object mode, you make transformations to objects as a whole, rotating them, moving them, or scaling them. In surface mode you edit the individual vertices, lines, and faces of the object.

There is also a coordinate readout system. In Figure 6-9 the location of the mouse is shown in the Top view. At the top right of the screen, the current position of the mouse within the coordinate system is shown. By convention, the current position of the mouse is shown in the X,Y,Z order. This feature turns the mouse into a digital ruler. The coordinate readout system can be turned on or off.

Measurements are made with arbitrary units. You can translate the relative sizes of a bee's part in a technical illustration into Imagine's arbitrary units. A four-inch wing span might be translated to 400 Imagine units. This allows you to precisely lay out the bee in the modeling program.

The 3D drafting tools are optimized for creating the basic elements of an object: polygons. A polygon is composed of vertices, lines, and faces. You can simply draw a polygon on the screen using points and lines and cover it with faces. The surface on the bee's wing was created this way. However, creating 3D surfaces on irregular shapes like the head would be difficult to build by drawing points and lines on the screen. There are more than 25,000 polygons on this bee. Generating the polygons one by one would be extremely tedious.

Creating 3D Objects from 2D Outlines

As 3D software technology has evolved, programs are taking on more and more of the labor content of building complex models by automatically generating 3D objects from 2D outlines. Although 3D drafting may be required to develop an outline shape, all the methods listed here reward a comparatively small effort with a harvest of polygons.

- *Extrusion* spins or sweeps a 2D outline through 3D space to create a new object.

- *Skinning* covers a 2D skeleton with a skin.

- *Sculpting* splits, joins, or slices objects and uses magnetism to mold them into new objects.

- *Procedural modeling* uses mathematical models to generate 3D objects.

Each method can generate complex polygonal meshes with hundreds or thousands of polygons using a simple shape as a starting point.

Extrusion

Extrusion builds 3D objects out of contours. This is a good modeling technique for objects that are radially symmetrical. An example is a pawn (see Figure 6-11). The contour of the pawn was drawn on the screen. Then it was spun on its ver-

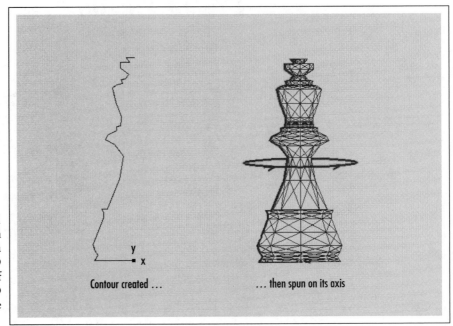

Figure 6-11
Extrusion generates a complex 3D object out of a simple 2D outline

Contour created ...   ... then spun on its axis

tical axis using an extrusion command. The chess piece's surface is created. You can see the polygons forming the surface of the 3D pawn. The artist has to draw the contour of the chess piece, but the creation of the final object is automated. The process is called extrusion and it pays huge returns for a small investment of time.

Skinning

Skinning also generates 3D surfaces using a key slice method similar to the one used in the Forms Editor of Imagine. The key slices of a shape are created as 2D shapes, then Imagine draws a skin of polygons around the shape like slats around the hoops of a barrel (see Figure 6-12).

Sculpting

Sculpting is analogous to wood carving or stone sculpture. You begin with a simple 3D object and sculpt it into a more detailed object. You can also "glue" other objects onto the shape or mold the surface of the shape. For example, you can begin with a plane and pull its polygons up to form a mountain. Or

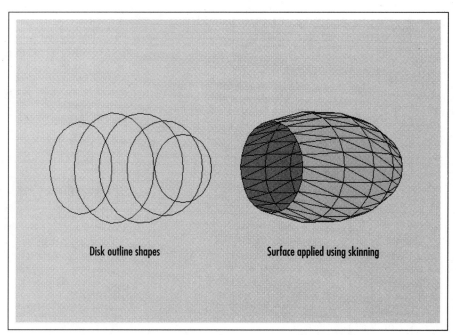

Disk outline shapes   Surface applied using skinning

Figure 6-12 Skinning draws a surface of polygons over 2D outline shapes

Tip: Bee Plans Are Elsewhere

The complete story of how the bee was constructed is provided in Appendix D.

you can use tools that use one object to cut up another, much as a cookie shape is cut out of dough with a cookie cutter.

Procedural Modeling

For sheer return on labor investment, nothing beats procedural modeling. Procedural modeling uses code to generate very complex objects like trees or geography. For example, the program Vista Pro generates entire landscapes based on geographical data. Procedures that mimic the physical behavior of particles have become common in advanced 3D programs. An object can be made to explode, shattering into a cloud of polygons. Or a wave pattern can be automatically generated, useful for modeling animated flags, ocean waves, or clothing. Other procedures mimic the behavior of such optical artifacts as lens flare.

Combining Modeling Tools

Modeling photorealistic subjects in a desktop environment is challenging. There is a great deal of creativity involved in solving the technical challenges offered by limited means. For example, in the case of the bee, the specifications called for a bee that had hair. A bee has thousands of hairs. The polygon count for the bee could easily increase by 50 percent. Alan Henry knew he would not be able to model the individual strands of hair. He decided to "coat" the body with an image map of hair. He used a filter map to make the white areas of the map transparent. By wrapping the filter map around a slightly enlarged version of each body part, he made the hair look like it was standing on end...a very convincing illusion.

What's Ahead

A photorealistic model will undoubtedly tax your skill as a modeler and your knowledge of the tools. The balance of this chapter will introduce you to the most important drafting and modeling tools. Let's begin by describing the data system used by 3D programs to store and display 3D geometry.

THE WORLD COORDINATE SYSTEM

When you enter a 3D software program, you enter a 3D world. If you modeled it in 3D, it would look like a three-dimensional grid (see Figure 6-13). The world coordinate system helps the computer to locate points within the 3D world. If the room you are in right now were a world coordinate system, you could precisely describe the location of any object in it using a coordinate system.

A room has three sets of parallel planes at right angles to each other:

- The ceiling and the floor
- The east and west walls
- The north and south walls

In order to describe an object's location, you could say it is six feet from the east wall, two feet from the south wall, and one foot down from the ceiling.

Axes

Axes make it possible to move things. When you tell a friend to adjust a lamp shade, you say, "Move it over to the right and down." Your friend will move the lamp relative to the coordinate system of the room. However, when you

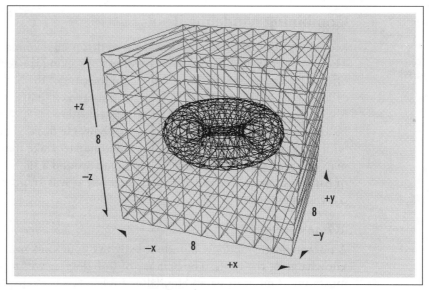

Figure 6-13 An object sits in a 3D grid called the world coordinate system

say, "turn it around," you are asking your friend to move it relative to its own axes.

The world coordinate system used by 3D programs works just like the system just described. X,Y,Z notation is used to precisely locate a point in the 3D world. For example, the notation X = 30, Y = 20, Z = 100 means the point is 30 units along the positive X axis, 20 units along the positive Y axis, and 100 units along the positive Z axis. When you see the notation 30,20,100, the order of the axes is assumed to be X,Y,Z. As indicated in Figure 6-13, each axis has a positive and negative value.

The Origin

In Figure 6-13 the donut-shaped torus lies at the very center of the world coordinate system, its *origin*. The origin provides a reference for all measurements in the 3D world. It's also the "point of origin" for all new 3D objects that enter the world. The origin has an X,Y,Z value of 0,0,0. When a primitive torus, for example, is created by Imagine, it places the torus's center at the center of the 3D world and arranges the object's surfaces around this point.

World Axes and Object Axes

The world coordinate system is absolute. It cannot be expanded, rotated, or moved. When objects are first created, they are aligned to the world coordinate system. But objects have their own axes. Just as you can tell your friend to move a lamp relative to the absolute coordinates of the room, you can move, rotate, and scale objects relative to the world coordinate system. This allows you to move objects to absolute positions within the 3D world. You can move objects along their own axes, to make a bird fly for example, or you can make an object move to an absolute position within the 3D world.

Figure 6-14 shows a very simple object, a cube. At the center of the cube are its axes. When the cube is first created in the 3D world, its axes are coincident with the world's axes.

The points or vertices at the corners of the cube have positions within the cube's own coordinate system. You could say, for example, that the front top vertex is located one unit along the positive X axis, one unit along the positive Z axis, and one unit along the negative Y axis. This precisely locates the vertex relative to the object's own origin point.

The same vertex is also relative to the world coordinate system. When you first create the object, the cube's top front vertex would have the same values in the world coordinate system, X = 1, Y = -1, Z = 1 or 1,-1,1.

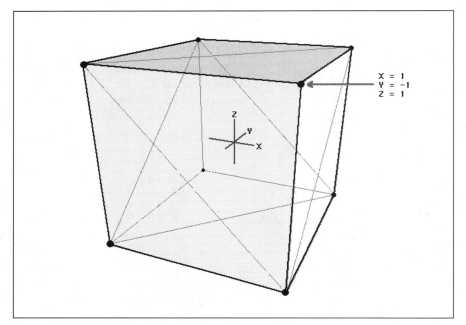

Figure 6-14 Objects have their own coordinate systems

The shape of the cube can be changed by adding vertices, deleting vertices, moving, or rotating them. For example, removing four of the box's eight vertices creates a triangle (see Figure 6-15).

Remember that an object's surface is composed of polygons. These polygons can have three or four vertices. The face of the polygon is attached to each of the vertices. It is the face that is rendered, not the lines and vertices. When you delete a vertex, you automatically delete the faces attached to it. Most programs allow you to delete the face and not the lines and vertices. This allows you to poke holes in objects without affecting their shape.

Modifying Object Geometry Through Transformations

Everytime you transform an object, or add or delete polygons to it, you change the database out of which the scene is created. Unlike a draw program, which keeps track of lines and points on the screen, a 3D program stores the absolute positions of points and lines as 3D coordinates. The computer has a very pow-

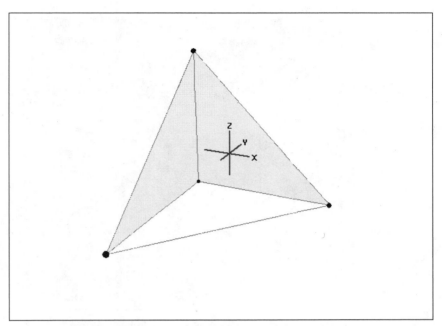

Figure 6-15 A pyramid is created by deleting four of the cube's eight vertices

erful calculating machine at its heart, and when you are making changes in the 3D workspace, a steady stream of data is sent to the CPU and math coprocessor. The math coprocessor makes calculations that translate into geometry viewed on the screen. When you zoom in on a part of a model, the system's math coprocessor works overtime rebuilding the screen according to the new viewpoint. In the case of very elaborate models, the perspective window's refresh rate can slow to a crawl, especially in solid or shaded mode. The shading used in shaded mode exacts a toll on the system's ability to process the thousands of calculations each zoom or rotation requires.

Changing the viewpoint, however, does not change the object's geometry. In order to make a change to an object's geometry, you must change the rotation, scale, or position of its vertices.

Transformations: Rotating, Scaling, and Moving

Rotating, scaling, and moving objects and vertices are the most basic kinds of changes you can make to a scene. Figure 6-16 shows a box with four vertices scaled to a second position within the world coordinate system.

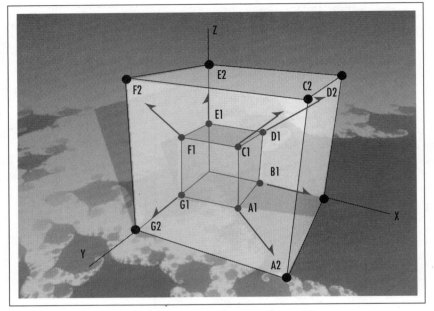

Figure 6-16 Scaling the four vertices of a box to new positions

The 3D program uses math to translate the vertices of the first box into the vertices of the second box. The vertex at position C1 is transformed into position C2 by adding a fixed value to its X,Y,Z coordinates. Using matrix notation, the math underlying the scaling translation might be written as,

C2 = C1 + D

where D is a numeric value. A transformation that remaps the object's coordinates in this way is called scaling.

Scaling

Many programs, including Imagine, allow you to scale the box interactively. However, some objects may require precise transformation. A ceiling fan, for example, is composed of four identical blades rotated about a center (see Figure 6-17).

Many 3D programs allow you to transform objects in very precise ways. For example, Imagine's Transformation Requester provides a data entry box where you can enter values for transformations. The blade, for example, was copied and then repeatedly pasted down and rotated in precise increments about a center.

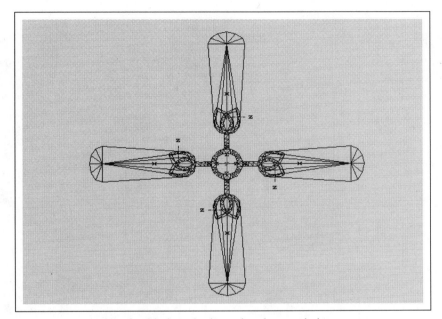

Figure 6-17 A ceiling fan blade is duplicated and rotated about a center

Rotating

Rotations are always made around one of the three axes of the object or the world coordinate system. Figure 6-18 shows how an object is rotated in 3D coordinate systems.

Programs allow you to rotate the object with the mouse in one of the orthogonal views or through a data entry box, such as Imagine's Transformaton Requester. In the case of Imagine, the rotating, moving, and scaling transformations are activated by clicking on one of the transformation buttons at the bottom of the screen (see Figure 6-19).

Rotations, movements, and scaling directions can be confined to one or more axes in 3D programs. Scaling an object along its horizontal X axis, for example, is accomplished in Imagine by deselecting the Y and Z buttons at the bottom of the screen. (Buttons are "up" or "down." In the figure, the X, Y, Z buttons are on.)

The Loc button at the bottom of the screen is a toggle switch. When clicked on, transformations are made according to the object's own internal coordinate system. The default condition is off. In this state, transformations to the object are made relative to the world coordinate system.

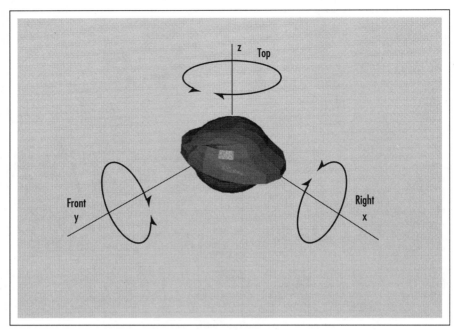

Figure 6-18 Use this diagram to understand how objects are rotated

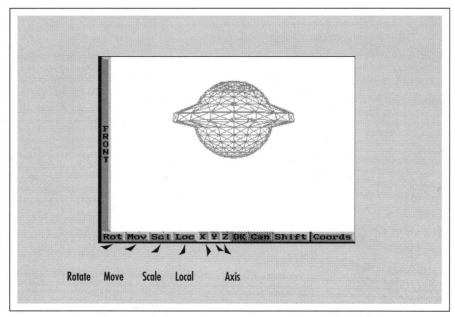

Figure 6-19 The transformation buttons in Imagine's Detail Editor

Remember that basic transformations to an object are made to its axes rather than its polygonal mesh. The center of origin for an object is an infinitely small point from which the three axes extend. When you move an object, you actually move its axes. Because the polygons making up the object are attached to this point, they move along with the axes. This makes it much easier to manipulate objects.

In Imagine, the axes are 32 units long by default. When you scale an object, you scale its axes, and the polygons that are arrayed around the axes move accordingly. If you look back to Figure 6-16, you can see the effect of transforming the size of the axes.

You can also move an object's axes relative to the polygonal mesh. You may want to move the object's center of rotation to one side. The bee's wings, for example, rotate at their base rather than their center. Imagine allows you to move the axes interactively with the (SHIFT)-(M) key combination.

The Transformation Requester

Imagine, like many 3D programs, also provides an alternative method for making precise transformations. The Transformation Requester shown in Figure 6-20 is called up by pressing (ALT)-(T) or selecting Transformation from the Object menu. This brings up a box which allows you to transform the object relative to its own axes or to absolute coordinates in the world coor-

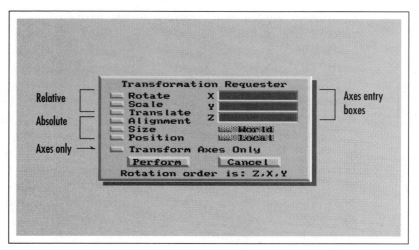

Figure 6-20 Imagine's Transformation Requester allows you to precisely transform objects

Tip: Steps to Take in Moving Object Axes

Press the (SHIFT) key, and while keeping it depressed, press the (M) key. This places Imagine into move axes mode. You can now release the (SHIFT) and (M) keys and move the axes with the mouse. Here are the transformation keys:

- (SHIFT)-(M) moves the axes
- (SHIFT)-(R) rotates the axes
- (SHIFT)-(S) scales the axes

dinate system. The Transform Axes Only button has the same function as the Loc button in the Detail Editor. Changes made to the object's axes can be made without changing the size, orientation, or position of the polygonal mesh.

The data entry boxes at the top right allow you to enter positive or negative values for transformations.

The buttons arrayed on the left side of the Transformation Requester allow you to perform two types of transformations. You can make transformations relative to the object's own axes or relative to the world coordinate system. For example, you may want to move the axes or object to an absolute position within the world coordinate system or to a position relative to the object's own axes.

This flexibility is necessary when you are creating objects divided into parts. The bee's wings, for example, may be rotated into a position relative to the bee's body. Then the axes can be moved to the wing's base and rotated into an orientation that allows the wings to flap up and down relative to the bee's body.

When creating an object, it's best to align the main part of the object to the world coordinate system. This allows you to use the world coordinate system's origin as a reference point for all the parts of the bee's body, for example. If the bee is used within a more elaborate scene, the main part of the body can be transformed or animated within the world coordinate system of the scene.

Objects in the real world have a kind of world coordinate system as well: it's called gravity. In the real world, we rarely have trouble figuring out up and down. The tools used for transforming objects in 3D programs allow us to create worlds where objects behave as if they were conforming to natural laws. A bee can be made to flap its wings and fly in a beeline from one absolute position within the 3D world to another.

One final note: Imagine's transformation tools are also available in the Stage Editor.

What's Ahead

The next section gives you practice working with 3D geometry and shows you how to build a very simple object from scratch.

EXERCISE: CREATING A BEE'S WING SURFACE

In this exercise, we'll use Imagine's drafting tools to create the surface of a bee's wing. The wing can be created by simply drafting it on the screen. You'll learn to use Imagine's point, line, and object editing modes. Figure 6-21 shows the wing geometry of Alan Henry's bee.

We're going to create the wing surface without the veins. (Alan Henry tells how the veins were created in Appendix D.) Figure 6-22 shows the vertices and

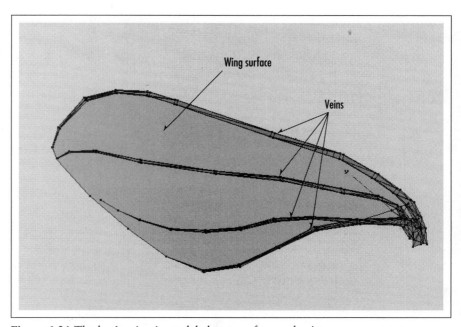

Figure 6-21 The bee's wing is modeled as a surface and veins

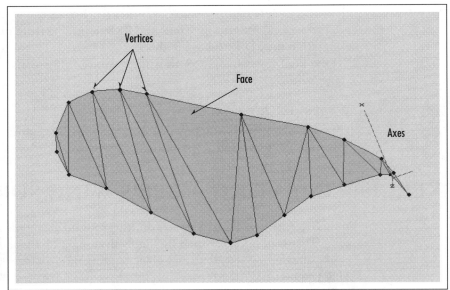

Figure 6-22
The wing surface
shown as a
polygonal mesh

lines that make up the bee's wings. Imagine creates triangular meshes, so the wing is subdivided into triangles. The interiors of triangles have faces. It's these faces that are rendered.

Let's now re-create the wing in Imagine's Detail Editor.

Creating the Wing: Step-by-Step

Enter the Detail Editor. If you are already inside the Detail Editor, make sure that there are no objects loaded. Press (right) (ALT)-(A) to select all the objects in the scene and then (right) (ALT)-(D) to delete all objects.

Laying Down the Axis

Every object has its own axes. When you move or transform an object, you actually change the object's axes, not its polygons. Construction of the bee's wing begins with laying down an axis. In Imagine, Axis is listed as a primitive on the Primitives submenu of the Functions menu, shown in Figure 6-23.

1   In the Functions Add submenu, click on Axis.

An axis is added at the center of the 3D world. It has three lines at right

Figure 6-23
Primitives are
added to the
scene from the
Functions Add
submenu

angles to each other, with a lighter dot at the intersection. Pressing (F1) picks the axis, readying it for editing.

2 Pick the axis either by clicking on the yellow point at its intersection or by pressing (F1).

You have now made the axes active. The easiest way to create the wing is to work in one of the orthogonal views, laying the wing out flat, just as if you were building it out of wood, flat on the ground. Create the wing in the Front view.

3 Change to full-screen Front view by clicking on FRONT at the left side of the viewing window.

You are now ready to draw the shape of the bee's wing.

Drawing the Bee's Wing

Figure 6-24 shows the shape you are going to draw on the screen. One of Imagine's editing modes, Add Lines, allows you to draw the outline on the screen. Imagine is modal in operation, meaning the editing system can be switched from one level of object detail to another. When you first enter the

Tip: Using an Axis as a Dummy Object

Because an axis does not have faces, it won't appear when you render a scene. This makes an axis valuable as an invisible object. Dummy axes are useful in model creation. For example, they allow you to group several objects and rotate these objects about the dummy axes.

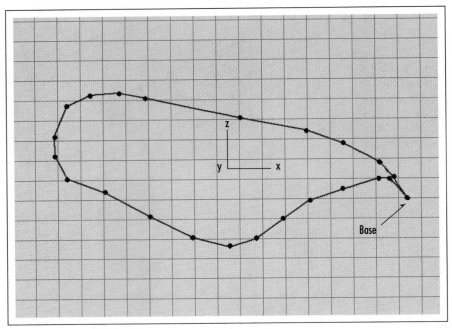

Figure 6-24 Drafting the bee's wing

Detail Editor, the system is in Pick Groups mode. In order to add vertices and lines to the scene, switch the editor into Add Lines mode. Add Lines mode allows you to lay down vertices and lines simultaneously.

Imagine's editing modes are found in the Mode menu, shown in Figure 6-25.

4 In the Mode menu, click on Add Lines. The axis turns black.

The information line at the top of the screen shows that you are in Add Lines mode. Now vertices and lines are visible.

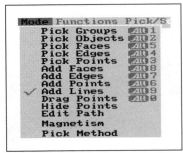

Figure 6-25
Imagine has many different editing modes, according to level of detail

Clicking on the screen adds points and lines to the object. Using the diagram shown in Figure 6-24, draw the outline very roughly on the screen. Later you'll see how to match the shape more closely to the one in the figure. Begin at the base of the wing.

5 Draw a rough outline of the bee's wing, beginning with the base of the wing. To complete the outline, click on the starting point again.·

If you make a mistake, use the (right) (ALT)-(U) Undo command. This cancels the last action.

Editing Vertices

Compare the wing you drew with the drawing. To edit the shape of the wing, you'll need to move individual vertices. Switch to Drag Points on the Mode menu.

6 Click on Drag Points mode in the Mode menu.

7 Click on a point and adjust its position by dragging it. This changes the shape of the object interactively.

Adding Vertices Using Fracture

You may have accidentally omitted a vertex in drawing the shape. Imagine has a feature that allows you to add a vertex between two existing points by fracturing it into two shorter lines. If the curve looks flat, the new vertex can be moved to create a smoother curve. The command Fracture splits faces or the edges of a polygon, but you cannot fracture vertices, because they are infinitely small. Let's add a vertex to the bee's wing. Switch to an edge editing mode first.

8 Click on Pick Edges mode in the Mode menu.

Now select the edge to fracture.

9 Select an edge by clicking on the two points that define it. The edge turns blue, and the two points defining it turn pink.

The edge is now picked, ready for transformation. The next step is to select the Fracture command.

10 Click on the Fracture command in the Functions menu. A new point is added between the existing points of the picked edge.

Tip: Creating Round Surfaces with Flat Edges

The bee's wing is flat. An airplane wing is rounded with sharp edges. Imagine allows you to treat the edges differently than the body of the wing. The polygons along the edges can be picked with the selection tools and assigned flat shading. The Sharp command on the Functions Make submenu is executed after the edges are picked. You can also give flat surfaces round edges using the Make Soft command.

Move the new point out slightly to create a more rounded curve.

11   Switch to Drag Points mode.

12   Click on the new point and move it out until the curve becomes smoother looking.

In adding vertices to the curve of the bee's wing, you are making it smooth. Remember that another method for creating smooth surfaces is to assign Phong shading to it. (In Imagine, the Phong button is automatically on for a surface when it is created.) However, the bee's wing is flat, not rounded, with a sharp edge, so we choose to add extra edges to the outline shape. When the wing is assigned surface attributes, turn the Phong shading off to give the wing flat shading.

Adding Faces to the Outline Shape

Right now the bee's wing has no faces. You can see its shape in wireframe, but if you rendered it, it would not appear. This is confirmed when you attempt to view it in the perspective window as a solid or shaded object. Before viewing the object, you need to change into an object viewing mode.

13   Switch to Pick Objects mode in the Mode menu. The vertices disappear, and the wireframe becomes blue.

This indicates that you are in object mode. Now switch to the perspective window.

14   Click on the PERSP button at the top right of the screen. The screen changes to full-screen perspective window.

The bee's wing should appear as an outline shape in the perspective window.

15 Select Solid from the Display window. The outline shape disappears from the screen.

Try viewing the wing in shaded mode as well. In both cases the bee's wing disappears. Before you add faces to the wing, you need to return to the Front view.

16 Click on the FRONT button at the top right of the screen.

Now add faces to the wing.

17 Click on Add Faces mode in the Mode menu. The wing is now displayed as lines and vertices.

To add faces to the outline, click on each of the three vertices that define a face.

18 Beginning with the base point at the right of the wing, cover the bee's wing with faces. Click on each of three points in turn.

As you click on each point, it turns reddish brown. When you click on the third point, edges are added between points. Since each new face that you create shares an edge with the old face, you should begin each new face by selecting the two vertices that make up the edge of the old face.

You can check your progress by toggling between the Front and perspective windows. Set the display mode as shaded and watch as the bee's wing appears as a series of gray triangles.

When you have created the last face of the wing, you save the wing.

19 Click on Pick Groups mode. The wing turns blue.

20 Press (ALT)-(S) to call the save box. Navigate to the \IMAG\OBJECTS subdirectory. Save the wing as BEEWING.OBJ.

You have now created and saved the bee's wing surface.

EXTRUSIONS

In the exercise you just performed, an object was created by drawing an outline on the screen and then filling in the shape with faces. The bee's wing, however, is flat and has no thickness. You could create a 3D object by drawing its surfaces on the screen, but this method is practically impossible for surfaces with complex curves.

This is where the 3D program's ability to transform the geometry of objects comes into play. The math that underlies transformations (moving, scaling,

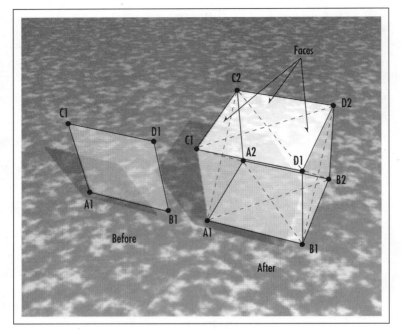

Figure 6-26 Transformation of a 2D shape into a 3D object

rotating) can also be used to generate the surfaces of 3D objects. Figure 6-26 shows the most basic transformation, *extrusion*.

A flat 2D plane with coordinates at A1, B1, C1, and D1 is extruded to A2, B2, C2, and D2, respectively. As extrusion progresses, faces are added along outer edges of the extrusion. The result is a polygonal mesh stretched between the first and second plane.

Types of Extrusions

Here are the types of transformations, including the extrude type we used in the last exercise:

- **Extrude:** Create a 3D object by projecting a 2D shape along a path.

- **Spin:** Extrude a 2D shape by rotating (spinning) it on its Z axis.

- **Sweep:** Create a surface of revolution by spinning a 2D contour on its Z axis. (This is called *lathing* by some programs.)

- **Conform:** Create a 3D shape by wrapping a 2D shape over a sphere, cylinder, or along a path.

- **Replicate:** Create a series of 3D objects along a path using a 2D shape as a template.

Spin and sweep are used to create radially symmetrical objects like wine glasses and chess pawns. In a later exercise we will practice with the Spin command.

Conform creates a 3D object by conforming a 2D shape to a sphere, cylinder, or path. This is a good tool for creating such objects as labels on cans or sails of ships.

You use replicate to duplicate an object along a path.

The next section shows you how to prepare the 2D outlines used in the extrusion process.

Creating 2D Shapes for Extrusion

There are a variety of ways to create the 2D shapes for extrusion. Outline shapes create objects with open ends. Filled shapes create solid objects.

3D Primitives

The disk and plane primitives (loaded from the Add menu) are used as templates for extrusion. Deleting the disk's central vertex creates a circle outline.

Importing 2D Shapes

Most 3D programs allow you to import a 2D shape into the editor for extrusion. You can import DXF shapes created in draw programs. You can use draw programs like CorelDRAW and Adobe Illustrator as your drawing tool.

Drawing Shapes on the Screen

Shapes can be drawn on the screen using the Add Lines editing mode in the Mode menu. This method was used to create the outline of the bee's wing. Using the Extrude command, you can then give depth to this wing.

Extruding in Imagine Step-by-Step

There is considerable variety in the way extrusion is implemented in 3D programs. Some programs devote a separate program module to extrusion. Imagine implements extrusion in a call-up box. This section shows you how to use Imagine's extrusion parameters. Keep in mind that you can perform the same types of extrusions in other programs.

In Imagine, extrusion is always made along the object's Y axis, from the front of the object to the back; and rotations are around the Z axis. Imagine gives you a lot of control over the shape, length, and rotation of molds through parameter boxes associated with each mold type. Extrusions are created by following this process:

- Create the 2D shape in the Front view.

- Pick the 2D shape.

- Call the Mold command to pop the Mold Requester on the screen.

- Select a molding method.

- Alter the parameters for the extrusion path in the mold parameters box.

- Click on Perform.

Each type of mold command creates a different kind of object. Replicate produces copies of an object along a path; Spin creates a continuous shape. Let's look closer at the way extrusions are shaped in the mold parameters box.

Exercise: Creating the Body for a Toy Drum

The utility of extrusion in modeling is best demonstrated with an example. In this exercise, we'll use extrusion to create the body of a toy drum. Enter the Detail Editor. Make sure all objects are removed from the workspace by selecting Pick All from the Pick/Select menu and pressing the (ALT)-(D) (delete) key combination.

Instead of drawing the outline of the drum on the screen, load a disk from the Primitives Type box and use that.

1 Press (F5). This brings up the Primitives Type box.

2 Click on the Disk primitive. A disk parameters box appears.

You can specify more or fewer sections for the circle. The more sections you add, the smoother the curve of the drum. For now, use the default number of sections.

3 Click on Perform.

The disk appears on the screen, but it is small. Let's scale it up.

4 Press F1 to pick the disk.

5 Press the S key to activate scaling, or click on the Scl button at the bottom of the screen. Click on the disk and drag it, scaling it until it fills the screen.

The disk is a 2D object. Imagine extrudes an object along its Y axis, from the front of the object to the back. This means that objects like the disk should be extruded in the Front view.

Imagine calls the process of extruding 3D objects from 2D shapes *molding*. (Extrude is a specific mold command.)

6 Select Mold from the Object menu or press ALT-E (see Figure 6-27). From the Mold Requester, click on Extrude. An Extrude Data box pops on the screen.

The Extrude Data box allows you to perform a number of transformations that change the shape of the extruded object. The default settings suit our purpose.

7 Click on Perform.

The disk is transformed into a cylindrical 3D object. Figure 6-28 shows the new object in the perspective window in shaded mode. Let's undo the extrusion and create a variation.

8 Press ALT-U to cancel the extrusion.

Instead of a solid object, create a hollow cylinder out of a hollow outline. To create the hollow outline, delete the point at the center of the disk.

9 From the Mode menu, select Pick Points. Click on the point at the center of the disk. The point at the center of the disk turns pink to indicate it is picked.

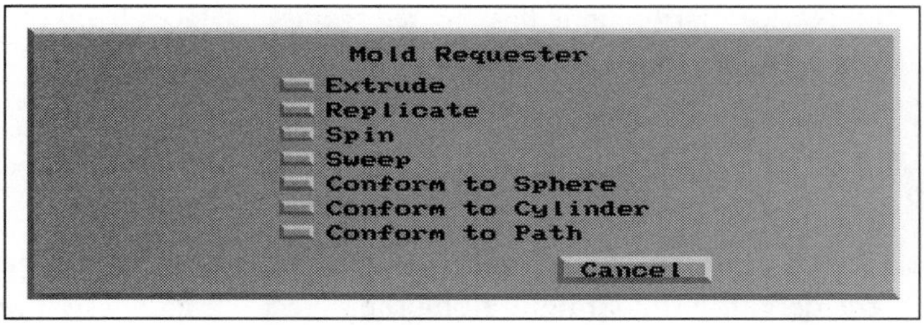

Figure 6-27 The Mold Requester

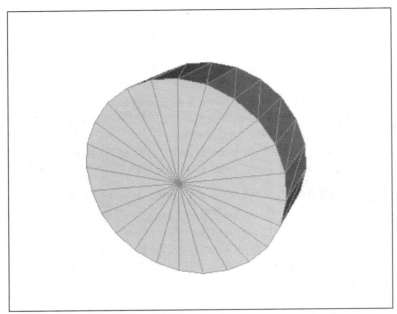

Figure 6-28 Extrusion transforms the 2D disk into a 3D object

10 From the Functions menu select Delete (or press ⒜⒧⒯-Ⓓ). All of the faces disappear.

If you are in solid or shaded mode in the perspective window, the object will disappear.

11 Change to Pick Objects mode. Call the Mold Requester by pressing ⒜⒧⒯-Ⓔ. Click on Extrude. Enter 500 for the length of the extrusion. Click on Perform. The hollow circle extrudes into a cylinder (see Figure 6-29).

Notice that Imagine has created triangular faces from the outline of the 2D object to its projected position in 3D space.

Changing the Path and Shape of the Extrusion

So far, you've seen the kinds of transformations that can be performed along the default path: straight along the object's Y axis. Most programs, Imagine included, allow you to create a path along which the extrusion will occur.

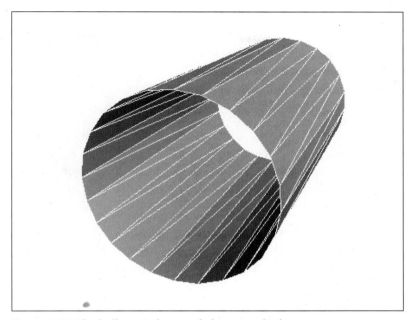

Figure 6-29 The hollow circle extruded into a cylinder

Each mold command has a unique parameters box associated with it, but the parameters break down to two basic activities. You can determine the *shape* of the extrusion path and how that path *transforms* over time. You can also define how smooth to make the extrusion (see Figure 6-30).

Specifying the Type of Extrusion

At the top left of the box, you choose whether you want a straight path (the To Length button) or a user-defined path (the Along Path button).

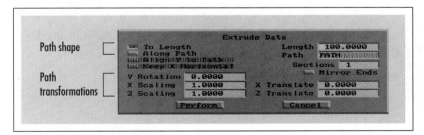

Figure 6-30 Extrude Data box

Straight Extrusions

Extrusions by default travel along a straight line in the Y direction. You set the length of the extrusion in the Length box at the far right of the Extrude Data box.

Extrusions Along Paths

Extrusions can also be made to follow paths. Figure 6-31 shows a plane extruded along a zigzag path. To extrude along a path, click on Along Path and enter the path name in the Path data box on the right.

When you choose Along Path, you are provided with two more options. You can either align the 2D shape to the path (it will follow it like a car follows a mountain highway) or keep the 2D shape aligned to the world's X axis.

Mirror Ends

By default, when you extrude a solid outline such as a disk, it arrives at the end of the path in the same orientation as the beginning position. Mirror Ends flips it around at the end.

Transforming the Shape of the Extrusion

You can also determine how a 2D shape is transformed over the length of the extrusion. For example, you can cause the shape to rotate as it follows along a path. Figure 6-32 shows what happens to an extruded disk when the transformation parameters are changed.

Extrusions can be made to rotate around the Y axis, scale from small to large along the X or Z axes, translate (skew) in either the X (horizontal) or Z (vertical) directions, or move in the X or Z directions as the extrusion takes place.

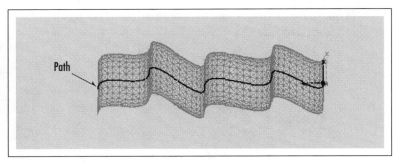

Figure 6-31 A path creates complex extrusions

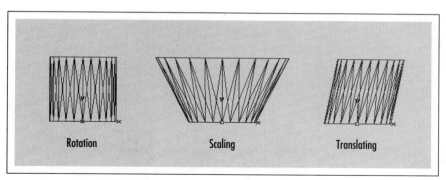

| Rotation | Scaling | Translating |

Figure 6-32 Shapes created by altering the extrusion parameters

Determining Detail

The Sections parameter box specifies how many polygons will be created. The more sections the object has, the smoother the curves of the extruded object.

Changing the Object's Center of Rotation

Extrusions that use rotations employ the object's Z axis as the center of rotation. For example, a disk is spun into a sphere. If you move the disk's axis off-center, the disk will travel at a distance from the center of the axis, creating a torus (see Figure 6-33).

To generate an object this way, follow these steps:

- Create a 2D shape.
- Pick it.
- To put Imagine into axes only mode, use the transformation (SHIFT) key combination, (SHIFT)-(M).
- Use the mouse to reposition the axes.
- Press the (SPACEBAR) bar to confirm the change.

Remember that pressing the (SHIFT) key first is important in putting Imagine into *change axes* mode. For more precision, move the axes by calling the Transformation Requester and entering precise values there. Click on the Transform Axes Only button. This transforms the axes, not the object.

What's Ahead

In the next exercise, we'll practice using the Spin command.

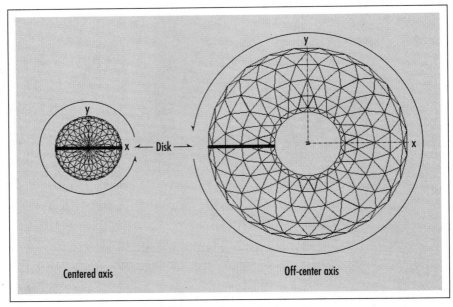

Figure 6-33 Disk spun on its axis and off-center to its axis

Exercise: Creating a Martini Glass

In this exercise you will create a martini glass by drawing its contour and spinning this contour around 360 degrees. Figure 6-34 shows the shape we will create. Here are the steps:

- Create and position the object's axis.
- Pick the axis.
- Change to line mode.
- Draw the 2D shape.
- Select the mold tool that will perform the transformation.
- Select the parameters of the transformation.
- Perform the transformation.

We'll draw the outline of the glass in the Front view and then spin it on its axes 360 degrees. The result will be a martini glass.

Figure 6-34 The martini glass formed by spinning a 2D shape

1 Enter the Detail Editor or clear it of objects.

2 Change to full-screen Front view by clicking on the FRONT button at the left side of the Front view.

Objects must have axes, so first we add an axis for the martini glass.

3 Select Add from the Functions menu and then Axis.

The martini glass contour used as the template for the extrusion is shown in Figure 6-35. Because we will spin the template 360 degrees, we need only create the contour. To understand why, think of the way a revolving door spins on its axes. Each door in the revolving door sweeps the entire 360 degrees.

Now draw the martini profile.

4 Pick the axis by pressing (F1).

5 Switch to Add Lines mode.

6 Draw a very rough version of the profile.

You don't have to be precise, because you are going to adjust the shape in Pick Points mode. If you make a mistake, select Undo from the Project menu or use the (right) (ALT)-(U) hot key combination.

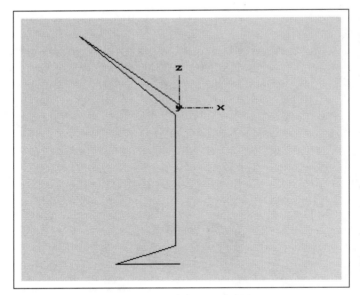

Figure 6-35 The 2D template of the martini glass

7 Change to Drag Points mode.

8 Change the shape of the martini glass to match that of Figure 6-35.

Because the profile will be spun, placement of points along its Z axis is important. You'll see what happens when the line formed by the stem is coincident with the object's Z axis.

9 Line the stem's points up with the Z axis.

You are now ready to use the Mold Requester to spin the profile.

10 Change back to the object mode.

11 Select Mold from the Objects menu or use the hot key combination (right) (ALT)-(E).

12 Click on Spin.

When you choose Spin, the Spin Data box pops on the screen. Leave the spin radius at its default (360 degrees).

13 Click on Perform.

Your screen should now look like Figure 6-36. This is a glass with a very thin stem!

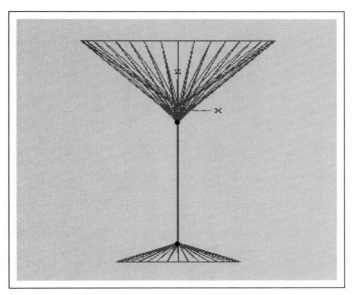

Figure 6-36 The spun shape of the martini glass

You can make the stem thicker by moving the points that define the *stem* of the glass to the left of the axis. Try moving the points as an exercise. Figure 6-37 shows what the shape looks like once the points have been moved.

Spinning an object on an axis is a valuable method for creating radially symmetrical objects. This was the primary tool used by Alan Henry to create the parts for the bee. An example is the bee's antenna. His method was to create a contour outline of the antenna, spin it, and bend it. Figure 6-38 shows the development of the antenna. This approach has the advantage of creating a simple object with relatively few polygons.

Extruding Along Curved Paths

By default, most 3D programs will extrude the object along a straight path. You can make the object rotate in a spiral around a straight path or move the destination point off-center. But these linear transformations don't result in complex, irregular curves. Complex winding paths, like the branch of a tree, require a different approach.

The bee's antenna created by Alan Henry, was a straight tube bent in the middle. Some insects, however, have antennae that curve in complex ways.

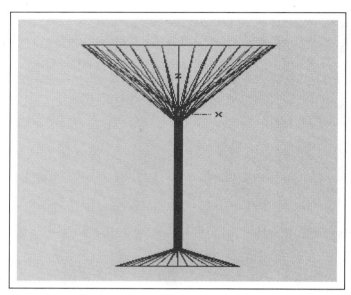

Figure 6-37 The enlarged stem

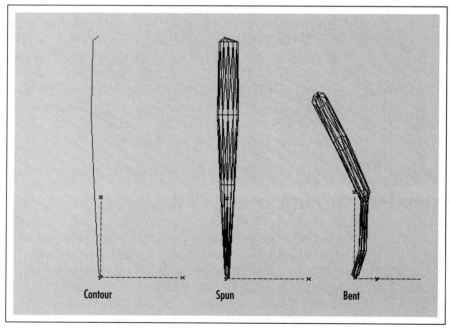

Contour Spun Bent

Figure 6-38 The bee's antenna as an outline, spun on its axes, and bent

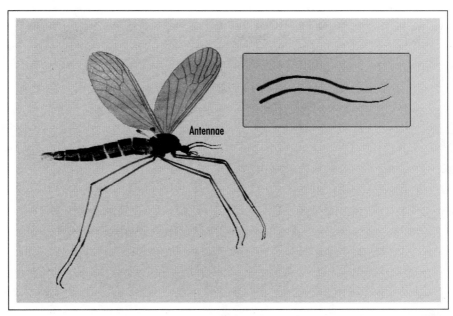

Figure 6-39 The gnat's antennae are curvilinear, making them more difficult to model

Figure 6-39 shows a gnat and its antennae. The enlarged antennae are shown on the right.

You can model the antennae with a hollow outline, just as Alan did with the bee's antennae. However, extruding a hollow circle straight along the Y axis would produce straight antennae that would be difficult to bend into the flowing lines you see in the figure. The solution is to make the hollow outline follow a curved path. This is a good approach for objects like garden hoses or necklaces.

Creating Paths out of Spline Curves

The 2D shape can be forced to follow a path you've drawn on the screen. Most 3D programs give you the ability to create *spline* curves for this purpose. Spline curves use a mathematical model optimized for curves. Figure 6-40 shows a spline curve and its control points.

The control points shown on the figure as small black boxes are what makes manipulation of the curve possible. The user clicks on a black square and interactively "rocks" the curve into another shape.

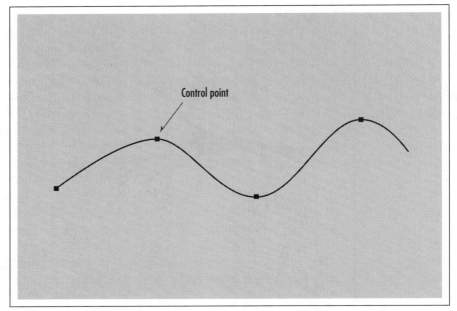

Control point

Figure 6-40 Spline path with its control points

In the version of Imagine bundled with this book, spline paths can be created in the Detail Editor. The best way to understand the method is by doing an exercise.

Exercise: Creating the Gnat's Antenna

In this exercise, you'll create a curved antenna using Imagine's spline curve functions.

In Imagine you create spline paths out of axes. Figure 6-41 shows a spline path created by connecting axes. Notice the location of axes along the curve of the path. The axes act as control points for the areas of the path immediately around them. Moving or rotating the axes causes the curve to change shape.

Creating the Spline Path for the Antenna

Figure 6-42 shows the path you'll create for the antenna. Notice the axes along the path. Here are the steps we'll take:

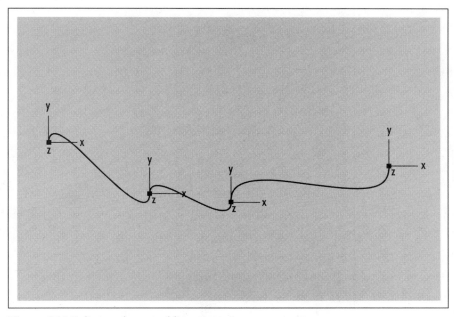

Figure 6-41 Spline path created by connecting axes

⊕ Use the Function menu's Add Axis command to lay down a series of axes.

⊕ Adjust the placement of the axes and rotate and scale them.

⊕ Using the Multi-mode (SHIFT) key, choose the axes in the order and the direction in which you want the path to follow.

⊕ Choose the Make Path command in the Object menu for open paths or the Make Closed Path command for closed paths.

Remember that extrusions are always carried out along the Y axis of an object (or path). For this reason, creating the path in the Top view is best, since the hollow cylinder extrudes toward the back of the 3D world.

1 Switch to the Top view and make it full screen. From the Functions Add submenu, choose Axis. A brown axis is added to the center of the world.

Now copy and paste the four axes making up the path.

2 Press (F1) to pick the axis. Press (ALT)-(C) or choose Copy from the Object menu to copy it to the clipboard.

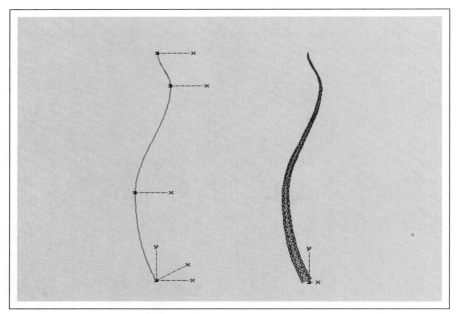

Figure 6-42 The gnat's antenna created by extruding a disk along a curved path

3 Press Ⓜ to place Imagine in move mode. Move the axis to the bottom of the antenna (see Figure 6-42).

Now let's add another axis.

4 Press ⒜⒧⒯-Ⓟ. The pasted axis appears at the center of the screen.

5 Press Ⓕ①️ to pick the new axis. Press Ⓜ and move it to the location of the second axis as seen in Figure 6-42. (Roughly place it. You can adjust it later.) Repeat steps 4 and 5 until the third and fourth axes are added to the screen.

Now we'll create a path using these four axes.

6 Press down on the ⓈⒽⒾⒻⓉ key. Beginning with the bottom axis, click on each of the axes in turn while holding down the ⓈⒽⒾⒻⓉ key. All four axes turn blue.

The order of selection is important because the first axis you select becomes the starting point for the path, and the other axes follow in order. Now create the path. The Object menu contains the Path commands. You can make an

Tip: Using Sort to Line Up Axes

In most cases, picking the axes in order in Multi-mode works. However, Impulse recommends that as a housekeeping chore, after you have picked the series of axes in order, use the Sort command to make sure they fall in order.

open or closed path. If you chose Closed Path the last axis would be connected to the first axis. Let's make an open path.

7   From the Object menu, select Make Path. Three axes disappear, and a blue line appears in their place.

Editing the Path

The path is close to the shape that we want, but not close enough. Imagine provides an Edit Path mode.

8   Click on Edit Path in the Mode menu. The axes of the path reappear.

You can move or rotate path axes. Moving them or rotating them in more than one view creates curves that twist in all directions. We'll keep it simple. We'll modify the shape of the path in the Top view using the axes. To move an axis, click on it and then press the move (M) key. The axis will now move independently of the object. To rotate an axis, click on it and press (R). Pressing (SPACEBAR) makes the change.

9   Move and rotate the axes until the curve approximates the gnat's antenna. Exit from Edit Path mode by clicking on Pick Objects in the Mode menu.

Creating the Cylinder for the Antenna's Radius

If we were creating an antenna with lots of detail in its surface geometry, we might elect to draw our own shape from scratch. Instead we'll keep it simple and work from a 3D primitive.

10   Press (F5). Click on Disk. Enter a value of 5 for the radius of the disk and 6 for the number of sections.

Entering a low value for the number of sections keeps the antenna simple, a memory conservation technique. Now we'll move the axes to the beginning of the path. This step is not necessary in most cases, because Imagine automatically extrudes the object at the beginning of the path.

11 Press (F1) to pick the disk. Press (M) to move it. Move it until its axis coincides with that of the path. Press (SPACEBAR) to confirm.

Now turn the disk into a hollow disk by deleting the point at its center (see Figure 6-43).

12 Switch to the Front view and zoom in (click on the ZI button) until the circle displays large. Enter Pick Points mode, click on the point at the center of the disk, and delete it. A hollow shape is created.

Because you specified only six sections for the circle, it has a six-sided polygon shape. This is fine for the detail we are working with. Now let's extrude the shape.

13 Change to object mode. Switch back to the Top view.

Since we'll be extruding the disk along the path we built, we need to first determine what name Imagine gave to the path when we built it.

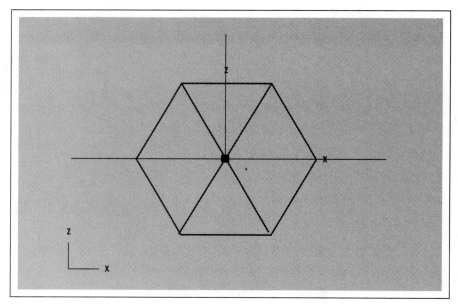

Figure 6-43 The disk in the Front view, lined up with the path

14 Press (ALT)-(F) or choose Find Requester on the Pick/Select menu.

You should see the path listed as AXIS.1. Make a note of that. Now we'll extrude.

15 Make sure the disk is still picked. Choose Mold from the Object menu or press (ALT)-(E). Click on Extrude in the Method box.

The Extrude Data box is shown, as in Figure 6-44. Set the parameters according to the values you see in Figure 6-44.

16 Click on Along Path to make the disk follow the path. Enter AXIS.1 in the Path box to tell Imagine what path to follow. Create the path with 50 sections. (Fewer sections create a crude path.)

At this point, if you clicked on Perform, you would create a garden hose shape. The cylinder would have the same size all along the length of the hose. We want the antenna to grow smaller as it progresses to the end of the path. To do that, use the transformation controls at the bottom of the Extrude Data box. Scale the disk in its X and Z directions. You can't scale it in the Y direction because the path is by default the antenna's Y length.

17 Enter .1 in both the X and Z Scaling boxes.

The disk will shrink to one-tenth of its size by the time it reaches the end of the path.

To force the disk to follow the path (like a car following a hilly road), we have one more option to choose.

18 Click on the Align Y to Path button.

Now we're ready to create the antenna.

19 Click on Perform.

An antenna is created, thick at one end and thin at the other.

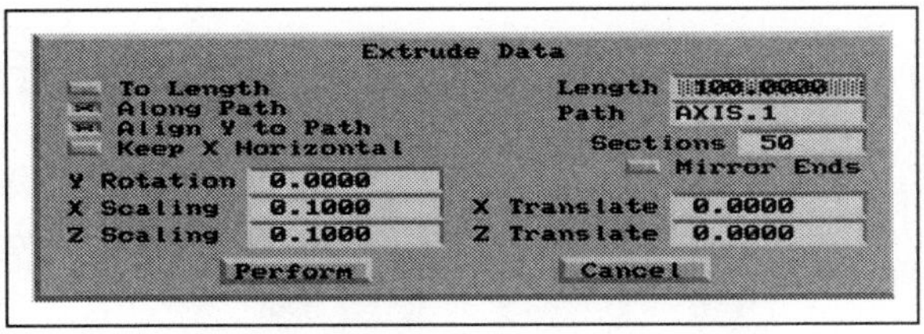

Figure 6-44 Determining the extrusion's shape in the Extrude Data box

Imagine's Alternate Path Method

Imagine offers a second method of constructing paths. The Add Open Path and Add Closed Path commands add small paths to the workspace that can then be edited using the Edit Path mode. The steps are

- Change to object mode.

- Choose Add Open Path or Add Closed Path from the Functions menu.

- Choose Edit Path to change the shape.

- Optionally use the Fracture command to create more control points for the path.

- Choose object mode to use the path.

Extrusion: A Summary

The objects we created, a martini glass and an antenna, both began as 2D outlines. These outlines were then projected through 3D space. They were either projected along the Y axis or spun around the Z axis. In each case, a surface of polygons was created.

You have sophisticated control over the shape of the 3D object. The Move and Scale transformation commands allow you to alter the size and direction of the 2D shape as it sweeps through the world coordinate system, creating the polygonal mesh of the model. Giving the 2D shape a path to follow allows you to add a second level of complexity to the curves in the object.

What's Ahead

The next section introduces another technique that allows you to generate 3D objects out of 2D outlines. However, the process of skinning is quite different from extrusion.

Adding Detail to the Surface Through Skinning

Skinning stretches a skin of faces over outline shapes. Figure 6-45 shows how a lamp shade is created out of four hollow disks using skinning. Here is how the lamp shade was created:

- The first disk was prepared by loading a disk primitive and then deleting the point at the center of the disk.

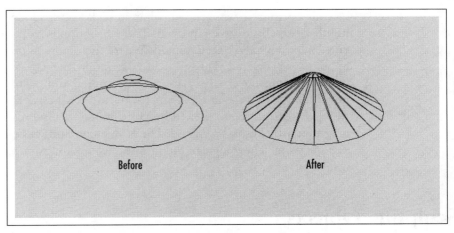

Figure 6-45 Skinning adds a "skin" of faces to 2D outline shapes

- ◉ The disk was copied, pasted, moved, and scaled three times.

- ◉ The four disks were picked in Multi-mode.

- ◉ The Skin command was executed.

The hollow disks are stacked on top of each other. By varying their size and location, you can create a shade with a less symmetrical shape.

Skinning an object works in a similar manner to key slicing, used in Imagine's Forms Editor, to create organic shapes with long, flowing curves. The shape is drawn over 2D shapes or slices. Because the shape of the surface is interpolated from one 2D shape to another, each shape or slice must have the same number of vertices.

The easiest way to ensure that all slices have the same number of vertices is to begin with a master shape, either drawn on the screen or created from a primitive. The master shape is copied into the clipboard and repeatedly pasted down. Then each slice can be sized or edited, so long as the number of vertices is not altered. Use the transformation commands to move, rotate, or scale the objects. You can also alter the shapes of individual slices in Drag Points editing mode.

Suggested Exercise

Create an airplane wing using skinning as a modeling technique. Figure 6-46 shows how an airplane cross section was created.

A disk primitive was loaded. Then in Pick Points mode, the points at the middle of the disk were removed. These become the top and bottom of the wing. The two halves are reunited. Where the points of the two halves overlap, one set is deleted. Then in Add Edge mode, the gap is closed again. This created the master cross section. It was copied and pasted. Each copy was moved and scaled using the Transformation Requester for precision. Then the cross sections were picked in Multi-mode, beginning at the part of the wing that attaches to the plane. The Skin command was executed. This created the wing. The wing can then be duplicated and rotated to the other side of the plane.

Sculpting Objects

So far, we've created 3D objects either by building them out of polygons (the bee's wing) or by projecting a 2D shape into 3D space. Modeling techniques that use extrusion or skinning depend on the user's ability to previsualize the shape that will be created. A spiraling staircase, for example, requires some planning and calculation on the user's part, perhaps even a sketch, before the parameters are set for the extrusion.

3D programs include model building tools that are a bit more intuitive than extrusions for most people. These are program functions that "sculpt" existing objects. Instead of projecting an object in space, you add, subtract, or multiply 3D shapes. Figure 6-47 shows the effect of Imagine's slice tool.

The sphere is sliced in two by the plane. The two primitives create four more that can be used for model building: two bowl shapes, a disk shape, and a matching plane with a hole in it. These parts can be used in a variety of models.

Some of the construction tools that help you sculpt objects include

- **Boolean operations:** Use these tools for combining and subtracting objects to form new objects.

- **Splitting objects:** Use these tools for splitting parts of objects to form new objects.

- **Joining objects:** Use these tools for fusing objects into one object.

- **Magnetism:** Use this tool for creating a new shape by creating regular or irregular bulges of the surface of an object.

- **Fracture:** Use this for adding complexity to the surfaces of objects.

The following sections review each of these in turn.

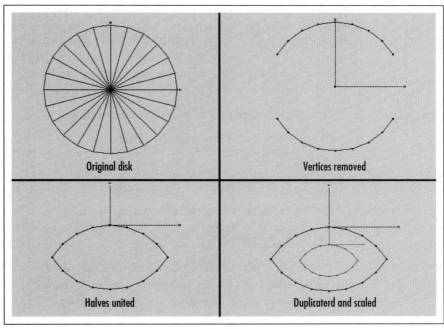

Original disk

Vertices removed

Halves united

Duplicaterd and scaled

Figure 6-46 The airplane's cross section is created by chopping the middle out of a disk

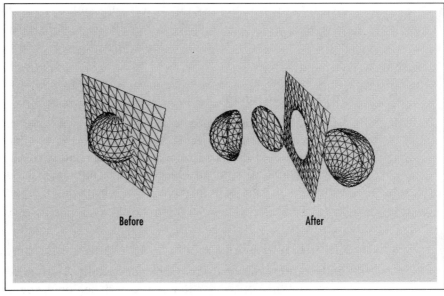

Before

After

Figure 6-47 Slicing a plane with a sphere creates a basket full of model building blocks

Boolean Operations: Creating New Objects with Slice

Boolean is a special type of math. The math is used to create the surfaces that result when one object is made to intersect another. The process is calculation-intensive, so if the two surfaces intersect in a lot of places in complex ways, slicing can often take a lot of time to perform. To slice two objects in Imagine:

- Create two objects or load two primitives.
- Bisect one object with the other.
- Pick them in Multi-mode.
- Select Slice from the Object menu.
- Pick the newly formed objects.
- Execute the Merge command.

Often slice leaves isolated edges around the areas where intersection occurred. Imagine's Merge command is a housekeeping command like Sort. It deletes extraneous faces formed when two objects are sliced. Select all the sliced objects and execute the Merge.

Error Messages

Sometimes when you slice one object with another, Imagine complains that some faces are too close together. Moving one object relative to the other usually fixes the problem. In creating the example image for Figure 6-47, the sphere had to be moved back slightly in 3D space.

Splitting Objects

An object by definition has only one axis. It's possible to subdivide an object into two objects. When an object is divided in two, the new object is given its own axis. Figure 6-48 shows a face on a disk before and after the Split command.

In Imagine, to split an object, change into faces mode and use a pick method to pick a face or group of faces. Then select the Split command in the Functions menu.

Joining Objects

Join performs the opposite operation as split. Two objects are joined (see Figure 6-49). Notice that the new object has only one axis. The example demonstrates that objects do not have to be physically joined. To join objects,

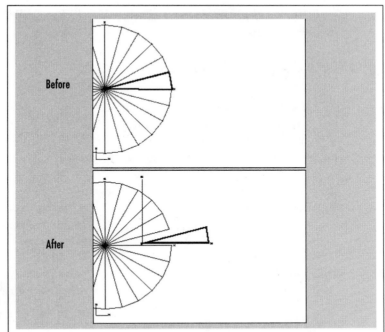

Figure 6-48
Split creates
two objects

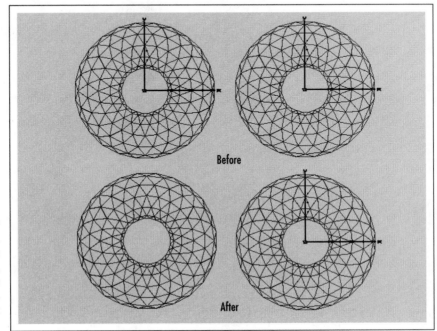

Figure 6-49
Even though
the two objects
are separated,
giving them one
axis creates a
single object

pick them in Multi-mode and execute the Join command found in the Functions menu.

Modeling Complex Surfaces

The honeybee in Color Plate 5 has very lifelike detail on the surface of its body. On the top of the bee's head, you can see a fine mesh of hairs, looking like a military brush cut! The head itself has a lumpy, uneven surface. Also, the head has a relatively simple shape. Figure 6-50 shows the bee's head stripped of its surface.

Most of the "apparent" detail in the image is applied using surface shading and modeling techniques such as image-mapping and procedural texturing. For example, the bee's hair is applied using a filter map (or *opacity* map as it is sometimes called). Alan drew tiny hair patterns in a paint program on a white background. Then he wrapped the map around a slightly enlarged version of the head. Because the white areas of the map are rendered transparent, the little black hair lines appear to float above the surface of the bee's body.

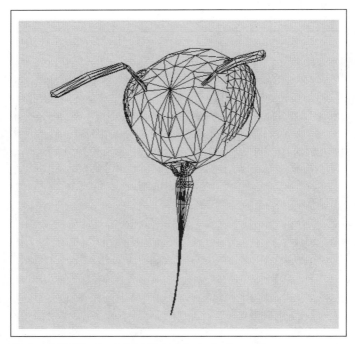

Figure 6-50 The bee's head has relatively few polygons

Image maps, textures, and shading work well as a modeling technique for minute detail on a surface, seen from a distance. But when the viewpoint is close to the surface, or the basic shape can best be described as "lumpy," a different approach is required.

Strategy for Modeling Complex Surfaces

Earlier in the chapter, we looked at the entire bee as a modeling project and used a "divide and conquer" approach: Divide the model into its constituent parts and conquer each part as a unique modeling project. Figure 6-51 shows the bee's head divided into modeling projects.

Separated into its parts, the bee's head yields a handful of simpler projects: the eyes, the antennae, the mouth, and the two parts to the tongue. The parts become a small kit that can be assembled with digital glue. The parts are rotated into position and glued together using such commands as Join and Group. The eyes, for example, were created by loading a sphere primitive, squashing it, and removing one side of the sphere. The half-sphere was rotated into position and duplicated on the other side.

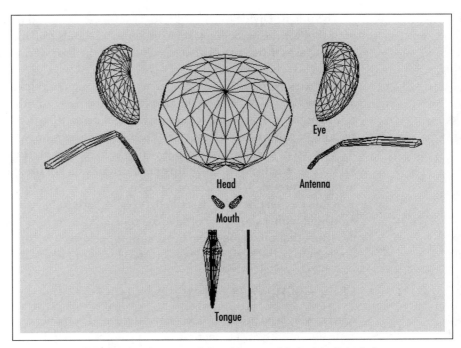

Figure 6-51 The bee's head as a modeling kit assembled with digital glue

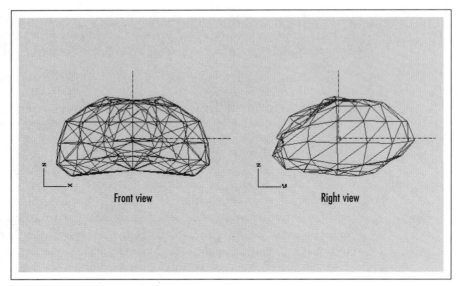

Figure 6-52 The base of the bee's head

The rule is: Divide the model into its simplest parts and then choose the simplest tool for the modeling task. This approach holds true for objects with complex surfaces. Even an unbroken surface, like the base of the bee's head, can be approached this way (see Figure 6-52).

The trick is to see the simple forms underlying the thicket of detail. In creating the bee, Alan Henry saw an extrusion project. Another Imagine modeler might see a Forms Editor project. The Forms Editor is ideally suited for creating organic forms like the bee's head. Another example is the space helmet we created in Chapter 2. Starting with a sphere, and working with the Forms Editor's interactive tools, a lumpy head can be quickly roughed into shape and imported into the Detail Editor for refinement.

Some modelers can be described as conservative. They prefer to do all their modeling with a simple set of favorite tools. Extrusion has been so basic to 3D modeling that many modelers use it almost exclusively for modeling 3D shapes. For example, the bee's head was created by Alan Henry using extrusion.

How the Bee's Head Was Modeled

Alan saw a basic profile in the shape of the real bee's head and decided to generate and modify it. He then turned to surface editing tools to give the surface bumpiness. To create the dent for the mouth, for example, he selected and moved vertices in the mouth area. Figure 6-53 shows the steps in the creation of the head.

An outline shape of the head was created (1), extruded using the Sweep command (2), and rotated into position and surface edited (3). Notice that the side profile (3) shows the polygonal mesh that makes up the head. A vertex is shown in the process of being moved; it's attached to the mouse cursor. This is a vertex in the bee's mouth area that is being moved back to create the cavity for the bee's mouth. This is how most surfaces were "sculpted" in the bee.

Modeling Tools for Bumpy Surfaces: Fracture and Magnetism

Extruding, splitting, joining, and slicing produce objects with smooth 3D surfaces. Two methods of giving surfaces bumps and dents have already been reviewed: with surface modeling tools like image maps and procedural textures, and surface editing tools such as the Drag Points mode in the Detail Editor. All of the methods for developing 2D outlines also apply. For example,

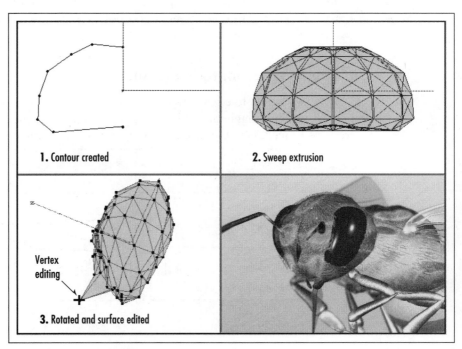

Figure 6-53 Modeling the bee's head by using extrusion and surface editing

you can generate the geometry for landscapes in a program like Vista Pro, which specializes in creating landscapes. Then the geometry can be exported as a DXF (Data Exchange Format) file and imported into many 3D programs.

Special procedural modeling tools are also popular as program add-ons (3D Studio's IPAS routines) or special-effects options in programs like Imagine. For example, Imagine has special effects that create animation effects, such as grow, ripple, explode, or fireworks.

More and more programs include procedures that automate the process of increasing the polygon count in surface areas of models. The following sections discuss two of them implemented in Imagine: Fracture and magnetism.

Using Fracture to Subdivide Polygons into Smaller Units

Fracture is sometimes called *tessellate* by other programs. Fracture divides faces or lines into smaller units. When building outlines for extrusion, the command is useful for adding more vertices to curves. Fracture is also useful for adding detail to the surface of an object (see Figure 6-54).

In the exercise that follows, you'll practice using this command along with magnetism. When importing logos or other objects from other programs, the Fracture command allows you to add polygons to areas of the model that require additional detail.

Using Magnetism to Mold Surfaces

Magnetism works like real magnetism. The command turns the mouse into a magnet with a "magnetic field" that pulls a variable number of points away from a surface. Lines and faces are dragged along with the points. The result is

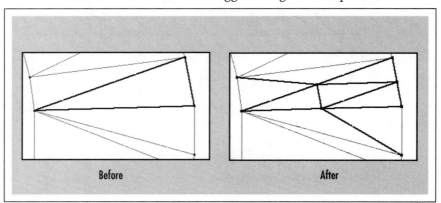

Before   After

Figure 6-54 Fracturing a face

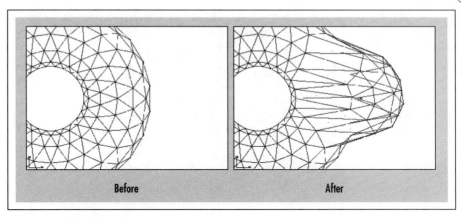

Figure 6-55 Torus before and after magnetism

a bulge in the object (see Figure 6-55).

In animations, you can transform a surface into a bulge by using *morphing*. Morphing is a program function that creates the in-between steps in the transformation of one object into another. In the case of the torus in Figure 6-55, a bump would appear to grow on the surface of the torus. 3D morphing was popularized in the movies *The Terminator* and *The Abyss*.

Magnetism has a number of parameters that make it useful for reshaping surfaces by pulling the vertices into a variety of shapes: a cone, a bell, or a dome. In the next exercise, we'll create a bumpy surface using the Magnetism command.

Exercise: Creating a Mountain Range with Magnetism

In this exercise, we're going to load a primitive plane and use the Magnetism command to create a jagged mountain out of it.

Enter the Detail Editor. If you're already in the Detail Editor, remove all objects from the workspace by selecting Pick All and then Delete ((ALT)-(D)). First we'll create a large, flat surface with lots of polygons.

1 Press (F5) to call the Primitive Types submenu.

2 Click on the Plane button.

This brings up the Plane Parameters box. We'll create a plane with about four times the default polygon density.

3   Enter a value of 200 for the width and height of the plane. Enter a value of 20 for the horizontal and vertical sections that will compose the plane. Click on OK. The surface is created.

Let's bring it a little closer to the point of view.

4   Press the ⑦ key or choose Set Zoom from the Display menu. Enter a value of 1.4 in the Zoom factor box.

Now we're ready to use the Magnetism command. Magnetism is used only in the Drag Points mode of the Detail Editor. Magnetism is toggled on or off.

5   Press ⒡ to pick the plane.

6   Choose Drag Points mode on the Mode menu. The orthogonal views now show the vertices that make up the plane.

The points you now see on the screen can be "magnetically" pulled away from the surface. Magnetism must be turned on before you can use it.

7   In the Mode menu, highlight the Magnetism option. A submenu pops up.

8   Click on the On/Off submenu option to turn Magnetism on. You are returned to the editor.

Notice that the information line at the top of the screen now reads: "Detail Editor: Drag Points, Magnetic". This indicates magnetism and Drag Points mode are active.

Magnetism pulls selected points away from a surface. The shape and size of the bump that is created is specified in the Magnetism Parameters box. The box can be called from the keyboard or from the menu.

9   Choose Magnetism Setup from the Mode menu or press (ALT)-(M). The Magnetism Parameters box pops up (see Figure 6-56).

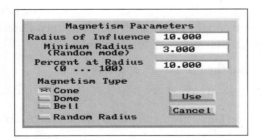

Figure 6-56 Magnetism Parameters box

The following parameters can be set with this box:

- The shape of the magnetic field: Cone, Dome, or Bell.

- The size of the magnetic field: Radius of Influence.

- Percentage of points affected at the outside radius of the magnetic field: Percent at Radius.

- The smoothness of the bulge: Random Radius.

The outer edge of the bulge (the radius) is fairly smooth in the cone, dome, and bell modes. The Random Radius button makes the radius irregular. This creates more natural-looking bumps.

By default the size of the area affected by magnetism is very small. Let's create a dome-shaped bump on the plane. We'll make the dome occupy most of the surface of the plane. The dome will provide us with the basic shape of the mountain.

10 Enter a value of 100 for Radius of Influence. Click on Dome. Click on Use. This creates a dome with a radius of 100 units wide.

Picking a Point in One View and Moving It in Another

When magnetism pulls points away from a surface, it is at right angles to the surface. The orthogonal views do not allow movement at right angles to the view. For example, in the Front view, you can move a point along the Z and X axes, but not the Y axis. There's a way around this limitation. Imagine allows you to select a point in one view and move it in another. The trick is to use Multi-mode. It's important that you keep the (SHIFT) key depressed during the next two steps.

11 Press the (SHIFT) key. Keeping it depressed, click on the point at the center of the plane in the Front view. Release the mouse button but do not release the (SHIFT) key. The vertex at the center of the plane turns red.

12 In the Top view, select a location along the vertical line formed by the Y axis, just above the red dot. Press down on the mouse button and hold it.

13 Let go of the (SHIFT) key. Keep the mouse key depressed while moving the mouse cursor up. The mouse magnetically pulls a dome shape up from the surface.

You're about to create a dome shape roughly like the one you see in Figure 6-57.

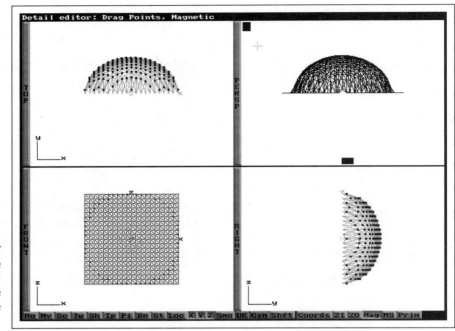

Figure 6-57
The dome shape is "magnetically" pulled out of the flat plane

Change to shaded view mode on the Display menu and move the perspective window slider up to the top of the window. This tips the plane back so that you can see the dome shape in perspective.

We've created a pretty smooth dome. Let's rough it up.

14　Call the Magnetic Parameters box. Change the shape to Bell. Change the radius of influence to 30. Click on Use.

15　In the Front view, randomly move the points about on the surface. When finished, the Front view should look something like Figure 6-58.

Switch to full-screen perspective to see the irregular "hill" created by manipulating surface polygons with magnetism, as shown in Figure 6-59. Notice that there is a great deal of polygon density at the top of the dome, but the sides are composed of relatively few long polygons. We can give the sides of the hill more polygons by picking them and fracturing them. First we need to switch into Pick Faces mode.

16　Switch to Pick Faces mode in the Mode menu.

17　From the Mode menu, select Drag Box from the Pick Method submenu.

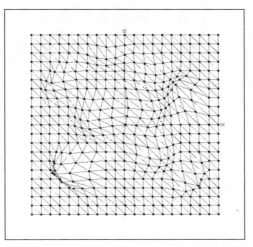

Figure 6-58 Magnetism can give the surface an irregular pattern

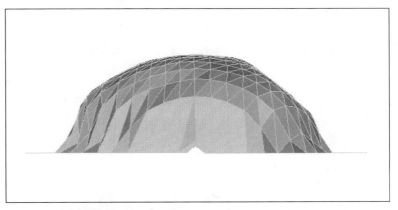

Figure 6-59 The bumpy surface in perspective

18 Press (SHIFT) to enter Multi-mode. While keeping the (SHIFT) key depressed, drag a box around the faces at the base of the hill. The selected faces turn blue, and the selected vertices making up the faces turn pink (see Figure 6-60).

Now we'll fracture the faces.

19 Select Fracture from the Functions menu. The faces are subdivided.

Now we'll switch back to Drag Points mode and massage the dome into a mountain range.

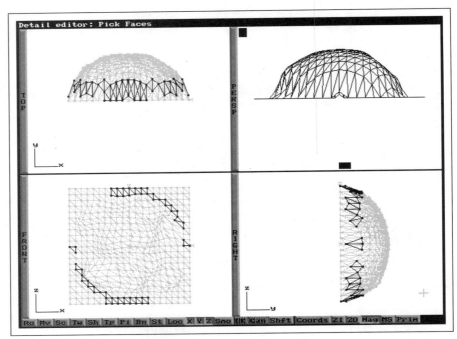

Figure 6-60 Faces selected for fracturing

Figure 6-61 A mountain range is created

20 Switch to Drag Points mode.

You must be in Click mode before Drag Points will work.

21 Select Click from the Mode menu's Pick Method option.

Now, using your mouse, pull points on the surface until you create a mountain range that looks something like Figure 6-61. Magnetism can be used on any kind of surface.

SUMMARY

This chapter has provided a broad overview of modeling strategies and techniques. There is a wide variance in the way modeling techniques are implemented in 3D programs. As your modeling skills improve over time, you will develop your own idiosyncratic methods for modeling scenes.

Now that we have built objects, given them textures and brush maps, and adjusted them for the lighting, it's time to take the pieces of the picture we have been building and put them together in the Stage and Action editors. We'll set up the camera, and make some adjustments to the lighting and the sky. Then we'll press the shutter on the virtual camera. We'll render.

Ready? Let's go.

Staging and Rendering Scenes

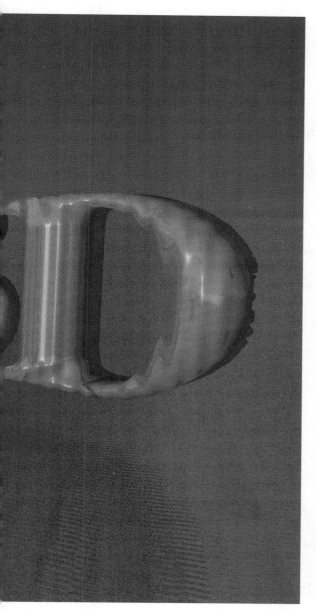

Up until now, we've test rendered low-resolution scenes using the perspective window as the camera view. A light is added to the scene automatically. It sits right in front of the object, perpendicular to it. A flat blue background is automatically added to the scene. The default camera sits at a fixed distance from the scene, and it is fitted with a *normal* lens. In photography lingo, a normal lens on a camera shows the view as the eye would see it.

The scene is also rendered in scanline mode. Such optical effects as shadows and true reflections are not shown until you render using ray-trace mode in the Project Editor.

Quick Render gives us a view of the object as a cheap camera with a built-in flash might record it. This is fine for test rendering the scene, but for the final image, the scene has to be *staged*. Staging a scene means assembling and arranging objects, setting up and adjusting the camera, and lighting the scene. Imagine implements these functions in a separate editor, called the Stage Editor. Other programs may incorporate object creation and staging in a single editor.

Once the scene has been staged, it is ready to be *rendered*. Rendering converts the scene into a 2D still image or animation and saves it to the hard drive. It can then be imported into an external program for further processing. 3D programs provide options for rendering. You can change the size and color depth of the image or animation to match the output requirements. For example, if you create an image for print, you will probably render the image in a high spatial resolution and 16.7 million colors. This chapter provides an overview of assembling and lighting scenes, setting up cameras, and rendering the final scene to the hard drive.

WORKING WITH 3D EDITING SYSTEMS

A modeling project can be a simple rendered object or a complex animation. The files that you use in the process of creating the image or animation can include image maps, special procedural texture files, staging information (placement of lights and camera), as well as the object files and the 3D program files. Most 3D programs provide some means of organizing the data that is used in the creation of a scene. When you create a project in Imagine, the system automatically creates a special directory structure in the program root directory for storing scene objects and staging information, as well as the rendered images or animations. Figure 7-1 shows the directory structure.

Each new project is given its own project directory, and each project directory includes object and image subdirectories. You can store all the objects in a scene in the object subdirectory. In this book objects are centralized in the OBJECTS directory.

You cannot enter the Stage or Action editors to assemble a scene without first opening a project.

Imagine's Editing System

So far, you have not had to enter other editors to complete exercises. In this chapter, we'll be working with Imagine's entire editing system in creating a scene. This section provides you with a road map through the system.

The process of creating and modifying scenes is called editing. Most 3D programs divide editing functions (object creation, staging, and rendering) into three or more modules. Figure 7-2 shows the organization of Imagine's editing system.

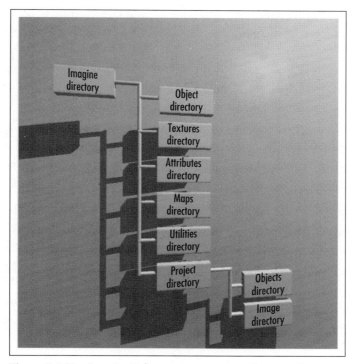

Figure 7-1 Use Imagine's directory structure to keep projects organized

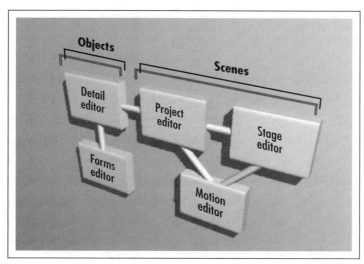

Figure 7-2 Imagine's editing system is organized into five modules

Objects are created in the Forms and Detail editors. Scenes are created and rendered in the Project, Stage, and Action editors. Here's the focus of each editor.

- *Forms Editor* uses a unique modeling technique optimized for creating organic 3D objects. Objects are saved and later imported into the Detail Editor for finishing.

- *Detail Editor* uses a variety of modeling techniques for modeling detailed, photorealistic objects. It includes the Attributes Requester, used in applying image maps and procedural textures to objects. Objects are saved for later import into the Stage Editor.

- *Project Editor* sets up a directory and the rendering parameters structure for the images and animations of a project. Final rendering is done here.

- *Stage Editor* assembles a scene; adds lights and camera. Animations are created here. Scene information is saved in a special staging file.

- *Action Editor* is an adjunct to the Stage Editor. Its primary role is as an editor for animations. It is used for setting such scene attributes as ambient light level.

Notice the order and connections between editors in Figure 7-2. During a modeling project, you are likely to jump back and forth between editors as you adjust surfaces and global lighting conditions and perform test renders. The order and connections indicate the most common pathways between editors.

Exercise: Opening a Project

This section shows you how to open a project in the Project Editor, a necessary "clerical" step before entering the Stage Editor to create and render a scene.

Remember that you move from editor to editor from the Project menu at the top left of the screen. You can also access the Project menu at startup, by choosing New from the Project menu. If you are presently in the Detail Editor, save your objects by picking them, grouping them, and saving them in Group Objects mode. Then enter the Project Editor.

1   From the Project Editor's Project menu select New or use the (ALT)-(N) shortcut. A Project Name box pops on the screen (see Figure 7-3).

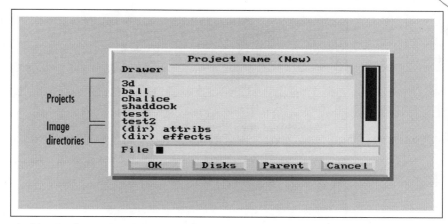

Figure 7-3 The Project Name box

The box provides a window on the Imagine directory, showing project directories and source file directories. Project directories appear simply as names in the Project Name box. If you looked at the directory names using the DOS DIR command, you would see that project directories are actually named with the extension .IMP. For example, the DOS path name for the TEST directory is \IMAG\TEST.IMP.

Naming the Project

When you name a new project, you automatically create a dedicated directory structure for project objects, scene, and image files.

2   Enter the word **BALL** in the File entry box and press (ENTER). You can use upper- or lowercase spelling.

When you press (ENTER), the screen changes to the Rendering Subproject screen shown in Figure 7-4. A brief review of this screen is included here. More detailed instructions for using its options are provided in the section near the end of the chapter, "The Rendering Subproject Screen." When you create a new project, you must create an associated subproject. The relationship between projects and subprojects is analogous to the relationship between filing cabinet drawers and file folders (see Figure 7-5).

Think of the drawer as a project directory and the file folders as image directories. As in a real filing cabinet, this drawer can have many folders in it. Let's open a "file folder" for the BALL project.

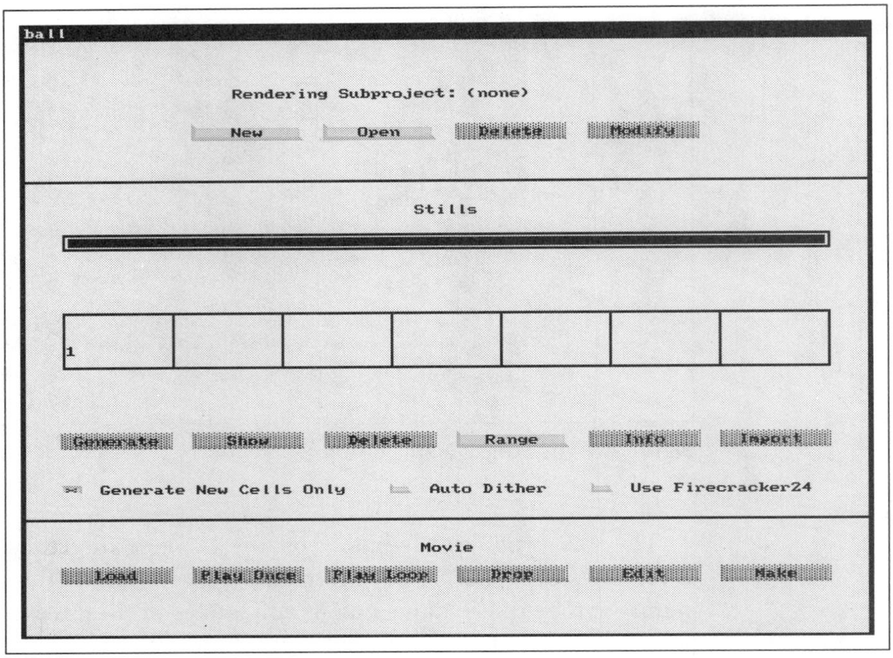

ball

Rendering Subproject: (none)

New   Open   Delete   Modify

Stills

1

Generate   Show   Delete   Range   Info   Import

☒ Generate New Cells Only   ☐ Auto Dither   ☐ Use Firecracker24

Movie

Load   Play Once   Play Loop   Drop   Edit   Make

Figure 7-4 Rendering Subproject screen

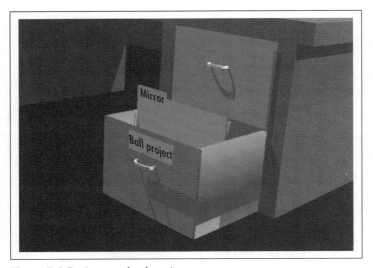

Figure 7-5 Projects and subprojects

3 Click on the yellow New button. A new box pops on the screen (see Figure 7-6).

This box allows you to name the project.

4 Type MIRROR in the File entry box and press ⟨ENTER⟩.

Imagine creates a subdirectory for the rendered image. Then a Rendering Subproject box pops on the screen (see Figure 7-7). This box allows you to specify the type of image that will be rendered to the hard drive. It will be discussed in more detail at the end of this chapter. For now, we're going to leave the values at their defaults.

5 Click on OK to remove the Rendering Subproject box from the screen.

You are returned to the Rendering Subproject screen. Notice that the previously grayed out options are now active.

Figure 7-6 Rendering Project Name box

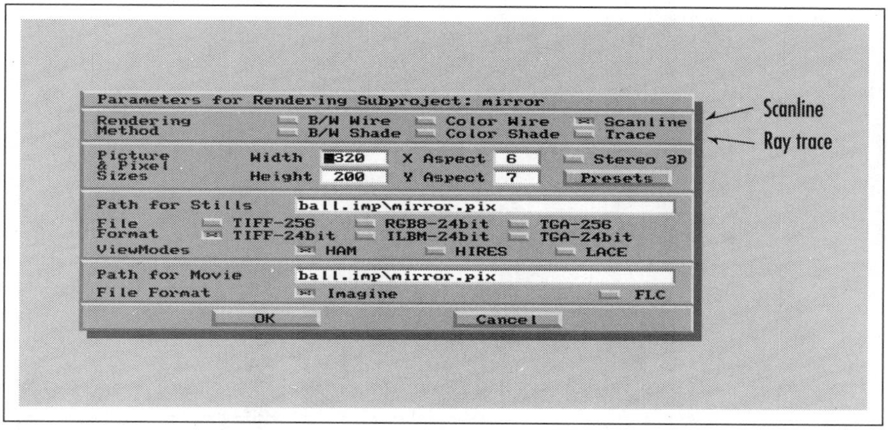

Figure 7-7 Rendering Subproject parameters box

What's Ahead

In this section you've learned how to open a project and a subproject in anticipation of rendering a scene. We can now enter the Stage Editor to assemble a new scene from objects created in the Forms and Detail editors.

EXERCISE: STAGING A SCENE

With a project opened, you're ready to enter the Stage Editor to create the scene. In this exercise you'll load objects into the Stage Editor and stage them.

1 Choose Stage Editor from the Editor menu.

Your screen will look like Figure 7-8. The screen looks similar to the Detail Editor screen. However, in this editor the commands and controls are oriented to creating scenes rather than creating objects and adding surfaces to them. Many of the menu choices are specific to animations. The focus is on modeling scenes, so animation functions will be mentioned in passing but not reviewed.

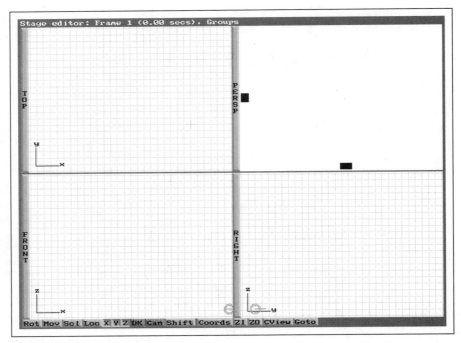

Figure 7-8 The Stage Editor

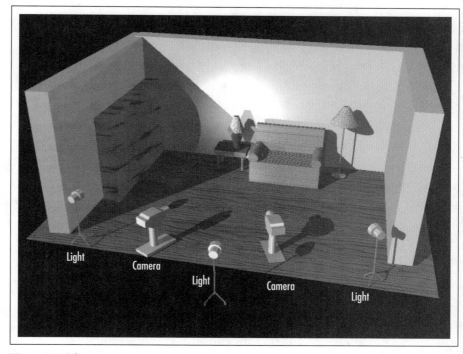

Figure 7-9 The set

How Scenes Are Created

You load objects into the Stage Editor and arrange them. Then lights and camera are added to the scene. Think of the Stage Editor as the stage in a theater or a Hollywood movie set (see Figure 7-9).

To create a scene in a movie, the crew brings the objects created in the scenery shop to the stage and arranges them. A trio of objects for the exercises in this chapter has been created: a mirror ball, a 3D logo, and a ground object. They are grouped and saved in a file called MIRROR.OBJ. They can be found in the \IMAG\OBJECTS directory.

2   Press (ALT)-(L). The Object Filename load box appears. Load the file MIRROR.OBJ from the \IMAG\OBJECTS directory.

3   Zoom out by clicking twice on the ZO (Zoom Out) button at the bottom of your screen.

Your screen should look similar to Figure 7-10.

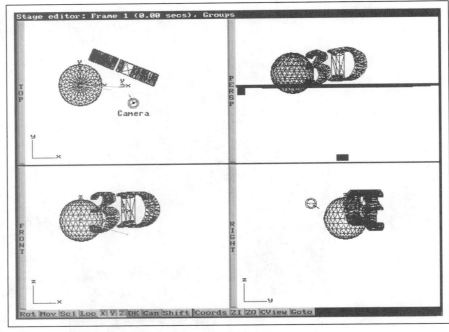

Figure 7-10 MIRROR.OBJ loaded into the Stage Editor

The Default Camera View

When you first enter the Stage Editor, there is a camera already placed in the scene. The camera appears as a symbol in the orthogonal views. (You can see it in the Top and Right views of Figure 7-10.) Its symbol is a double circle with a dot and a line signifying the orientation of the camera. By default, it points at the center of the 3D world—a small distance away—33 degrees up and to the right.

Changing to the Camera Viewpoint

When MIRROR.OBJ is loaded into the scene, Imagine shows the objects from the same point of view as seen in the Detail Editor. Like a real camera, you can move Imagine's camera around in a scene and even change its lens from normal to wide or telephoto. Let's change to camera view.

4   Select the Display menu. Select Camera View.

The perspective view at the top right of the screen changes to the camera view. Your screen should now look like Figure 7-11. The perspective window now shows the camera view. Because the camera by default is close to the center of the world, and pointing down at it, all we see of the mirror ball scene is the plane. The sphere and 3D logo are out of camera range. The camera must be moved to a position where the entire scene is visible.

Changing the Camera View

Imagine's camera can be moved about the scene freely because the camera is an Imagine object. It's a special object because it has no surface, so it cannot be rendered or made to appear in a reflection. Like other Imagine objects though, it has an axis. The same kinds of transformations permissible on other objects (move, scale, rotate) can be performed on the camera object. We'll use Imagine's transformation commands to adjust the camera manually.

5   Click on the ZO button twice to zoom out on the scene.

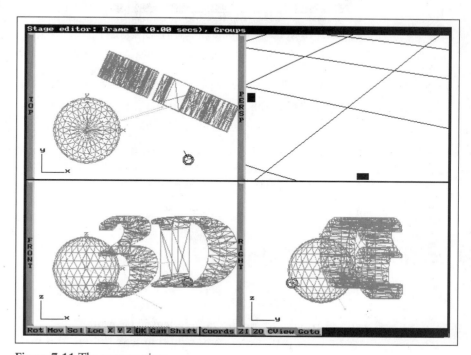

Figure 7-11 The camera view

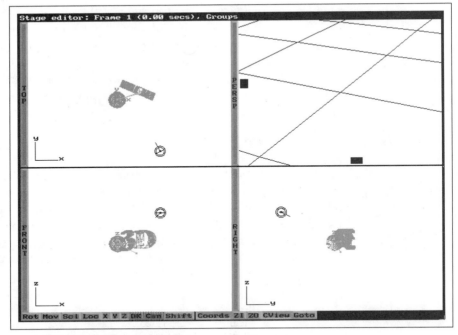

Figure 7-12 The new camera positions

You can pick the camera in the same ways as other Imagine objects.

6   Click on the camera object to pick it. The other objects turn brown and the camera turns blue.

7   Press the ⓜ (move) key. Drag the camera in the Top view and Right view until it's in the position indicated in Figure 7-12. (Press the (SPACEBAR) to confirm the transformation.)

In moving the camera back, the camera view now shows the entire scene.

Creating a Camera Target

Moving the camera this way is not very easy because the camera view does not update until you have moved the camera to its final position. It's also difficult to see exactly where the camera lens is pointing.

Imagine provides a command that gets around this problem. The method is to keep the camera locked to a target area of the scene as you move it. In this manner, no matter where you move the camera, it always points at the target area. The command is called Camera Re-Track.

Aligning the Camera Using the Re-Track Command

You can select Re-Track from the Object menu or press the (ALT)-(K) key alternative. When you call the command, a box pops on the screen (see Figure 7-13).

The Re-Track command aligns the camera to the object you name in this box. (To see a list of objects in the scene, call the Object List box using the Find Requester hot key combination, (ALT)-(F).)

Creating a Camera Target from a Dummy Axis

The Re-Track command realigns the camera to an object's axes. The object's axes may be too high or too low in the scene for the angle that you want. The solution is to create a dummy camera target that does not render. Imagine provides a perfect dummy: an axis. Remember that an axis does not have a surface, so it won't render. We can use it as a camera target. Let's do that now. First we'll add an axis to the scene.

1.   From the Add submenu on the Object menu, select Axis. An axis is added at the center of the 3D world.

If you call up the Object List by using the (ALT)-(F) hot key combination, you will see that Imagine named the axis "TRACK" when it created it. Let's move the new TRACK object into position.

We want to have the camera point at the middle of the scene. Right now the target sits below the scene. We'll move it so that it is centered in the scene.

2.   Press (F1) to pick the new target object. Press (M) and move it to the center of the three objects.

Now we'll retrack the camera to the TRACK dummy axis.

3.   Press (ALT)-(K) to bring up the Track Object box. Enter the name TRACK in the box. The camera realigns to the TRACK object.

Figure 7-13 Track Object box

Your screen should now look roughly like Figure 7-14. If your view does not match the figure, repeat steps 2 and 3. Move the track object and retrack until the camera view is close to that of Figure 7-14.

Automating Camera Re-Track

Having to type the name of the camera target object every time you change the camera position can be tiresome. Imagine provides a way of automating this process. In the Action Editor, you can force the camera to always track to the TRACK object. Let's do that now.

4   Save the scene by using the (ALT)-(S) hot key combination or choosing Save Changes on the Project menu.

5   Click on Action Editor in the Project menu.

The Action Editor screen, shown in Figure 7-15, is quite different from previous screens, so let's pause here and describe its layout and controls.

THE ACTION EDITOR SCREEN

The Action Editor is an extension of the Stage Editor. For example, aligning the camera to an object must be performed here. Controls for changing the style of lights and adding global effects like fog are found here.

The Viewing System

In the Action Editor, the focus is on what happens to objects over time, not the geometry of objects. For this reason, the objects are not shown onscreen. When you edit objects or scenes in the other editors, you edit concrete entities: polygons, objects, and groups of objects, as well as their surface attributes. In the Action Editor, the edit is made on something more abstract, the actions of objects over time.

Animation and the Screen Layout

The animation capabilities of the Action Editor are not covered in detail. However, it is necessary to explain the editor from the point of view of animation because global controls for scenes use the Action Editor's layout and

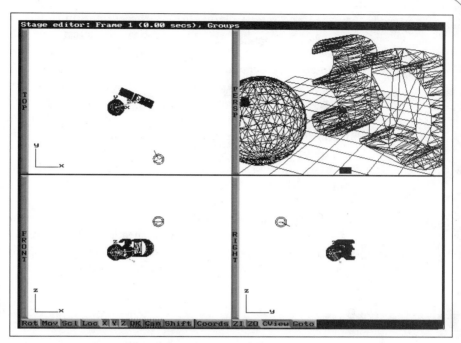

Figure 7-14
The new
camera view

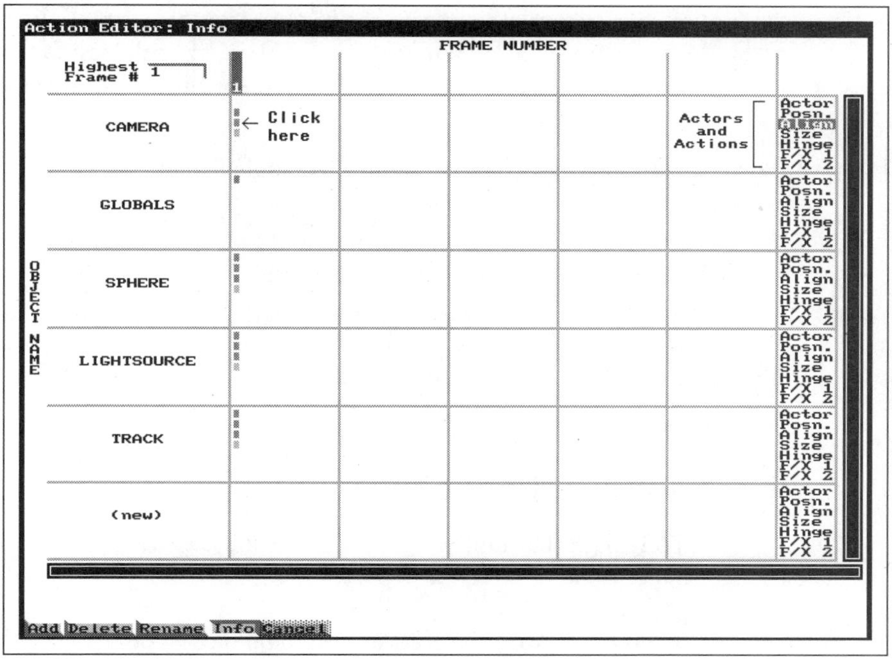

Figure 7-15
The Action
Editor

system. The screen layout breaks the animation down to frames and lays them as a grid of boxes. Each grid box stores ten animation frames. On the left of these grid boxes is a list of objects in the scene. On the right is a list of parameters associated with these objects. The colored rectangles beside the object name are called *actors*. Actors act as buttons that call up program functions and parameter boxes. They are associated with the objects in the scene. You can add or subtract actors using the Delete and Add buttons at the bottom of the screen. The Info button allows you to change the parameters of an existing actor.

When you first enter the Action Editor, there is only one frame set up for editing. You can create additional frames for an animation by changing the value in the Highest Frame # box at the top left of the Action Editor screen. Right now the mirror scene animation has only one frame in it so the Highest Frame # is 1. Notice that frame "1" heads up the column of colored dots. As you move your mouse over these rectangles, the corresponding parameter at the right of the screen lights up. The parameters describe what each actor does.

Editing Modes

The colored rectangles to the right of an object name act as on and off switches. For example, to release the camera from its current alignment, click on the Delete button and then click on the blue rectangle beside the CAMERA object name. This deletes the current alignment of the camera. Here are the Action Editor editing modes:

- *Add* creates a colored rectangle for an object.
- *Delete* removes a colored rectangle from an object.
- *Rename* allows you to change an object's name.
- *Info* allows you to change action or actor parameters.

The easiest way to switch from one mode to another is to click on the buttons at the bottom left of the screen.

Action Editing Step-by-Step

To realign the camera to the TRACK object, we will take the following steps:

- Click on the Delete button.
- Click on the colored rectangle (actor) beside the object to delete it.

- Click on the Add button.

- Replace the actor with a new one.

- Click on the Info button to change to information mode.

- Click on the new rectangle to bring up a parameters box.

- Change the parameters and exit from the parameters box.

- Save the changes.

Let's practice the editing steps. We'll align the camera to the TRACK dummy axis. Notice that both the CAMERA and TRACK objects are listed in the Object Name column. Let's first delete the camera's current alignment.

1   Click on the Delete button at the bottom left of the screen. Then click on the blue rectangle beside the CAMERA object. This deletes the current alignment.

2   Click on the Add button at the bottom of the screen. Now click *twice* in the space vacated by the previous deletion to add a new blue rectangle to the CAMERA object.

Figure 7-15 shows where to click on the screen. When you click twice, a box pops on the screen (see Figure 7-16). The first two options on the box are for animations. Choose the third option.

3   Click on Track to Object.

A new box pops on the screen (see Figure 7-17). The box provides options for tracking an object during an animation. We need only enter a name for the object we want to track.

4   Enter the word TRACK in the Object Name box (as shown in Figure 7-17). Click on OK. You are returned to the Action Editor.

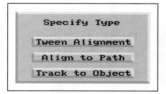

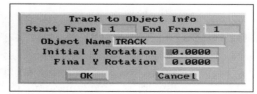

Figure 7-16 Specify Type box   **Figure 7-17** The Track to Object Info box

5   Save the changes by choosing Save Changes in the Project menu.

6   Enter the Stage Editor.

Now when you return to the Stage Editor, and you have camera view turned on, the camera view is aligned to the new target axis, TRACK.

Move the camera and then use the (ALT)-(K) Camera Re-Track command. The camera view is updated automatically by the hot key combination. This is a very efficient way to move the camera around in a scene.

What's Ahead

You can now move the camera about the scene by moving the camera or its target. In the movie world, moving the camera around a scene is often called *dollying* because the camera is set up on a platform with wheels. In the next section you'll see how to show a closer or wider view of the scene by simulating the lens on a camera.

SIMULATING A CAMERA LENS IN 3D SOFTWARE

If you have ever used a 35mm still camera or a video camera with an adjustable lens, you will readily understand the effect of changing the focal length of cameras in 3D programs. As you change the length of the digital lens, you see more or less of the scene through the camera view. The focal length of still and movie cameras is measured in millimeters. The focal length that matches the view seen by the naked eye is roughly 50mm. Figure 7-18 shows how focal length affects the view of an image seen through the view finder of a 35mm camera.

The camera on the left is adjusted so that the view of the object matches that of the naked eye (50mm). The view on the right shows the same object viewed with the lens "shortened" to 28mm. As you can see in the view of the object at the bottom right, the object is distorted. It is stretched sideways, and the surrounding scene is included in the picture. The 28mm lens is called a wide-angle lens.

Changing the Camera's Focal Length

The virtual camera in 3D programs allows you to simulate optic effects digitally. In Imagine, you simulate the effect of shortening or lengthening the lens by changing the length of the camera object's Y axis.

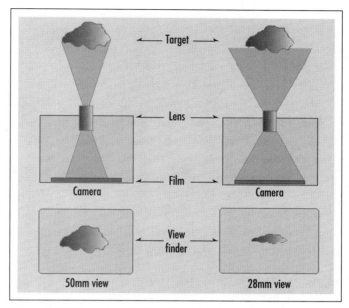

Figure 7-18 Changing the focal length of a lens

Tip: Further Reading

Showing wide-angle views of scenes has practical application in 3D architectural applications. It is also a well-documented technique in fine art photography. Appendix B recommends texts covering the technology and aesthetics of camera optics.

Imagine's camera lens points along the Y axis of the camera object. To change the focal length of the lens, change the length of the camera object's Y axis. Figure 7-19 shows a telephoto, normal, and wide-angle view of the mirror scene produced by changing the Y axis length.

Creating Telephoto Views

Doubling the Y axis length narrows the field of view. This is called a *telephoto* shot in photography. Telephoto shots bring objects closer, but perspective is flattened.

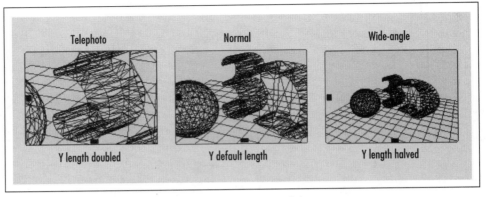

Figure 7-19 Telephoto, normal, and wide-angle view of the scene

Creating Wide-Angle Views

Halving the Y axis produces a wide-angle shot that pushes the object into the background and exaggerates its horizontal width.

Changing the length of the camera's Z axis does nothing since the height of the camera is not factored into lens length changes. You can change the length of the X axis, but there's no purpose in doing so. The length of the lens is a ratio of the size of the X and Y axes, so doubling the X and Y axes at the same time does nothing. Change the camera focal length by changing the length of its Y axis.

What's Ahead

In the next section we'll practice by creating a wide-angle view of the mirror ball scene.

Exercise: Creating a Wide-Angle View of the Scene

Let's change the view of the current scene to a wide-angle view. If you do not have MIRROR.OBJ loaded in the Stage Editor and the camera positioned to give you a view of the scene as shown in Figure 7-14, do that now. (Don't forget to change to camera view.) First we're going to select and pick the camera.

1   Find the camera by pressing (ALT)-(F). This pops up the Object List box.

2   Click on CAMERA in the Object List box. This selects the camera.

3   Press (F1). This picks the camera.

The best way to scale the Y axis is to use the Transformation Requester.

4   Press (ALT)-(T). This brings up the Transformation Requester.

The Transform Axes Only button has been grayed out because the camera object cannot be separated from its axes. Now we're going to reduce the length of the Y axis by half to create a wide-angle view of the scene.

5   Click on the Scale button and change the value of the Y data entry box to .500. (Don't forget to press (ENTER) after entering the new value.) Then click on Perform.

The perspective view should now show the scene from a distance. Let's move the camera closer to the scene.

6   Use the (ALT)-(K) Re-Track command to realign the camera with its target. You may have to move and realign the camera several times.

When you are finished, your screen should look roughly like Figure 7-20. The wide-angle view of the scene from a close range distorts the image in a hor-

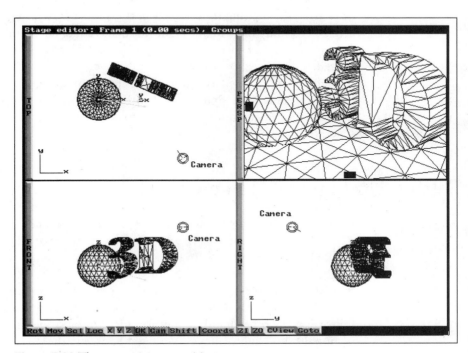

Figure 7-20 The camera's new position

izontal direction. This is the effect we've sought. Let's look at the scene in full-screen shaded perspective.

7   Click on the PERSP button to change to full-screen camera view.

8   Choose Shaded from the Display menu.

Your screen now looks like Figure 7-21. The shaded camera view gives a preview of what the scene will look like in the final render.

What's Ahead

We have now composed the scene. It's time to turn our attention to lighting.

ADDING LIGHTING TO A SCENE

Chapter 3 showed you how to make surfaces alternately shiny, dull, reflective, transparent, or rough. Chapter 5 explored the complex relationship between colored light sources and the colors on surfaces. In this final section on lighting, we step back from the object to the camera's position.

Getting the lighting to look "natural" is most frustrating to beginning 3D artists. Not only does digital light not behave like natural light, but lighting objects is a matter of practice and aesthetics. This section will help get you started.

Lighting is discussed as it is implemented in Imagine, but bear in mind that other programs have similar types of lights. However, the way the lighting model is implemented in the program makes the subject of lighting a bit idiosyncratic.

Setting Up Lights in Imagine

Imagine provides two places where lights are added to a scene: in the Attributes Requester of the Detail Editor or in the Stage Editor's Object menu option, Add Light Source. In the Detail Editor you make any object become a light by clicking on the Light button in the Attributes Requester. You can then alter the light using the transformation buttons or the Transformation Requester. Invisible lights are simply axes with no polygons. In the Stage Editor, on the other hand, a light is added to the scene as a generic omnidirectional "sun" light. Clicking on Light Source in the Add submenu creates a light that is placed at the center of the 3D world. This light is then moved

Figure 7-21 Full-screen shaded camera view

into position. In the Action Editor, the light can be changed to a conical or cylindrical light, and you can make it cast shadows. Like all lights in Imagine, you can change its color in the light parameter box. Some Imagine users create all the lights in the scene in the Detail Editor. Others create most of the lights in the Stage Editor. Deciding which approach to use comes down to personal preference.

Stage Editor Default Lighting

Unlike the Detail Editor, the Stage Editor does not use default lighting. When you first enter the Stage Editor, the world is totally dark. You must add lights to make objects visible.

In order to see a quick render of the scene, you must add a light prepared in the Detail Editor to the scene or use a light added to the scene from the Object menu's Add menu.

What's Ahead

In the next exercise, we'll practice adding a light to a scene in the Stage Editor.

Exercise: Adding a Light Source to the Scene

If you are continuing from the previous exercise, the MIRROR.OBJ group should already be loaded. Otherwise, load the TUTORIAL project and the FAN subproject. Then enter the Stage Editor. Make sure that the MIRROR.OBJ group is loaded and that your camera position and camera view match those of Figure 7-20.

1 Click on Add in the Object menu. A submenu pops on the screen (Figure 7-22).

2 Click on Light Source on the Add submenu. A small brown circle with a yellow dot at its center appears at the middle of the 3D world. This is the light source.

3 Press (F1) to pick the light source and (M) to move it. Move the light source until it is beside the camera.

Your screen should look like Figure 7-23. It's a good idea to place a light near the camera because everything the camera sees will be illuminated. Let's now quick render the scene to see the effect of the light.

4 Quick render the scene.

When finished, the rendered scene should look similar to Figure 7-24. There are a number of observations to make about this scene:

- By default, when a light is added, it a spherical light that radiates in all directions. The light is a white light at an intensity level of 256. It does not cast shadows.

- Quick render uses scanline mode to create the scene, so reflections of objects in other objects cannot be seen, nor will shadows from

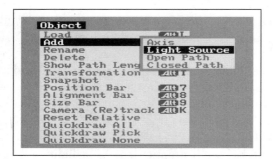

Figure 7-22 The Add submenu

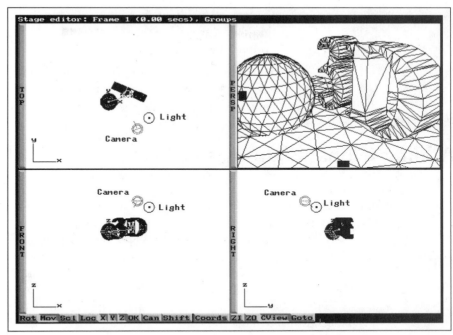

Figure 7-23
The new position for the light source

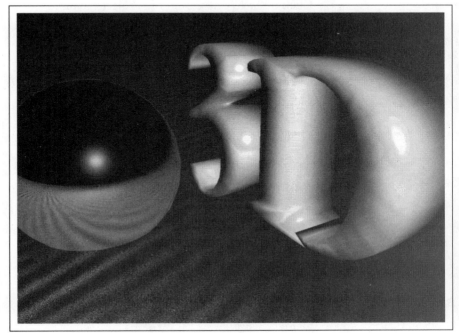

Figure 7-24
The quick rendered scene

shadow-casting lights be visible. However, you can see the reflection of the ground in the sphere. This is a special attribute of the ground object.

⊕ The scene is quite dark and made to look dramatic because it is lit strongly by one light from a high angle. We need to add more lighting to the scene to give it a brighter, more natural look.

Adding Global Lighting to a Scene

In a natural environment, a single source light such as the one we have used would be supplemented by the diffuse light of other light sources. This light is called *ambient* light.

As mentioned earlier, such global lighting effects as ambient light, fog, and global brush maps are added to the scene in the Action Editor. Color Plate 11 shows the same scene after global lighting has been added and the scene ray traced. The changes to the scene's appearance are dramatic.

Let's enter the Action Editor to make the lighting changes. In exiting the Stage Editor save the scene first.

5　Click on Save Changes in the Project menu.

6　Click on Action Editor in the Project menu.

Using the Globals Info Box for Scene Lighting

Global lighting controls are found in the Action Editor's Globals Info box. The box is called by clicking on the small orange rectangle in the column beside the GLOBALS name. Figure 7-25 shows where to click on the screen. When you click on this box, Globals Info pops on the screen (see Figure 7-26).

The Globals Info box ranks with the Attributes Requester and the Transformation Requester in importance in the Imagine workspace. The box allows you to:

⊕ Restrict lighting effects to specified frames in an animation

⊕ Use an image as a backdrop for the scene

⊕ Use an image as a global reflection map

⊕ Set the ambient light levels in the scene

⊕ Create a sky

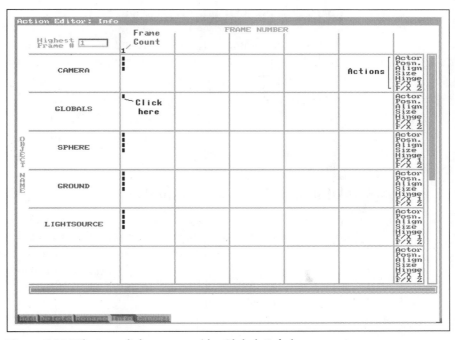

Figure 7-25 Where to click to pop up the Globals Info box

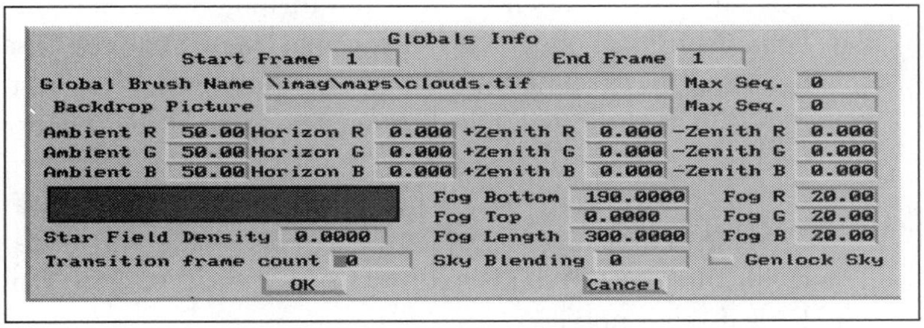

Figure 7-26 Globals Info box parameters

- Create a bank of fog in the scene
- Create a star field for a night sky

Boxes are provided for entering the image's name and the DOS path to the file's location on the hard drive. Remember that Imagine images must be in 24-bit TIFF format. The other options are set by changing values in data entry boxes.

Adding a Global Reflection Map to a Scene

Global reflection maps were discussed in Chapter 3. For the present scene, we'll add a sky with clouds in it to give the objects in the scene a "natural" environment to reflect.

7 In the Global Brush Name entry box on the Globals Info box, type in the path to the CLOUDS.TIF map in the MAPS directory: \IMAG\MAPS\CLOUDS.TIF. Press (ENTER) after typing the path and file name in the box (see Figure 7-26).

Adding a Backdrop to the Scene

Imagine allows you to specify a paint image as a backdrop in a scene. You could, for example, put a scene of mountains in the background. The image size of the backdrop must be the same size as the image size you specify for the scene or animation. It must also be in 24-bit TIFF format. For example, if you were creating a 640 by 480 pixel image, you would use a 640 by 480 24-bit TIFF image as the backdrop.

Changing the Ambient Light Level

The light that filters into the room through the blinds, mixing with interior lighting, gives a room a very diffuse and slightly colored general light level. The light at different times of the day can also have a color cast. Dawn light has a reddish cast. Midday light is blue. The ambient light controls in the Globals Info box allow you to adjust the ambient light levels and color-tint the scene.

The color values work just like all other light data entry systems in Imagine. You can give the light a dominant tone by adjusting the respective levels of the RGB data boxes. The range is 0 to 255, from black to white. Let's do that now.

8 Enter a value of 50 in each of the red, green, and blue Ambient RGB data entry boxes. Use Figure 7-26 as your guide.

Notice that as you change the RGB values, the color swatch just below the Ambient controls changes colors.

Creating a Sky

Imagine's Horizon and Zenith controls allow you to color the sky. When you look at a setting sun, the sky directly over your head (the zenith) is dark blue,

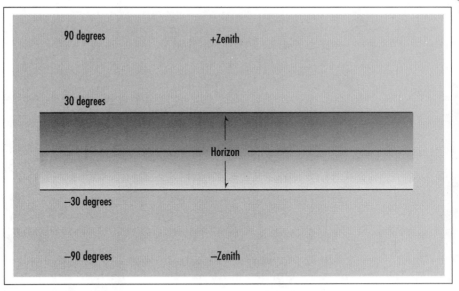

Figure 7-27 Sky color bands

and it changes gradually to reddish blue at the horizon. Near the horizon the change from blue to red is accelerated. Imagine gives you control over these kinds of gradations in the sky.

The sky begins at the horizon and extends *up* 30 degrees and *down* 30 degrees. The positive zenith is at 90 degrees (straight up) and negative zenith is at -90 degrees. Figure 7-27 shows the way the sky is divided up.

The sky is black by default. Entering values in the Horizon and Zenith data boxes creates colored skies.

Sky Blending

By default, Imagine will make the transition between the zenith and the horizon quite abrupt. Sky Blending (at the bottom of the Globals Info box) determines how the sky will blend between the horizon and the zenith. A value of 255 is a complete blend, a value of 0 is an abrupt change.

Adding Global Fog

Global fog is one of two ways of simulating fog in a scene: by creating a fog object or by creating a bank of fog covering the entire scene. Creating a fog object was discussed in Chapter 4. This section discusses global fog.

Real fog is an effect you may use occasionally. But fog has another application. You can use fog to simulate the fall-off of light as it travels over a distance. That's what we are going to use it for in the mirror ball scene.

Exercise: Adding Global Fog to a Scene

You can set the color of the Fog in the fog RGB data entry boxes at the bottom right of the Globals Info box. We'll use values that make the light appear to fall off to a dark-gray mist.

1 Enter a value of 20 in each of the Fog RGB boxes. The color swatch will turn dark gray. This is the color you see in the background in Color Plate 11.

Imagine allows you to define whether the fog is a bank hugging the ground (Fog Bottom) or a heavy mist hanging overhead (Fog Top). We'll enter a value of 190 for Fog Top. Since the camera is angled down, we won't see the top of the fog.

2 Enter a value of 190 for Fog Bottom.

Now we'll determine the thickness of the fog. Global fog thickness works just like object fog thickness. A Fog Length of 1 will completely cover the scene in fog. A Fog Length of half thickness is calculated by measuring the distance in Imagine units between the camera and the object and then dividing the distance in half. Use the coordinate display and your mouse to find the camera's distance from the target object. The distance between the camera and the target object in the mirror ball scene is 800 Imagine units. To make the background quite foggy, use 300 as the fog length.

3 Enter a value of 300 for Fog Length. As usual, remember to press (ENTER) after changing a value or name.

Creating a Star Field

The parameters box also includes a data entry field for creating a starry background. We won't create a star field for this image. Creating a starry field is very easy in Imagine. All you have to do is enter a value in the Star Field Density box. The value must be less than 1. A very small value like .02 works best. The sky fills with a random pattern of stars.

Test Rendering the Scene

We have now adjusted global lighting. Let's return to the Stage Editor to do a quick render.

1 Click on OK to exit the Globals Info box.

2 Click on Save Changes in the Project menu.

3 Click on Stage Editor in the Project menu.

4 Click on Quick Render.

The scene now sparkles with lively color. The test render looks similar to Color Plate 11, but it lacks the reflection of the 3D logo in the mirror ball. This reflection won't appear in the scanline rendering used by the Quick Render option in the Stage Editor. It will appear when you ray-trace the scene in the Project Editor. You'll learn how to do this later.

LIGHT TYPES: SPHERICAL, CYLINDRICAL, AND CONICAL

Chapter 5 outlined the three different types of lights available in Imagine. Figure 7-28 shows the three types of lights and their patterns.

Lights appear on the screen as unfilled circles with dots in the middle. When you change a light to a cylindrical or conical light, a small line appears, pointing in the direction of the light.

- *Spherical* lights radiate in all directions. This is the default light when you add a light source to the scene in the Stage and Detail editors.

- *Cylindrical* lights radiate along the positive Y axis. The light produces a spotlight. You control the size of the spotlight by changing the size of the light's X axis.

- *Conical* lights radiate a cone of light along the positive Y axis. The ratio between the X and Y axes determines the width of the cone at its farthest extreme.

Spherical lights are rather difficult to place and move around a scene because they radiate light in every direction. Cylindrical and conical lights radiate an adjustable beam of light. These lights have to be aimed and focused.

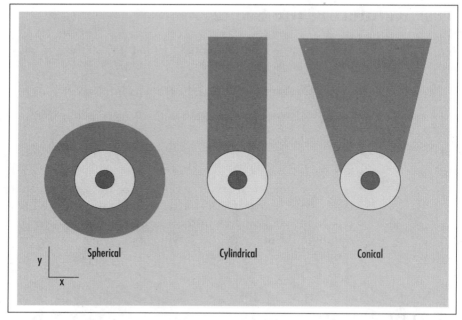

Figure 7-28 The three types of lights and their light patterns

Locking Lights to Targets

Imagine allows you to lock individual lights to specified objects. Lights are given targets in the same way as the camera. In fact, any object can be made to align to any other object, making some kinds of animations easy to do. For example, after aligning a spotlight to a 3D chair, you are then free to move the chair anywhere in the scene. The spotlight automatically follows it. Or you can give a spotlight its own target: a dummy axis, added to the scene using the Add Axis command.

Light Editing Step-by-Step

When lights for a theatrical stage are installed, they are first mounted, then pointed at the target area, then colored, focused, and tested in conjunction with the other lights in the scene. Lighting a scene in Imagine follows an analogous process. A light is mounted, it is aimed and focused and then test rendered. Here is the step-by-step process:

⬤ In the Stage Editor, add a light to the scene using the Add Light Source command.

⬤ Roughly place the light in the scene using transformation commands.

⬤ Save the scene.

⬤ In the Action Editor, click on the actor beside the light's name to call the Light Source Info box.

⬤ Select a light type and set its parameters.

⬤ Exit the Light Source Info box.

⬤ If appropriate, adjust the light's size using the Size parameter.

⬤ If appropriate, align the light to a target in a scene.

⬤ Save the changes.

⬤ Test render.

⬤ Return to the Stage Editor.

When you return to the Stage Editor, the light automatically realigns to the target. The steps just outlined will be elaborated on in the next exercise.

Exercise: Setting Up, Focusing, and Coloring a Spotlight

In this exercise, we're going to turn the light in the mirror scene into a spotlight. This spotlight will point at the same target axis as the camera. This keeps the spotlight centered in the camera view as we move the target axis. We'll adjust the size of the spotlight and then test render the scene.

In order to follow along in this exercise, make sure the BALL project and MIRROR subproject are opened. The Stage Editor screen should look like the one in Figure 7-23. Note the placement of the lights and camera in relation to the ball and 3D logo. Your camera view should be close to the one shown in this figure.

Lights are mounted (added, positioned, rotated, and scaled) in the Stage Editor, but all other lighting controls for lights are in the Action Editor.

1 Enter the Action Editor.

When you add a light to a scene, Imagine automatically gives a name to it.

Naming Lights

Light objects will show on the object name list on the left side of the screen. Lights added in the Stage Editor using the Add Axis menu choice are automatically given a generic name: LIGHTSOURCE. (This is an Imagine internal name, not a DOS file name.) As you add more lights, Imagine increments the file extension:

LIGHTSOURCE

LIGHTSOURCE.1

LIGHTSOURCE.2

LIGHTSOURCE.3
and so on…

As the list grows, these names will not help you remember the position of the light in the scene. Imagine allows you to specify more descriptive names, but first it will help to know something about naming conventions.

Creating a Basic Lighting Setup

The jargon of professional theatrical lighting supplies useful names you can use for 3D lights. Figure 7-29 shows the names and locations of traditional stage or movie lights. Here are the lights and their roles in lighting a scene:

- **Main light**: The brightest light in a scene is aimed at the same spot as the camera. A spherical light in this position radiates in all directions, making the whole scene visible. This is also a good position for a sun light in outdoor scenes. A cylindrical or conical light in this position simulates a spotlight in stage lighting.

- **Fill light**: This light is usually, but not always, lower in intensity than the main light. It lightens the shadow areas not reached by the main light. Use a spherical light in this position to bring out the detail in shadow areas. A colored cylindrical or conical light with a small radius can be used for adding highlights to surfaces.

- **Back light**: A back light is sometimes called a *rim light*, from the rim of light created along the back of the heads of actors in old black-and-white movies. Placing a spotlight in this position allows you to give the back edge of an object a bright halo, effectively separating a dark object from a dark background. Often this light is colored for effect.

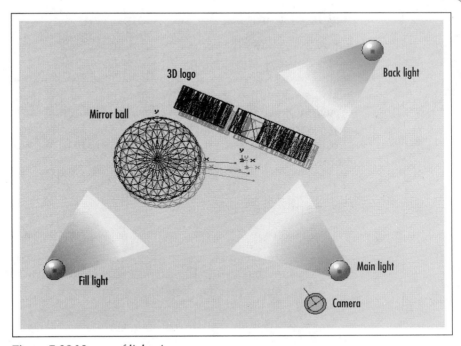

Figure 7-29 Names of lights in a scene

Lighting is a complex subject because it encompasses aesthetics as well as optics. 3D software programmers have consistently borrowed their metaphors and modeled their tools after artificial light photography. The best place to learn the mechanics and aesthetics of lighting is in photography lighting reference texts. Appendix B lists some of them.

In the next part of this exercise, we'll name the light we have added to the scene "MAIN LIGHT" and then align it to a target. First we need to switch the Stage Editor into rename mode.

2   Click on the Rename button at the bottom of the screen.

3   Click on the LIGHTSOURCE object name.

A New name box pops on the screen. It contains the current name for the object.

4   Delete the existing name and type in the name MAIN LIGHT. Leave a space between the words *MAIN* and *LIGHT*. The light is renamed as MAIN LIGHT.

Angle of Lighting for the Main Light

Figure 7-30 shows the vertical position of the light relative to the scene. The main light is usually placed above objects, at an angle ranging between 33 degrees and 45 degrees. This is the usual angle for outdoor scenes. The highlights and shadows created by the light's angle look "natural" to an audience brought up on a diet of film and television. You can reposition the light while in the Action Editor by clicking on the light green rectangle associated with "Posn." (position), but it is easier to position the light by eye in the Stage Editor.

Changing the Light Type

We will now change the light from the default type, spherical, to conical.

5   Click on the Info button if you are not already in information mode. Then click on the orange/red rectangle associated with MAIN LIGHT's actor. The Light Source Info box pops on the screen, as shown in Figure 7-31.

Altering a Light's Parameters

The Light Source Info box allows you to change a light source's parameters.

- **Spherical, Cylindrical, or Conical:** You can make the light a spherical, cylindrical, or conical light.

- **Cast Shadows:** The light can cast shadows. Usually the main light is a shadow-casting light. Remember that the darkness of shadows can be controlled by altering the level of ambient or fill lights.

- **Diminish Intensity:** This toggle switch does not cause the light intensity to fall off over distance, as you might expect. Rather, it has the same effect as turning down the intensity of the lights in a scene.

- **Red, Green, Blue Intensity:** Changing the values of the three color data boxes changes the color of the light. The color swatch beside the three data boxes changes accordingly.

Let's change the light to a conical light that casts shadows and is medium gray in color.

6   Click on the Conical light button.

7   Click on Cast Shadows.

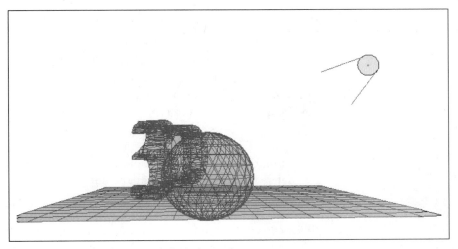

Figure 7-30 Vertical position of a light in the scene

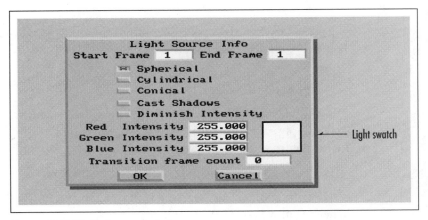

Figure 7-31 Light Source Info box

8   Change each of the RGB values to 200. Don't forget to press (ENTER) after changing each of the values.

9   Click on OK to exit the Light Source Info box.

You have created a conical light with a very narrow beam. This beam is directed along the default orientation of the light. This means the light is not directed at the scene; it's directed at the back of the 3D world. Let's realign the light.

Aligning a Light to a Target

Positioning a spherical light in a scene is relatively easy because the light radiates in all directions. However, cylindrical lights and conical lights radiate light in a beam along their Y axis. In the next part of the exercise, we'll align the light to the same target axis used for the camera. To begin, we'll delete the light's existing Align actor and replace it.

10   Click on the Delete button to change to Delete editing mode.

11   Click on the blue Align rectangle beside the MAIN LIGHT object name to delete the current default alignment.

12   Click on the Add button to change to Add editing mode.

13   Click *twice* in rapid succession on the space left empty when the blue Align rectangle was deleted. (Make sure that the Align name is highlighted in the far right column.) A Specify Type box pops on the screen.

The Specify Type box provides options for animating the light. We'll choose Track to Object.

14   Click on the Track to Object button. The Track to Object Info box pops on the screen.

Again, the Track to Object Info box provides choices related to animation. We'll simply enter the name of the target object in the Object Name entry box. Remember that the target we used for the camera was called TRACK.

15   Enter the name TRACK in the Object Name box.

Now the conical light source will "track" the dummy axis named TRACK. When we move the TRACK axis, the lens of the camera and beam of the light will point at its new position.

Changing the Size of the Spotlight

Remember that the radius of the spotlight created by the conical light is determined by the light's X and Y axes. By default, axes in Imagine are 32 units long. If we rendered the scene right now, the conical light would act like a spherical light, because the light pattern is very wide (see Figure 7-32). Look at what happens when we leave the X axis at its default, but increase the length of the Y axis (see Figure 7-33).

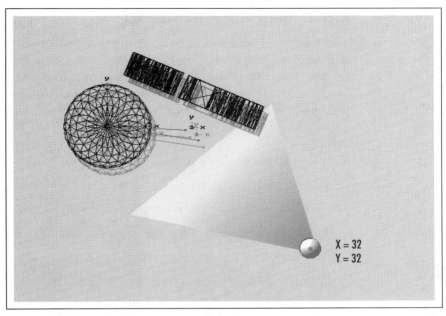

Figure 7-32 Conical light source at its default axes size

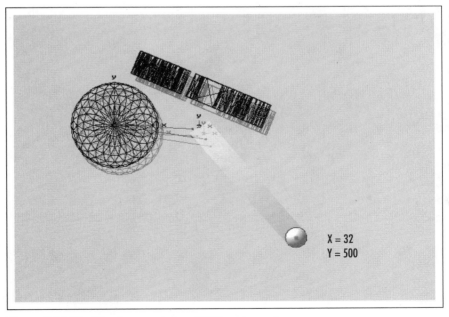

Figure 7-33 The Y axis extended to 500 Imagine units

Determining the Y Axis Length

The Y axis size is arrived at by measuring the distance between the light and the target in the Stage Editor. (Turn Coordinates on in the Display menu and use the mouse to get the location of the light source and the location of the target.) The distance between the light and target is 500 Imagine units. The X radius of the spotlight is 32 Imagine units. Making the X radius larger will increase the size of the spotlight. Figure 7-34 shows the X radius increased to 200 units.

Let's enter these values in the Light Source Info box.

16   Change to information editing mode by clicking on the Info button.

17   Click on the pink rectangle associated with the MAIN LIGHT's size.

18   Change the X size of the light's axes to a value of 200. Press (ENTER).

19   Change the Y axis size to 500. Press (ENTER).

Changing the light's size in the Stage Editor has the same effect as using Size in the Action Editor. Now let's save the changes and quick render the scene.

20   Choose Save Changes from the Project menu.

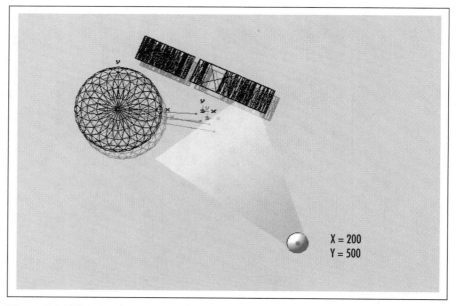

Figure 7-34 The X radius increased to 200 units

Figure 7-35 The quick rendered scene with the spotlight

21 Choose Stage Editor from the Project menu.

22 Quick render the scene in the Stage Editor.

Figure 7-35 shows what the scene should look like quick rendered. Because Quick Render uses scanline rendering, the scene appears without shadows. However, you can see the size and shape of the spotlight formed by the conical light.

Suggested Exercises

The next section outlines general rules for lighting scenes. Using the controls just described, experiment with lighting setups.

TIPS AND TECHNIQUES FOR NATURAL LIGHTING

As a rule it is a good idea to keep lighting simple in a scene. The single light illuminating the mirror ball and 3D logo adds drama to the scene. However, in some scenes, the lighting may require many lights. For example, many lights are used to add highlights to objects. (Remember that adding lights increases

Tip: Turning Lights On and Off

While you test multiple lights, keep a record of the intensity values for each light. Then selectively turn lights off by reducing their RGB intensities to zero. Use the Source Light Info box to make the changes.

render times.) Scenes that look "natural" usually follow the conventions of film and photography lighting. This section includes a number of guidelines that will help you achieve natural lighting.

Color of Lights

Most lighting conditions in the real world are either warm or cool. Warm lighting has a reddish glow to it, cold lighting is blue or violet. Interior rooms usually look best bathed in white light that has a little red added to it. Cool white light (ultraviolet) is found in factories and areas where brighter light is needed. Cool light gives a "brighter" appearance to lit objects. Sunlight has the color of cool white light.

Recommended Natural Lighting Setup

A recommended natural lighting setup is a medium-gray light (RGB value of 200) paired with a tinted fill light. A fill light is up to half the brightness of the main light. It "fills in" dark areas with color and detail. A pale-gold fill light will warm up a scene.

Shifting the Overall Color of a Scene

Global ambient lighting can be used to cause a color shift in a scene, toward blue, for example, in a night scene. Setting a global ambient color to a very dark reddish gray adds a slight mix of red to all objects in the scene.

General Rules in 3D Lighting

The following are recommendations for lighting scenes:

- **Keep one light close to your camera.** Many of the old movie cameras had a light built on top to assure that what the camera saw would be illuminated. Handheld cameras with built-in flashes are based on the same principle.

A light close to the camera should be adjusted as your scene develops. With the addition of other lights to the 3D scene, it will not always be necessary to work with a "camera light."

Camera lights can also pose a problem, sometimes known as *specular glare*. This is caused when a light source reflects a specular highlight off the surface of an object that is perpendicular to the camera lens. Large white "glares" or highlights are very apparent (especially on flat-faced objects like walls) when the camera angle and light angle are the same for the object's face. If a light is producing an undesirable glare on a flat surface, try moving the light farther to one side of the camera.

Add a fill light. Most scenes need more than one light. When portrait or still life photographers set up their lights, many rely on the use of a fill light to bring out form in areas that are not reached by a front light. A fill light is usually placed to the far left or right of the camera and is usually less bright than the main front light.

Tinted fill lights work well to give the illusion that a colored light (like a golden sunset) is dimly glowing in the distance.

Add lights to a scene one at a time. Many modelers add as many as five lights to a 3D scene. Multiple lights are tricky. Add them one at a time and test render the result of each light before you add another.

Never start with pure white lights. Two gray lights illuminate a scene more evenly and naturally than one white light. If you want the specular highlights on some objects to be pure white, and you want other colors on other objects, control this with the Specular setting of the objects attributes.

Remember that two gray lights can have a greater "additive" brightness than one white light, so use much lower values in multiple light scenes.

Use one sun light. Outdoor lighting situations that represent our "real" world should only cast one shadow.

What's Ahead

So far we've been using Imagine's low-resolution scanline renderer to create previews of our scenes. In the next section we'll use the Project Editor's rendering facilities for creating high-resolution, ray-traced versions of scenes. Ray tracing will bring out the refractions, reflections, and shadows missing from scanline renders.

RENDERING THE SCENE IN THE PROJECT EDITOR

The Project Editor is used at the final stage of a modeling project. The default rendering parameters create low-resolution (320 by 200, 256-color) images. This is the resolution of Quick Render in the Forms, Detail, and Stage editors. This section shows how to use the rendering facilities in the Project Editor to create high-resolution (640 by 480, 24-bit) images.

If you are continuing on from an earlier exercise, then the subproject MIR-ROR will already be open for the BALL project we have been working on. If you are entering the Project Editor from startup, open the BALL project and the MIRROR subproject.

   1   Enter the Project Editor.

Your screen should now look like Figure 7-36. Let's review the controls on this screen.

The Rendering Subproject Screen

When you first enter the Rendering Subproject screen, many of the options are grayed out, including those buttons associated with generating, showing, or deleting image files. After opening a subproject, and setting image parameters in the Subproject Rendering box, the grayed out options become active. You can then render the scene.

Screen Layout and Controls

Notice that the Project name ("ball") is at the top left of the screen, and the subproject name is on the next line down, centered.

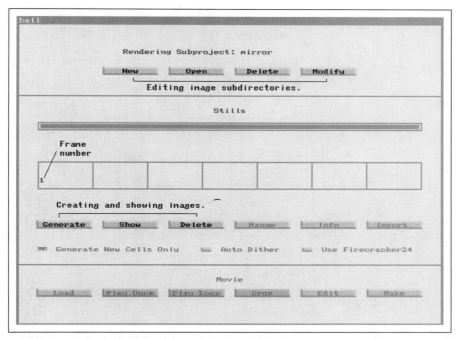

Figure 7-36 Rendering Subproject screen for MIRROR

Like the Action Editor, the Project Editor has been optimized for editing animation frames. In the grid of boxes at the center of the screen, the first frame of our one-frame animation is entered in the first column.

Many of the controls on the screen are specific to animations. This discussion is narrowed to seven controls.

Editing Subprojects

The four buttons at the top of the screen allow you to open and close subprojects and their associated file directories. The directory structure for Imagine projects and subprojects is shown at the beginning of the chapter, in Figure 7-1.

- *New* opens a new subproject. When you open a subproject, a subdirectory is created for the images you render. It uses the name of the subproject for the file name and adds a .PIX extension to it. For example, in the MIRROR subproject, a subdirectory is created beneath the BALL directory called MIRROR.PIX. When you start a new subproject, you have to set the image rendering parameters.

- *Open* places a file load box on the screen. A list of existing subprojects is presented. Click on the subproject you want to open.

- *Delete* deletes a subproject and its associated directories and pictures.

- *Modify* changes the rendering parameters associated with the subproject. Clicking on the Modify button brings up the Rendering Subproject parameters box.

Selecting Frames for Rendering

In an animation, the boxes in the grid at the center of the screen are filled with numbers. You are given the option of rendering a single frame from the animation or a range of frames. Since our animation has only one frame, only one number appears in the animation grid.

Creating and Showing Images

There are three buttons below the animation grid used for creating, showing, and deleting images.

- **Generate:** Click on this button to begin the rendering process. Set the rendering parameters and select a frame from the animation grid before generating the image.

- **Show:** Click on the Show button to view a rendered image.

- **Delete:** Delete a rendered image.

This completes the overview of the Project Editor screen. Let's continue with our exercise. First we'll change the rendering parameters for the scene.

2 Click on the Modify button. This brings up the Rendering Subproject parameters box shown in Figure 7-37.

Setting Up the Rendering Subproject Parameters

The Rendering Subproject parameters box has a number of settings that determine how your image will appear when it is created by Imagine and stored on disk. More specifically, the options in this box allow you to set the image's spatial and color resolutions. *Resolution* refers to the detail and color depth of your image. A screen 640 pixels wide by 480 pixels high is the pixel resolution of the common PC video standard, VGA.

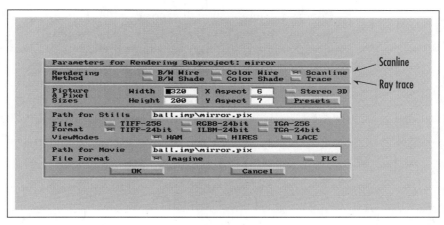

Figure 7-37 The Rendering Subproject parameters box

- **Spatial resolution:** Spatial resolution refers to the density of dots on the screen, measured horizontally and vertically.

- **Color resolution:** Color resolution is also called the *color depth* of the screen. It refers to the number of colors that can be displayed at one time on the screen. Standard VGA allows for the display of only 16 colors at a pixel resolution of 640 by 480, while Super VGA allows the system to display 256 colors at the same pixel resolution.

Higher spatial resolution translates to more dots on the screen and finer details. More color resolution translates to more colors in the picture and more detail in shadows, shiny surfaces, and reflections.

The Rendering Subproject parameters box is broken up into areas with mutually exclusive choices. The areas are divided by lines that look like grooves in the box. For example, the rendering methods (B/W Wire, B/W Shade, Color Wire, Color Shade, Scanline, and Trace) are grouped in this way. Choosing one method of rendering the image excludes all others.

Specifying the Rendering Mode

By default, Imagine uses Scanline rendering. This is a very fast way of simulating the play of light in a scene. But complex interaction between object surfaces and light (such as the bending of light in water or glass or complex reflections) cannot be simulated using this method. So far, the tests you have seen of the mirror ball scene have been in scanline mode.

Compare Figure 7-24 with Color Plate 11. Figure 7-24 is the scene rendered in scanline mode. Color Plate 11 is the scene rendered in ray-trace mode. Notice, that in scanline mode, the floor's reflection in the mirror ball has been simulated, but not the reflection of the 3D logo. Because ray tracing simulates the complex behavior of light, it is much more computation-intensive, and it takes longer to render a scene or animation. In the case of the mirror ball scene, the ray-trace render takes about twice as long as the scanline render.

Let's choose to ray-trace this scene. The Trace selection, below Scanline, means *ray trace*. Click on this button to change the rendering type to ray tracing.

3   Click on the word Trace.

Notice that the X moves to the box beside Trace. This indicates that ray tracing, to the exclusion of all other methods, has been chosen.

Specifying Spatial Resolution

Now that we have told Imagine that our scene is going to be ray-traced, we turn our attention to the spatial resolution of the image. Imagine allows you to create very detailed images. Image size is measured in pixels, the tiny dots that make up a picture. Imagine creates pictures up to 16,959 pixels in height by 16,959 pixels in width. That's many times bigger than the 640 by 480 screen on your monitor now. It's also well beyond the detail you'll require for print or film work.

Enter the spatial resolution of the image in the Picture & Pixel Sizes area of the box, just below the Rendering Method section. Instead of entering values in the text boxes beside Width and Height, we'll use the Presets pop-up box.

4   Click on the button marked Presets (it's at the far right of the box). A new box pops up on the screen (see Figure 7-38).

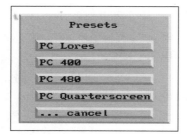

Figure 7-38 The Presets box

Tip: Users with Low-Resolution VGA Cards

If you do not have a computer equipped with a high-resolution color card, you will have to load the image into Picture Man for Windows for viewing. The next chapter shows you how to do this.

This box presents you with a list of five choices for the spatial resolution of the image.

   5 Click on the PC 480 button.

This selects the 640 by 480 spatial resolution, which is common on IBM PC VGA cards. The Presets box disappears from the screen.

Now we are going to set the image's color resolution. This is done in the next section of the box.

   6 Click on the TGA-24bit button.

We will create a *Targa* image with 16.7 million colors. Targa is a word used to describe high-color resolution images. We're going to use Picture Man for Windows to display the image, so it's not important if your video card does not display True Color. (See the Glossary for a definition of *True Color.*)

The Viewing Resolution Buttons

Ignore the settings in the next set of boxes. Imagine will automatically determine your graphics system's capability and adjust itself accordingly. Note that the preview image will not look as good as the image saved to the hard drive. You will load the image in Picture Man for Windows for viewing the final render.

Animation File Format

Ignore the next option. This option chooses the file format for animations. We will not animate the scene.

   7 Click on OK. This returns you to the Rendering Subproject screen shown in Figure 7-39.

Rendering the Scene

Figure 7-39 shows the location of the frame number on the screen.

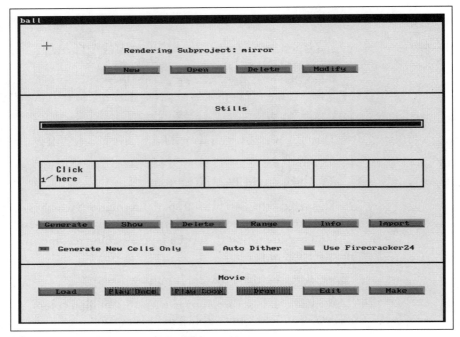

Figure 7-39 The Rendering Subproject screen

8   Click on 1 now. It becomes highlighted.

This selects the scene you have just created for rendering.

9   Now click on the Generate button.

This initiates the rendering process. If you look at the very top of the screen, you'll see that the progress of the rendering is displayed. Once the render is complete, an asterisk appears under the number 1 which you clicked on earlier. This indicates the frame has been saved to the hard drive.

10   Click on the Show button.

The scene will be displayed. It should look like the scene in Color Plate 11.

What's Ahead

The image saved to the hard drive was previewed in Imagine. Imagine does not show the image with its complete complement of colors. The next chapter will show you how to use the image processing program, Picture Man for Windows, to display and retouch the images.

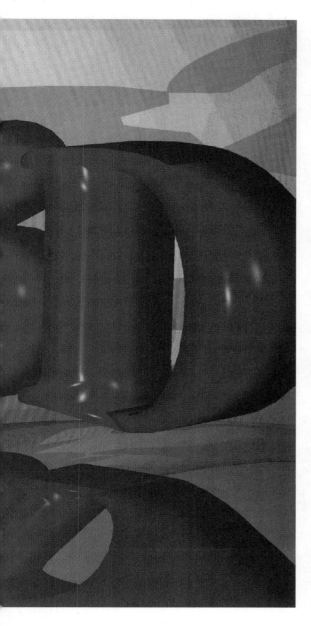

Creating Maps and Processing Images

For creating 3D images, an image processing program is the most useful software tool after the 3D program itself. An image processing program prepares images for use in the 3D program as backdrop pictures, image maps, or animated surfaces. The same program can be used for "photo retouching" a 3D image. You can add titles to pictures, create motion blur effects, place parts of images out of focus, and change the overall color tone of the image. Figure 8-1 shows the kinds of transformations you can make to the mirror ball scene created in the last chapter.

The image was processed using Aldus Gallery Effects. The program can give an image the appearance that it was created using traditional art tools. Figure 8-1 shows the effect of image processing the mirror ball scene with the Chalk and Charcoal, Craquelure, Poster Edges, and Watercolor effects.

321

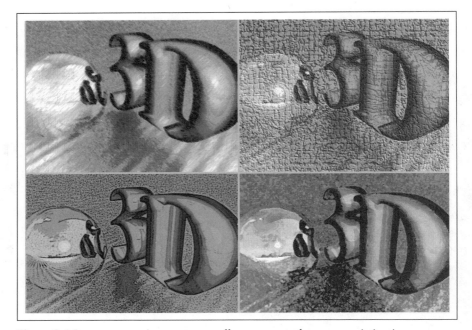

Figure 8-1 Image processing programs allow you to enhance an existing image

Image processing programs can play an important role in preparing images for other media, like print or television. Color balances can be adjusted and certain colors (such as red and blue) selectively muted or brightened. The program can also act as an image translation program, allowing you to translate a 3D image into a form useful to other programs, such as Windows multimedia programs or DOS programs like Autodesk Animator Pro or Paul Mace Multimedia GRASP.

All of the image creation and manipulation activities mentioned so far fall under a single name: *image processing.* Programs like Adobe Photoshop and Aldus Photostyler are called image processing programs. Adobe Photoshop has become the dominant professional tool for preparing images for print and multimedia.

One of the programs on the disk included with this book, Picture Man for Windows, is an all-purpose image processing tool. This shareware program was created by Russian programmers Igor Plotnikov, Alex Bobkov, and Mike Kuznetsov. Picture Man can convert files between different file formats and resolutions. Picture Man can also bend, rotate, stretch, resize, flip, clip, and warp images or parts of images. It can change an image's contrast and color intensity. It uses special image processing routines called *filters* for exotic effects like mosaic and faceted glass.

In this chapter you'll learn how to use Picture Man for Windows to create and image process images, using tutorial images as examples. Before we do that, let's see how Picture Man for Windows fits in the larger picture.

WHY A WINDOWS PROGRAM IN A DOS BOOK?

The launch of Microsoft Windows has produced an explosion in graphics programs for the PC. Before the advent of Windows, the graphics program developer had to write a special low-level program called a *driver* for each of the many graphics card chips in the marketplace. This made the installation and running of graphics software a nightmare for users. After installation, the user was often faced with a cryptic interface, and saving images to the hard drive for further processing in other programs became a task for translation programs. Memory requirements for graphics programs demanded sophisticated memory management techniques only DOS gurus can handle with aplomb ... well, most of the time.

Microsoft Windows has changed all that. Now the video hardware manufacturers release Windows drivers with their products. This frees the graphics software to concentrate on program features rather than software services for video cards. Software developers write their programs to work with standard Windows file loading, saving, and windowing routines, so users have a jump start on understanding new Windows programs.

Windows does offer significant drawbacks to the 3D artist. Because of the layers it places between the operating system and the application software, most graphics processing routines are slowed down to a crawl. Also, compared to DOS applications, animations under Windows are sloooow: two to four times as slow. That's murderously slow for animators. All but a handful of 3D program developers prefer DOS because of its speed.

The process can be summarized in the following way:

- Create 3D images and animations in a DOS program.

- Process images (not animations) under a Windows program.

- Play back animations or run image slide shows under DOS.

The best draw, paint, and image processing programs have been developed for Windows because of the way it simplifies the graphics Tower of Babel. When the project calls for integrating images and animations from a variety of incompatible sources (scanner, 3D program, draw program, paint program), the shuffle between programs can slow the production to a crawl. Windows' data sharing between applications, clipboard facilities, and multitasking saves wear and tear on the brain and speeds up program development.

The best 3D animation creation and playback programs have been developed for proprietary programs running under DOS because of the need for raw speed. Animation consumes computer resources ravenously. DOS delivers more processing power to the program than Windows.

PICTURE MAN FOR WINDOWS OVERVIEW

This section briefly introduces the Picture Man for Windows program interface and its image processing tools.

Picture Man and Windows

Picture Man runs under the Windows Program Manager. Program settings and commands are implemented as menus. It also makes certain commands available as icons organized as a vertical button bar, the toolbox.

When you first run Picture Man, the two basic elements of the program, the floating toolbox and the floating image processing window, appear on top of the Windows desktop. Picture Man, unlike other programs, doesn't take over the display system and fill the screen. You can move the toolbox and image processing window around independently, using the standard Windows drag-and-drop method.

Floating the toolbox and image processing window on top of other program windows facilitates switching between Picture Man and the other program. You can also run several Picture Man sessions at once. Figure 8-2 shows Picture Man's toolbox and image processing window.

Setting Up Picture Man for This Chapter

If you have 4 megabytes of memory or less on your computer, close all other Windows applications when you run Picture Man. This will allow Picture Man to use more memory for image processing. Run it entirely in the foreground, with the Program Manager minimized in the background. This will keep the desktop uncluttered, making it easier to find program options.

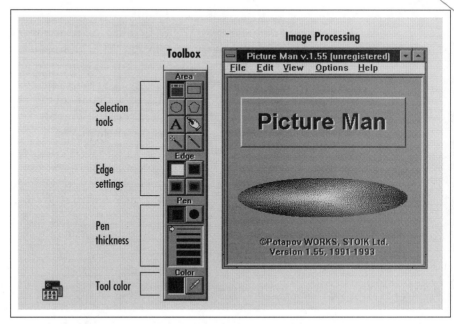

Figure 8-2 Picture Man image processing window and tool box

Picture Man for Windows uses most Windows conventions, so experienced Windows users should have no trouble with most program functions. For example, the location and methods used for file loading and saving are standard for a Windows graphics program. However, the way that Picture Man for Windows processes images requires special mention.

Picture Man for Windows includes tools for drawing, processing, and painting the screen in the toolbox. It places the image in a separate image processing window that includes almost 50 image processing commands. Unlike other graphics programs, the tools in Picture Man's toolbox do not have default image processing functions. The Freehand drawing tool, for example, shown as a hand with a piece of chalk in the floating toolbox, won't actually do anything if you click on it and then attempt to draw on the screen. Before you use a tool on an image, you have to select an image processing command first. For example, to draw on the screen with the Freehand tool, you must

◉   Click on the Freehand tool.

◉   Select an image processing command on the Edit menu.

◉   Draw on the screen.

Think of the toolbox as a set of 7 different tools (screwdrivers, brushes, drills), each with 46 different attachments. In order to perform work on the image, you choose the tool and then the attachment. When the image processing operation finishes, the "attachment" falls away. You have to reattach an image processing command at the start of *each* image processing operation, even a repetitive one. You'll be reminded of this point several times in this chapter.

Picture Man for Windows has a basket full of tools. Like the tools in your private workshop (or the utensils in the kitchen), you'll develop your own idiosyncratic way of using them. A pair of pliers often doubles as a hammer. This chapter will introduce you to the tools and give you practice in using them. You can get help on tools from the Help menu in the image processing window. Help is available on tools and their functions from a standard indexed Windows help system.

Let's now explore the contents of the toolbox and the image processing window. We'll start with the toolbox.

The Toolbox

The toolbox contains selection tools as well as the settings for tools. These are divided into sections:

- Selection tools
- Edge settings
- Pen thickness settings
- Tool color settings

Picture Man provides a helpful way of deciphering the icons used on the toolbox. The Options menu contains the names of tools and settings, listed according to the toolbox categories. The current tool choice in a category has a check mark beside it.

The toolbox contains the following tools and settings.

Area Tools

These tools are for selecting areas of the screen:

- Whole Image
- Rectangle
- Ellipse

Tip: Make the Windows Background Neutral Gray

When minimizing all but the Picture Man toolbox and window, Windows' standard "wallpaper" appears in the background. The patterns and colors on this background may influence your judgment of images loaded into the image processing window. Your perception of a color is often dramatically affected by neighboring colors. The color gray is often used as a background because it contains all the colors of the spectrum. It's called "neutral" for this reason. It's a good idea to make the Windows background a neutral gray so that it does not "color" your judgment of image colors.

- Polygon
- Text
- Magic Wand
- Freehand
- Pen

Edge Settings

Use these to set how hard or soft to make the edges of tools:

- Sharp
- Smooth low
- Smooth medium
- Smooth high

Pen Type

There are two pen or brush shape settings:

- Square
- Circle

Pen/Brush/Line Size Settings

These are measured in pixels. The size ranges from 1 to 11 in two-pixel increments.

Color Setting

You are provided with two different methods for selecting the current tool color:

- Color Selector

- Eyedropper

Clicking on the Color Selector brings up a color selection box. You can choose a color from the spectrum of colors presented in the box.

Clicking on the Eyedropper icon turns the mouse cursor into a very precise color selection tool. To use the Eyedropper, you select a point on the screen. The color of that point becomes the current tool color.

The Image Processing Window

The image processing window uses a menuing system for organizing program commands. Program commands are grouped according to function. For example, commands that create, modify, and save files are grouped under the File menu. All the image conversion tools are located in the File menu. All the image processing tools are located in the Edit menu. The other menus allow you to set program options.

The File Menu

The File menu contains commands for opening files, scanning facilities, saving, converting files, and printing options.

The Edit Menu

Image editing activities are grouped under the Edit menu. The Undo command allows you to cancel the last change you made to an image. There are a variety of tools for transforming, color altering, area filling, and image processing pictures. The clipboard facilities are located here.

The View Menu

The view menu gives you options for zooming in and out of images, adjusting your monitor's color gamma (important in print work), and options for arranging the Picture Man desktop. For example, you can remove the toolbox from the screen.

The Help Menu

Picture Man uses the standard Windows help system. Basic program functions and tool descriptions are located here.

What's Ahead

The next section describes Picture Man's color reduction and file translation tools.

DITHERING AND CONVERTING IMAGES

Many users of this book will not have a dedicated file translation or image viewing program. This section shows you how to view high-resolution color images in Picture Man and convert them to images with fewer colors for use in other graphics display systems or programs. Let's begin with loading and viewing an image. We'll load the image you created at the end of the last chapter. If it is not available, choose another high-resolution (24-bit) image.

Opening a File for Viewing

Run Picture Man for Windows. A file is opened using standard Windows hard drive navigation methods.

1 Choose Open from the File Menu.

An Open file pop-up box will appear on your screen (see Figure 8-3).

2 In the Type box, choose True Vision TARGA as the file type.

We previously saved the mirror ball scene in this file format. Now we'll navigate down the project directory tree to find a file named PIC0001.TGA, the name given to the mirror ball rendering by Imagine.

3 In the Drives box, select the drive where you installed Imagine.

4 In the Directories box, select the Imagine directory: \IMAG.

5 In the IMAG directory choose BALL.IMP.

6 In the BALL.IMP directory choose MIRROR.PIX.

The file PIC0001.TGA appears in the File Name box (see Figure 8-4).

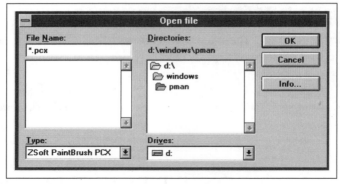

Figure 8-3 Open File pop-up box

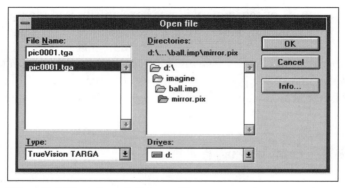

Figure 8-4 The mirror ball scene file

7   Double-click on this file.

The image loads into Picture Man. Remember that the image was stored as a 24-bit (16.7 million colors) True Color image. If you do not have a video card capable of displaying 24-bit images (or do not have Windows set up to display these images) the image will appear with fewer colors.

Choosing a Color Standard for Images

Both Imagine and Picture Man do all their internal color processing using 24 bits. It's best to generate and process images using 16.7 million colors, *even if your system is not capable of displaying this many colors.* Here's why:

⊕   It is much easier to remove detail from a picture than add detail to it.

⊕ You can create a master image at the highest quality, then make color-reduced copies for distribution.

Common PC Video Standards

There are two PC video standards: one for the computer games market and one for business communications.

The Games Market

The most common color standard in the PC games market is 320 by 200, 256 color. As users upgrade their systems, the standard is quickly evolving to 640 by 480, 256 colors. The low color and pixel resolution of the 320 by 200 standard allows game programmers to create very fast animations. Detail on the screen is not important; it's the action of the game.

Business Communications

The data display requirements of the business market, from word processors to electronic slide shows, demand higher pixel resolutions. Text and detailed graphics are too crude and blocky at the lower resolution. The minimum standard for the business communications market has a higher spatial resolution and a lower color resolution: 640 by 480 at 16 colors. There are five times as many pixels on a 640 by 480 screen than a 320 by 200 screen. The difference is dramatic. Here's our recommendation for developing images and animations for the games or business markets:

⊕ Render at the pixel resolution of the finished image.

⊕ Render 24-bit True Color images.

⊕ Color-reduce the True Color image for distribution.

Color display systems vary widely in their capabilities, but they break down to the following common color resolutions at 640 by 480 pixels.

⊕ True Color: 16.7 million colors

⊕ Hi-Color: 32,000 colors

⊕ Super VGA: 256 colors

⊕ Standard VGA: 16 colors

Super VGA is the minimum recommended requirement.

Tip: Users of True Color and Hi-Color Systems Read This

The next section provides information about viewing True Color images on Super VGA systems. If you have set Windows to a Hi-Color or True Color mode, reset the system to Super VGA mode. To change your system to Super VGA display, use the Windows setup facility in the Program Manager or run SETUP.EXE in the Windows main directory. Choose the 640 by 480, 256 color driver that came with your graphics card.

Fast View and Optimized Display

Images and systems with a limited color range use a palette system to display colors. A palette is a range of colors stored in the video system or at the beginning of an image file. When an image is displayed, the video system uses the palette to map colors to pixels on the screen.

Fast View

The fastest way for the computer to display a True Color image on a Super VGA system is to try to quickly match the colors in a standard palette to the colors in the image. In the case of the mirror ball scene, the computer will choose yellows to display the gold part of the 3D logo.

Optimized Palette

There is a second, much slower method. The second method is based on the fact that most images have a lot less than 16.7 million individual colors in them. The mirror ball scene, for example, contains mostly golds, grays, and blues. The computer analyzes the image and creates a palette that is optimized for the image. The process of converting an image from one color depth (24-bit) to another (for example, 8-bit) is called dithering.

Let's look at the visual difference between these options. Figure 8-5 shows a portion of the mirror ball scene displayed as True Color, Fast View, and dithered.

On a True Color system the image displays in full color. In Fast View, Picture Man analyzes the image very quickly, and roughly matches the current system palette to the image. The result is an image that breaks up into dots. Many of these dots will be the wrong color. In the case of optimized display,

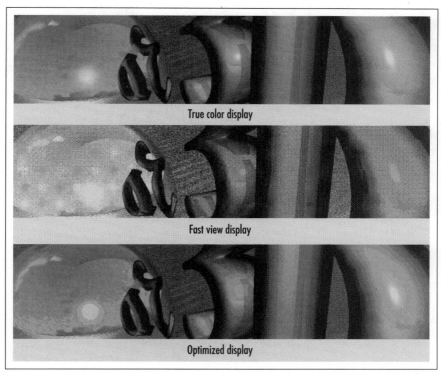

Figure 8-5 Image shown in True Color, Fast View, and optimized (or dithered) displays

Picture Man spends more time analyzing the image and creates a unique palette optimized for the image. This causes a delay, but the final image is a closer approximation of the original True Color image.

In the True Color version of the image, there is a gradual change of color between shadows and highlights. Notice, however, the *color banding* that occurs in both the Fast View version of the image and the optimized version. The smooth gold tones of the *D* in the 3D logo break up into bands of color.

Optimizing Images with Color/Dither Options

Picture Man allows you to optimize display of an image using the Color/Dither Options in the View menu. Let's use these options to modify the way images are displayed. (This assumes you have set Windows to Super VGA display.)

Click on Color/Dither Options in the View menu. A box pops on the screen (see Figure 8-6).

Figure 8-6 The Colors pop-up box

Setting Up the Display

The Colors box provides options for displaying images. The option that switches the display from Fast View to optimized and back is found at the bottom left of the Colors box: the Fast View switch. On a True Color system, a palette is not used, so Fast View is disabled (grayed out). On Super VGA systems, Fast View is automatically selected when you first enter Picture Man. (There is an X beside it.)

The other options in the box allow you to specify how you want the image displayed. Here are the options:

- **Color Depth:** Select from one of eight color display options.

- **Dithering:** Select the optimizing method.

- **Numbers of colors:** This is an alternative method for setting the number of colors in the image.

Repaint After Processing

Repaint after processing is used when the system is set for Super VGA display. Turning it on causes the screen to *refresh* (redisplay the image) after each image processing or transformation operation. This is important when the image processing operation changes the colors in the image. On Super VGA systems the image processing operation may introduce new colors in the image not in the current palette. Picture Man will re-optimize the palette and repaint the image on the screen.

Repaint Button

The Repaint button is used when you make a change to one of the options. Clicking on it causes the image to repaint.

Resetting the Display System Step-by-Step

Here are the steps for switching video display options:

- Select Dither/Color Options from the View menu.
- Select the Color Depth of the displayed image.
- Select the Dithering option.
- Turn off Fast view.
- Turn on Repaint after processing.
- Click on Repaint to preview the image.
- Click on Ok to confirm.

Color Converting Images

After you have set the dithering and coloring options, all images that you load into Picture Man subsequently will be displayed at the new color resolution. You can save these images to the hard drive at the new color resolution as well. This makes Picture Man useful for batch-reducing a series of True Color images.

Saving images stores the optimized palette created by Picture Man with the image, so you can use the image in programs that consult the image's palette before displaying the image. For example, you may want to convert a series of True Color images to Super VGA images for distribution. Here are the steps:

- Set Color/Dither Options for the image. (Make sure you turn off Fast View.)
- Select Save As from the File menu.
- Choose the file format type.
- Name the image.
- Select OK.

The image is saved at the new color resolution. Note that when you return to the image processing window, the file name at the top of the screen changes to the name of the saved file.

File Formats

Picture Man supports a wide variety of file formats, from 24-bit file formats like Truevision Targa to single-bit black-and-white color. You can dither a 24-bit image to 1, 4, 8, 15, 16, 24, or 32 images, in black and white, color, and grayscale. This makes Picture Man useful as a conversion utility in desktop publishing, multimedia, and electronic slides. For help in understanding what the names of file formats signify, use Picture Man's help system. One of Picture Man's strengths is that it supports an amazing range of file formats. The Help menu contains information on each of the file formats supported.

IMAGE PROCESSING WITH PICTURE MAN

This section shows you in general terms how Picture Man is used as an image processing tool. Let's begin by defining terms used throughout this section. Because the pixel lies at the very heart of image processing it is defined first.

Pixels

A *pixel* is the smallest, irreducible picture element in an image. The image is divided into a grid of pixels (for example, 640 pixels in width by 480 pixels in height) and displayed on the screen as small dots of varying intensity and color. Pixels are stored in image files as a series of bytes. These bytes are streamed from the hard drive into a section of video memory. True Color images store the color of each pixel as 24 bytes.

Filters

A *filter* is a generic name for computer procedures that process these tiny picture elements. Filters get their name from the fact that they alter the color of pixels in an image, just like a photographic filter alters the color of light rays entering a lens. Filters use mathematical algorithms to determine how each pixel will be altered in an image. For example, a filter might make all neighboring pixels the same color. This would have the effect of breaking up the image into small blocks of color. Or it might reduce the intensity of the blue component in an image by a specified amount. This would be used to remove a blue cast from an incorrectly exposed photograph.

Most filters work on groups of pixels. All pixels of a certain color will be modified, for example. Or a pixel is compared with the pixels near it and an algorithm is used to calculate new color values for neighboring pixels. Filters produce the most interesting effects on 24-bit True Color images. 24-bit images usually have pixels that have slightly different values from neighboring pixels. Sixteen-color images usually have large areas of the same color. Eight-bit (256-color) images have more gradual color changes between pixels. Four-bit (16-color images) have much larger areas of flat colors with sharp boundaries between colors. Because of these differences, the image processing filters will often have greatly different effects on 24-bit, 16- and 256-color images.

Size of Filter

Many filters allow you to adjust the size of the area the filter acts on. The range is between 2 pixels and a grid of 15 pixels by 15 pixels. Filter sizes are discussed further in the section, "The Processing (Filter) Tools."

Repeated Processing

Images can be processed again and again for effect. Some filters add detail to an image and others remove detail from a picture. Fractal-like patterns emerge as the same image is processed again and again. It's a good idea to save images regularly as you do this, so that you can return to an earlier stage and head off in a new direction.

Image Processing Tools

Picture Man image manipulation tools are capable of creating a very wide range of effects. Image processing is sorted into four groups on the Edit menu:

- **Transformation**: These commands alter an image's shape.

- **Tune**: These commands alter an image's overall color.

- **Fill Area**: These commands fill all or parts of the screen with colors.

- **Processing**: These commands use filters for altering pixels.

Interactive Use of Tools

The image processing steps in Picture Man are somewhat confusing at first because of the many options you are given and the complexity of their interaction. In simple paint programs, you simply click on an icon that looks like a pen and begin drawing. You may also have the option of altering the pen's thickness. Picture Man gives you many more options. For example, the Pen tool can draw an edge that has four levels of softness or hardness. The shape of the pen's "tip" can squirt out circles or squares. You can vary the thickness of the line it lays down. But that's not all. You can attach any of the 46 image processing tools to the pen. This multiplies your choices exponentially. For example, you can attach an image to the Pen tool and paint the image on the screen, only in the dark areas of the screen image!

Image Processing Step-by-Step

However complex the interactions of tools become, they are based on a simple series of steps. Here they are:

- From the File menu, choose Open. Select and load an image.

- Choose an Area tool from the toolbox.

- Choose an image processing filter from the Edit menu.

- Use the Area tool to apply the image processing filter to the image.

- Double-click either on the inside or outside of the selection area to begin processing.

A gauge pops on the screen showing the progress of the image processing operation. You can press (ESC) to cancel the image processing operation at any time.

How Repeated Processing Works

Picture Man is designed to allow you to process an image by degrees. The last area processed is automatically selected when you want to process an area with the same tool again and again. All you have to do is double-click inside or outside the selected area to accept the current selected area. However, when you change the Area Selection Tool a new area must be selected. The "Preserve Mask" option under the options menu allows you to preserve the previously selected area, even when Area Selection tools are changed. H is on by default. Here's the method:

- Turn on Preserve Mask in the Options menu if it is not already turned on.

- Select an Area tool from the toolbox.

- Select an image processing tool from the Edit menu.

- Select an area of the screen.

- Process the area by double-clicking on the inside or outside of the bounding box.

- Select a different image processing tool from the Edit menu.

- Process the area again.

- Select a different Area Selection tool...

- Process the area again.

- ...

Inverting a Selected Area

The selected area is highlighted by a bounding box. Clicking on the inside of the bounding box processes the interior of the selected area. Clicking on the outside of the bounding box processes the area outside the bounding box.

Canceling the Selected Area

You can cancel a selected area by pressing the (ESC) key and then clicking once anywhere outside the bounding box.

USING THE AREA TOOLS

This section introduces you to the Area tools. Area tools are affected by the current Edge setting, Pen shape, and width of tools. You can change these settings at any time. This allows you to blend the current tools with the background. For example, you can place a rectangle on the screen. When Edge is set to maximum softness, the rectangle's edges will blend with the background image.

Area Tool Functions

Now let's review how each Area tool functions. Descriptions will follow the order of the Area tool icons in the toolbox, from the top down and from left to right. Remember that you can check to see which tool is currently selected in the Options menu.

Time-Saving Tip: Use Rectangle to Restrict the Processing

> Many filters have no effect on solid backgrounds. When working with shapes on solid color backgrounds, use the Rectangle tool to restrict image processing to the shape and its immediate vicinity.

Whole Image

The Whole Image icon looks like a coarse drawing of the screen. This tool selects the entire image for processing.

Rectangle, Ellipse, Polygon

These three geometric icons allow you to create a rectangular, oval, or many-sided selection area. Shapes are drawn on the screen by dragging a bounding line shape to the required size. Once sized, the bounding line shape can be moved to a new location or resized. Double-click inside the bounding line shape to process the interior of the selection area. Click on the outside of the shape to process the exterior area. Pressing (ESC) and clicking once outside the bounding shape will cancel the image processing process. You must then re-select the image processing tool.

Creating a Many-sided Selection Area

The Polygon tool creates an irregularly shaped selection area. Here's how to use this tool:

- Select the Polygon tool.
- Select an image processing tool.
- Click on the screen.
- Click on the screen at a second location to create the first edge.
- Click on another location to create a second edge.
- Repeat ...
- When you have defined all but the last edge, double-click on the screen. Picture Man will draw an edge between the last mouse click and the first mouse click.

- You can modify the selection area by dragging the points at intersections of the polygon.

- Double-click inside or outside the bounding shape to begin processing.

The irregular-shaped area will be image processed.

This tool allows you to trace a shape on the screen. Use a very soft edge to soften the shape of the selection area. Use lots of points to define a detailed shape.

Text

The Text icon in the toolbox is in the shape of the letter *A*. Picture Man provides excellent tools for adding titles to images.

Picture Man lets you use the PostScript or TrueType fonts installed for use by Windows programs. However, creating a title in Picture Man is quite different from other paint or draw programs because Text is not an object added to the screen but rather a *selection area*. Instead of pasting opaque text on the screen, you image process the area under the text using Picture Man's image processing tools. You could, for example, use a mosaic filter to create a mosaic pattern in your image in the shape of the letter *A*. This creates a lot of opportunity for experimentation.

Using the Text Tool for Titling

To create a title follow these steps:

- Select the Text tool from the toolbox.

- Select the Edge setting from the toolbox.

- If appropriate, select the color for the title from the Color selection box at the bottom of the toolbox. Or use the Eyedropper tool to select a color from the image.

- Select an image processing tool from the Edit menu. (For solid text, select Fill Area, then Color, then Plain.)

- Click on the screen where you want to place the bottom left letter of your title.

- When you click on the screen, a Text parameters box pops up. Select the font, font style, and size for the text.

- Type the text in the text entry box at the bottom of the text parameters box. As you type the text it appears in a preview box.

- Edit the text and click on Ok when you are finished.

- The bounding box for the text you entered in the box appears on the screen.

- Adjust the size and position of the bounding box on the screen.

- Click on the inside or outside of the bounding box.

The text is created. This is a lengthy method of creating plain solid titles, but the same method opens up creative opportunities when you use other image processing tools. An example is shadowed text.

Creating Shadowed Text

To create a shadowed title, first create the shadow text, then create the title on top of it:

- Click on the Text tool in the toolbox.

- Select the softest edge.

- From the Edit menu select Tune, then RGB control, then TV. The TV control panel pops on the screen.

- Increase the contrast and decrease the brightness of the controls until the preview image is close to the shadow color for the text. Click on OK.

- Click on the screen where you want to place the bottom left of the title.

- Select a font, style, and size.

- Enter the text in the text entry box. Click on Ok.

- Move the box to where you want the shadow to appear.

- Double-click on the inside of the box.

- The soft-edge shadow is placed on the screen.

- Now select the hard Edge setting.

- Select a color for the title.

- From the Edit menu, select Fill Area, Color, Plain.

- Click on the screen a little up and to the left of the shadowed text.

Caution: Check Your Edges!

Sometimes new users are puzzled by the fact that text looks fuzzy. The culprit is usually a very soft Edge tool. Check the Edge setting before image processing.

- When the text parameters box appears, accept the previous selections. Click on Ok.
- Double-click on the inside of the bounding line box.

The solid text appears to hover over the screen.

Freehand

Freehand is the name of the tool represented by the icon of a hand holding a piece of chalk. This tool works like a piece of chalk dragged across a chalkboard. Use the Pen shape and size as a way of altering the shape and size of the chalk "line." The chalk line is not continuous, so don't try to create outline shapes with this tool. Use the Pen tool or a geometric tool.

Magic Wand

The Magic Wand tool is found at the bottom left of the Area section of the toolbox. It looks like a wand with a sparkle on the end of it. It is used to select areas by color. When you select a color, it creates a bounding box around all the areas in the image of the same color. This is useful when you want to restrict image processing to one color. For example, you may want to tint all the blues in the picture. Here are the steps in its use:

- Select an Edge setting.
- Click on the Magic Wand tool.
- Select an image processing tool from the Edit menu.
- Select a color on the screen and click the Magic Wand on it.

All instances of the color you chose now have bounding boxes around them. The Edge setting causes significantly different results using the same processing filters.

While RGB controls allow you to change a specified component color in all the colors on the screen, the Magic Wand allows you to select and process a specific color or range of colors on the screen. For example, you can select all the candy-red pixels on the screen while leaving purple untouched. Use the Magic Wand to "tune" specified colors.

The Wand Tool Parameters

The Wand tool has an options box called from the Options menu choice. The Wand Tool parameters box allows you to narrow or widen the range of colors selected by the wand. Moving the Tolerance to the right means that a wider range of similar colors will be selected. A Tolerance of 0 means that only colors with identical RGB values will be selected by Magic Wand.

Changing the Color Model

Either the RGB model or HSV model can be used when choosing colors. The RGB model selects colors based on the value of the red, green, and blue components of colors. The HSV model selects colors based on their hue, saturation, and value (intensity).

Creating Solid Selection Areas with the Magic Wand

Turning on the Unifold option in the Magic Wand box restricts the Magic Wand to colors adjacent to the area you click on. This allows you to select common colors in one part of the image. If the Unifold box is not checked, all areas of similar color in the image will be selected.

Pen

The Pen tool icon is shaped like an old ink pen with a nib. The Pen tool works similarly to the Freehand tool except that Pen can be used to draw continuous lines. Drag slowly with the pen for continuous lines, fast for discontinuous lines. Using a softer edge, the Pen tool can be used as a blending tool.

IMAGE PROCESSING TOOLS

The image processing tools allow you to transform images: to resize them, change their color, put solid shapes like text on them, and to apply special effects to parts or all of the image. Let's review the image processing tools in the order that they occur on the Edit menu:

- Transformation
- Tune
- Fill Area
- Processing

Transformation Tools

The transformation tools perform such image manipulation functions as resizing, clipping, flipping, and rotating images. They also include tools that create distorted images. The transformation tools, as they are presented on the submenu, are described here.

- **Size:** The Size tool resizes an image smaller or larger.
- **Clip:** Clip out a rectangular area of the image with this tool.
- **Flip:** Flip an image vertically or horizontally with this tool.
- **Rubber:** Rubber allows you to distort the image interactively using a grid system. You can stretch and distort the image in very fluid ways. Figure 8-7 shows the mirror ball scene undistorted. Figure 8-8 shows the same scene distorted with the Rubber tool.
- **Deformations:** The Deformations tool creates more structured distortions of images. The image that you create looks like it has been reflected in curved surfaces: concave and convex mirrors and cylinders. Figure 8-9 shows the mirror ball scene highly distorted by the Deformations concave mirror tool.
- **Rotate:** Rotate allows you to turn an image on its side or upside down.

Color Tuning and Balancing Images

The Tune submenu gives you access to Picture Man's RGB editing tools. You can perform such functions as changing the image's overall balance of colors. For example, you can remove a greenish tone in a badly exposed scanned picture. You can brighten a dark image. The submenu also includes special-effects color processing tools.

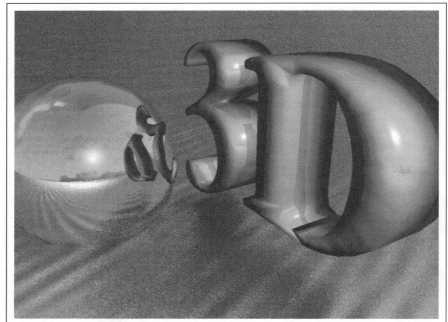

Figure 8-7
The original
mirror ball scene

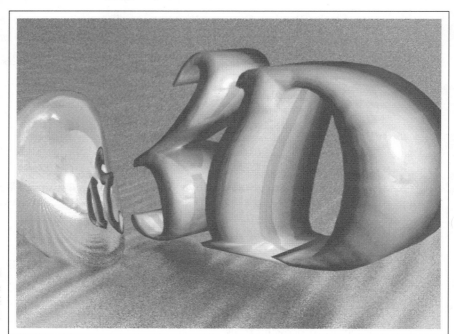

Figure 8-8
Mirror ball scene
altered with the
Rubber tool

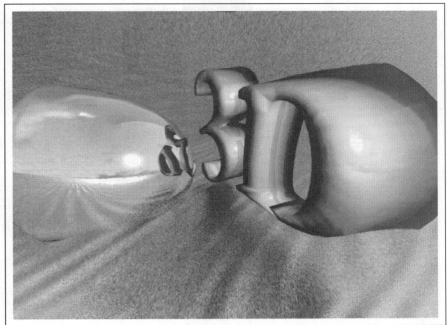

Figure 8-9
The Deformations
concave mirror
distortion

RGB Control

Selecting RGB control pops up a submenu that gives you two different ways of individually altering the red, green, and blue colors in the image: TV or Linear.

TV

When you choose TV, a slider panel pops on the screen. The panel works like the color tuning controls on a television set. You can alter the amount of color in the image (color saturation), the image's contrast (the spread between the darkest and lightest areas of the image), and the image's brightness. Turning the color slider all the way down turns the image into a "black-and-white TV" image. As you slide the controls up and down, Picture Man previews the changes. A permanent change to the image is not made until you click on the Ok button.

Linear

Linear provides an alternate way of changing an image's color. Separate control is provided over each RGB color. This allows you to increase or decrease the red, green, or blue components of a color.

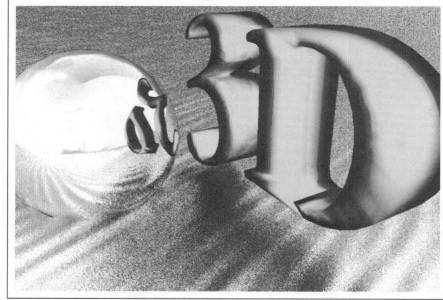

Figure 8-10
Equalization
performed on
the mirror
ball scene

Gamma Correction, Expand, and Equalize

These controls allow you to alter the intensity of colors in the image in a number of non-linear ways. Figure 8-10 shows the mirror ball scene processed with the Equalization tool.

See the Help menu for specific help on each of these controls.

Filling Areas with Color

The Fill Area tools allow you to fill selected areas of the screen with colors and images.

Let's review the color fill tools in the order they are presented on the Fill Area submenu.

Color

Selecting Color brings up two choices: Plain or Fluctuated.

Plain

Plain fills an area of the screen with the current color. Change the current color by clicking on the color selection tools on the toolbox.

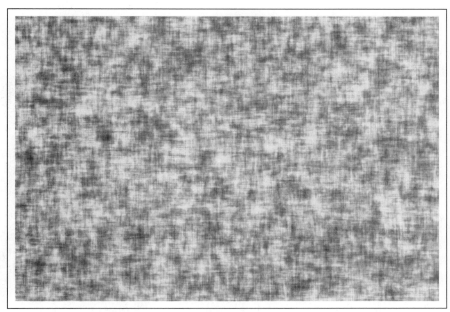

Figure 8-11
Mirror scene
processed with
Fluctuated

Fluctuated

Choosing Fluctuated pops up a parameters box. The selected area is converted to a random pattern based on the current selected color. Figure 8-11 shows the mirror scene processed using Fluctuated.

The Fluctuated tool creates an interesting pattern for an image map. Changing the Fluctuated parameters intensifies the effect.

Gradient

Figure 8-12 shows a gradient of colors. The Gradient tool fills the selected area with a horizontal, vertical, or radial gradient of colors. When you choose the type of gradient you want to perform, a parameters box pops on the screen. The box allows you to choose the beginning and ending colors for a gradient fill.

Pattern

Pattern allows you to use an image as a pattern. Figure 8-13 shows the mirror image used as a soft-edged pattern on the gradient background.

Try using the Pen tool and a soft edge to paint an image on top of another.

Figure 8-12
A gradient from
white to black
of colors

Figure 8-13
Mirror scene used
with Pattern

Touching Up One Image with Another

Use the Pattern tool in conjunction with the Pen tool to retouch a heavily processed image with the original image. For example, if you have softened an image, you can bring back the sharp outlines of the original with the Pen tool. Here's the method:

- Load and heavily process an image.

- Save it under a new name.

- Select the Pen area tool.

- Select the softest edge.

- Select a round pen shape.

- Select a medium thick line for thickness.

- In the Edit menu select Fill Area, Pattern, and Scaled.

- An Open File dialog box appears. Select the original unaltered image.

- Using the Pen tool, selectively restore parts of the processed image with the original image.

This is a good method for emphasizing certain parts of an image or restoring parts of a heavily processed image. A picture of a person can be blurred, and then the face restored to its original sharpness.

Patch

This tool creates a streak of colors across the selected area based on the pixels at the edges of the area. Figure 8-14 shows the effect of using the Patch command on the mirror ball scene.

Patch doesn't work with all the Area selection tools. It doesn't work outside a selection area.

Patch creates excellent motion blur effects.

You can create a patch on a certain area of the screen and then clip it. The new clipping can then be saved as a tilable image map.

The Processing (Filter) Tools

The Edit menu's Processing tools are analogous to photo retouching tools. They smooth, sharpen, add or remove detail from pictures, and produce special-effects images. All the tools have parameters.

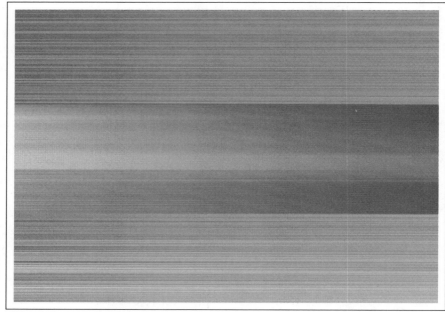

Figure 8-14
Streaks formed
by the Patch
command

Filter Size

Filter tools are applied to blocks of the image. The filter size determines the width and height (between 2 and 15 pixels) of the blocks. For example, a filter size of 4 and 8 means the image will be processed in 4-by-8 blocks. You can use a large filter size in conjunction with the Mosaic tool to break the picture into blocks of color. A small size will create a more pixelated look. Setting the filter size has different effects according to the tool.

In the following sections, compare the original mirror ball scene (Figure 8-7) to the image processed versions.

Smoothing

Picture Man has several different methods of blurring an image. Smoothing creates the effect closest to camera blur. Figure 8-15 shows the effect of Smoothing on the mirror ball scene.

Smoothing softens the image. It is very useful in compositing (putting together) images. When laying one image on top of another, soften the background image. This keeps attention focused on the foreground. Smoothing can also "polish away" small defects in an image.

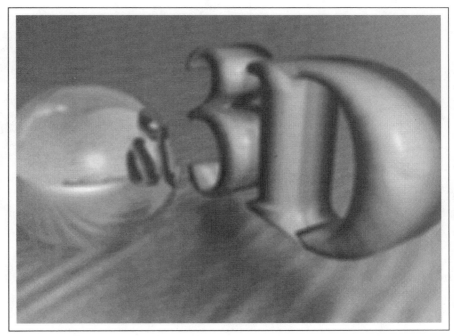

Figure 8-15 The effect of the Smoothing filter

Suggested Exercises

Reload the mirror ball scene. As we review each menu choice, image process this scene. Choose Undo from the Edit menu after each processing session. In cases where you make successive changes to an image, when you are finished, choose the Reload command from the File menu.

Sharpening and Heavy Sharpening

Figure 8-16 shows the effect of the Sharpening filter. Sharpening makes an image look crisper. It is often used to sharpen blurry, out-of-focus print images. Images in the JPEG (.JPG) format are slightly blurry because of the compression method used when they are saved. When importing a JPEG image into Picture Man, sharpen it slightly using this tool.

Heavy sharpening is primarily used for special effects. Repetitive sharpening removes detail from a picture. Use Sharpening to bring out the contours and edges in an image. Then process the image with another tool like Emboss or Contour Outline to enhance the remaining detail.

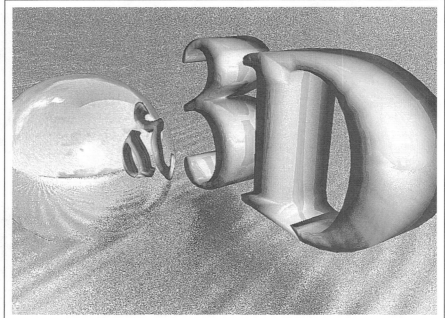

Figure 8-16
Sharpening
the image

Spot Removing

Figure 8-17 shows an image processed with the Spot Removing filter. Spot
Removing removes groups of attached pixels from the screen, replacing them
with the group's median color. Setting the filter size determines how many pixels are included in the group. At small filter sizes, Spot Removing is useful for
cleaning stray pixels and scratches from scanned images, but the image is softened. Sharpening will restore the image to crispness, but some detail will be lost
in the process.

Maximum and Minimum

Figure 8-18 shows an image processed with the Maximum filter. Maximum
and Minimum are image reduction tools. They remove detail from the image,
breaking it into small patches of colors. Maximum makes the image darker and
Minimum makes the image brighter. You can determine how big to make the
patches by setting the filter size.

   If you process an image over and over again using Maximum it will become
black. Minimum used repeatedly makes an image white. If you have red shapes

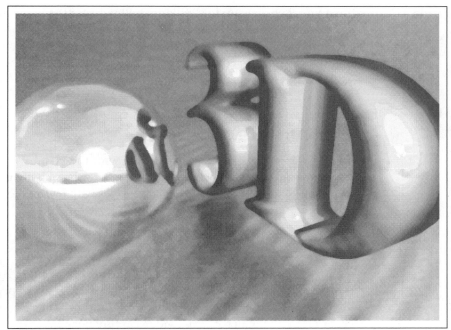

Figure 8-17
Image processed
with the Spot
Removing filter

Figure 8-18
Image processed
with the
Maximum filter

on a white background, Maximum will increase the white area of the image, decreasing the size of the red shape. Minimum will increase the red shape's size. Maximum and Minimum reduce the number of colors displayed on the screen, but not the image's color format. A True Color image reduced to 16 colors is still a True Color image. To convert the image to a 4-bit 16-color image, you need to file-convert it.

Hand Drawing

Figure 8-19 shows an image processed with the Hand Drawing filter. Hand drawing converts a high-color resolution image into an image that looks like a pencil sketch or a pastel painting. On images with fewer colors the image looks like an outline drawing.

Cleaning Background

Figure 8-20 shows an image processed with the Cleaning Background filter. This filter processes flat areas of the image, averaging the pixels according to the filter size. Edges are not processed. The authors of Picture Man recommend it for cleaning up images from video capture boards.

Contour Outlining

Figure 8-21 shows an image processed with the Contour Outlining filter. Contour Outlining lightens the edges of image shapes, separating them from their background.

Mosaic

Figure 8-22 shows an image processed with the Mosaic filter. This filter changes the image into a mosaic of rectangles. Each rectangle is the average of the area the rectangle covers. You can alter the size and shape of the rectangles by changing the filter size.

Emboss

Figure 8-23 shows an image processed with the Emboss filter. Emboss transforms the image into a kind of bas-relief. The filter reduces most of the image into a single color, creating flat areas with edges of bright color.

Embossing works best on images that have areas of high contrast, so it's a good idea to increase the contrast of the image before embossing it. The filter

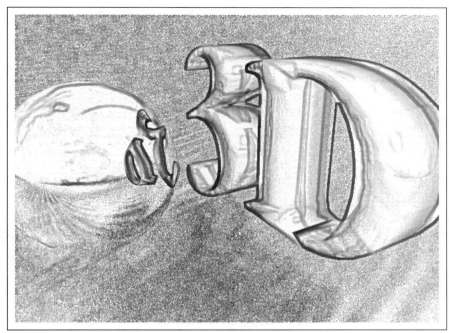

Figure 8-19
Image processed
with the Hand
Drawing filter

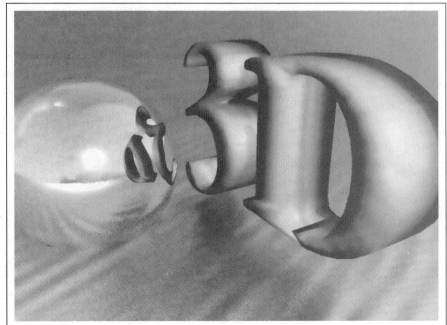

Figure 8-20
Image processed
with the Cleaning
Background filter

Figure 8-21
Image processed
with the Contour
Outlining filter

Figure 8-22
Image processed
with the
Mosaic filter

Figure 8-23
Image processed
with the
Emboss filter

works best on 16- and 256-color images because they naturally have sharper edges. Color-reduce a 24-bit image like the mirror scene image to 256 or 16 colors. Use the Edit menu's Tune controls for increasing the contrast of the image. Use the Sharpen or Contour Outlining tools to increase the contrast at the edges of shapes in the image.

Select a color before embossing an image. The selected color will be used as the base color for the embossed image. For example, to make images look like they've been etched in stone, choose a gray color and then use Emboss.

Faceted Glass

Figure 8-24 shows an image processed with the Faceted Glass filter. As you might expect from its name, Faceted Glass makes the image look like it is being viewed through a layer of faceted glass.

Scatter

Figure 8-25 shows an image processed with the Scatter filter. Scatter gives neighboring pixels a random value. It produces a grainy, blurred look, like a

Figure 8-24
Image processed
with the Faceted
Glass Filter

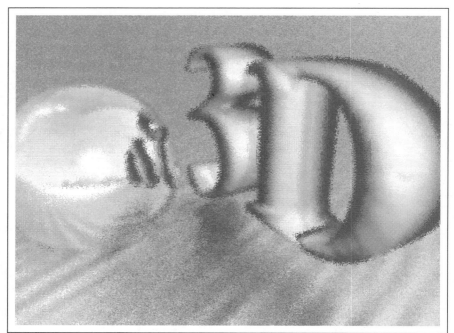

Figure 8-25
Image processed
with the
Scatter filter

photograph greatly enlarged, instead of out of focus. The effect is similar to looking through pebbled glass.

Combining Images

The Paste From tool on the Edit menu allows you to combine images. When you load a file with the Paste From command, a parameters box pops on the screen. What makes this tool particularly useful is its transparency parameters. The Paste options box gives you the following options in pasting one image on top of another:

- Make the blacks in the incoming picture transparent.

- Make the whites in the incoming picture transparent.

- Make all the colors in the incoming picture transparent.

A slider bar at the bottom of the parameters box allows you to set the transparency level. For example, you can create a semitransparent title on a background by setting the transparency level at 50 percent.

What's Ahead

The next section provides some tips on making the image processing session more productive.

IMAGE PROCESSING PRODUCTIVITY TIPS

Picture Man is a laboratory for images. Here are some time-saving program options.

Running Multiple Sessions

Some Windows programs, such as Adobe Photoshop, allow you to load images into Windows on your screen, so that you can work on several images at once. Imagine has this facility, but it uses a more indirect way of achieving this editing convenience. The strategy is to run several Picture Man sessions at once. Here are the steps:

- Run Picture Man, and then go back to the Program Manager and run it again.

- Load an image in one Picture Man session and process the same image in the other for a side-by-side comparison.

- Open several Picture Man sessions and process the image in several different ways. Choose and save the most pleasing images.

The Reload Command

Image processing often involves extensive trial and error. The Reload command in the File menu reloads the current image from the disk, saving you the trouble of searching for the file.

Saving Your Work

Saving your work regularly while image processing is important. Picture Man allows you to undo the last action, but several image processing steps later, you may decide you don't like the direction you have taken. In image processing programs, once an image is changed, it cannot be rebuilt easily. Save provisional versions under different names.

What's Ahead

In the next section, you'll gain some practice using the tools. You'll also learn how to work with several tools interactively.

EXERCISING PICTURE MAN'S TOOLS

Picture Man is especially powerful when you combine the tools for creative effects. In this section, you'll practice using the tools and combining them. You'll also learn how to use Picture Man as an image processing utility for Imagine maps and images.

Creating Map Textures

Picture Man for Windows can be an inexhaustible source for maps that can cover areas of a 3D scene. In this exercise, we'll apply a filter to an image to produce a second image that can be used as a map image.

Tip: Cycling Through Images

Use ⟨ALT⟩-⟨TAB⟩ to move from one program window to another.

Converting a Photograph to a Pastel Image

The first effect we'll create is the conversion of a photograph to a pastel, "hand-drawn" image. Included on the disk is an image called CORNCURL.JPG. It's from the Aris Entertainment Deep Voyage MediaClips™ collection. It can be found in the \IMAG\MAPS directory. Open this file. (In the Open File dialog box select JPEG as the file type and navigate to the \IMAG\MAPS directory.) Figure 8-26 shows what it looked like before and after image processing.

First we're going to retouch the photograph, then we are going to apply an artistic effect to it. Note that this image is rather blurry. Before we do transform it, we should sharpen it up.

1 Select the Whole Image area tool in the toolbox.

2 From the Edit menu, choose Processing, then Sharpening.

The image is processed. It becomes much sharper. Now to give the image a more "hand drawn" look:

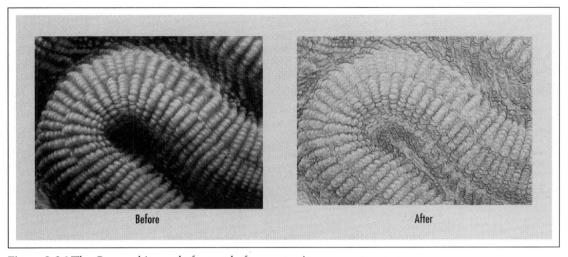

Before   After

Figure 8-26 The Corncurl image before and after processing

Tip: Save Often!

> Save work between steps. Remember not to use Save but Save As, so that you preserve your original. Use a name like TEMP.JPG. This saves the image temporarily. Overwriting this image at a later stage keeps your hard drive from becoming cluttered.

3   From the Edit menu, choose Processing and then Drawing.

4   Leave the filter size setting at its default. Click on OK.

The color image on your screen has the delicacy of color missing from the printed page.

Embossing Images

The Emboss filter is very popular in image processing. Picture Man has a particularly good Emboss tool because you can set the background color. We are going to use a picture of a lion to practice with the Emboss tool. Load LION.JPG from the \IMAG\MAPS directory. Figure 8-27 shows the lion image before and after embossing.

The lion is quite small. Let's increase its size.

1   Select the Whole Image area tool.

2   From the Edit menu, select Transformation, then Size.

3   A Size parameters box pops on the screen. Enter values in the Width and Height boxes that at least double the size of the image. Then click on OK.

The lion head is doubled in size. It is also quite soft, as a result of doubling its size. Images with sharp edges and a high degree of contrast work best with the Emboss tool. Let's sharpen the image.

4   Select the Whole Image area tool in the toolbox.

5   From the Edit menu, select Processing and then Sharpening.

6   Select a medium gray from the Color selector box at the bottom left of the toolbox.

7   From the Edit menu, choose Processing, then Emboss.

We've created an embossed lion.

Figure 8-27 The lion before and after embossing

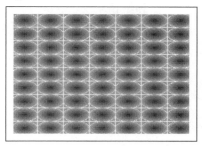

Figure 8-28 Tiled pattern created from scratch

Creating Textures from Scratch

Picture Man's drawing tools create images from scratch. In this exercise, we use the Gradient tool to create a pattern; then we clip and tile. The finished image will look like Figure 8-28.

1   Choose New from the File menu. Accept the 640 x 480 pixel default size.

2   Select the Ellipse area tool and the sharpest edge.

3   From the Edit menu, choose Fill Area, then Gradient, then Radial.

4   When the Gradient dialog box comes up, click on the Center color box and select a dark blue from the Color Selector dialog box.

5   Click OK and then select a cyan color for the Border color.

6   Click OK in the Gradient box.

7   Use the Ellipse cursor to draw a two-inch wide by one-inch high ellipse anywhere on the screen. Double-click inside the ellipse to fill it with the gradient.

Now we will clip the color shape.

8   From the Edit menu, select Transformation, then Clip.

9   Use the cursor to draw a rectangle around the ellipse.

10   Move the cursor to one of the sides of the selection box. When the double-ended arrow cursor appears, hold down the left mouse button until it changes to a hand with a finger extended.

11   Keep the button depressed while you drag the side of the rectangle until it just touches the ellipse. Repeat this with all four sides so that the selection box is just touching the ellipse on all sides.

12   Double-click inside the selection box to clip the rectangular area of the screen. Resize the Picture Man window to get rid of the scroll bars.

13   Select the Magic Wand area tool.

14   Select the softest edge.

15   From the Options menu, select the Magic Wand parameters box.

16   From the Magic Wand parameters box set Tolerance to 0, check the RGB radio button, and make sure that Unifold is off (not checked) before clicking OK.

17   From the Edit menu, select Fill Area, then Gradient, then Radial.

18   When the Gradient dialog box comes up, choose a dark magenta and a pink for the gradient. Click on OK.

19   Use the Magic Wand cursor to click on a white part of the image outside the ellipse. Notice how the softer edge altered the effect.

We want the final image to be smaller than the one we've been working on:

20   From the Edit menu, choose Transformation and then Size.

21   Change the Width and Height numbers to one-quarter of their values and then click OK.

22   Save the resulting small image as TEMP.JPG.

23   From the File menu, select an image size of 640 x 480 pixels.

24   Select the Whole Image area tool.

25   From the Edit Menu, select Fill Area, and then Pattern, and then Tiled.

The screen is tiled with the pattern we clipped from the screen.

SUMMARY

Picture Man for Windows is quite a powerful image processing tool. It has the flexibility to meet most image processing challenges. For additional help on the program consult the Help menu in the image processing window.

This completes the first part of this book. Our subject has been 3D modeling and image processing. In the next part of the book, the focus will be on what you can do with the tools.

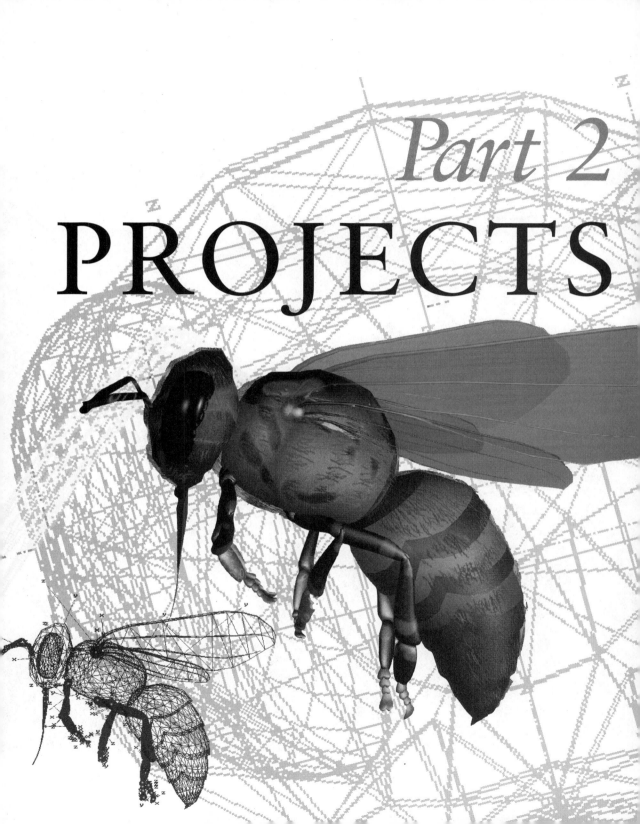

Part 2
PROJECTS

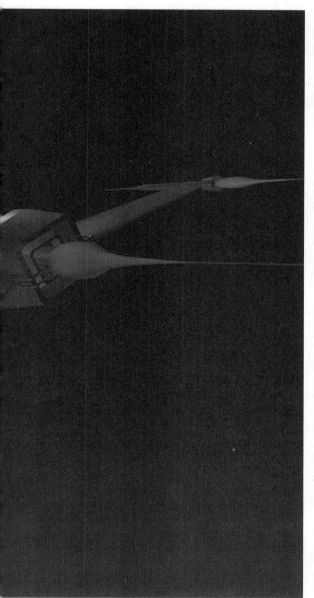

CHAPTER NINE

Modeling Workshop

Featured Artist: Alan Henry

Alan Henry, pictured in Figure 9-1 is an F-16 pilot with a need for speed in 3D rendering. He may spend a lot of time in the air, but he is well-grounded in 3D. He has a degree in mathematics and has won awards in the AmiEXPO art and video contest. Alan creates 3D models for a variety of clients, including a 3D software vendor.

The purpose of this workshop is to practice with the tools found in the Detail Editor. Key concepts and model-building techniques will also be reviewed. The key topics covered include Imagine's Spin, Sweep, and Extrude commands, plus Paths. While this workshop covers many of the Detail Editor's tools, it is not inclusive. The most common commands and techniques have been selected for review.

ALAN HENRY'S MODELING TECHNIQUES

Alan Henry writes: "Probably the most perplexing part of modeling is figuring out how to begin. Which tool or procedure will produce the most expeditious and desired results?

Figure 9-1 This chapter features Alan Henry, an award-winning 3D modeler

"Regardless of what object you build, you need to view it broken down into as many primitive shapes as possible. Generally, the more complex the object is, the more parts you will have to break it into. Some of these smaller parts may be more organic in shape and difficult to duplicate by merely altering primitives. These objects will be built manually (Add Axis, Add Line, etc.) and either spun or extruded as necessary.

"Probably the best approach to building an object is having a plastic model of the subject (or something similar) at the computer with you. Whenever possible, I recreate the plastic model pieces as closely as possible in the Detail Editor and then hold each plastic part directly against the computer monitor and scale and stretch the object to more closely match it. If you are unable to obtain a plastic model of your subject, try to dig up a tri-view diagram of it (many book stores carry very detailed books on trains, planes, automobiles, etc.). Another alternative is using photographs of the subject. At a minimum, you should use a front-quarter and rear-quarter view.

"The least reliable method of modeling is using your memory to re-create the object. However, in the absence of any suitable diagrams or models, don't hesitate to use your imagination. Sometimes the most fascinating images are created by not imposing strict 'real world' constraints in the object's construction."

Modeling the Fan

Figure 9-2 shows the ceiling fan that we will build in this workshop. Like most relatively complex modeling projects, this one will be broken down to manageable subprojects. Each subproject is independent. However, the difficulty

Figure 9-2 The ceiling fan

level will increase as you move through each subproject. Once completed, the objects can be grouped together to form the ceiling fan.

Structure of the Subprojects

Step-by-step instructions are provided for creating the object in each subproject. You don't have to build all the parts to the fan. Because the parts have to fit precisely together, in some cases you will load the completed part and follow along as the steps taken in building it are described.

This chapter gives you a chance to revisit tools and techniques first introduced in Chapter 6.

At the conclusion of each subproject, you should have a good understanding of why a specific method was used to build the object and how to incorporate these techniques into future projects.

The subprojects are short and self-contained so you can take breaks in between and experiment with tools.

Animating the Ceiling Fan

We'll build the ceiling fan so that it can be animated in the Stage Editor. Some tips on using the Stage Editor's animation tools are given later in the chapter.

SETTING UP THE PROJECT

The first order of business is to open a ceiling fan project.

1   Enter the Project Editor and select New from the Project pull-down menu. Enter TUTORIAL for the file name and click on OK.

This creates a project directory called TUTORIAL.IMP. Opening a project is a necessary prelude to entry in the Stage and Action editors.

SUBPROJECT 1: CREATING THE FAN BLADE

The object will be built in the Detail Editor. We will first create the shape of the blade as you would see it looking straight up at it. The base shape for the fan blade will be a disk. This will be supplied by the Detail Editor's Add Primitive command.

Creating the Base Shape

In this section we'll use a disk as the base shape from which to form the blade.

2   Enter the Detail Editor.

3   Select Add Primitive from the Functions menu. Select Disk from the pop-up box. In the parameters box leave the radius at 50 units, and click in the Sections box and change the value to 12. (Don't forget to press (ENTER).) Click on OK when finished.

4   Enter the Front view by clicking on the bar beside the lower left window.

5   Pick the disk by clicking on its axis (it should change to blue).

Seen from above, a fan blade can be conceived as a disk stretched along the X (horizontal) axis. Let's stretch the disk now.

6   Select Pick Points from the Mode menu.

7   Select Pick Method from the Mode menu and select Drag Box.

8   Hold down the (SHIFT) key and, while simultaneously holding down the left mouse button, draw a box around the rightmost eight points (including the center point). They will now change to a red color to indicate they are picked.

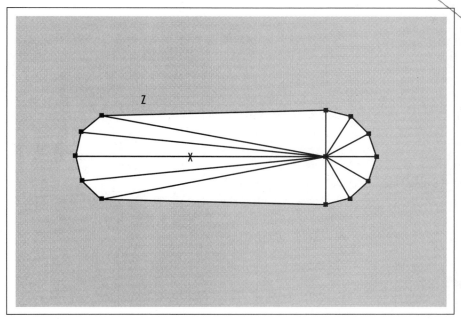

Figure 9-3 Beginning profile of the fan blade

9 Select Transformation from the Object menu. Click on Position and type 200 for the X coordinate (press (ENTER)). Select Perform when complete.

The blade's profile is beginning to take shape (see Figure 9-3). We now see the basic shape of the fan blade, narrow at the point where it attaches to the fan's center, and wide on the perimeter. Let's now shape the outer edge of the fan blade.

10 Click on the Scl (scale) button at the bottom left of the window. Depress the Z and Y buttons to deselect them. This constrains the scaling operation to the X (horizontal) axis.

11 Hold down the left mouse button and move the cursor downward. As you move the cursor down, notice how the right end of the blade flattens. Scale the points down to 70 percent of their original size. Keep an eye on the readout at the top right of the screen. When you get to a value of 0.70, let go of the mouse button. Press the (SPACEBAR) to complete the scale operation. Unpick the current points by clicking anywhere on the screen.

12 Using the same method as step 8, pick the left five points.

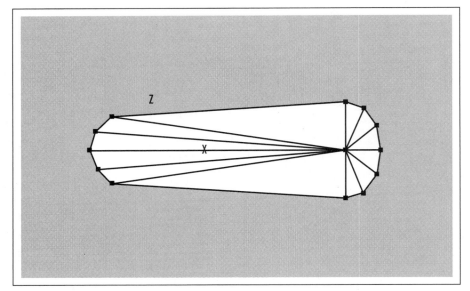

Figure 9-4 The left points of the blade reduced in size

> 13 Scale the right points to 80 percent, in all three axes. Your screen should look like Figure 9-4 when finished.

The basic shape of the blade has now been created. Let's return to Objects mode.

> 14 Select Pick Objects from the Mode menu.

Extruding the Fan Blade into a 3D Object

We've created a fan blade that is very thin. Let's give the blade thickness.

> 15 Under the Object menu select Mold and pick the Extrude option (or press (ALT)-(E)). Type 5 for the Length and click on Perform.

The object now has a thickness of five units. Let's look at it from another view.

> 16 Click on the Right bar on the right side of the screen. Toggle back and forth between the Right and Front views to view the shape from these two angles.

You can also preview the object's shape by clicking on the PERSP bar at the top of the right side of the screen and selecting Shaded from the Display menu. Move the sliders at the side and bottom of the screen to see the shape of the blade.

Adding a Wood Surface to the Fan Blade

In this section, we're going to add a surface to the fan blade using an image map. We'll use Imagine's default mapping parameters for the blade, but provide a review of how maps are altered to fit some objects better. Before completing the next step you must convert the file RICHOAK.JPG in the \IMAG\MAPS directory from a JPEG (.JPG) to a TIFF (.TIF) file. See Chapter 8 for tips on using Picture Man for Windows for file conversion.

17 Select Attributes from the Object menu (or press (F7)) and click on the Brush 1 button. You are prompted to select the brush file name. Navigate to the \IMAG\MAPS directory and select the RICHOAK.TIF file name. This is a small scan of oak wood.

Once the image map is loaded, the map parameters box pops on the screen. Imagine automatically wraps the blade with the image map. We want the oak map to be applied as a flat map in the X and Z directions, so accept the default wrapping method and the other defaults. However, this is a good point to review how Imagine applies image maps to objects.

Remember that images, when applied to objects, have their own unique axis. This axis can be viewed by clicking on the Edit Axes button found in the map parameters box.

18 Click on the Edit Axes button.

Figure 9-5 shows the default placement of the map. This map bounding box defines the area that the blade will be covered by in the image map. Even though a large yellow bounding box is shown, the brush's image is defined by the area in the upper right quadrant.

We made the blade five units thick. Imagine is smart enough to extend the map through to the other side of the blade. However, there will be some cases when the map will not appear on the other side of an object like this. When using the Flat X/Flat Z wrap method, the depth of the image map is defined by the Y axis.

19 Click on the RIGHT name bar to see the fan blade in cross-sectional view.

Figure 9-6 shows the bounding box of the image map surrounding the fan blade. Imagine has correctly set the map's Y depth.

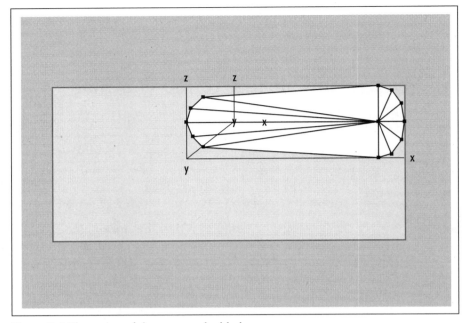

Figure 9-5 Placement of the map on the blade

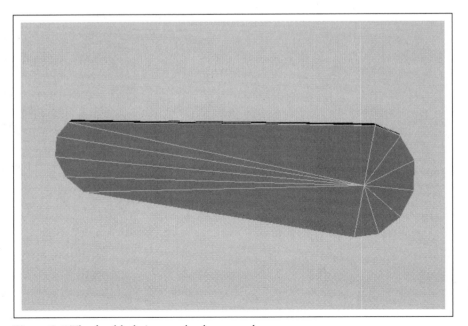

Figure 9-6 The fan blade is completely covered

In future, if a map fails to cover an object, place it slightly in front of the object and lengthen its Y axis through to the other side. While in the Edit Axis mode, the axis can be moved and rescaled by using the Mov and Scl buttons (bottom left), respectively.

20 Hit the (ESC) key to exit the Edit Axis mode and click on OK to accept the map parameters settings. This returns you to the Attributes Requester.

Adding Surface Attributes to the Fan Blade

A wooden fan blade is shiny. In this section, we're going to load a predefined set of surface attributes that match the specular and hardness surface qualities of a wooden fan blade.

21 Click on Load at the bottom of the Attributes Requester box. Select the \IMAG\ATTRIBS. This is the directory where Imagine's attribute files are located. Click on the file, OAKWOOD.ATR. Click on OK.

Defining the Blade's Edges

By default, objects are given Phong shading. But some objects, like the blade, have round bodies and sharp edges. It is possible to give Phong-shaded objects sharp edges using Imagine's Make Sharp command. The command applies flat shading to selected polygons. By flat shading the polygons along the edges of the blade, we make them look sharp.

Check to make sure that the Phong button is toggled on (it has an X beside it).

22 Select OK when finished.

Now we select the polygons along the blade's edge.

23 Select the Right view. (Center the blade if necessary by pressing the () key and then clicking at the center of the blade. Zoom in by clicking on the ZI button.)

24 Select Pick Edges from the Mode menu. Ensure your Pick Method is Drag Box (the Drag Box choice should have a check mark beside it). Select Zoom In from the Display menu.

The Make Sharp command in the Functions menu instructs Imagine to render the selected edges as flat. In picking the edges to make flat, be careful not to select the round edge along the outside of the blade. It is easier to select the correct points in the Right view.

25   Holding down the (SHIFT) key, draw a box around the 11 points lined up vertically on the right side of the object (the picked edges will change to blue).

26   Under the Functions menu select Make Sharp. Repeat the operation for the 11 points on the left side.

Now save your work.

27   Change back to Pick Objects mode. The blade turns blue. Select Save from the Object menu. Navigate to the \IMAG\OBJECTS menu. Name the object FANBLADE.OBJ and click on OK.

Quick Rendering the Blade

Let's take a look at a quick render of the blade.

28   Adjust the object blade so that it is centered and fills the screen. (Make fine zoom adjustments by pressing the forward slash key (/), to increase or decrease the object size by small percentage points.)

29   Make the perspective view full screen and ensure Shaded mode is selected in the Display menu. Move the bottom slider about 1 inch to the right and the side slider about 1 inch from the top. This adjustment will change the perspective angle of the object so the light source won't glare on the blade surface. Your screen should look like Figure 9-7.

30   Select Quick Render from the Projects menu and click on OK when ready.

After a period of time, your fan blade will be displayed in living color. If everything went well, you should be looking at a fairly realistic oak fan blade (see Figure 9-8).

This completes subproject 1, the creation of the fan blade.

SUBPROJECT 2: CREATING THE FAN BODY

This exercise creates the fan base plate, along with the downrod, brass motor housing, and wire box for the light kit.

Enter the Detail Editor, ensure you are in the Quad view and that there are no existing objects loaded. In the Mode menu, ensure that your Pick Method is Click.

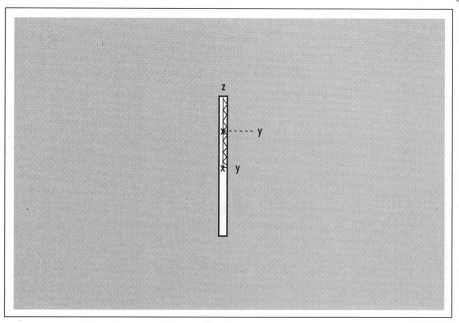

Figure 9-7 The perspective view of the fan blade

Figure 9-8 The rendered fan blade

Creating the Profile Shape

At the end of the Chapter 6, we created a martini glass using Imagine's Spin command. You drew half the profile of the martini glass and spun it 360 degrees on its Z axis. Like the martini glass, the fan housing for the ceiling fan is radially symmetrical, and it lends itself to the same approach. Figure 9-9 shows the fan housing contour we will create in this section.

The object's shape is too complex to be formed from a primitive. It has to be built from the ground up. Because the parts of the fan have to fit together precisely, the fan body is provided on disk (FANBODY.OBJ in the \IMAG\OBJECTS directory). The next four steps show how it was created. Load FANBODY.OBJ and read through the steps.

You begin by laying down an axis, then the points and edges of the contour to this axis.

31 First an axis is laid down by selecting Add Axis from the Functions menu.

32 The axis is picked by clicking on it.

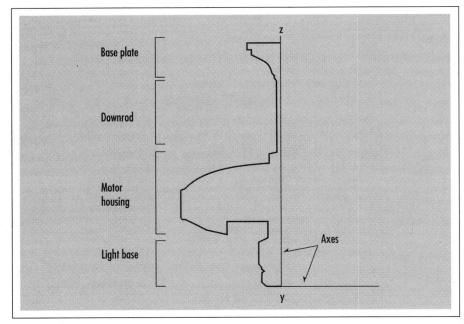

Figure 9-9 The fan housing contour

33 Add Lines mode is selected in the Mode menu.

34 Figure 9-9 shows the various parts of the fan housing: base plate, down-rod, motor housing, and light base. Starting at the top, the profile is drawn with points and edges.

Using Spin to Create the 3D Shape of the Fan

With FANBODY.OBJ loaded, continue along with the exercise. In this section we use the Spin command to create the fan body.

35 Pick the fan body object by clicking on its axis (it will change to blue or purple).

36 Select Mold from the Object menu and click on Spin. Click in the # of Sections box and enter 20 (press ⟨ENTER⟩). Click on Perform.

The fan body is created as a 3D object (see Figure 9-10). What you now see is the 3D shape of the fan body. A ceiling fan seen from afar might use fewer sections. This one will be seen close-up, so we've given it 20 sections.

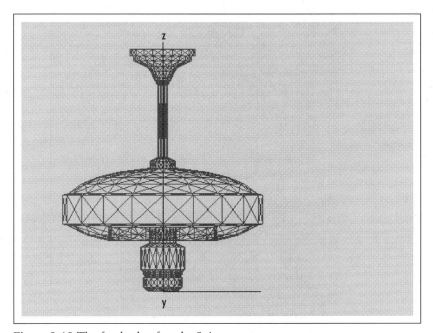

Figure 9-10 The fan body after the Spin

Applying the Brass Surface

In this section, we'll apply a brass surface to the fan body.

37 Select Attributes from the Object menu (or press (F7)) and click on Load. Navigate to the \IMAG\ATTRIBS directory and click on BRASS.ATR. This will give the fan body a brass finish. Click on OK when finished.

38 Finally, before leaving the Attributes Requester, make sure that the Phong button is toggled on (it will have an X beside it). This will render the spun object with smoothly shaded curves. Select OK when finished.

Making the Edges Sharp

If we rendered the fan body right now, it would not have sharp edges. We will now designate the edges that will be flat-shaded to make them look sharp.

39 While in the Front view, zoom in on the object until the base plate and the top half of the motor housing fill the screen.

Your screen should look like Figure 9-11. Notice the horizontal lines in the wireframe that will be converted to sharp edges.

40 Select Pick Edge mode and ensure your Pick Method is Drag Box.

41 Use the (SHIFT) key to put the Detail Editor into Multi-mode. Pick one horizontal line at a time so you don't include the edges along the side of the fan body. Starting from the top, pick the edges composing the first horizontal line. Once picked, select Make Sharp under the Functions menu. Repeat this procedure for the edges of the second and third lines, the edges that divide the base plate from the downrod and the downrod from the motor housing.

Now we are going to create hard edges on the bottom part of the fan body. Figure 9-12 shows which lines to choose.

42 Using the (↓) key move the viewing window up until your view matches that of Figure 9-12. Continue making hard edges at the indicated places.

43 Switch back to Pick Objects mode. (The fan body turns blue.) Select Save from the Object menu. Name the object FANBODY.OBJ and click on OK.

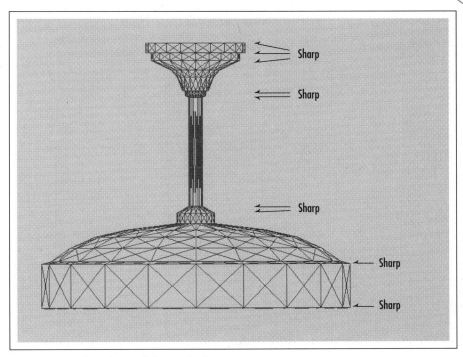

Figure 9-11 Edges that will be made sharp

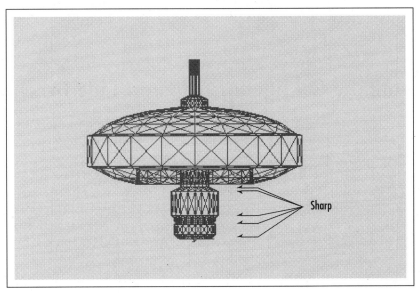

Figure 9-12 Hard edges for the bottom part of the fan body

Viewing the Rendered Fan Body

Let's now preview our work.

44 Enter the perspective view and move the side slider about one inch below its present position. Zoom out to see the entire object. Select Quick Render from the Projects menu and click on OK when ready.

After rendering, your screen should look like Figure 9-13. The fan body has now acquired a flat yellow coating, but it does not look very much like brass! Setting an object's attributes to resemble brass is only the first step in creating a realistic brass appearance. In order to complete the illusion, the object needs to reflect the colors and lights of its surroundings. Since Quick Render uses scanline rendering, we won't see the reflections on the fan body until we ray-trace the scene.

SUBPROJECT 3: CREATING THE FAN BLADE BRACKET

In this subproject we're going to create the bracket that holds the blades to the fan body.

Enter the Detail Editor, ensure you are in the Quad view and there are no existing objects loaded. Be sure your Pick Method is Click (under the Mode menu).

Creating the Outline for the Fan Blade Bracket

Unlike the fan blade, the bracket's shape cannot be formed by shaping a primitive object. The bracket needs to be built from scratch in a similar manner to the fan body.

The bracket shape is included on disk as BRACKET.OBJ in the \IMAG\OBJECTS subdirectory. It has been created to precisely align with the other sections of the fan. Load BRACKET.OBJ from the \IMAG\OBJECTS directory and read through the next five steps (45 to 49) to see how it was built. Figure 9-14 shows the BRACKET.OBJ shape.

45 An axis is added in the Front view.

46 The axis is picked by clicking on the dot at its corner. Add Lines mode is selected.

Figure 9-13 The rendered image

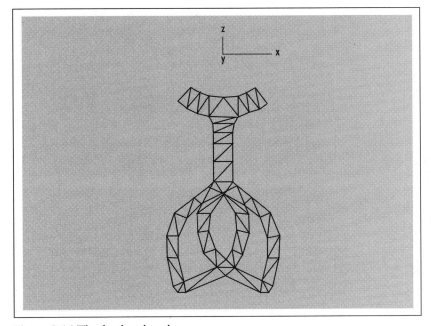

Figure 9-14 The fan bracket shape

47 The outline of a fan blade bracket is drawn, as shown in Figure 9-14. Once the shape is created, the outline is filled in with faces.

Review: Adding Faces to an Object

Lines or Edges cannot be rendered. In order to see an object, the object must have a surface (faces). A face can be defined by selecting any three points on the outline while in Add Face mode. With the exception of the Sphere object, all surfaces defined in Imagine are made up of at least one triangular face. Look at Figure 9-14 to see the pattern of the faces that cover the bracket's surface.

Bending the Bracket

In order for the bracket to fit around the thick blade, it will be bent.

48 Pick Points mode is selected, then Drag Box for the Pick Method, and then the Right view. Figure 9-15 shows the shape of the bend for the BRACKET.OBJ on disk.

The shape is shown in Pick Points mode. Notice how points have been moved away from the Z axis, along the Y axis.

49 In order to pick the points to move, the Front view is selected, where they are picked, and then back to the Right view to move them. When the points are picked, they are moved in the Y direction. Moving them along any other axes would change the shape as seen in the Front view. The Mov button (bottom left of window) is used to move points, deselecting the X and Z buttons (just to the right of the Mov button).

Giving the Bracket Thickness

Once the bracket is shaped, it is ready for extrusion. Make sure BRACKET.OBJ is loaded. Perform the next operation.

50 Under the Object menu select Mold and pick the Extrude option. Type 3 for the length and click on Perform. The object now has a thickness of three units.

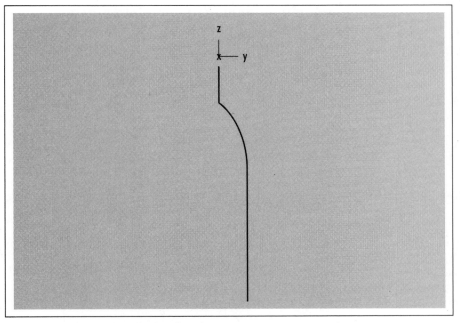

Figure 9-15 The bend in the bracket shape

Giving the Bracket a Surface

We are now ready to give the bracket a brass surface.

51 Select Attributes from the Object menu and click on Load. Navigate to the \IMAG\ATTRIBS directory and click on BRASS. Click on OK.

52 Before leaving the Attributes Requester, ensure that the Phong button has been toggled on. Select OK when finished.

We will now create the sharp edges for the new object.

53 While in the Right view, zoom in and center on the top half of the bracket. Change to Pick Edges mode. You will see the bracket in outline, as shown in Figure 9-16.

Notice the section that is offset to the left. There are two sets of vertical edges in that section that run parallel to each other (making up the front and rear faces). These are the edges we want to make sharp.

54 Select Pick Edges mode and ensure your Pick Method is Drag Box.

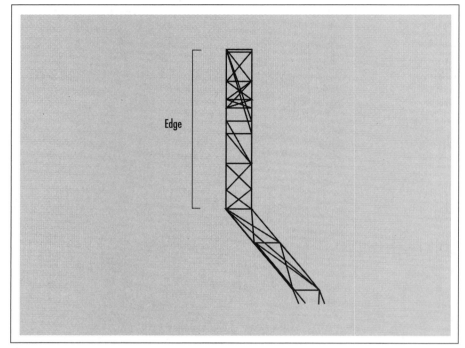

Figure 9-16 The top of the bracket in profile

55 Select Make Sharp for the edges that make up the left side of the vertical section, and then repeat the procedure for the vertical edges on the right side of that section.

56 Select Save from the Object menu. Navigate to the \IMAG\OBJECTS directory. Name the object BRACKET.OBJ and save it.

Finally view the bracket with its new surface.

57 Quick render the bracket.

SUBPROJECT 4: CREATING THE LIGHT SHADE

In this subproject, we'll create a schoolhouse-style frosted glass shade. We'll draw the base plate, downrod, motor housing, and the light base's approximate shape freehand. This shape is on the disk in the \IMAG\OBJECTS directory as SHADE.OBJ.

Enter the Detail Editor. Ensure you are in the Quad view and that there are no existing objects loaded. Be sure your Pick Method is Click (under the Mode menu).

Load SHADE.OBJ from the \IMAG\OBJECTS directory and read the description of how it was created (steps 58 and 59). Figure 9-17 shows the outline shape that will be used to extrude the light shade.

The procedure used to create the shade contour is identical to that used in creating the fan body.

58   The Front view is entered.

59   An axis is added to the screen, then the light shade shape is drawn on the screen (Figure 9-17).

Extruding the Light Shade

Now we'll use Imagine's Spin command to create the shade. Make sure that SHADE.OBJ is loaded.

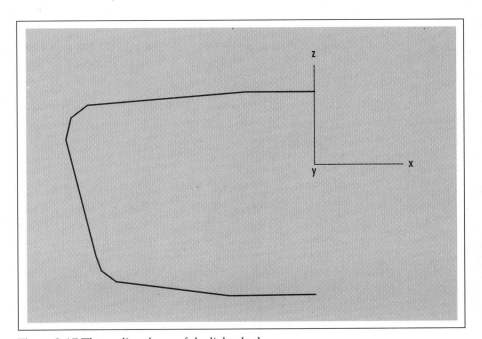

Figure 9-17 The outline shape of the light shade

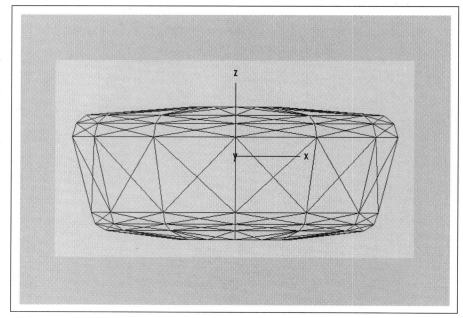

Figure 9-18 Wireframe view of the light shade

60 Pick the shade by clicking on its axis (its color will change to blue). Select Mold from the Object menu and click on Spin. We will leave the # of Sections set at the default: 12. Click on Perform.

The light shade is created; Figure 9-18 shows a wireframe view.

Giving the Light Shade a Surface

In this section, we'll give the light shade a frosted glass surface.

61 Select Attributes from the Object menu and click on Load. Navigate to the \IMAG\ATTRIBS directory and click on FROSTED.ATR. Click on OK when finished.

62 Finally, before leaving the Attributes Requester, make sure that the Phong button is toggled on. This renders the spun object with smoothly shaded curves. Select OK when finished.

63 Select Save from the Object menu. Name the object SHADE.OBJ and click on OK.

SUBPROJECT 5: ASSEMBLING THE FAN

Now we'll assemble the fan. Enter the Detail Editor. Ensure you are in the Quad view and there are no objects loaded. Be sure your Pick Method is Click.

Aligning the Bracket and Fan Blade

Previously, we created a fan blade and bracket. In this section, we're going to align the bracket and fan blade.

64 Select Load from the Object menu. Load BRACKET.OBJ from the \IMAG\OBJECTS directory and click on OK. Center the bracket. Pick the object by clicking on the center of its axis.

Right now the bracket is in its construction orientation. We need to rotate the bracket 90 degrees to line up with the fan blades.

65 Under the Object menu select Transformation (or press (ALT)-(T)). Select the Rotate button and click in the X box. Change the value to -90 (press (ENTER)). Click on Perform when finished.

The bracket is now in the proper orientation. We're ready to load and reorient the fan blade. We'll provide the exact coordinates for placement of the bracket and fan blades.

66 Load the FANBLADE.OBJ. Pick the object and call the Transformation Requester. Select the Rotate button and click in the X box (enter 90) click in the Z box (enter -90).

67 Select the Position button and click in the Y box. Enter the value 131.8333 and press (ENTER). Then click in Z box and enter a value of -200.0833 and press (ENTER). Press Perform.

The fan blade is moved and rotated into a precise alignment with the bracket.

Grouping the Bracket and Fan Blade

Now we're going to attach the bracket and fan blade.

68 Pick the bracket (click on the center of the axis) and, while holding down the (SHIFT) key, pick the fan blade. Select Group from the Object

menu. A yellow line should connect the bracket axis to the fan blade axis.

The objects will continue to move independently of each other in Pick Objects mode, but in Pick Groups mode, they will move together.

Duplicating and Rotating the Bracket and Fan Blade

In this section we'll copy the bracket to Imagine's clipboard, rotate the current bracket, paste down the copy, and rotate it. We'll repeat these steps until all the blades for the fan have been created.

69 Ensure you are in Pick Groups mode. Enter the Top view. Recenter the grouped bracket and fan blade. Pick the bracket (both objects should become picked) and select Copy from the Object menu (or press (ALT)-(C)).

This stores a copy of the bracket in Imagine's clipboard.

In previous sections we rotated the bracket. It is no longer aligned to the world axes. Therefore, we have two options for rotating it into position on the fan: Rotate its local Y axis or rotate it in the world's Z axis. Either option will achieve the same results because the object's Y axis is aligned to the world's Z axis. Use the Transformation Requester for precision.

70 Call the Transformation Requester ((ALT)-(T)). Click on the Rotate button. Click in the Z box. Enter 90 and press (ENTER). Select the World button. Click on Perform.

Copying and Pasting the Other Brackets and Fan Blades

Now we are ready to duplicate the bracket and fan blade.

71 Select Paste from the Object menu. This pastes a copy of the bracket down in its original position. Pick it (press (F1)) and rotate it using the Transformation Requester. Click on the Rotate button. Enter -90 degrees for the Z axis. Click on the World button.

72 Repeat step 71, but this time rotate the object 180 degrees using the World's Z axis. Finally, paste one last time to add the fourth and final

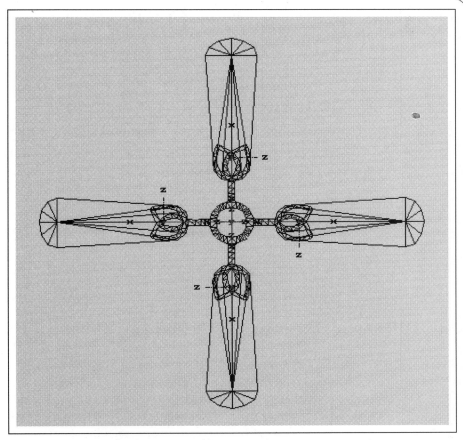

Figure 9-19 The four brackets and blades grouped

bracket and blade. You should now have four bracket and fan blade combinations forming a circle (see Figure 9-19).

73   Select Pick All from the Pick/Select menu. Select Group from the Object menu. Select Save from the Object menu. Name the object BLADES.OBJ and click on OK.

This saves all four brackets and blades as a group. Now we will clear the Detail Editor in preparation for grouping more objects.

74   Select Delete from the Functions menu when saving is complete. This will clear the editor of all objects.

Grouping the Fan Body and Light Shade

75 Switch to the Front view. Load the FANBODY.OBJ.

It should already be positioned correctly.

76 Load the SHADE.OBJ.

Again, it should already be in the correct alignment with the fan body.

77 Now pick the fan body by clicking on its axis. Next, select Pick All from the Pick/Select menu. Select Group from the Object menu. You now have one complex object made up of the glass light shade parented to the fan body.

78 Select Save from the Object menu. Navigate to the \IMAG\OBJECTS directory. Name the object BODY.OBJ and click on OK.

We have now grouped the fan body with the light shade.

SUBPROJECT 6: STAGING THE FAN SCENE

In this subproject we'll assemble the fan blades and fan body and rotate the blades. In order to stage the scene, we need to create a project file.

Enter the Project Editor. (Step 1 opened a new project called TUTORIAL. If you do not have the project open, select Open from the Project menu. Navigate to the \IMAG directory if you are not already there. Select the project, TUTORIAL.)

Creating a Subproject

In order to render the final animation, we need to tell Imagine what rendering mode to use and at what resolution to create the final animation.

79 In the Rendering Subproject section (top quarter of the screen) there are four buttons labeled New, Open, Delete, and Modify. Click on the New button and enter FAN as the file name. Click on OK when done.

The Subproject Parameters box pops on the screen.

80 Accept the defaults for now. Click on OK.

Staging the Ceiling Fan Scene

Now we are going to enter the Stage Editor to add lighting and a camera view to the scene.

81 Select the Stage Editor from the Editor menu.

82 From the Object menu, select Load. Navigate to the \IMAG\OBJECTS directory. Load the file BODY.OBJ and click on OK.

83 Load BLADES.OBJ from the same directory.

We now have a complete ceiling fan. Figure 9-20 shows the shaded perspective view of the ceiling fan.

Now we'll add a light to the scene.

84 Select Add Light Source from the Object menu.

A circle with a dot in it will appear at the center of the fan, representing the light. Move the light to a new position.

85 Press (F1) to pick the light. Call the Transformation Requester ((ALT)-(T)). Click on the Position button and enter X 1472, Y –1064, and Z 327. (Press the (ENTER) key after each entry.) Click on Perform when finished.

Figure 9-20 A shaded perspective view of the ceiling fan

Let's add a second light to give the fan interesting lighting.

86   Repeat steps 84 and 85, except enter X –520, Y –1757, and Z –919 for the second light's position.

Adding a Camera and Target

87   Pick the Camera (it's the circle with a directional pointer near the fan). (Or use the Find Requester (ALT)-(C).) Again, call the Transformation Requester. Select Position. Enter X 371.9999, Y –830, and Z –568.

Now let's add the camera target.

88   Select Add Axis from the Object menu. Just below the fan's base plate an axis should appear.

The target will be used to align the camera to the scene. Let's position it.

89   Call the Transformation Requester. Select Position. Enter X 0, Y 0, and Z –154.

This will slide the axis down from its present position to a position at the center of the fan's motor housing.

Now we'll align the camera to the target.

90   Select Camera View from the Display menu.

This changes the perspective window to the camera view of the scene.

91   Select Camera (Re)track from the Object menu (or press (ALT)-(K)). Enter track in the Track object? box.

The camera now points directly at the axis (which is named "track" by default).

92   Select Save Changes from the Project menu (or press (ALT)-(S)).

The scene is saved.

Setting Up the Global Lighting Conditions

We are now ready to add global lighting to the scene. Global lighting is adjusted in the Action Editor.

93   Select the Action Editor from the Editor menu.

Looking down the left side of the screen, you'll see the GLOBALS element. Use the orange Actor box beside it to call up the Globals Info box where scene lighting is adjusted.

Ensure you are in information mode, selected by clicking on the Info button at the bottom of the screen.

94 Click on the orange Actor box for the GLOBALS element. The Globals Info pop-up box will appear.

95 Click in the End Frame box and change the value to 20 (press ⟨ENTER⟩).

We are now going to add a global brush map to the scene. This gives the reflective surfaces on the fan something to reflect.

96 Click in the box labeled Global Brush Name. Enter the complete path for the file CLOUDS.TIF, \IMAG\MAPS\CLOUDS.TIF, and press ⟨ENTER⟩.

Now we'll give the scene some ambient light.

97 Notice that there are three data entry boxes for ambient lights. Enter a value of 40 for each of the Ambient RGB colors. Click on OK when done.

98 Click on Save Changes in the Project menu.

The Final Render

We are now ready to create the final render of the scene.

99 Enter the Project Editor.

Now we'll modify the rendering parameters.

100 Click on the Modify button.

The Rendering Subproject box pops on the screen.

101 Set the following rendering parameters:

- X: Trace
- Width: 640
- Height: 480
- TGA-24bit

Click on OK.

Figure 9-21
The ceiling fan rendered in ray trace mode

102 Click on the number 1 in the first square of the grid at the middle of the screen.

103 Click on the Generate button.

The scene renders. The information bar at the top of the screen shows progress in rendering. When rendering is complete, a star appears underneath the frame number in the first grid box.

104 Click on the Show button beside the Generate button.

Your screen should now look like Figure 9-21.

SUMMARY

Alan Henry writes about the project: "My approach may or may not have been the most optimal method, but it was the most logical and simplistic for my own style of modeling. The intent of this workshop was to introduce you to the various tools that are used in modeling with the Detail Editor. By gaining hands-on knowledge of their functions you can now build your own modeling techniques."

Animation Workshop

In this chapter we once more enter the workshop of Alan Henry. This time the subject is animation. Alan will animate a worker honeybee. We will not build the bee in this chapter. The bee object is provided on disk in the \IMAG\OBJECTS directory. Color Plate 6 shows the finished model of the worker bee. A description of how the bee was made is provided in Appendix D.

HOW THE BEE IS ANIMATED

The animation workshop shows you how to animate a bee. The honeybee flies in from the left side of the screen at a distance, approaches the monitor screen, pauses, and zips away.

THE FLYING HONEYBEE: STEP-BY-STEP

Complex objects or scenes are often very slow in rendering as single images. When you animate a complex object like a bee in the scene, the rendering time increases exponentially. A modest two-second animation can easily multiply rendering time by a factor of 60. Although you can preview an animation in wireframe, it is often the rendered version that reveals jerky animated motion. Animators often test render the scene at low spatial resolution (160 by 120 pixels is common), but there is another approach that works especially well for test renders.

Rendering with a Substitute Object

Animators often replace stationary objects in a scene with simple "place holders" representing complex objects. They'll also use a substitute object for the animated object itself. The substitute object is a simple representation of the object, usually formed out of primitives with simple geometry. In this workshop, we'll adopt this approach in test rendering the bee.

Once the simple bee's motion is fine-tuned, you can then substitute the complex bee.

The Plan of Attack

Our initial setup and trial animations will use two substitute objects representing the bee: one with wings up and the other with wings down. Each of these objects consists of three simple spheres (the body) and two planes (the wings), which are loaded from the Add Primitives submenu of the Functions menu. These objects will be assembled and then animated.

Creating the Project

Animation will be performed in the Stage and Action editors. In order to enter these, we need to create a project.

1 Select New from the Project menu and name the project BEE.

Now we'll open a rendering subproject.

2 Select New from the Rendering Subproject screen. Name the subproject FLY. When the parameters pop-up box appears, select scanline rendering, the best resolution, and the FLC file format from the "movie" section of the box. Click on OK when finished.

FLC Animation File Format

The FLC animation file format was developed by Autodesk for its 2D animation program, Autodesk Animator Pro. It stores the individual frames of your animation in a single file with the extension .FLC. This standard has been widely supported by other vendors. The animation you create will require some type of player program to play it back, or a program such as Video for Windows that will convert the animation to a another form. The DOS multimedia program, Paul Mace GRASP, is recommended. See Appendix B for more information about this program.

Preparing the Bee Object for Animation

In this section, we'll load the bee object and prepare it for animation.

1. Enter the Detail Editor and select the Front view. Choose Load from the Object menu and select the BEE.OBJ included with this tutorial. Click on OK when the object has been selected.

Removing the Tongue

The bee object as it is stored on disk requires some editing. First we'll remove the bee's tongue, which is sticking out right now in anticipation of a tasty bit of nectar.

2. Change to Object mode by selecting Pick Objects from the Mode menu. Select Find By Name from the Pick/Select menu. When the Object Name pop-up box appears, type tongue. The bee's tongue will change color to brown, indicating that it has been selected. Press (F1) to pick it. Select Delete from the Functions menu or press (ALT)-(D).

Rotating the Wings Up

The bee will flap its wings up and down. In order to give the bee this motion throughout its flight path, we need to create two bee objects, one with its wings up and one with its wings down.

1. Change back to Pick Groups mode. Change to the Right view. First, rotate the wings into their upward extended position. Select Find Requester from the Pick/Select menu or call the Find Requester by press-

ing (ALT)-(F). Select the name SPHERE.1. Three objects will change to the brown (selected) color: Front Wing, Hind Wing, and Wing Root (right side of bee). Select Pick Select from the Pick/Select menu (all three objects turn blue).

Now bend the wing up and back. Alan studied the wing's movement and noticed that it rotated as it extended up. He rotated the wing to the extended position manually. To do this use the Transformation Requester. We'll supply you with exact coordinates.

2   Select Transformation from the Object menu, click on Alignment, and enter X **38.3063**, Y **28.1688**, and Z **0.3771**. (Press (ENTER) after each entry.) Click on Perform.

3   Change to the Front view. Repeat the same procedure as outlined in step 1 for rotating the bee's left wings. The grouped objects are labeled SPHERE. The Alignment coordinates for the right wing's position are X 38.3063, Y -28.1688, and Z -0.3771. Note the negative values for Y and Z.

The bee's wings should now be rotated into position. From the right side, the right wings overlap the left wings. Your screen should look like Figure 10-1.

4   Choose Pick All from the Pick/Select menu. Select Save from the Objects menu. Navigate to the \IMAG\OBJECTS menu and name the object B1.HLD.

Rotating the Wings Down

We'll use the same object to create the down position of the wings.

5   Repeat the steps (1, 2, 3) for picking each wing group and altering the coordinates for their alignment with the following coordinates:

⊕   SPHERE.1: X 179.7081, Y -85.9241, Z 117.2121

⊕   SPHERE: X 179.7081, Y 85.9241, Z -117.2121

Your screen should now look like Figure 10-2. These are coordinates Alan determined were best for the bee's wings in the down position.

6   Choose Pick All from the Pick/Select menu. Select Save from the Objects menu and name the object B2.HLD.

Figure 10-1 The bee's wings rotated up

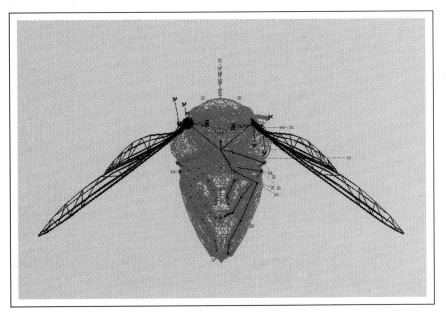

Figure 10-2 The bee's wings in the downward position

Creating the Substitute Object

Now we'll create the substitute object, using the fully formed bee as our basis.

1   With the B2.HLD still present in the Detail Editor, switch to the Right view. Center the bee in the display, either with the arrow keys or by selecting Re-Center from the Display menu and clicking on the center of the bee's thorax.

Adding and Duplicating Primitive Spheres

We are now going to add the primitive shapes that will stand in for the bee. They will be crude but effective.

2   Select Add Primitive from the Functions menu (or press (F5) and click on Sphere). Enter **6** for both the Circle and Vertical Sections and deselect the Stagger Points button. Click on OK when finished. A brown sphere appears in the center of the screen.

3   Choose Pick Select from the Pick/Select menu (or press (F1)). Click on the Mov (move) button at the bottom of the screen and, while holding down the left mouse button, position the sphere at approximately the center of the bee's head.

4   Click on the Rot button at the bottom of the screen and select the X button beside it to restrict rotation to the X axis. Again, holding down the left mouse button, rotate the sphere forward (top tilted to the left) approximately 66 degrees. Watch the readout at the top right side of screen as you do this.

5   Select Copy from the Object menu and click on the Mov button again. This time, move the sphere to the center of the bee's thorax. Press the (SPACEBAR).

6   Select Paste from the Object menu (or press (ALT)-(P)).

A copy of the sphere appears over the head.

7   Again, select Copy and click on the Mov button. Position the sphere at the center of the bee's abdomen.

8   Select Paste from the Object menu. A copy of the sphere now appears over the thorax.

9 Click on Rot and select the X button (see step 4) and rotate the abdomen sphere backward -30 degrees. This will align the sphere closely to the actual bee object's abdomen. Press the (SPACEBAR).

Shaping the Three Spheres into the Bee's Shape

You have three major sections of the bee created, but they don't look much like the bee. Let's fix that. We'll bend and squash the spheres into a better likeness. Figure 10-3 shows what the spheres will look like when you are finished.

1 Starting with the abdomen sphere object, click on the Scl button at the bottom of the screen and select the Loc (local axis) button. Ensure that only the Z button is depressed.

Selecting the Loc button allows manipulation of an object based on its own axis rather than the world axis. In other words, as in the case with the abdomen object, with its Z axis angled forward 36 degrees, scaling the object along its own Z axis maintains the object's original symmetric shape. Scaling the object using the world axis would cause the object to grow vertically and result in a distorted, asymmetrical object.

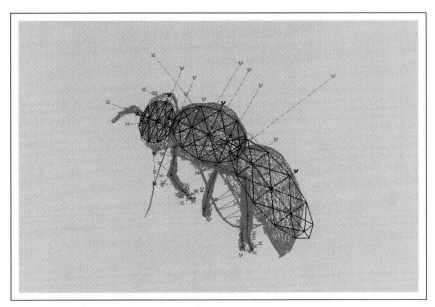

Figure 10-3 The resized primitive spheres

2 Hold down the left mouse button and scale the object to a factor of approximately 2.4, as shown in the readout at the upper right corner of screen. Press the (SPACEBAR) when finished.

3 Pick the sphere object that represents the thorax by clicking on its axis.

4 Click on the Scl button and ensure the Loc and X, Y, and Z buttons are selected. Scale the thorax sphere to a factor of 1.20. (Do not press the (SPACEBAR) yet.) Now, deselect the X and Y buttons. Scale the object along its Z axis to a factor of 1.20. Press the (SPACEBAR).

5 Select the sphere that represents the head. Use Select Next in the Pick Select menu or press the (ALT)-(N) key combination to single out the head sphere.

6 Click on Scl and select the Loc and the Z button to deselect X and Y scaling. Scale the head sphere to a factor of .65. Press the (SPACEBAR).

Scaling the Spheres in the Front View (X Axis)

Now scale the three spheres to the width of the bee's body.

7 Switch to the Front view.

8 With the head sphere still picked, click on Scl and select the Loc and X buttons (Z and Y deselected). Scale the head sphere to a factor of 1.20. Press the (SPACEBAR).

9 Pick the thorax sphere. (Switch back to the Right view temporarily to do this.) Scale this object along its local X axis to a factor of 1.5. Press the (SPACEBAR).

10 Pick the abdomen sphere. Scale this object along its local X axis to a factor of 1.5.

Grouping the Three Spheres

Now group the three segments into a single object and position the body's axis correctly.

1 Switch to the Right view.

Use the Select Next command (ALT)-(N) to choose the three spheres in the next step.

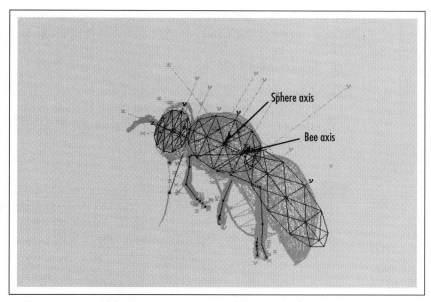

Figure 10-4 The grouped spheres and the axes for the bee and sphere

2　First pick the middle (thorax) sphere object, then, holding down the
(SHIFT) key, pick the head and abdomen objects. Choose Group from the
Object menu.

Figure 10-4 shows the grouped spheres and the location of their axes.

Creating the Substitute Object's Center of Gravity

When you grouped the three spheres, the first object you picked became the
parent object. This is signified by the lines that radiate from the parent object's
axis. The axis of the parent object can be considered the center of gravity or
rotation for the object. When this object moves, it moves relative to this center
of gravity. Placement of this axis is critical in producing realistic animation. An
aircraft would appear awkward if its roll axis was offset to the end of a wing
tip. As the aircraft maneuvered in the animation it would have an unnatural
look. Normally, as one wing rises the opposite wing drops, leaving aside the
effects of pitch and yaw. However, in a displaced roll axis, the wing tip where
the axis was located would not roll opposite the other wing. Instead, it would
remain stationary while the other wing and the fuselage pivot up (or down).
If every object within the group must maintain a specific axis position, and the

overall object's main axis doesn't correspond conveniently to one of these axes, an axis can be added (Add Axis) and used as the parent by grouping the overall object to it.

In this case, we'll use the center sphere's axis as the center of gravity.

1　Hold down the (SHIFT) key and press the (M) key to move the center sphere's (thorax) axis. Holding down the left mouse button, move the thorax sphere axis to correspond with the real bee's thorax axis. Press the (SPACEBAR).

Now we move the Y axis forward.

2　Select Transformation from the Object menu and click on Alignment. Enter 0.0 for the X and Y coordinates and –180 for the Z coordinates (press (ENTER) after each entry). Select the Transform Axes Only button and click on Perform (this aligns the Y axis forward which, in turn, defines the direction the object faces when it follows a path).

Now remove the bee object from the picture.

3　Select Find Requester from the Pick/Select menu. When the Object List requester appears, select the thorax object. Press (F1) to pick the bee object.

4　Select Delete from the Functions menu.

Figure 10-5 shows the wingless bee substitute.

Adding the Wings

In this section, we use a plane primitive for the substitute bee's wings.

1　Change to the Front view.

2　Choose Add Primitive from the Functions menu and select Plane. Enter 300 for Width, 100 for Height, and 1.0 for the Horizontal and Vertical Sections. Click on OK when done. This object represents the wing.

3　Select Pick Select from the Pick/Select menu or press (F1).

4　Select Pick Points from the Mode menu. Click on the point at the upper right corner of the plane and choose Delete from the Functions menu.

5　Select Pick Group from the Mode menu. Hold down the (SHIFT) key and then press the (M) key. Holding down the left mouse button, move the

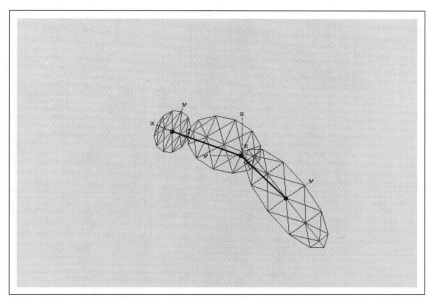

Figure 10-5 The bee substitute without wings

Plane object's axis to the lower right corner of the object. Press the (SPACEBAR).

6   Click on the Mov button (without the (SHIFT) key) and move the object so that its axis just touches the left side of the bee's head (see Figure 10-6).

7   Go to the Right view and move the wing so that it just touches the first segment on the thorax near the head. Deselect the X and Z buttons to allow the wing to move on the Y axis only. Figure 10-7 shows where to move the wing.

8   Click on the Rot button and select the X button. Rotate the wing -108 degrees (indicated in the upper left of the screen). Switch to the Front view and select the Y button. Rotate the wing 81 degrees. Press the (SPACEBAR). Your screen should now look like Figure 10-8.

Now duplicate the wing on the other side by copying the wing to the clipboard and pasting it down again.

9   Select Copy from the Object menu.

10 Select Transformation from the Object menu and click on Scale. Enter -1 for the X coordinate and press (ENTER). Click on the World button

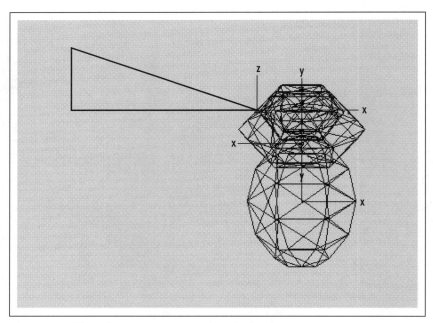

Figure 10-6 The substitute wing moved to the head

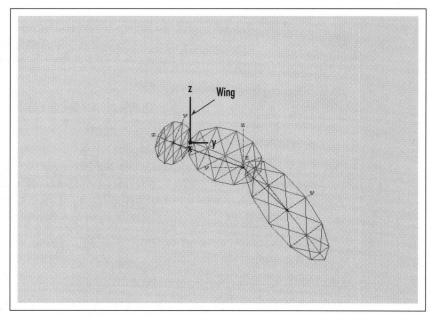

Figure 10-7 The wing moved in the Right view

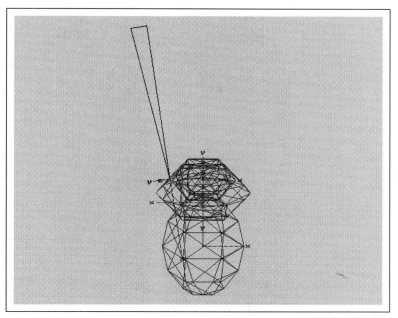

Figure 10-8 The repositioned wing in the Front view

and, finally, click on Perform. This creates a mirror image of the wing object.

11 Click on the Mov button and deselect the Y and Z buttons. Move the new wing just to the right of the bee's head.

12 Select Paste from the Object menu. The original wing reappears in its original position. Figure 10-9 shows the two wings in position.

13 Switch to the Right view. Select the middle (thorax) object. Select Pick All from the Pick/Select menu and select Group from the Object menu.

14 Choose Save from the Object menu and name the object B1.OBJ. Click on OK.

15 Switch to the Front view. Pick the left wing by clicking on its axis. Click on the Rot button and select Y. Rotate the wing -144 degrees. Click on OK when done.

16 Repeat the process for the right wing, except rotate it 144 degrees.

17 Switch to the Right view. Pick the thorax object. Select Save from the Object menu and name the object B2.OBJ. Press the (SPACEBAR).

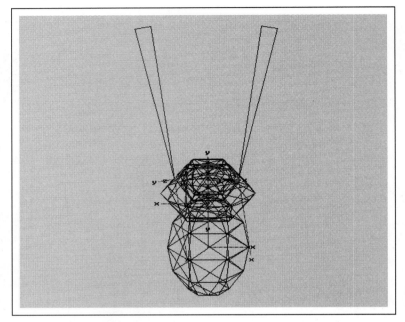

Figure 10-9 The wings in position

CREATING THE ANIMATION
PATHS FOR THE BEE

Although the expression "make a bee line" has long accustomed us to the idea that bees can fly in very straight lines, much of the time, bees follow curved paths. Imagine's spline technology allows you to define those curved paths. You will be familiar with splines if you have worked with draw and paint programs that allow you to interactively create curved lines by manipulating control points along the line. Using spline paths for animation produces very smooth motion. (Spline paths are covered in Chapter 6. See Figure 6-40 in that chapter.)

The bee flies in from the left, slows down as it approaches the screen, pauses, turns around, and speeds up as it flies away to the right. Look ahead to Figure 10-11 to see the shape of the paths. Imagine allows the user to define acceleration and deceleration along paths. We will work with two separate paths: the approach to the screen and the fly away. These paths will share a common point: at the screen where the bee pauses.

Tip: Creating Spline Paths

Spline paths can be added and edited in either the Detail or the Stage editors. The tools for editing the spline paths are identical, however some are named differently depending on which editor you are working in. The following are the tools used for editing a path in the Detail Editor cross-referenced with their sister tools in the Stage Editor:

Detail Editor	Stage Editor
Add Path (Functions menu)	Add Path (Object menu)
Edit Path (Mode menu)	Edit Path (Mode menu)
Fracture (Functions menu)	Split Segment (Path menu)
Delete (Functions menu)	Delete Point (Path menu)
Pick Object/Group (Mode menu)	Pick Groups (Mode menu)
Save (Object menu)	Save Path (Path menu)*

* While editing a path in the Stage Editor, Imagine will automatically query you as to whether you want to save the path when you exit the Edit Path mode.

We create the spline paths in the Stage Editor.

1. Enter the Stage Editor and switch to the Top view.

2. Select Add Open Path from the Object menu. A pop-up box appears requesting you to name the added path. Navigate to the \IMAG\OBJECTS directory and name it PATH1.OBJ. Click on OK.

An axis appears in the center of the screen with a line running along the Y axis. This is the base path object for the path the bee follows throughout the animation.

3. Choose Pick Select from the Pick/Select menu or press (F1).

4. Select Edit Path from the Mode menu.

Three points now appear on the line. Notice that each point has its own axis. The center point defines the path object's local axis, and the two end point axes are used to define an object's orientation as it moves across each specific location. For example, if the axis rotates 30 degrees around the Y axis, an object following the path will rotate 30 degrees in the Y axis as it passes over that point. Additionally, Imagine interpolates the object's orientation as it moves between two adjacent points, based on the difference between each point's axes orientation.

The point closest to the front is the beginning point for the path. Since we want the bee to fly toward us, we need to move the front point to the beginning position.

5 Pick the point at the front of the path. This will be the bottom point in the Top view.

To make it easy for you, the beginning and end points for the path have been plotted.

6 Choose Transformation from the Object menu and click on Position. Enter X -939.6262, Y 713.8725, and Z 37.3333. Press (ENTER) after each entry. Click on the Alignment button, enter Z -92.3997 and press (ENTER). Click on Perform.

This orients the point's Y axis. The bee will fly in from the left. Now position the point just in front of the screen, where the bee pauses and looks out at you.

7 Select the point at the other end of the path. Choose Transformation from the Object menu and click on Position. Enter X -165.6321, Y -696.2404, and Z 17.6951. Click on the Alignment button and enter Z 167.1975. This orients the end point's Y axis to allow the bee object to rotate toward you and slightly to the right of the screen. Click on Perform.

The path in the Top view should look like Figure 10-10.
Now we'll add a slight direction change in the bee's flight path.

8 Select the point at the back of the path (at the top of the Top view) and select Split Segment from the Path menu.

This will cause a new point, or axis, to appear midway along the path. Notice that its orientation is an exact interpolation between the two end points.

9 Pick the new point, select Transformation from the Object menu, and click on Position. Enter X -228.4997, Y 540.7396, and Z 27.5142.

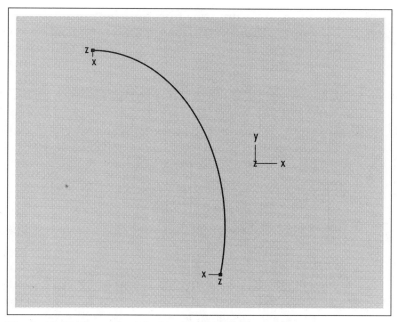

Figure 10-10 The path of the bee in the Top view so far

Click on the Alignment button and enter X `-0.9128`, Y `0.0909`, and Z `-123.3421` Click on Perform when complete.

This curves the path up and to the right, as seen in the Top view.

10   Select Pick Groups from the Mode menu. Imagine asks if you would like to save your edited path. Answer *yes*, and be sure the name is PATH1.OBJ. Click on OK when done.

One more path!

11   Select Add Open Path from the Object menu and name it PATH2.OBJ.

12   Choose Pick Select from the Pick/Select menu or press (F1).

13   Select Edit Path from the Mode menu and click on the bottom point.

14   Select Transformation from the Object menu and click on the Position button. Enter X `-165.6321`, Y `-696.2405`, and Z `17.6951`. Click on the Alignment button and enter X `0.0`, Y `0.0`, and Z `167.2010`. Click on Perform.

15   Pick the point farthest from the front.

16   Select Transformation from the Object menu and click on the Position button. Enter X 379.7355, Y 291.8677, and Z 51.3333. Click on the Alignment button and enter X 0.0, Y 0.0, and Z -88.8004. Click on Perform.

17   Select the front (bottom) point and choose Split Segment from the Path menu.

18   Click on the newly created point and select Transformation from the Object menu. Click on Position and enter X -17.5782, Y -628.3076, and Z 1.8476 (press (ENTER) after each entry).

19   Click on the Alignment button and enter X 8.5551, Y 20.4403, and Z -36.9931. Click on Perform.

20   Choose Split Segment from the Path menu and again, click on the newly created point.

21   Click on the newly formed point. Select Transformation from the Object menu. Select Position and enter X -193.2725, Y -24.9458, and Z 46.7759. Click on Alignment and enter X 1.6124, Y 9.5282, and Z -7.8523. Click on Perform.

22   Choose Pick Groups from the Mode menu and save the object.

The paths should now look like Figure 10-11.

We've created the bee objects and the paths, now let's set the stage and begin animating.

SETTING THE STAGE

Before we add any objects to the Stage Editor, we need to tell Imagine how many frames will be in our animation. We'll do this in the Action Editor.

When you leave the Stage Editor, Imagine will inform you that the last changes were not saved. We do not need to save anything at this point. Click on the Yes button when prompted.

1   Enter the Action Editor.

In the upper right corner there is a box labeled Highest Frame #.

2   Click in the box and enter 100 (press (ENTER)).

Notice that the grid along the top fills in with frame numbers, from 1 to 100. Now return to the Stage Editor.

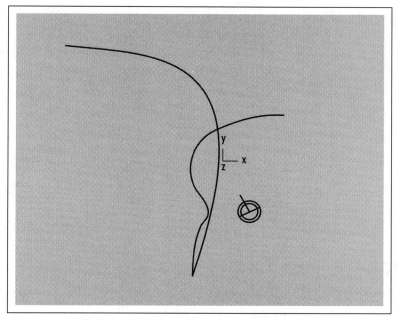

Figure 10-11 The two bee flight paths and the camera in the Top view

3 Select Save Changes under the Project menu. Return to the Stage Editor.

This time, when you enter the Stage Editor, you'll be asked for a frame number.

4 Enter 1 and press (ENTER).

Positioning the Camera

Right now, the camera is pointing at the center of the world. We'll position it at the front of the path.

1 Select Find Requester from the Pick/Select menu and click on the object named Camera.

2 Press (F1) and then (ALT)-(T).

3 Click on Position and enter X -101.9995, Y -1178.0006, and Z 66.6667. Click on Perform.

Adding and Positioning the Lights

1 Select Add Light Source from the Object menu and press (F1).

2 Select Transformation from the Object menu and click on the Position button. Enter X 2175.9998, Y -765.3331, and Z 672.0000. Click on Perform.

Now add a second light.

3 Select Add Light Source from the Object menu and press (F1).

4 Press (ALT)-(T) and click on the Position button. Enter X -616.0001, Y -1950.6666, and Z -65.3319. Click on Perform.

Figure 10-12 shows the positions of the lights and camera.

Adding a Camera Target

Notice that the camera is pointing away from the path. We'll add a target for the camera to point at.

1 Select Add Axis from the Object menu and press (F1).

2 Select Transformation from the Object menu and click on the Position button. Enter X -231.9995, Y -48.6655, and Z -2.3320. Click on Perform.

3 Select Save Changes from the Project menu.

4 Switch to the Action Editor.

Locking the Camera to Its Target

To align the camera to the target, delete the existing alignment button for the target object and add a new alignment button.

1 Select Delete from the Functions menu.

2 Each object loaded into the Stage Editor is listed down the left side of the Action Editor. Place your cursor in the area just to the right of the block labeled CAMERA. While in this area, align the cursor with frame number 1 and the word *Align* (found on the right side of the screen). Click on the small blue rectangle found at that position. It will disappear.

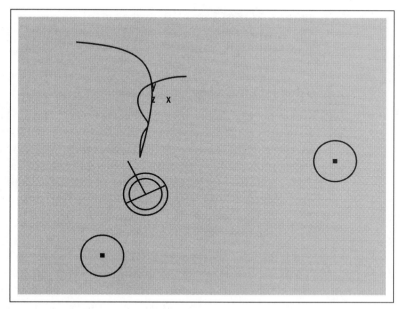

Figure 10-12 Positions of the lights and camera

Now we'll align the camera to the axis we created.

3   Select Add from the Functions menu.

4   Place the cursor in the vacated space for the alignment actor and click twice. (The first click indicates beginning frame and the second click indicates end frame. In this case both are frame 1.) A pop-up box will appear. Click on Track to Object. A Track to Object Info requester will appear next. Click in the box labeled Object Name and enter the word t r a c k (press (ENTER)). Click on OK.

The camera is now aligned to the axis we added earlier.

Adjusting the Global Settings

Now we'll adjust the global settings for the scene. The first adjustment we'll make is to the world size for this scene. A size setting of 0 forces Imagine to scale the world size to fit all of the objects loaded. This can sometimes speed up rendering time and prevent objects from not appearing because they are outside the world limits.

1. In the GLOBALS area, align the cursor on the Size line and frame 1. Click twice. When the Sizing Info requester appears, enter 100 in the End Frame box. Then change the X, Y, and Z boxes to a value of 0. Click on OK.

2. Select Info from the Functions menu.

3. Click on the Actor line in the GLOBALS area. The Globals Info requester will appear. Change the End Frame number to 100. Change all three of the Ambient RGB values to 20. This determines how dark the shadows will be. Change the Horizon RGB values to 175, 200, and 255, respectively. This sets the color of the background horizon. Change the +Zenith RGB to 100, 150, and 255. This sets the color above the horizon. Change the -Zenith RGB to 0, 125, and 0. This sets the color below the horizon. Click on OK when done.

4. Find the objects labeled LIGHTSOURCE, LIGHTSOURCE.1, and TRACK. Use the slider bar on the right side if necessary. These objects' Actor bars should extend from frame 1 to 100. If they do not, click on each object's Actor bar and change the End Frame value to 100. This ensures that the lights don't turn off midway into the animation.

5. Click on the orange Actor box beside the PATH object. Leave the Start Frame as 1 and the End Frame as 54. Click OK when done.

6. Click on the orange Actor box beside PATH.1. Line up the cursor with frame 55. (Use the slider box at the bottom of the screen to do this.) Click twice. Leave the Start Frame at 55 and change the End Frame to 100.

Adding the Honeybees to the Scene

1. Click on the slider bar at the far right until you can see the object listed as "(new)". Switch to Add mode. Double-click on the Actor bar at Frame 1. Select Normal Object. Navigate to the \IMAG\OBJECTS menu. Load B1.OBJ and click on OK. Ensure the object's Start and End Frames are 1 and click on OK.

Notice the object's label on the left side of the screen. Instead of listing the object as B1.OBJ, it says SPHERE.XX. Imagine's internal name for the object rather than its file name is used. Let's rename the object to make it easier to find in the future.

Tip: Take a Break

Next we are going to add the two honeybee objects to the scene. This is a little tedious so you might want to take a break.

2   Click on the Rename button at the bottom of the screen. Rename the object as B1.OBJ.

Now comes the tedious part. We're going to make the bee's wings flap by alternating between the object with the bee's wings up (B1.OBJ) and the bee's wings down (B2.OBJ) positions.

3   Change back to Add mode. On the Actor line, add the B1.OBJ to every odd frame. For example, click on frame 3, select B1.OBJ, click on OK, double-click on 5, select B1.OBJ, and so on. Make sure the Start and End Frames are values for the current frame. Continue to frame 99.

4   Again, on the same Actor line, add B2.OBJ to every even frame number (frames 2, 4, 6, and so on) up to and including 100.

5   Select Delete from the Functions menu and click on the Posn. bar for the bee at frame 1.

6   Select Add from the Functions menu and double-click in the same position (Posn. bar/frame 1). Click on Follow Path. Set Start Frame to 1 and End Frame to 54. Click in the Path Name box and enter PATH. Change the Deceleration Frames to 15. Click on OK when finished.

7   Repeat step 6, but double-click at frame 55. Set Start Frame to 55 and End Frame to 100. Change the Path Name to PATH.1 and the Acceleration Frames to 20. Click on OK when done.

8   Select Delete from the Functions menu and delete the bee's Align bar at frame 1.

9   Select Add from the Functions menu and double-click on the bee's Align bar at frame 1. Click on Align to Path (faces the bee in the direction of the path). Set Start Frame to 1 and End Frame to 100. Click on the Keep Y Horizontal button (this maintains the bee's pitch orientation throughout the animation). Click on OK when complete.

The Size parameter beside B1.OBJ allows you to scale an object larger or smaller during an animation. Deleting the Size bar beside B1.OBJ forces Imagine to use the size of the object as it is recorded on the hard drive. Since we will be switching from the real bee to its substitute, we want Imagine to use the default size of the object. This is a precautionary measure since our animation does not actually change the size of the bee.

10   Select Delete from the Functions menu and delete the Size bar at frame 1.

11   Select Save Changes from the Project menu.

We're finished — now we can animate!

PREVIEWING THE ANIMATION

Let's preview our animation.

1   Return to the Stage Editor. When prompted for the frame number, select frame 1.

2   Select Camera View and Solid from the Display menu. This provides a solid-shaded preview of the animation.

3   Select Make from the Animate menu. Press the (ENTER) key to accept the default values for the Start, End, and Step values. Imagine takes a few moments to render the animation in wireframe.

4   When the rendering has finished (Cancel disappears from the center of the screen), select Play Loop from the Animate menu. While the animation is playing, move the slider bar in the Animation Controller to the left until you reach an acceptable speed.

As you can see, the substitute bee renders quickly. It is much more efficient and faster to use a simple object when fine-tuning animations. Additionally, the screen redrawing time, when switching between views, is much shorter. Once you have created a fully adjusted animation path, you can swap the real bee for the substitute bee. The next section shows you how to do this.

USING THE REAL BEE

One method of exchanging the real bee (B1.HLD) for the substitute bee (B1.OBJ) is to return to the Action Editor. There, while in information mode, you select each entry on the Actor line of the bee object, change the .OBJ extension to a .HLD extension, and then choose Saving Changes again.

A much faster method is to exit Imagine to DOS, change to the \IMAG\OBJECTS directory, and rename the B1.OBJ and B2.OBJ files to B1.OLD and B2.OLD. Next, rename the B1.HLD and B2.HLD files to B1.OBJ and B2.OBJ. (Use the REN rename command, for example, you would type REN B1.OBJ B1.HLD.) It is very important to rename the files in this order or you could overwrite the substitute bee before you have had a chance to rename it.

RENDERING THE FINAL ANIMATION

Now let's return to the Project Editor to do the final render. First we'll select the frames to render. Load the BEE project and the FLY subproject.

1. In the Project Editor, click on the Range button. We'll use the default Start, End, and Step settings. Press (ENTER). All of the frames highlight.

2. Click on the Make button and answer *yes* to "Lock the Palette?", and *yes* to the question about deleting files. This creates an animation with a single color palette, and deletes the single frame files that are compiled into a single animation file at the end of the animation rendering process.

Imagine will now begin the long task of rendering your animation. Be careful not to interrupt the rendering process since the picture files are deleted after they are no longer needed.

SUMMARY

Alan Henry's bee animation workshop shows you how to use Imagine's powerful animation capabilities to make objects follow animation paths. The same approach can be used for flying logos or kites. Animation tools vary widely between 3D programs, but some of the key concepts (paths, acceleration, and test rendering with simple objects) are common across programs.

Tutorial on Imagine

It's rare that software exudes personality. Most of the spreadsheet programs and word processors you may be using are as bland and bloodless as a military barracks. Extremely functional—but you wouldn't want to live there.

Imagine is bursting with personality. It has acquired some of the idiosyncrasies and maverick quality of the Commodore Amiga itself. The IBM-PC version of Imagine bundled with this book is identical in its interface to the Amiga version that precedes it by eight years. (Imagine evolved from a program called Turbo Silver.)

Don't try to approach Imagine without taking into account that it comes from a different microcomputer culture: the millions of Amiga users. The Amiga is a graphics enthusiast's hardware and software environment. Try to argue the merits of an Apple or Intel machine with an Amiga owner, and you'll soon find you are dealing with a fanatic. The Amiga was created with graphics, animation, and music in mind. Although it is extremely well suited

Amiga Conventions

Here are a few notable Amiga conventions that may trip up DOS power users:

1. Jargon: IBM-DOS dialog boxes are called *requesters*. Buttons are called *gadgets*. Directories are called *drawers*.

2. (ALT) keys: The IBM-PC keyboard left (ALT) key is not used. All (ALT) commands use the *right* (ALT) key.

3. Data and words entered into boxes must terminate with the (ENTER) key. Clicking on the OK button means you have finished using a pop-up box; it does *not* confirm changes to the box.

to multimedia, it has never enjoyed much success in the white-collar world of North American corporate computing. (In Europe its design has been more readily embraced.)

Impulse's Imagine on the PC shows its Amiga heritage right in the interface. The version bundled with this book is virtually identical in its functionality and layout to the Amiga version of the program that preceded it. For some PC users habituated to the metaphors and practices of PC programs, mousing around in Imagine may raise hackles and lead to frustration. But once you crawl over the initial hurdles, you'll be surprised at how quickly you'll be on your feet running. Experienced users soon learn to appreciate the speed it brings to modeling and animating. Imagine is slow in becoming *friendly* … but it becomes a good friend of the modeler indeed.

Imagine is no upstart. It is approaching a decade on the market. Mike Halvorson, its designer, answers many of the technical support calls himself. Most of the methods Imagine uses are implemented for very good reasons. Once you've found all of Imagine's features, you'll come to admire its depth and quality. It is a mature product that incorporates the suggestions and needs of thousands and thousands of users.

WHAT YOU WILL NEED FOR THIS TUTORIAL

- Imagine installed
- Memory configured according to the Installation Notes at the beginning of the book
- A basic knowledge of MS-DOS

IMAGINE'S INTERFACE

Imagine uses a modern graphical user interface (GUI) that allows you to draw on the screen with a mouse or quickly choose program options by clicking areas of the screen. These areas might be menu bars, selection lists, buttons, or boxes requesting information from you (called *requesters* in Amiga jargon or *dialog boxes* in PC jargon). Some pop-up boxes on the screen allow you to enter file names or program values. You'll learn how to use these methods of interacting with Imagine as we go along.

When you first start Imagine, you are presented with a welcome screen (Figure A-1). From this screen you can jump to various program modules.

Using the Menu Bar to Move Between Editors

The narrow brown band at the top of the screen is called an information bar. It provides information about program status.

1   With your mouse cursor situated anywhere on the screen, press the *right* button and keep it depressed.

Figure A-1 Imagine's opening screen

Notice that the bar at the top of the screen changes to a menu bar: "Editor Project." A menu bar provides access to program functions. This particular menu bar has two main menus of commands. Let's see what they are.

2   Let go of the mouse key and move the mouse cursor over the word *Imagine* on the menu bar. Click with the left mouse button.

The Editor menu drops down, covering part of the screen. Your screen should look like Figure A-2. Notice that the Editor menu bar lists the modules that you can jump to from this screen (Detail, Forms, Cycle, Stage, Action, Preferences).

3   Move the mouse over the word *Imagine* at the top left and click once. Then move the mouse cursor down until the menu choice, Forms Editor, is highlighted. Click once.

Your screen should now look like Figure A-3.

Working with Object and Scene Menus

The Forms Editor is one of Imagine's object editing modules. Its menuing system is similar to those found in the majority of modules, including the Forms, Cycle, Stage, and Action editors.

Quad View

The screen is divided into four different viewing screens, offering four different views of the object. Access to object or scene editing commands is through three principal means:

- A menu bar at the top of the screen
- Keys or key combinations that allow you to use the keyboard to access program functions
- Button bars

The Menu Bar

The menu bar at the top of the screen is similar to the menu bar found in the opening screen. In object and scene editing screens the menu bar keeps most of

Figure A-2 The drop-down Editor menu

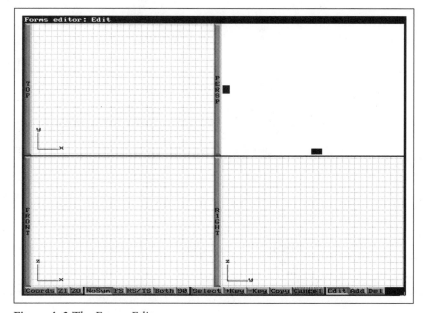

Figure A-3 The Forms Editor

the program options hidden while you work in the viewing windows creating objects.

4 Click on the menu bar, release the button, and then run the mouse cursor along the menu bar.

As you do this, menus drop down. Imagine commands are organized into groups. For example, listed on the Object drop-down menu are such familiar operations as setting up the program to create a new object (New), loading an existing object (Load), saving an object you have created (Save), and forcing an object to line up with the grid (Snap to Grid).

Check Marks

Notice that some menu items have check marks, such as those in the Display menu (Figure A-4). Menu items with check marks are usually a group of mutually exclusive commands that perform similar functions. For example, in the Display menu, Wireframe, Solid, and Shaded refer to three different viewing options. By default Wireframe view is selected. If you select Solid, the check mark moves from Wireframe to Solid. The check mark confirms that Solid is the current viewing mode. When you load an object and view it in the perspective window, it will appear as a solid object.

Canceling Drop-Down Menus

You can cancel a drop-down menu by clicking on the screen anywhere outside of the menu.

Using the Keyboard to Access Commands

You may have noticed that many menu items have keyboard alternatives listed in light gray beside menu items. If you look at the Object drop-down menu, you will see that the first three menu items (New, Load, and Save) have keyboard equivalents listed as (ALT)-(N), (ALT)-(L), and (ALT)-(S). These key combinations allow you to activate commands in the editor from the keyboard, without having to click on the menu bar with the mouse. Imagine does not use the *left* (ALT) key. When keyboard commands are called for, use the *right* (ALT) key.

Let's bring up the Object Load box using a keyboard combination.

5 If the Object menu is open, cancel it by clicking anywhere outside of it.

6 Press the *right* (ALT) key, and while holding it down, press the (N) key.

This brings up the New object dialog box. An Object Load box will pop onto the screen. When the box appears, cancel it by clicking on Cancel located at the bottom of the box. Keyboard shortcuts (also called *hot keys*) can improve productivity dramatically because you do not have to "mouse around" the menu bar.

Many hot keys do not require the use of the (ALT) key. For example, the left (SHIFT) key places Imagine into Multi-mode, allowing you to select several objects (or parts of objects) at once. It works in conjunction with other commands. Some commands, like Move, can be activated by pressing a single key, (M); and some commands use the function keys at the top of your keyboard.

The Button Bar

Imagine provides another kind of shortcut for the 3D modeler working in the Object and Scene editors. This is the button bar. It's the yellow bar of buttons stretching along the bottom of the screen. Placed here are the most common commands in the editor. Clicking on any of these buttons has the same effect as using keyboard alternatives.

We'll leave the Forms Editor to explore some of Imagine's other features.

Using Information Boxes

When you do not have a project open and attempt to enter the Stage or Action editors, an error box advises you that a project has *not* been opened. Let's try that now.

7   Open the Editor menu and click on Stage Editor.

By now you should know what "open the Editor menu" means: Move the mouse cursor to the menu bar, click, and move the mouse cursor over the Editor menu. It drops down. When you click on Stage Editor, a box pops on the screen (see Figure A-5).

Figure A-4
The Display Menu with check marked items

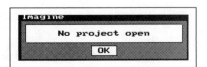

Figure A-5 Pop-up box

Any box that appears on the screen when you perform some action, or when a program function has concluded, is called a pop-up box or a requester. Some of these boxes simply give you information. An example is the "No project open" box.

In order to proceed, you must click on OK to confirm that you have seen the message.

8   Click on OK.

In this case, clicking on OK removes the box from the screen and jumps you into the Project Editor. A Project File Name box automatically pops on the screen (see Figure A-6).

How to Use File Boxes

Creating a new project requires that you name a project. Imagine uses a Project Name box to open and name a project. Let's work with the New Project Name box.

9   Open the Project menu and click on Open.

Figure A-7 labels the parts of the Project Name box. It has five main areas: a text entry box where the current directory can be specified, a window on the current directory, a scroll bar, a file name entry box, and buttons. The main parts of the box are labeled in Figure A-7. Let's review each of them in turn.

The Drawer

At the top of the box there is a text entry box called "Drawer." Drawer is an Amiga term describing a directory on the hard drive. Imagine allows you to specify the path name of the directory where you want the new project to be stored. The current path is also displayed in this box. As you navigate deeper into a directory tree, the Drawer text entry list is built just like a path in DOS (for example, D:\IMAGINE\OBJECTS\MARBLES\GRAY).

If you know the directory name you want, you can click in this box, delete the current path name, and enter the path name of the desired directory.

The Directory Window

Below the Drawer text entry box is the directory window. It is the large gray area in the middle of the Project Name box. You can see a list of names in this box. (Your list will differ from the one seen in Figure A-7.) The directory win-

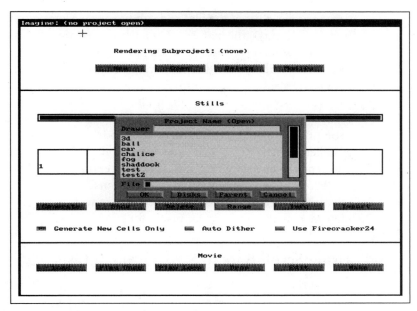

Figure A-6 The Project Editor

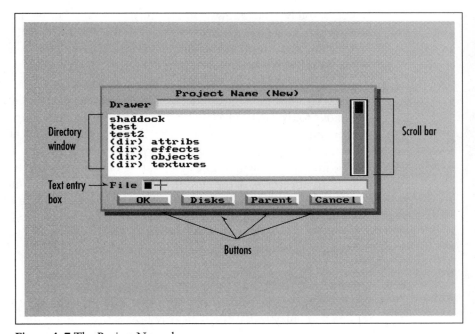

Figure A-7 The Project Name box

dow contains a list of the files and subdirectories in the current directory. Here Imagine displays the names of system directories and project directories. Imagine system directories have (dir) placed in front of their names. For example, "(dir) attribs" is the directory where a library of surfaces for objects (called *attributes*) are stored as a resource for various projects. Imagine project directories are listed without the (dir) prefix. For example, in Figure A-7, Shaddock is an existing project directory. If you did a directory listing at the DOS prompt, you would see that there is a subdirectory in the IMAGINE directory called SHADDOCK.IMP. The extension, .IMP, is added by Imagine when you type the project name in the File text entry box, but it is not displayed in this Project Name requester box. The extension is used internally by Imagine to distinguish between system directories and project directories. This is an idiosyncrasy that may be confusing for IBM DOS or MS-DOS users.

Using Scroll Bars to Step Through Lists

The list that appears in the directory box is too long to fit in the window. When you get to the bottom of a page in a word processing program, the screen automatically *scrolls up*, meaning the page moves up a line or more to reveal the next line. Similarly, to the right of the window in the project Name box is a vertical scroll bar that allows you to manually scroll up or down the directory window list. You drag the black square (slider) up and down, causing the list to scroll until you see the directory you want to change to. (*Dragging* means clicking on the slider with the left mouse button, and while keeping the mouse button depressed, moving the slider down.) You will notice that the slider will be larger in some directories than others. That's because the slider's size is shown relative to the larger black outline box that encloses it. A larger drag box means there are fewer files in this directory. A small drag box indicates that only a few of the files that are in the current directory are currently visible in the directory window. You will not be able to drag on the slider if a complete list of files and subdirectories in the current directory is shown in the directory window.

Notice that when you drag the slider it turns red. This is the program's way of giving you visual feedback. There is another way of moving the slider. You can click on the area just above or below the slider to cause the list to scroll down or up one window at a time.

Entering Text in Text Entry Boxes

The text entry box is the long gray box with "File" in front of it. The current position of the *text* cursor is indicated by a black rectangle in that box. Don't

Example: Navigating the Hard Drive

Let's assume you are lost and want to find your way to the directory where Imagine objects are stored. You have activated the object load requester by choosing Load from the Object menu.

1. Click on the Disks button.

2. In the directory window, click on the drive where Imagine is installed (C:\).

3. Click on \IMAG (the Imagine directory).

4. Scroll the directory list until you see "(dir) objects".

5. Click on "(dir) objects". You are now in the OBJECTS directory.

6. Now scroll down until you see the object in the file view window and double-click on the object name.

confuse the text cursor position (the black rectangle) with the mouse cursor position (the cross hairs). Remember: The mouse cursor allows you to click on program options or draw on the screen. The text cursor is found in a text entry box and allows you to enter data that will be processed by Imagine. When you begin a new project this is where the name of the project is entered. Always press the (ENTER) key at the end of a text or data entry. If you don't press (ENTER), Imagine will ignore your entry.

The Requester Buttons

Along the bottom of the Project Name box are a number of options presented as labeled 3D buttons. These buttons work like push buttons. Let's see what each button does. (Do not click on these buttons at this time. You'll get a lot of practice using them later.)

The OK Button

The OK button is used when you are finished with a box. Clicking on OK returns you to the program screen. The box disappears.

The Disks Button

Clicking on the Disks button will cause the Drawer text entry box to clear. The project list window now changes to a list of logical drives on your system. (Logical drives can include floppy disk drives as well as hard drive letters like

C: or D:.) When you click on a drive on this list, the drive letter is automatically entered in the Drawer text entry box. The directory window once more changes, now to a list of the directories on the drive you've selected.

The Parent Button

Clicking on the Parent button backs you out of the current directory to the next higher directory.

The Cancel Button

The Cancel button cancels all the changes you made since calling up the Project Name box. If you make a mistake, click on Cancel and start over again.

Creating a New Project

Let's start a new project.

1   If the Project Name box is not on the screen, call it up again by opening the Project menu, then highlighting and clicking on New.

Notice that the text cursor is in the File entry box by default.

2   Type the name `temp`. Press (ENTER).

You are now placed in the Rendering Subproject screen (see Figure A-8).

Grayed Program Options

Look at the yellow 3D buttons on the screen (Delete and Modify). Many of these buttons appear to be *grayed out*, meaning they are covered with a pattern of black dots. Graying out program options that are not currently active or available is a graphical user interface convention. Because a subproject has not been created, such menu options (such as Delete and Info) are not active.

Opening the Subproject

When you create animations using Imagine, you must open a subproject for the individual sequences that form the animation. (This is explained in Chapter 7.) Let's do that now. We are going to use the New button.

3   Click on New.

A Rendering Subproject Name box pops on the screen. This is similar to the Project Name box.

4   Type the word `exercise` and press (ENTER). A new box appears (see Figure A-9).

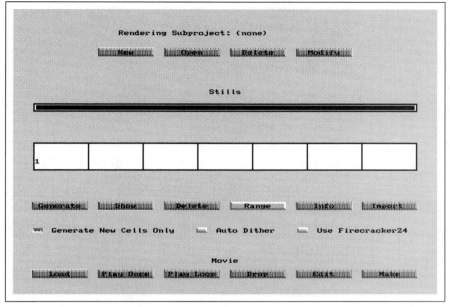

Figure A-8 Rendering Subproject screen

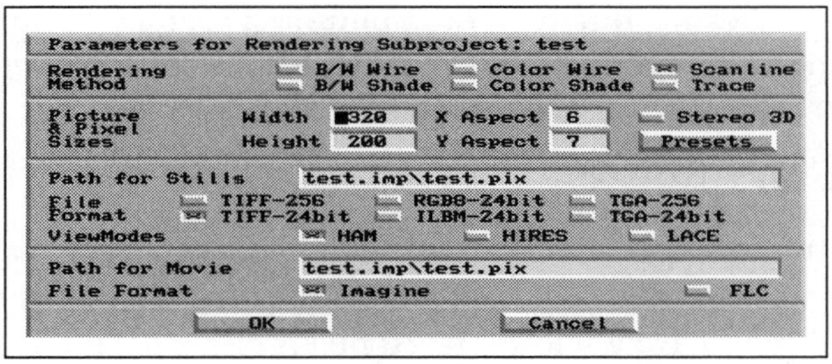

Figure A-9 The Rendering Subproject parameters box

Selecting Options Using Boxes

The Rendering Subproject parameters box illustrates several Imagine conventions associated with boxes.

Option Grouping

Notice that the box is divided by grooved lines into horizontal sections. For example, rendering options (titled "Rendering Method") are grouped at the top of the box. These options are related. In this example, the selected option tells Imagine what rendering method to use in creating the image or animation. By default, scanline images are created.

Option Buttons

The buttons we've used so far cause some program conditions to change, such as the OK button that causes a pop-up box to terminate. In the Rendering Subproject parameters box, some of the buttons are like buttons on old car radios. Selecting a new button releases the current selection. Currently selected options have buttons that look like they have been pressed down. They also have an X embedded in them. (At the top of the box, Scanline is currently selected.) Try clicking on the buttons within the Rendering Method group of options.

Defaults

Most program functions need some kind of value associated with them if they are to execute. Imagine gives these program functions standard values that you can change. For example, by default the image will be rendered as a scanline image. This will create a Phong-shaded image. You change to a ray-traced image by clicking on the Trace button. Program option boxes like the Rendering Subproject box allow you to change default values or options.

Data Entry Boxes

Data entry boxes are similar to text entry boxes. In the Rendering Subproject parameters box, the Width and Height data entry boxes currently show that the image will have a width of 320 pixels and a height of 200 pixels. (This is a low-resolution VGA mode.) You can change the values in these boxes in the same way you enter text in text entry boxes. Click on the box, delete the current value, type in the new value and press (ENTER). If you don't press (ENTER), you'll see the value change in the box, but the new value will not be processed by Imagine. Note: you can clear a data box by pressing (right) (ALT)-(X).

Other Boxes

Imagine's object and scene editors contain other types of boxes. Enter the Stage Editor by selecting Stage from the Project menu at the top of the screen. Load an object into the Stage Editor. Select Load from the Object menu and navigate to the OBJECTS directory. Load an object from this directory.

Normally you can select an object to manipulate by clicking on it. In a scene with many objects, this may get cumbersome. Imagine keeps an internal list of all the objects in a scene. You can see this list by pressing (ALT)-(F) (remember, use the *right* (ALT) key) or by choosing Find Requester from the Pick/Select menu.

Clicking on the name of an object in the Find Requester box *selects* that object. It will turn brown. An alternative way of selecting an object is to press (ALT)-(N) or choose Select Next from the Pick/Select menu. On a busy screen a selected object is much easier to find, because it will be colored brown. Once an object is selected it is easy to pick it. All you have to do is press the (F1) function key or choose Pick Select from the Pick/Select menu. The object will now turn purple, indicating it is picked.

Object Color Coding

Imagine gives visual clues as to whether an object in a scene is picked or selected. Here is the color coding:

- ⊕ Black: Dormant (not selected or picked)
- ⊕ Orange: Selected (ready for picking)
- ⊕ Purple: Picked (picked brown/selected object)
- ⊕ Blue: Picked (picked black/unselected object)

To *unpick* an object, click anywhere on the screen, or pick another object. Options can be found on the Pick/Select menu that allow you to unpick selected objects (Unpick Select) and unpick the last object that was picked (Unpick Last).

There is another way of selecting objects. If you know the name of an object, you can select it by name with Find By Name in the Pick/Select menu or

Hint: Picking Loaded Objects

When an object is first loaded into a scene it is placed at the very center of the 3D world. Often you will want to move it from this position. Because it is selected when it enters the scene, all you have to do to pick it is press (F1). It is then ready to be moved, scaled, or rotated.

Tip: Selecting More than One Object, Point, Edge, or Face

You can pick more than one object, point, edge, or face at a time. Use the left (SHIFT) key in conjunction with one of the Pick methods (Click, Drag Box, Lasso). The pick methods can be found at the bottom of the Mode menu.

by pressing (ALT)-(V). Type in the name of the object in the Find By Name requester and press (ENTER). The object you named will turn brown.

Don't worry about remembering the color coding. You'll soon be selecting and picking objects without thinking about it. Just remember that selecting objects makes picking easier. And remember that you cannot manipulate an object (or several objects) without picking them first.

SCHOOL'S OUT

This completes the tutorial in using Imagine's menus and boxes. Detailed information in using other program options are provided as you encounter them in the book.

A P P E N D I X   B

Resources: Books, Magazines, and Software

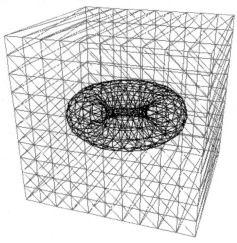

BOOKS

MS-DOS Reference

Up and Running with DOS 5, by Alan Simpson. Alameda, CA: Sybex, 1991 (ISBN 0-89588-774-6).

This is a concise introduction to the disk operating system (DOS). Read Chapter 17 ("Configuring Your System") to understand what the cryptic commands in your CONFIG.SYS file mean. Chapter 18, "Improving Performance," pulls the veil away from PC memory management. A well-organized, easy to follow introduction to the intricacies lurking under the hood in your system.

Imagine Supplementary

The Imagine Companion 2.0, by David Duberman. Redwood City, CA: Motion Blur Publishing, 1993.

> This book is a collection of tutorials, hints, and tips for users of Imagine 2.0 on the PC and Amiga. With over 14 well-illustrated and fully explained in-depth tutorials, such as the creation of a variable-transparency spotlight beam, it makes an excellent supplement to *3D Modeling Lab*. You can contact Motion Blur Publishing at 915A Stambaugh Street, Redwood City, CA 94063. Telephone: 415-364-2009.

Animation and Multimedia

Animation How-To CD, by Jeff Bowermaster. Corte Madera, CA: The Waite Group Press, 1994 (ISBN 1-878739-54-9).

> This comes with everything needed to make your own animations. The DTA Targa animator allows you to process the images output by Imagine as FLC animation files. Over 400MB of animation files. You can contact The Waite Group Press at 1-800-368-9369.

Multimedia Creations, by Philip Shaddock. Corte Madera, CA: The Waite Group Press, 1992 (ISBN 1-878739-26-3).

> Bundled with a reduced-color version of Paul Mace Software's Multimedia GRASP, this book shows you how to build multimedia programs, including information on integrating 3D into interactive multimedia shows. For users who want to create movies or business presentations on their computers or for distribution. Includes sound card interface.

Multimedia Madness, by Ron Wodaski. Indianapolis, IN: Sams Publishing, 1992 (ISBN 0-672-30413-9).

> Covers all aspects of multimedia, including animation, video capture, digital audio, MIDI, presentations, programming, and authoring. Includes detailed reviews of hardware and software products in each category, as well as a complete Shoppers' Guide of multimedia products. Includes two CD-ROM discs with more than 1 gigabyte of software demos, multimedia resources (video, audio, animation, music), and a complete edition of Nautilus CD, a CD-ROM magazine.

Lighting

Artificial Light Photography, by Ansel Adams. Boston, MA: New York Graphic Society, 1956.

> A classic text teaching the basics of lighting. At the time of this writing it was out of print. Worth searching out in used book stores. Ansel Adams' other photography books are excellent resources for 3D modelers.

Matters of Light & Depth, by Ross Lowell. New York, NY: Broad Street Books, 1992 (ISBN 1-879-17403-0).

> Written by an Academy Award-winning cinematographer, this book puts the emphasis on using lighting to create memorable images for video, film, and stills. The book is richly illustrated.

Computer Graphics and Art

Art Work, by Digital Image. Tokyo, Japan: Firefly Books, 1992 (ISBN 4-7661-0682-2).

> An exceptional compilation of Japanese computer graphics. Use this book as a source book for 3D artwork ideas.

Computer Graphics, by Foley, van Dam, Feiner, and Hughes. Reading, MA: Addison-Wesley Publishing Company, 1987 (ISBN 0-201-12110-7).

> The bible for computer graphics. A comprehensive textbook covering all aspects of computer graphics.

Image Lab, by Tim Wegner. Corte Madera, CA: The Waite Group Press, 1992 (ISBN 1-878739-11-5).

> A PC-based "digital darkroom" covering all areas of graphic processing and manipulation. Includes PICLAB, CSHOW, IMPROCES, Image Alchemy, and other graphics software on the bundled disk.

Treasury of Animal Illustrations, ed. by Carol Belanger Grafton. New York, NY: Dover Publications, 1988 (ISBN 0-486-25805-X).

> Over 600 engravings from eighteenth-century sources. All the Dover books provide copyright-free sources for images.

MAGAZINES

The following magazines keep you up to date on the fast-moving world of 3D art and animation. Look for ads for 3D clip art and image maps.

3D Artist, Columbine, Inc., P.O. Box 4787, Sante Fe, New Mexico 87502.

3D Artist is a tip and techniques guide to 3D graphics programs that run on PCs and other platforms or PCs only. Covers Imagine. Highly recommended. Their phone number is 505-980-3532.

Computer Artist, Penwell Publishing Company.

Available on the newsstand. Covers all aspects of 3D art, including 3D modeling and animation. Good source for ideas.

Computer Graphics World, Penwell Publishing Company.

Traditionally, this longstanding computer graphics magazine has covered high-end 3D animation systems, but it covers desktop systems as well. Keep tabs on the leading edge through this newsstand magazine.

Desktop Video World, TechMedia Publishing.

The focus is on desktop video, but the magazine includes coverage of 3D animation.

SOFTWARE

GRASP Multimedia, Paul Mace Software, Inc., 400 Williamson Way, Ashland, Oregon 97520.

Multimedia script-based authoring tool. GRASP directly supports the Autodesk FLC format. Using a script-based programming method, the program allows you to link animation sequences, put them to music, and add user interaction. You can contact Paul Mace Software at 503-488-0224.

A P P E N D I X C

Mike Miller's Train

Featured Artist: Mike Miller

Mike Miller is perhaps the world's best known ray-tracing artist. His work has appeared in several books, magazines, and on CompuServe. His company, Head Spin Studio, is located in Columbus, Ohio.

Mike writes: "I've been an artist for over twenty years and have been driven during that time to create illustrations in whatever medium I could get my hands on. Most of my personal and commercial artwork spans from hand drawings to finished paintings. I most enjoy fantasy and science fiction illustration. The computer art that I've produced in the last two years has been a new medium for me. Many of the procedures I follow for producing a work by hand are also followed when I'm creating a three-dimensional rendering on a computer. Probably the most important bit to this creation process is the idea."

GENERATING IDEAS FOR 3D ART

Mike describes the process he went through to create the train: "I don't start with a clean page or blank monitor and hope ideas will start flowing. Most of the ideas for my art pieces come from relaxing, looking through books, watching TV, and so on. My idea process goes something like this: I see something — perhaps a photo in a book that would make a nice rendering. I sketch it down on paper and pin it to my studio wall. In the case of a magazine I may just rip it out and pin that to my wall. Eventually I'm surrounded by ideas. When I'm set on a particular scene I want to produce, I look for more reference.

Finding Visual Reference

"For an illustrator or artist trying to achieve photorealism, reference is of considerable importance. My reference library, sometimes known as the morgue, includes illustrations, photos, books, magazines, movies. An artist can never have too much reference. When deciding on the model and rendering for this book, I reviewed some earlier drawings I had made. Some of these drawings were of a train and train station I had modeled and rendered earlier, but I was never satisfied with its complexity. Once deciding I would use Imagine to fulfill this train idea, I accumulated all the reference I had on trains. Not finding the style of train I was looking for I visited the local hobby store and bought two magazines on antique trains. From these magazines I found the train I liked and made a few hand sketches. Color Plate 1 shows the finished render of the train.

CREATING THE PROJECT DIRECTORY STRUCTURE

"Before starting my model in Imagine, I set up the directory tree. I started Imagine and created a new project and subproject. I exited to DOS, and created two new directories under the newly formed train directory. The directories I added were called TEXTURES and MAPS. Confining subdirectories for the project to the train directory helped me stay organized. With the scanned outline (stored as a TIFF image) on my hard drive, storage directories set up, and reference material by my side, I was ready to start modeling in Imagine.

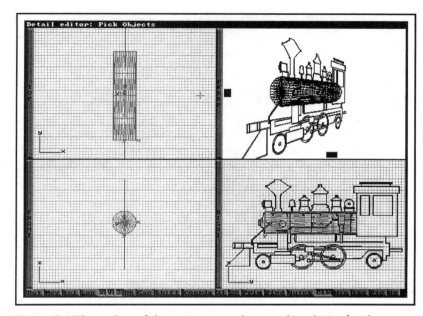

Figure C-1 The outline of the train was used as a scaling device for the parts of the train

CREATING A TEMPLATE FOR THE TRAIN

"In order to develop an accurate scale model of the train, I decided to create a template for it in the form of a hand drawing that was a straight-on side view of the train. I drew only the outlines of each part on the train: the wheels, spokes, window openings on the cab, and so on. I then scanned this outline into the computer as an eight-bit indexed black-and-white TIFF format image. I started Imagine and imported the outline train TIFF into Imagine's Detail Editor. This is done by choosing Convert Image from the Object pull-down menu. When I loaded the outline image, Imagine asked if faces should be added to the object. I said no. Imagine then created an outline trace of the TIFF. Imagine does a fairly good job at vector tracing a bitmapped TIFF. Without faces, this outline is a two-dimensional assembly of points and lines. I then rotated and scaled this outline (see Figure C-1).

"I dragged this profile to the side so that it would not interfere with newly formed shapes. This outline was not used as a model, but rather as a proportional scale for building the train shapes. It was used as a guide in creating correct profiles for spinning and extruding, and for correctly scaling each part into a virtually correct train. There are times when converted images are used as rendered objects, for example, in tracing type for logos or creating a framework for a complex shape.

BUILDING THE MODEL

"A word of advice before going ahead with the model building. It may be wise to determine what part or parts of your model would be the most difficult to model. Attempt to model those parts first, especially if these difficult parts are critical to your rendering or animation. Spending a week on a model only to leave the hardest parts for last may lead to project failure. If you're confident in your skills and your tools, then a good starting place for modeling is

1 Model the largest parts first.

2 Work from parent to child.

3 Add the smallest details last.

Creating the Engine Cylinder

"For the train I chose to start with the large cylinder tank that makes up the main body. This cylinder was created by adding the tube primitive with both ends closed. It was created with four sections. With the cylinder selected, I switched to full-screen Right view and moved the cylinder over the top of the train profile. I rotated and scaled this cylinder until it fit properly inside the outline profile.

Creating the Other Train Parts

"Each additional train part was sized and placed in the same manner as this first cylinder. The sweeps and extrusions were done over the top of the outline. For example, the train smokestack profile was created this way. While still in the Right view I created a new axis and selected it. I moved the axis so that it was centered in the smokestack outline-profile. I added lines to the axis that represented one-half of the smokestack profile and chose mold-sweep with a setting of 24 sections. This produced a 3D mesh of the stack in correct proportion in the Right view. I repeated this process of shape-fitting the train parts to the outline profile throughout the modeling process.

Assigning Textures

"As I modeled each train part, I would create a unique name for it in the Attributes Requester and load a simple texture (from the \IMAG\ATTRIBUTES directory) of its surface, and save the object to the hard drive. The textures were not the final textures. They were used to proof the mesh. By keeping them simple, I was able to do fast test renders. This is a good way to see how your model is progressing and to determine what edges of the mesh should stay sharp or smooth. Imagine will almost always default to creating smooth edges. You must select the edges you want to make sharp or smooth. As I modeled each part, I would go through the procedure of edge correcting and test rendering.

"Not all parts should receive an edge treatment. If the mesh you are creating will be joined (using the Join command) with another mesh object, all sharp edges will be lost. Joining will also destroy texture mapping. (You can get around this by grouping objects rather than joining them.)

Aligning the Axis for Extrusions

"Most of the train parts were created in the Right view of Imagine. That's because of the way real trains are constructed. Imagine always extrudes along the object's Y axis. When building each new part, the local Y axis needed to be rotated to align with the world X axis. This meant the part would extrude in the right direction. In some cases you might find the Top view is the best view for building faces for extruding. The local Y axis would then be rotated to align to world Z axis. All objects on the train were built as profiles that used either the mold Sweep or Extrude commands.

Building the Headlight Beam

"One of the last objects that was added to the train was the beam that is emitted from the headlight. This began as an open-ended primitive tube with one section. I selected all the points on one end and scaled those points to a smaller radius and aligned it to fit to the headlight. I then created the texture for it. To create the appearance of a beam of light I used an image map. This image was a gradient blend that traveled from pure white to a light gray. It was applied as a filter map to make it semitransparent along the length of the object. The result was a beam that was transparent on one end and 90 percent opaque on the other end (see Color Plate 1).

Test Rendering the Textures

"After all objects were built for the train it was now time to finalize the textures. Instead of test rendering final textures on the complex train shapes, I opened a new project and tested the textures on simple shapes: spheres, cylinders, and cubes. Since many of the train textures were reflective, I had to first create a surrounding world so that reflections had something to mirror. I created the textures for the sky, backdrop, and ground plane before finalizing the metallic train textures. If you are using a surrounding sphere for a sky or a global brush map for background reflections, subtle changes in their coloring will greatly affect the look of your reflective textures.

"For the surrounding sky I used an ellipse, scaled smaller in the Z direction, with a gradient image map. This image map was a 24-bit TIFF that had a light-blue center blending upward to a dark orange. I designed this gradient with the metallic-gold train texture in mind. This texture had the highest reflection setting. It is the orange tones in the surrounding sky that appear in most of the upper reflections of the gold train parts. Since this surrounding sky did not produce an interesting backdrop, I created my own backdrop using an image applied to a simple vertical plane. This is the sunset seen in Color Plate 1.

Creating the Sunset Image

"Here's how I created the sunset image. It was a TIFF rendering done in Imagine.

1. I created a gradient sunset blend in a paint program.

2. I created another image, beginning with a black background. With the air-brush tool set to a transparency of 80 percent and white paint, I slowly built up very soft white streaks on the black background. I converted this image to a negative image (white background with faint gray streaks).

3. I saved both of these images as 24-bit TIFFS.

4. I created a sphere object in Imagine and mapped the sunset gradient onto the sphere using the Flat X=Flat Z mapping parameter. I mapped the second image on top of the first as a filter map using the Flat X=Flat Z mapping parameter.

5. I test rendered the results.

"Since this second image contained almost all white except for the feathered gray streaks, the sunset gradient now had dark streaks running through the sky. The white areas in the second image became totally clear. Satisfied with the results, I loaded this multi-texture sphere into the Stage Editor and rendered an 800 by 600 TIFF image. This image was then mapped onto the plane used as a backdrop."

SUMMARY

Mike's train is an excellent example of the power of Imagine when it is in the hands of a skilled artist.

The Plans for Alan Henry's Bee

This chapter's focus is on modeling. We enter Alan Henry's modeling shop and learn how he approached the problem of modeling an organic object: a worker honeybee. Color Plate 5 shows the finished model of the worker bee.

BUILDING THE BEE

The worker honeybee has jointed legs, a segmented body, and wings. Here, you'll read how Alan Henry approached the task of modeling these parts.

Alan Henry writes: "The following is a description of how I approached the task of building a fairly realistic honeybee, complete with hair, pollen markings, and completely jointed extremities. While I will not take you step-by-step through the actual creation, it will give you a very good understanding of how I approached modeling the bee."

Finding the Reference Model

The first step in any modeling project for a photorealistic subject begins with finding a visual reference. In the small town Alan lives in, finding a model of a honeybee was difficult. Finding a live or dead bee proved fruitless. Alan finally found an excellent child's reference book at a local book store that had dozens of honeybee pictures taken at different angles, most full page. Now Alan had a suitable reference as a starting point.

Planning the Model

After finding a picture reference, the next step in the modeling process is to "divide and conquer the model"; break it into smaller subprojects. Alan studied the bee pictures and decided there were three major components that the bee could be divided into: the body, the legs, and the wings. Further analysis revealed each of the three parts could be further reduced. Figure D-1 shows a side view of the bee as it was finally created in wireframe.

Figure D-1 The wireframe bee

The final breakdown of each major component appears as follows:

Body

1. Abdomen
   a. Hair

2. Thorax
   a. Hair

3. Head
   a. 2 Eyes
   b. 2 Jaws
   c. 2 Antennae
   d. Tongue
   e. Hair

Legs

1. 2 Rear Legs
   a. Jointed Segments

2. 2 Mid Legs
   a. Jointed Segments

3. 2 Front Legs
   a. Jointed Segments

Wings

1. 2 Front Wings

2. 2 Hind Wings

3. 2 Hinge Joints

The approach taken in modeling the various sections of the bee depends on the expertise of the artist and his or her familiarity with the modeling program's tools. An object can be built by reshaping a 3D primitive (such as a sphere, tube, or cone) or using a specific tool in its creation. Or it can be created by spinning or extruding an outline. Imagine's Forms Editor could have been used to create the organic shapes, but Alan preferred to work entirely in the Detail Editor.

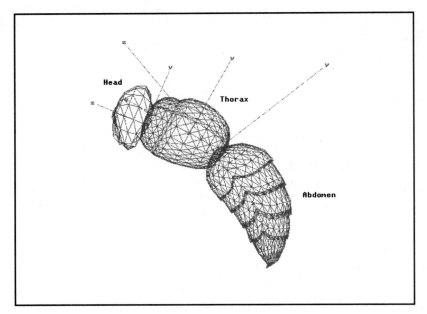

Figure D-2 The base shapes of the honeybee

Modeling the Body

Let's look at how Alan created each part in turn. Figure D-2 shows the parts of the bee that Alan modeled first.

Creating the Abdomen

Alan began with the abdomen at the bottom of the bee.

Creating the Geometry

Looking closely at the abdomen section of the bee, Alan noted that it is alternately colored yellow and dark brown. It is segmented, slightly bent, and quite hairy. Alan began by laying down an axis and drawing half of an egg-shaped object with a "stair-step" bump in each segment and stinger at the bottom. He used Imagine's Add Lines command to draw the shape freehand. Using the Spin command, he spun the object 360 degrees with 24 sections. While this gave him the general segmented shape, he still had to create the downward curve.

Adding Color to the Surface

Before changing the object's shape, he colored and added the dark brown stripes because selecting the individual faces is easier while the object is still symmetrical. The attribute setting of the bee's base color (yellow) is a matter of taste. He chose an orange-yellow color with a roughness and hardness setting to approximate a fuzzy appearance. He also added a linear texture to smoothly fade from the yellow base color to a darker brown at the stinger. This was not really a requirement to make the bee look real, but it gives it visual appeal. To add the brown stripes, he entered Pick Faces mode and selected faces that made a band around the object in the vicinity of each segment. With these faces selected, he then selected Preferences and changed the face's color from the orange-yellow color to the dark brown. The number of attribute settings that can be changed in Pick Faces mode is limited. One last thing that was required before bending the object was to make the edges that formed the segmented sections flat rather than rounded (Phong-shaded). He selected the edges that formed the segmented sections of the abdomen and chose Make Sharp from the Functions pull-down menu to give them a hard edge.

Bending the Abdomen

Once completed, Alan proceeded to give the abdomen its curve. This was achieved by entering Pick Points mode (with Drag Box as pick method) and selecting all of the points from about the middle segment to the stinger and rotating them by a few degrees in the proper axis to achieve the downward bend. Next, starting one segment closer to the stinger, he again selected all of the points from this new segment to the stinger and rotated them in the same direction as before. He repeated this until there were no more segments. This gave the object a smooth curve to one side.

Creating the Illusion of Bee Hair

Creating the individual strands of hair on the bee using polygons would have created a prohibitively large and complex model. Alan opted to use Imagine's surface modeling tools to simulate the look of hair. The basic strategy was to place a "skin" of hair over the abdomen. A copy of the abdomen was rescaled slightly larger than the original and pasted (using the Paste command) over the top of the abdomen object. A filter image map of hair was then wrapped around the object. The hair picture was created in a 2D paint program. It was simply a white background with single-pixel width black lines drawn randomly. A filter map makes the white part of the image transparent and the black or colored parts of the image opaque. The hair object was made slightly darker yellow and all specular, hardness, and roughness values were set to zero. This precluded shiny "hot spots" from appearing on the filtered (see-through) sections. The black lines of the filter map would now appear on the abdomen as dark-yellow hair.

Creating the Thorax

To create the center section of the bee's body (thorax), Alan started with a primitive sphere object. In loading the sphere object he toggled off the Stagger Points button. This created a thorax with symmetrical points. This made it easier to choose groups of points. While in Pick Points mode, he selected the bottom half of the sphere. He resized the picked points in all three axes to about 90 percent of their original size. This produced an acorn shape which, with an additional point moved here and there to create a slightly irregular shape, closely approximated the bee's thorax.

Surface Modeling the Thorax

The attributes setting was set to be identical to the abdomen with the exception of the selected texture. Instead of the Linear texture, he used the Spot texture found in the \IMAG\TEXTURES directory. After several trial and error attempts, he found a Spot setting that resembled pollen-like markings.

The hair was created exactly the same way the abdomen hair was created. He made a copy of the thorax object, slightly enlarged it, pasted it over the thorax, and applied a filter image map to it.

Modeling the Head

The head could have been made by squashing a primitive sphere object or by adding an axis and spinning a hand-drawn shape around it. Alan elected to use the latter method to keep the number of polygons on the backside of the head to a minimum. The shape he drew resembled an "M&M™" candy, a flattened disk shape with fewer points on the back of the head than the face. Once the shape was spun he picked several of the points in the vicinity of the bee's mouth and moved them slightly closer to the head's axis to form the opening where the jaws would attach. Figure D-3 shows the head seen from the Top view.

Next he picked a row of points running down the front of the bee's face and moved them slightly away from the axis to form a ridge (see Figure D-4).

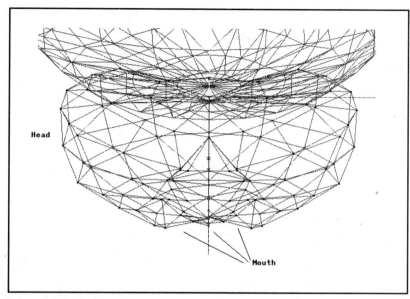

Figure D-3 The head seen from the Top view

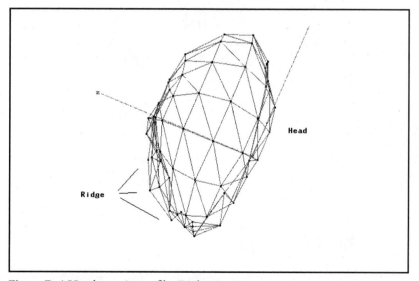

Figure D-4 Head seen in profile (Right view)

The use of Imagine's Hide Points mode is useful for this procedure. Selecting the points at the back of the head and hiding them prevented them from being accidentally selected while selecting the face points in Pick Points mode.

Coloring the Head

The surface attributes were set the same as the thorax, except the base color and the spot colors were altered slightly for contrast. Alan also used the Dots texture to simulate pollen spores on the bee's face.

The bee's hair was created in the same fashion as the other parts of the body.

Creating the Eyes

Figure D-5 shows the location of the eyes on the head. The eyes were created using a primitive sphere object that was squashed to about one-third of its original diameter in one axis. In order to help reduce the complexity of the model, Alan used Pick Points mode to pick and delete all the points that would not be visible once the eye was placed on the bee's head. The second eye was duplicated from the first. Placing the eyes correctly on the head was a matter of trial and error. Alan did several renderings to make sure that no edges were visible. Since the eyes are placed directly on the head object, just below the boundary of the hair object, some of the hairs appear to be growing out of the eyes, just like on a real honeybee!

Creating the Jaws

Figure D-6 shows the size and placement of the jaws. The jaws are two spun objects that resemble elongated eggplants. They were then flattened slightly and, using the same method as the abdomen, given a slight curve.

Creating the Antennae

Figure D-7 shows the antennae. These antennae were created using a spun object that looked like an inverted screwdriver. A variation of the Spot texture was applied to them. Each individual antenna was given its own characteristic bend.

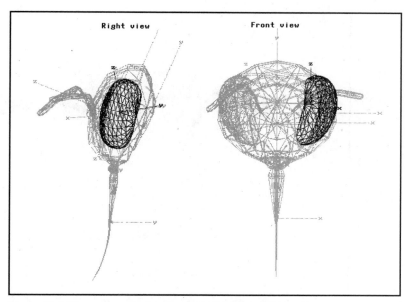

Figure D-5 The eye on the head seen in Right and Front views

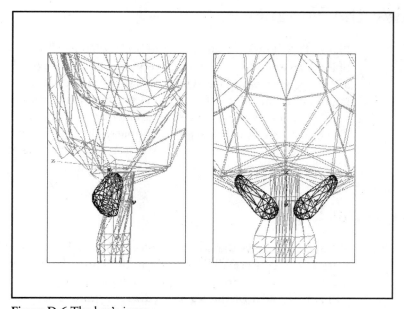

Figure D-6 The bee's jaws

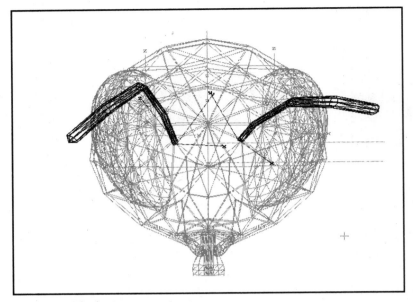

Figure D-7 The bee's antennae

Creating the Tongue

Figure D-8 shows the shape of the bee's tongue. The tongue consists of two objects: an extruded object and a very thin tube. The extruded object started as a V shape with wings (see Figure D-9). The shape was extruded with a tapering to about one-tenth of its original size through to the end of the tongue.

The attributes were set with a caramel color and given some transparency. The tube was made small enough to match the tapered end of the first part of the tongue and then curved slightly by rotating each of its midsections slightly. The same attributes as the extruded object were used.

Creating the Legs

Figure D-10 shows the honeybee's legs. Although there are six legs, each pair different, they were all derived from the same basic leg. Each pair was then scaled and bent to appear unique (see Figure D-11).

Each segment of the leg started as a primitive sphere. Using Pick Points mode, Alan selected different sections of the sphere and scaled or moved them as necessary to model each part of the bee's leg.

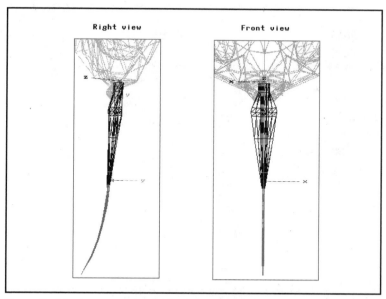

Figure D-8 Bee's tongue shown from Front and Right views

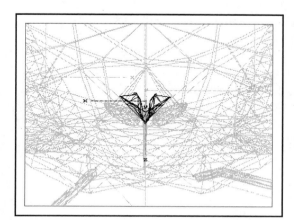

Figure D-9 V shape of the tongue seen from the Top view

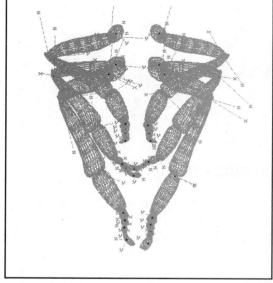

Figure D-10 The honeybee's legs seen from the front

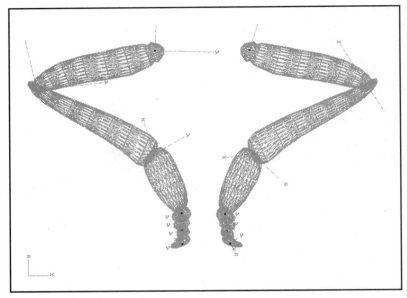

Figure D-11 Single pair of legs

When adding a primitive sphere ensure that the Stagger Points button is turned off. This creates a sphere object that has defined, regular segments that can be easily picked and altered.

Once each segment was created, Alan used the (SHIFT)-(M) axes movement command to move the leg segment's axis to the end of the segment. This provided him with a pivot point for arranging the segment.

The surface attributes for each segment are exactly the same. The base color was a dark brown with the spot texture applied. The legs did not use a hair object. The bee's little feet were given a light-brown color.

Creating the Wings

Figure D-12 shows a Front view of the wings. Alan also created the wings by duplicating and modifying a single object. The hind wings are miniature versions of the front wings. To build the wing object, Alan added an axis and in Add Lines mode drew the shape of the bee's wing, including a large root where it enters the bee's body (see Figure D-13). Using Add Faces mode, Alan filled in the outline.

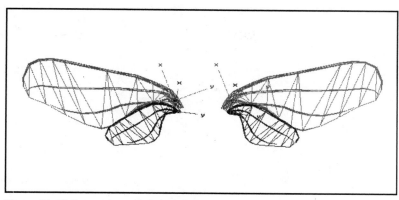

Figure D-12 Front view of the wings

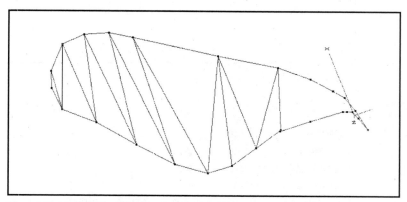

Figure D-13 Shape of the bee's wing

Creating the Veins in the Wings

Alan decided to model the wing's veins using tube primitives. Figure D-14 shows the veins of the wings. To begin, he loaded a tube primitive with enough sections to allow the tube to curve across the top of the wing. He scaled the tube's diameter to an appropriate thickness. Then, starting with the end at the root, he selected and moved each of the tube's segments to follow the curve along the top of the wing. As the tube got closer to the tip of the wing, he scaled it smaller and smaller. The tubes that make up the veins in the wing are different variations of the top tube.

Once completed, the entire object was made into one using the Join command. Alan then gave it a light-yellow base color with fairly high transparen-

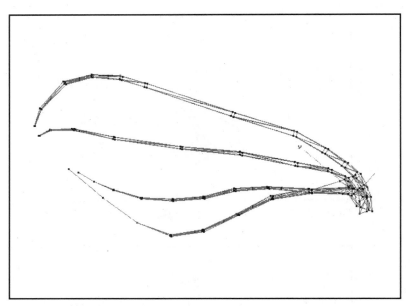

Figure D-14 Veins in the wings

cy settings. The hind wings are scaled-down versions of the front wings. The front and hind wings were placed in the correct positions with their root sections as closely matched as possible.

Alan knew that he was going to eventually animate the wings. He decided to create a pivoting socket: a sphere that could be rotated. He added a primitive sphere and scaled it down until it would just fit around both wings' root sections. He gave them the same attributes as the wings. Then he made them the parent object to the wings by picking them first, then the wings. Then he selected Group. By rotating this sphere approximately 30 to 40 degrees in the Y axis, the wings could be made to flap up and down.

THE BEE'S FINAL ASSEMBLY

As was the case with the eyes on the bee's head, there is quite a bit of trial and error in positioning all of the bee's parts. Alan moved, twisted, and bent the bee's legs more than 20 times before he found their orientation acceptable. He went through the same trial and error with the wings and antennae. (It's a good idea to save often when doing this.) Each positioning required a quick render to see the result. Because the bee is an organic object, arranging its parts cannot be reduced to precise measurement and rotation.

Alan Henry writes: "The honeybee is an example of how detailed an object can be while still being fairly simple to create. The bottom line is you can allow your imagination to extend far beyond chrome balls over a checkered floor."

APPENDIX E

Glossary

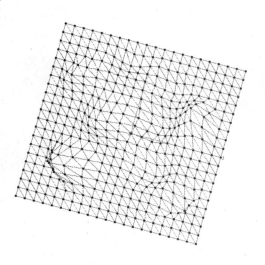

Altitude maps   Also called bump maps. A type of image map used to simulate bumpy surfaces. Uses the black-and-white color component in an image to simulate an uneven surface. Black is interpreted as a dent in the surface; white is interpreted as a bump.

Anti-aliasing   Process by which the jagged edges of bit-mapped images are softened by averaging the color of pixels along the edge of a shape with the background color or colors. Figure E-1 shows the top of the letter *B* with no anti-aliasing (on the left) and with anti-aliasing (on the right).

   Notice that the stair-step edge of the curve is smoothed out when anti-aliasing is used. Because the computer must average the pixels along the edge of shapes, anti-aliasing will slow down rendering considerably. Most artists use aliasing in the final stages of image production. 3D programs, and many 2D programs, offer aliasing as an option.

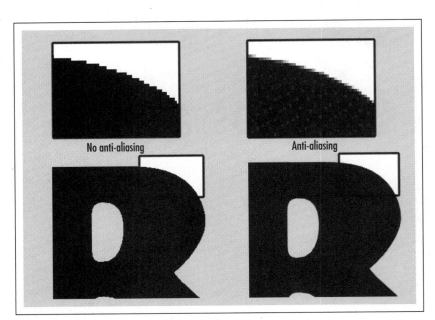

No anti-aliasing   Anti-aliasing

Figure E-1 Anti-aliasing applied to the letter B

ASCII (American Standard Code for Information Interchange) A computer code used for exchanging information between computer systems. DXF files are written in ASCII. *See also* DXF.

Attributes Imagine's term for the surfaces that you apply to objects. *See* Texture-mapping, Procedural texture, Brush-mapping, Shading.

Bezier curve A type of curve definition originally developed by Pierre Bezier in France in the early 1960s for car body design. A Bezier curve is formed from two end points and two or more control points along the curve. Figure E-2 shows a Bezier curve with its two control points.

Smooth, sloping shapes can be created by manipulating the control points. However, a Bezier curve is not as flexible for creating complex shapes as B-splines or NURBS (non-uniform rational B-splines). When you alter a Bezier curve, the entire curve between the control points is affected. The other types of curves allow you to localize control over segments of a curve, allowing more complex shapes to be created with fewer control points. *See* B-spline curve, non-uniform rational B-spline.

Bezier patch A type of curve definition used by 3D software. Complex surfaces like those of cars are modeled with *patches* that are applied like the

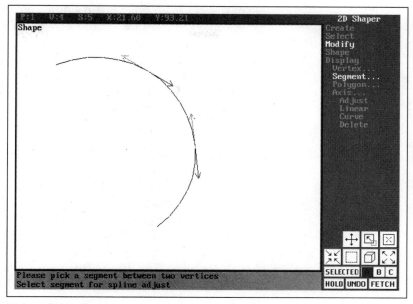

Figure E-2 Bezier curve

elbow patch of a jacket. A Bezier patch uses the Bezier curve algorithm (*see* Bezier curve) to define the surface of a 3D shape. Bezier curves are drawn through control points arranged along a curve. Bezier patches interpolate the curved surface of a three-dimensional object from these control points.

Bitmapped graphics Also called paint or brush graphics. A type of graphics display and storage where each dot on the screen (called a *pixel*) corresponds to one or more *bits* in memory or in a file. The computer screen (or more precisely, the screen's memory buffer) is mapped as a grid of tiny dots. The entire screen buffer is saved to the disk as a stream of bits. Since all that is stored is the color of each pixel, reading and displaying these files can be very fast. As the color depth and spatial resolution increases, the data rate goes up, increasing file storage size and hampering the speed of display. Animation file formats are in this format, although they use special software compression techniques for reducing the amount of information stored. (*See* FLC file format.) Graphics in PCX, GIF, TGA, TIFF, BMP, or LBM file formats store bitmapped images.

3D programs use vector graphics to store and display 3D objects and scenes. Vector graphics store the instructions for building objects.

As long as those objects remain simple, file storage size remains small and speed of display can be extremely fast. Extremely complex objects or scenes, however, can be computationally intensive as the computer has to perform thousands or millions of calculations to re-create a scene or animation. That's one of the reasons why final output of a 3D program is in the form of 2D bitmapped images. The images can be dumped onto videotape or used in a bitmapped animation program for fast playback.

Brush-mapping   Also known as *image-mapping*. Brush is an Amiga term for paint or bitmapped images. Brush-mapping is the application of surfaces to objects using bitmapped or paint images as reference maps. The bitmapped images are created in paint programs that use such *brushes* as paint cans, rollers, and pencils. Some 3D programs call brush-mapping *texture-mapping*. This often leads to confusion between the terms *texture-mapping* and *procedural texturing*. The latter is the application of surfaces to objects using algorithms. You might create a wooden floor, for example, using a fractal algorithm that simulates wood. In the case of brush-mapping, you might accomplish the same end by scanning a piece of wood from a photograph and then applying this image to a plane. The advantage of an image map is that complex surfaces can be simulated quickly and easily. The disadvantage is that the map is not 3D data, so it will become flat and lose resolution as you travel near it with a camera. *See* Shading, Procedural texture, and Texture-mapping.

B-spline curve   (Beta-spline) A mathematical formula for curves. *Beta-splines* are parametric curves whose shape is determined by control points. They are especially valuable for describing cross sections of 3D objects that are complex in shape, such as the curvature of cars.

B-spline patch   A type of curve definition used by high-end 3D software. Complex curved surfaces like those of cars are modeled with patches that are applied like the elbow patch of a jacket. B-splines are an evolutionary development of Bezier curves. (*See* Bezier patch.) While control points along a Bezier curve affect the entire curve, a B-spline control point provides increased local control over the segments of a curve nearest to a control point. Another advantage of B-splines is that they allow fewer control points to be used than a simple Bezier curve, which must increase the number of control points to create complex shapes.

Figure E-3 shows a complex shape drawn in 3D Studio (which uses B-spline technology). Note that the small crosses along the curve in the

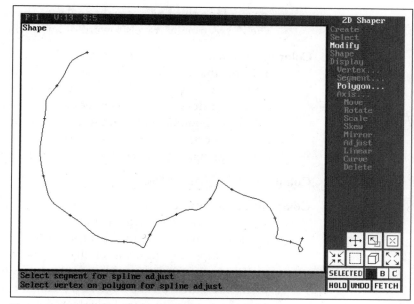

Figure E-3 Shape drawn by freehand tool in 3D Studio

illustration represent the control points for modifying the shape. *See* Bezier curve, Non-uniform rational B-spline.

Bump maps. *See* Altitude maps.

Bus The electronic signal path between the main microprocessor *(CPU)* and all the components that make up your computer system. Older PCs allow 8 bits and 16 bits of data to travel along this intercomponent pathway at a speed of 8 MHz. The older standard is called ISA (Industry Standard Architecture). Newer architectures, such as IBM's microchannel, the EISA standard, and innovations like VESA or PCI local buses, allow more data to flow at a faster rate and in larger chunks. For example, the popular VESA local bus architecture allows 32 bits to be transferred at the local speed of the microprocessor. Power-hungry 3D software benefits from the newer, more robust designs.

Cartesian coordinate system A method for plotting points either in a two-dimensional or three-dimensional space. On two-dimensional planes, the horizontal and vertical axes are at right angles and labeled X and Y, respectively. Using a grid system, any point on the plane can be plotted by assigning it a positive or negative X or Y value. Three-dimensional space adds a third axis at right angles to the X and Y axes, the Z axis. The Z axis usually travels toward or away from the eye.

Color depth   When referring to computer display, color depth is the number of colors that can be simultaneously displayed on the screen. A 4-bit (2 x 2 x 2 x 2) image assigns 4 bits of computer data to each *pixel* (picture element or dot) on the screen. Four bits of data allow 16 colors to be displayed simultaneously on a screen. As the bit depth increases, so does the number of colors. 24-bit color translates to 16.7 million colors, the limit of human vision. *See* True Color and 32-bit color.

Composite video   *See* NTSC.

Compositing Borrowed from old film animation cameras that built up an image by repeatedly exposing a single frame of film until a complex image is created. In computer programs, compositing is accomplished by superimposing one image on top of another and making one or more colors of one image transparent to the colors of another. Anti-aliasing, where the pixels on the edge of a shape are averaged with the background color to blur jagged edges, produces a problem when images are composited after they are created. The outline of the image in the foreground will show a dark or light ring of these pixels.

CPU   (Central Processing Unit) The brain at the heart of the computer's electronic system. The CPU fetches instructions and data from memory and processes them, effectively controlling all operations in the computer.

Digitizer   Any hardware device that converts analog information into a digital form that computers can process. Examples are mice and tablets, which translate your hand movements into binary numbers and, ultimately, coordinates on the screen. A video frame grabber is a specialized digitizer that converts a video signal into digital data that can be stored on the hard drive.

Dithering   Reduction of the total number of discrete colors in an image. Images are usually downgraded to fewer colors because the target computer system cannot display the full complement of colors in the image. This may be temporary, as when a True Color image is temporarily dithered for display on a low-resolution color display system. Some programs, such as Picture Man for Windows, which is bundled with this book, have color reduction options that permanently alter the color resolution of an image. The algorithms used by Picture Man's image color conversion option are slower but much superior to the algorithms used by Microsoft Windows. Often the resulting dithered image is indistinguishable from the original. This is true of images with a narrow range of colors or tones.

DXF   (Data Exchange Format) A standardized file format initiated by Autodesk to facilitate exchange of CAD files between incompatible computer programs and systems. The file is a standard ASCII text file that functionally describes an AutoCAD-compatible binary drawing file. DXF files are widely used to import the geometry of CAD drawing files into rendering programs like Imagine or Autodesk 3D Studio. *See* ASCII.

Extrusion   Transformation of a two-dimensional geometric figure into a three-dimensional object. Imagine's Mold commands create 3D objects this way.

Flat shading A type of surface shading given to 3D objects by 3D programs. Each polygon making up an object has a single illumination level across the surface of the polygon. (See Figure 1-26 in Chapter 1.) Note the case of flat shading. The sphere is not smooth because the individual polygons are visible. Flat shading is not very natural, but renders very quickly. *See* Wireframe shading, Gouraud shading, and Phong shading.

FLC file format   FLC is an acronym for flick, as in a movie "flick." It is an industry standard file format developed by Autodesk for animations produced by 2D and 3D animation programs. FLC format files store resolution-independent bitmapped images. The format uses a form of software compression called delta compression to store a series of images called frames. (A movie or a video is composed of a series of frames.) In delta compression, only the changes between frames are stored. This reduces file storage size and the data flow between the file on disk and the screen. Scenes where an object moves across a still background work best with delta compression. An example is a bird flying across a blue background. The first frame in the series is stored in its entirety, then just the bird's path across the screen is stored. The FLC delta compression format makes animation possible on IBM-stlye PCs unassisted by hardware compression.

FLI file format   An early industry standard file format developed by the developers of Autodesk Animator for the storage of low-resolution (320 x 200, 256 colors) animation files. The FLI format uses delta compression. *See* FLC file format.

Frame   A single image in the series of images that make up an animation. In video, a frame is composed of two full scans of the television monitor. In film, a frame is a single image on a strip of film. On computers, a frame is a full screen of data. While the rate of playback is fixed in the case of video (30 frames a second) and film (24 frames a second), the rate of playback in the computer environment varies widely.

Gouraud shading   Coloring applied to the surfaces of 3D objects by 3D software. Gouraud shading is the simplest form of smooth shading. The light's intensity is averaged across on entire face, from the pixels with the highest values at the edge of the polygon to the pixels with the lowest values on the other edge. *See* Figure 26 in Chapter 1. *See* Wireframe shading, Flat shading, and Phong shading.

Graphics primitive   A 3D object like a plane, cone, or sphere created by the program and made available to the user as a building block. The term also applies to simple geometric shapes predefined by 2D programs.

Hidden line removal   Sometimes called *hidden surface removal* when the reference is to object surfaces. A software algorithm is used to identify object lines that would be hidden from the viewer if the object were composed of solid surfaces. The most common algorithm in modern 3D software is the Z-buffer algorithm. *See* Z-buffer.

Image-mapping   *See* Brush-mapping.

Key frame animation   A traditional film method for defining animation sequences. In traditional animation the main animator draws the critical frames of the animation. Assistants draw the in-between frames. In computer animation, the animator defines these key frames and then has the computer draw the in-between frames. If an object is in one location in the first key frame, the computer will create the changes to the object as it moves to the next key frame.

Lofting   *See* Extrusion.

Map   A 2D raster or bitmapped image (such as those images produced by paint programs) that is used to cover a 3D surface, much as wrapping paper covers a package. *See* Mapping.

Mapping   Mapping is a 3D graphics term referring to the process of transforming a point or set of points to another point or set of points, as when an object is mapped to a new location on the screen. Mathematical algorithms determine how the object is transformed. It has a more specific meaning when used in conjunction with brushes (2D paint images applied to objects). *See* Brush-mapping.

Math coprocessor Originally a set of add-in boards for the computer, the math coprocessor has shrunk down to a single chip that sits next door to the CPU and off-loads floating point calculations, which it is optimized to do very efficiently. Floating point calculations allow for fractional results, something the CPU cannot do quickly. On many 80486s and higher, the math coprocessor is built into the CPU. This speeds up floating point calculations by four to five times or more, because the CPU does not have to send out the information over the computer's bus. A math coprocessor is an important addition to the 3D computing environment. *See* CPU, Bus.

Mesh *See* Wireframe model. 3D entities are often called meshes, models, or objects.

Mesh model A solid-shaded 3D object. The polygons that make up the surface of the object are given solid shading.

Model Also called *object* or *mesh*. A single 3D entity that forms part of a larger scene or animation. The term is often used to describe wireframe meshes or solid models. The process of creating 3D objects is called modeling. *See* Wireframe model, Solid model.

Modeling The process of building wireframe objects (models) in a 3D software program and applying surfaces to them.

Non-uniform rational B-spline (NURBS) A method of creating and editing 2D curves used by high-end 3D software. While Bezier curve control points only give global control over an entire curve, B-spline control points provide increased local control over *segments* of a curve near a control point. Non-uniform rational B-spline algorithms add the ability to adjust a segment's tension and bias. The result is more complex (that is, *non-uniform*) curves, better shape control, and the ability to model a larger class of shapes. *See* B-spline curve and Bezier curve.

Normal *See* Surface normal.

NTSC (National Television Standards Committee) Also known as composite video and RS-170A. An international organization that establishes technical standards for television broadcast signals. Television video signals are incompatible with computer display systems. While a computer signal will be split into red, green, blue, plus the vertical and horizontal timing signals, the NTSC signal is a composite of all of these, and is usually delivered on one wire. Special electronic circuits, boards, or boxes will convert computer signals to the NTSC standard or convert NTSC signals to the RGB standards of computer display.

Object   A generic term used to describe the individual entities that form part of a scene or animation. Objects can take two forms: wireframe mesh or solid model. Objects are often called *meshes* or *models. See* Wireframe model, Solid model.

Origin   The absolute center of the 3D world. It is usually given a value of 0,0,0 (X = 0, Y = 0, Z = 0).

Overscan   In television sets the image display exceeds the border around the picture tube. This results in a slight cropping of an image. When preparing visuals for television display, the cropping of computer visuals should be taken into account.

Patch   A type of curve definition used by high-end 3D software. Complex curvature surfaces like car surfaces are modeled with patches that are applied like the elbow patch of a jacket. *See* B-spline patch.

Phong shading   A type of shading given to the surface of 3D objects. Each pixel on the sphere's surface is calculated in relation to the light source and its color is adjusted accordingly. As you can imagine, the number of calculations that need to be performed on a Phong-shaded object is vast compared to Gouraud-, flat-, or wireframe-shaded objects. While Gouraud shading uses the pixels along the edges of a polygon for an approximation of lighting values, in Phong shading, each pixel in the image is measured and given a value. The number of calculations multiplies exponentially as the spatial resolution of the image goes up.

Photorealism   Accurate 3D modeling of surfaces, textures, lighting, and camera views in real or fantasy scenes. The resulting image is often indistinguishable from a photograph.

Pixel   Short for picture element. Video display systems divide the screen into a two-dimensional display of small square dots or pixels. A pixel is the smallest definable area of an image that can be displayed. The resolution of images is usually described in terms of the number of pixels in each horizontal line of the image by the total number of pixels in each vertical line of the image. For example, when a image is 640 by 480, the image is composed of a grid of pixels that are 640 pixels in width and 480 pixels in height. (This is the spatial resolution of common business displays and television.) At high resolution (for example 1024 by 768 pixels) images have a lot more detail and look sharper. A low resolution ("low res") image of 320 by 200 pixels has a mosaic pattern, caused by the size and shape of pixels. There is a stair-step pattern along curves.

Polygon   A planar shape with three or more line segments (vectors) that meet at their vertices. A planar shape is a shape whose vertices lie on a two-dimensional plane. Programs like Imagine use triangles to model the surface of 3D objects. Because all the vertices of triangles lie on a single plane, they are easy for Imagine to calculate. Quadrilateral (four-sided) polygons may or may not lie on a single plane and take longer to calculate.

Procedural modeling   Generating objects from algebraic equations. One of the three modeling methods used by Imagine. *See* Solids modeling.

Procedural texture   A mathematically generated surface applied to objects, such as a surface defined using fractal geometry. Not to be confused with *texture-mapping* or *brush-mapping*. Procedural textures use computer code to generate patterns on the surface of objects. The advantage of procedural textures is that you can simulate natural textures that do not lose their definition as the camera gets nearer to the object. In the case of texture maps, a layer of pixels is wrapped like a blanket around an object. As you approach the object, the pixels become apparent. *See* Texture-mapping, Brush-mapping, Shading.

Projection   Conversion of a three-dimensional view of an object to a two-dimensional representation.

Radiocity   A rendering method that attempts to reproduce the natural paths followed by light rays in a scene. Radiocity has the disadvantage of being computationally intensive because much of the light bouncing around in a scene never reaches the screen. *See* Ray tracing.

RAM   (Random Access Memory) Also called system memory. The live, volatile memory space where instructions and data used by the computer for computation are stored. The contents of RAM are lost when the computer is shut off. Data and programs are usually permanently stored on such large memory devices as hard drives, CD-ROMs, floppy disks and tape backup systems. RAM is the most important asset in 3D creation after CPU speed.

Ray tracing   A rendering method based on the physics of light. Normally light rays are emitted from a light source and either enter the eye directly or bounce off of surfaces before entering the eye. Calculating the path of light in a 3D world can be enormously time-consuming. (*See* Radiocity.) Ray tracing economizes by following (*tracing*) the light path from the observer's eye back to the light source, including reflections off of objects that are in the path of light. Figure E-4 shows the Top view in the Staging Editor. A single ray is traced from the camera view to the mirror ball and back to the light.

Ray tracing produces much more complex reflections than are possible with other rendering algorithms, such as scanline rendering. True refractions (light bending in water for example) and more complex reflections are possible with ray tracing. *See* Scanline rendering.

Reflection mapping   Simulating reflections in objects by mapping a 2D paint image of the reflected object onto their surfaces.

Refraction   Simulation of the bending of the path of light through transparent surfaces like glass. Refraction is a capability of ray-tracing software like Imagine. *See* Ray-tracing.

Render   The process by which objects in a scene are given surfaces, including such properties as reflections, background images, surface lighting, and

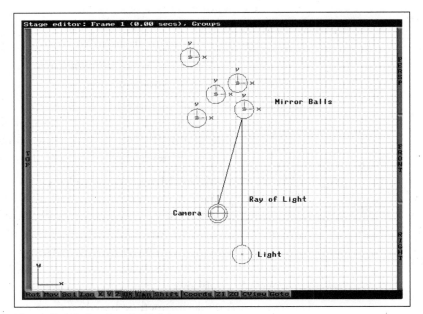

Figure E-4 Path taken by light ray

post-production special effects. The result is a 2D image file (bitmapped) that can be further processed in a paint or image processing program; output to tape, a printer, or a film camera; or simply displayed onscreen. It is the last step in the 3D creation process.

RGB color   Colors on television sets and computer displays are composed of the three primary colors: red, green, and blue. In the case of a television set, the three colors are mixed prior to transmission into what is called a *composite* signal. Computer systems keep these colors separated.

Scanline rendering   A scan line is a single horizontal line on a monitor. Many rendering programs convert 3D models to 2D images one scan line at a time, beginning at the top left of the image. Imagine's scanline rendering mode is an alternative to the ray-tracing method of reproducing a scene. Rather than following the path of a ray from the eye to an object and back to the light source, in scanline rendering mode each object is shaded individually according to the location of a predetermined light source. This speeds up the rendering process, compared to ray tracing. *See* Ray tracing.

Scene   In the context of this book, a scene is a collection of 3D objects edited and rendered as a single image. Sometimes a scene is called a *world*. *See* Model.

Shading   The technique by which objects are assigned colors, based on how light strikes the surfaces of those objects. Shading also refers to the methods by which polygonal models are rendered. These include wireframe, flat, Gouraud, and Phong.

SMPTE time code   SMPTE is an acronym for the Society of Motion Picture and Television Engineers, a trade association that sets standards for television and film. SMPTE time code is a data track laid down on a videotape or disk in the form of hours, minutes, seconds, and frames. SMPTE time code allows the elements of a production to be synchronized. So-called *frame accurate* systems use the data track to precisely locate a frame on a master or slave unit, or precisely line up one of the elements of a production to a specific frame (which can be a picture, sound element, or any kind of event).

Solid or surface model   A 3D object whose faces have been given solid shading. *See* Solid shading.

Solid shading   A shading method that uses hidden surface removal to represent objects on the screen. While in wireframe models you can see through to the other side of objects, in the case of solid shaded models, the polygons or triangles making up the object's surface are opaque. *See* Hidden line removal.

Solids modeling   Solids modeling is the creation of 3D objects from 3D primitives (sometimes called *graphic primitives*). One of the three modeling methods used by Imagine. *See* Procedural modeling.

Specular highlight   This is the small, intense circle of light formed when light rays fall on a shiny surface. The shinier the object, the smaller and brighter the specular highlight.

Spline curves   A type of mathematical model used to represent smooth curves. *See* B-splines and Non-uniform rational B-splines.

Staging   Imagine's term for adding lights, camera, and animation to a scene. The objects created in the Forms Editor, Detail Editor, and Cycle Editor are assembled in the Stage Editor. Light sources are added to the scene. The camera is adjusted.

Surface model   A solid *model. See* Solid shading.

Surface normal   A vector (line) perpendicular to a surface. Surface normals are used to calculate the effect of light on an object's surface.

System memory   *See* RAM.

Targa   A common file format for computer images originally developed by Truevision for its graphics cards. It is well supported on a wide variety of computer platforms. There are many flavors of Targa files, including compressed and uncompressed forms, and a range of color depths, including 8-, 16-, 24-, and 32-bit. It is the recommended format for color images exceeding 8-bit (or 256 color) format.

Texture-mapping   Texture-mapping is a general term describing the application of a texture to a 3D object using a mapping algorithm. Some 3D programs use texture-mapping to describe the application of a surface to an object using a 2D reference image (such as a scan of wood). This is confusing because texture-mapping can also refer to the application of surfaces to objects using mathematical algorithms like fractal geometry. Imagine uses the term *brush-mapping* to describe the application of surfaces to objects using 2D reference maps. *See* Brush-mapping for an extensive discussion about brush-mapping versus procedural mapping.

32-bit color   A file format (most commonly, Targa) that assigns the first 24 bits of a pixel to the RGB colors and the last 8 bits to special colors, called *alpha* colors. The alpha colors allow software and hardware to treat selected colors in the image in special ways. A certain hue of red, for example, can become transparent to the colors in a second image.

Transformation   A mathematical operation on one or more Cartesian coordinates. The object is either rotated, scaled, or moved from one set of Cartesian coordinates to another.

True Color   Also called 24-bit color or RGB color. True Color images can contain up to 16.7 million colors, the total range detectable by the human eye, although some scientists believe we detect far fewer colors. True Color display systems are capable of simultaneously displaying 16.7 million colors. Although the number of colors your analog VGA monitor is capable of displaying is infinite, the computer must process color information as digital data (bits and bytes). True Color systems (such as those using True Color VGA cards or 24-bit Targa cards) convert colors to levels of brightness. Each pixel on the screen is stored as 3 bytes. The first byte is the brightness level, from 0 to 255, of red. The second byte is the level of green, and third is the level of blue. Since there are three colors, each with 256 levels of brightness, 256 by 256 by 256 yields a total system palette range of 16.7 million colors.

24-bit color   *See* True Color.

Underscan   In computer display the image is displayed well within the borders of the picture tube. *See* Overscan.

Vector graphics   Graphics created and stored as instructions rather than dots on the screen. The form of graphics used by draw and 3D programs. The commands necessary for reproducing an object are stored rather than the dots on the screen that make up the object. *See* Bitmapped graphics.

VESA   (Video Electronic Standards Association) A vendor-supported standard for accessing the high-resolution modes on VGA cards. The original VGA standard developed by IBM supported such modes as 320 by 200 with 256 colors and 640 by 480 with 16 colors. Higher color modes that went beyond the original IBM specification, such as 640 by 480 with 256 colors, were implemented by VGA card manufacturers using proprietary methods. The VESA standard attempts to redress the chaos in the marketplace that resulted. Unfortunately, like most PC standards,

VESA compliance continues to have a wide margin of error in manufacturers' cards. The standard continues to evolve. Some VGA boards include VESA compatibility in the on-board BIOS. Some require that a small TSR (terminate and stay resident) be installed in memory before the application is called. A good place to install VESA TSRs is the AUTOEXEC.BAT file. See your video card's documentation for help.

Wireframe model   A 3D object with a wireframe surface composed of edges and no solid faces. In many 3D programs (such as Imagine), the object is created and edited as a wireframe model. Wireframe models allow you to edit the far side of an object, normally obscured from view when objects are shaded. Wireframe models also display very quickly because only the edges on the surfaces of objects have to be created, not the surfaces in between. *See* Solid model.

Wireframe shading   One of the four types of shading methods used by 3D software. In wireframe shading only the edges of the polygons or triangles making up the surface of the object are rendered. This is an extremely fast way of displaying objects in a scene, or test rendering models. *See* Flat shading, Gouraud shading, and Phong shading.

World coordinate system   The method for plotting the position of objects in 3D software. In Imagine, the world coordinate system is 1024 units in every direction by default, although it can be made larger or smaller. The X, Y, and Z axes intersect at the center of the screen by default. *See* Cartesian coordinate system for a discussion of this method.

Z-buffer   A location in computer memory used by 3D software for storing information about an object's depth. In the world coordinate systems used by 3D software, X, Y, and Z are the three axes that determine an object's position in 3D space. The X axis corresponds to right and left, the Y axis corresponds to up and down, and the Z axis corresponds to front and back. Storing the object's position along the Z axis gives the 3D software access to information about the object's depth, useful in hidden line removal algorithms. (*See* Hidden line removal.) For example, as an object is rendered to a location on the screen, the 3D program checks to see if a previous object at that location is in front of the current object. If it is, the previous object's surface takes precedence. In the case of a single object, the front part of an object takes precedence over the back surface.

Index

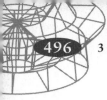

Books have a substantial influence on the destruction of the forests of the Earth. For example, it takes 17 trees to produce one ton of paper. A first printing of 30,000 copies of a typical 480 page book consumes 108,000 pounds of paper which will require 918 trees!

Waite Group Press™ is against the clear-cutting of forests and supports reforestation of the Pacific Northwest of the United States and Canada, where most of this paper comes from. As a publisher with several hundred thousand books sold each year, we feel an obligation to give back to the planet. We will therefore support and contribute a percentage of our proceeds to organizations which seek to preserve the forests of planet Earth.

WALKTHROUGHS AND FLYBYS CD

Phil Shatz

Fly around buildings before they exist, tour the inner workings of imaginary machines, and play electronic music while watching the motion of atoms. Welcome to the world of animated PC demos, a new area of technology and design that relies on high-powered PCs, an assortment of graphics animation software, a Sound Blaster board, and some special tricks. The Walkthroughs and Flybys CD presents breathtaking computer animation and music including over 300 megabytes of Autodesk 3-D studio movies.

ISBN: 1-878739-40-9, 128 pages, 1-CD-ROM, $29.95, Available now

VIRTUAL REALITY CREATIONS

Bernie Roehl, Dave Stampe, John Eagan

Walk, jump, fly, bound, or beam through virtual worlds, exploring them from your mouse or keyboard. With the included REND386 software and special Fresnel 3-D glasses, it's easy to build machine simulations, molecular models, video game environments, and much more. REND386 runs on any 386 or 486 system with a VGA adapter. No special VR hardware is required but many peripherals are supported. You'll find details on connecting special LCD glasses to view environments in 3-D, as well as instructions for making gloves that allow you to reach out and manipulate your creations.

ISBN: 1-878739-39-5, 300 pages, 1-5.25" disk and Fresnel viewers, $34.95, Available June 1993

MULTIMEDIA CREATIONS

Philip Shaddock

Jump in to multimedia with Multimedia Creations and its powerful built-in GRASP program and utilities. Whether novice or professional, you'll get everything you need to create your own electronic brochures, interactive educational games, multimedia kiosks, digital real-time movies, and music videos. Hands-on step-by-step examples teach you animation, color-cycling, how to manipulate color palettes, synchronize sound effects and MIDI music to your presentations, and much more. The accompanying disks provide fully commented examples that you can run, modify, or incorporate into your own programs.

ISBN: 1-878739-26-3, 450 pages, 2 5.25" disks, $44.95, Available now

Send for our unique catalog for more information about these books, as well as our other outstanding titles, including:

Master C: Let the PC Teach You C and Master C++: Let the PC Teach You Object-Oriented Programming: Both book/disk software packages turn your computer into an infinitely patient C and C++ professor.

Workout C: Hundreds of C projects and exercises and a full-featured compiler make this an unbeatable training program and value.

OOP in Turbo C++ and OOP in Microsoft C++: Master teacher of the programming art, Robert Lafore, takes the prospective C++ programmer from the basics to the most complex concepts. It is also a comprehensive reference guide for all levels of programmer.

Flights of Fantasy: Programming 3-D Video Games in C++ Learn to use 3-D animation to make commercial quality video games. Plus it includes a complete flight simulator program and the full source code for the simulator.

Fractals for Windows: Create new fractals and control over 85 different fractal types with a zoom box, menus, and a mouse! Comes with WINFRACT, a powerful Windows version of FRACTINT for DOS, this package is faster than lightning at computing mind-bending fractals.

Virtual Reality Playhouse: Jack-in to the world of Virtual Reality with this playful book/disk package. Eight demos with VR simulations let you create your own personal digital dimension.

Nanotechnology Playhouse: This book and disk set is an accessible introduction to nanotechnology (the science of making devices, materials, objects of all kinds, one atom at a time). It includes multimedia demos to give you a taste of tomorrow.

Artificial Life Playhouse: Turn your PC into an experimenter's lab to find out more about this exciting new area of scientific exploration. Eight demo programs are included.

This is a legal agreement between you, the end user and purchaser, and The Waite Group®, Inc., and the authors of the programs contained in the disk. By opening the sealed disk package, you are agreeing to be bound by the terms of this Agreement. If you do not agree with the terms of this Agreement, promptly return the unopened disk package and the accompanying items (including the related book and other written material) to the place you obtained them for a refund.

SOFTWARE LICENSE

1. The Waite Group, Inc. grants you the right to use one copy of the enclosed software programs (the programs) on a single computer system (whether a single CPU, part of a licensed network, or a terminal connected to a single CPU). Each concurrent user of the program must have exclusive use of the related Waite Group, Inc. written materials.

2. Each of the programs, including the copyrights in each program, is owned by the respective author and the copyright in the entire work is owned by The Waite Group, Inc. and they are therefore protected under the copyright laws of the United States and other nations, under international treaties. You may make only one copy of the disk containing the programs exclusively for backup or archival purposes, or you may transfer the programs to one hard disk drive, using the original for backup or archival purposes. You may make no other copies of the programs, and you may make no copies of all or any part of the related Waite Group, Inc. written materials.

3. You may not rent or lease the programs, but you may transfer ownership of the programs and related written materials (including any and all updates and earlier versions) if you keep no copies of either, and if you make sure the transferee agrees to the terms of this license.

4. You may not decompile, reverse engineer, disassemble, copy, create a derivative work, or otherwise use the programs except as stated in this Agreement.

GOVERNING LAW

This Agreement is governed by the laws of the State of California.

LIMITED WARRANTY

The following warranties shall be effective for 90 days from the date of purchase: (i) The Waite Group, Inc. warrants the enclosed disk to be free of defects in materials and workmanship under normal use; and (ii) The Waite Group, Inc. warrants that the programs, unless modified by the purchaser, will substantially perform the functions described in the documentation provided by The Waite Group, Inc. when operated on the designated hardware and operating system. The Waite Group, Inc. does not warrant that the programs will meet purchaser's requirements or that operation of a program will be uninterrupted or error-free. The program warranty does not cover any program that has been altered or changed in any way by anyone other than The Waite Group, Inc. The Waite Group, Inc. is not responsible for problems caused by changes in the operating characteristics of computer hardware or computer operating systems that are made after the release of the programs, nor for problems in the interaction of the programs with each other or other software.

THESE WARRANTIES ARE EXCLUSIVE AND IN LIEU OF ALL OTHER WARRANTIES OF MERCHANTABILITY OR FITNESS FOR A PARTICULAR PURPOSE OR OF ANY OTHER WARRANTY, WHETHER EXPRESS OR IMPLIED.

EXCLUSIVE REMEDY

The Waite Group, Inc. will replace any defective disk without charge if the defective disk is returned to The Waite Group, Inc. within 90 days from date of purchase.

This is Purchaser's sole and exclusive remedy for any breach of warranty or claim for contract, tort, or damages.

LIMITATION OF LIABILITY

THE WAITE GROUP, INC. AND THE AUTHORS OF THE PROGRAMS SHALL NOT IN ANY CASE BE LIABLE FOR SPECIAL, INCIDENTAL, CONSEQUENTIAL, INDIRECT, OR OTHER SIMILAR DAMAGES ARISING FROM ANY BREACH OF THESE WARRANTIES EVEN IF THE WAITE GROUP, INC. OR ITS AGENT HAS BEEN ADVISED OF THE POSSIBILITY OF SUCH DAMAGES.

THE LIABILITY FOR DAMAGES OF THE WAITE GROUP, INC. AND THE AUTHORS OF THE PROGRAMS UNDER THIS AGREEMENT SHALL IN NO EVENT EXCEED THE PURCHASE PRICE PAID.

COMPLETE AGREEMENT

This Agreement constitutes the complete agreement between The Waite Group, Inc. and the authors of the programs, and you, the purchaser.

Some states do not allow the exclusion or limitation of implied warranties or liability for incidental or consequential damages, so the above exclusions or limitations may not apply to you. This limited warranty gives you specific legal rights; you may have others, which vary from state to state.

SATISFACTION REPORT CARD

Please fill out this card if you want to know of future updates to
***3D Modeling Lab,* or to receive our catalog.**

Company Name: _____

Division/Department: _____ **Mail Stop:** _____

Last Name: _____ **First Name:** _____ **Middle Initial:** _____

Street Address: _____

City: _____ **State:** _____ **Zip:** _____

Daytime telephone: (_____) _____

Date product was acquired: Month _____ **Day** _____ **Year** _____ **Your Occupation:** _____

Overall, how would you rate *3D Modeling Lab*
- ☐ Excellent ☐ Very Good ☐ Good
- ☐ Fair ☐ Below Average ☐ Poor

What did you like MOST about this book? _____
_____

What did you like LEAST about this book? _____
_____

How did you use this book (problem-solver, tutorial, reference...)?
_____

What is your level of computer expertise?
- ☐ New ☐ Dabbler ☐ Hacker
- ☐ Power User ☐ Programmer ☐ Experienced Professional

How did you find the pace of this book? _____

Please describe any problems you may have encountered with installing or using the utilities: _____
_____
_____

What computer languages are you familiar with? _____
_____

Please describe your computer hardware:

Computer _____ Hard disk _____

5.25" disk drives _____ 3.5" disk drives _____

Video card _____ Monitor _____

Printer _____ Peripherals _____

Sound Board _____ CD ROM _____

Where did you buy this book?
- ☐ Bookstore (name): _____
- ☐ Discount store (name): _____
- ☐ Computer store (name): _____
- ☐ Catalog (name): _____
- ☐ Direct from WGP ☐ Other _____

What price did you pay for this book? _____

What influenced your purchase of this book?
- ☐ Recommendation ☐ Advertisement
- ☐ Magazine review ☐ Store display
- ☐ Mailing ☐ Book's format
- ☐ Reputation of Waite Group Press ☐ Other

How many computer books do you buy each year? _____

How many other Waite Group books do you own? _____

What is your favorite Waite Group book? _____
_____

Is there any program or subject you would like to see Waite Group Press cover in a similar approach? _____
_____
_____

Additional comments? _____
_____

Please send to: Waite Group Press
Attn: 3D Modeling Lab
200 Tamal Plaza
Corte Madera, CA 94925

☐ **Check here for a free Waite Group catalog**